Tailoring Identities

Tailoring Identities

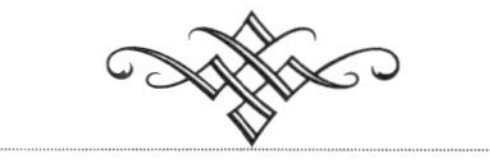

Craft, Technology, and Style in Benin, West Africa

Elizabeth Ann Fretwell

INDIANA UNIVERSITY PRESS

This book is a publication of

Indiana University Press
Herman B Wells Library
1320 East 10th Street
Bloomington, Indiana 47405 USA

iupress.org

For customers in the European Union with safety or GPSR concerns, please contact
Mare Nostrum Group B.V., Mauritskade 21D, 1091 GC Amsterdam, The Netherlands.
Email: gpsr@mare-nostrum.co.uk

First Printing 2026

Cataloging information is available from the Library of Congress.
ISBN 978-0-253-07534-5 (hdbk.)
ISBN 978-0-253-07535-2 (pbk.)
ISBN 978-0-253-07537-6 (ebook)

Chapters 3 and 4 are derived in part from
"The Tools of Tailoring as Technologies-in-Use in
Twentieth Century Benin, West Africa,"
published in *History and Technology*, 2021,
copyright Taylor & Francis.

CONTENTS

ACKNOWLEDGMENTS

I want to begin by thanking the tailors and other artisans who have welcomed me into their homes and workshops over the past two decades. I have learned so much from them at different points in my life and in different capacities. They taught me how to make things and how to recognize the joy and value of a well-made trouser or pot, but I also learned other life lessons that shaped me not just as a scholar but also as a collaborator, worker, mother, and community member.

Vice President Fidel Ouèdjo and Romauld Koussougbe in Bohicon, Didier Kloué in Za-Kpota, and Lydia Abadadhoué in Bohicon were vital to the success of my fieldwork. Lydia allowed me to spend months in her shop, and my apprenticeship was crucial to the early development of the dissertation that eventually became this book. Romauld and Fidel were always ready to introduce me around and invite me to meetings and ceremonies. Didier guided me within the rapidly changing politics of artisanship in the mid-2010s.

In Bénin, Marc Esse helped identify community members and often served as translator. We spent many hours traveling around on his moto (I have the scars from exhaust burns to remind me) to do pre-interviews and collect oral histories. He and his family are also great friends. Marcel Djedatin helped me navigate Bohicon politics while Florencia Adjoghidje completed the tedious work of transcribing interviews collected in multiple languages. Finally, Serge Agbo at Bohicon's Fongbexwé spent months teaching me Fon and helping me with transliteration and translation, although all errors remain my own.

This project also benefited from the assistance of multiple institutions in Bénin. Artisan associations at the local, regional, and national levels granted me permission to conduct my research and connected me to members. Affiliations with the Department of History at the University of Abomey-Calavi and with the director of cultural heritage in the Ministry of Tourism helped me secure a visa. The staff at the National Archives was always ready to bring out another carton even when I was not entirely sure where to find tailors in the archive. Urbain Hadonou formerly at the Royal Palace of Abomey provided feedback and office space in Abomey very early in this project.

This book also benefited from the assistance of archivists and others beyond Bénin. In Dakar, the West African Research Center provided an affiliation and helped me secure a homestay with the Guèye family in Mermoz, who made a two-month research stay there a wonderfully rewarding experience. I also thank archivists and librarians at the Archives Nationales du Sénégal, the Archives Nationales d'Outre-Mer in Aix, the Schomburg Center for Research in Black Culture, the National Museum of African Art, and the Fundação Pierre Verger.

The many years of fieldwork and archival research that went into this book would not have been possible without the financial support of the University of Chicago's Division of the Social Sciences; Department of History; African Studies Workshop; France Chicago Center; Center for the Study of Race, Politics, and Culture; and Center for the Study of Gender and Sexuality. Additional research was conducted with a Summer Research Fellowship from Old Dominion University's Office of Research and a National Endowment for the Humanities Summer Stipend.

The book also benefited from the feedback of countless scholars over the years. John Cropper read every chapter, most of them many times, and his advice always led to better writing and tighter arguments. Emily Lynn Osborn was a wonderful advisor in graduate school and is a mentor into the present. Rachel Jean-Baptiste and Leora Auslander encouraged me to think critically about postcolonial Africa and material culture, respectively. At Chicago, I found the African Studies Workshop to be a particularly productive space, and I appreciate all the feedback I received from its regular attendees, especially from Jennifer Cole and the late Ralph Austen. At ODU, my colleagues Nick Abbott, Brett Bebber, Megan Nutzman, Tim Orr, John Weber, Miller Wright, and Liz Zanoni invited me into their reading group, providing much-needed deadlines and feedback on chapter drafts. I also presented portions of this research at conferences hosted at University Dar es Salaam, Queen's University, University of North Carolina at Chapel Hill, University of Wisconsin-Madison, College of the Holy Cross, University of Memphis, Northwestern University, and University of Alberta, and at the annual meetings of the American Historical Association and African Studies Association. Comments from years ago are still with me today.

Friends provided a much-needed respite from the project, even though it occasionally came up in conversation with them too. In Bénin, Marc, Soni, Opa, Richard, Reed, Orlando, Mike, and Tia made downtime a pleasure. Visits to the Ouanta family in Natitingou and Fagla in Lalo were weekend getaways. In Chicago, my grad school friends, Francisco, Maru, Kai, Amanda, Kyle, and Ariana, were an endless source of inspiration and fun. Giana has remained my friend since childhood, spotting me dinners and drinks during the lean years of graduate school and after.

My biggest debt of gratitude is to my family. My two favorite artisans, my brother Matt and my father Chuck both passed away recently. They supported my academic pursuits and international travels in a myriad of ways and taught me the importance of hard work and creatively modifying materials. My mother, Cheryl, was my biggest booster for attending college and beyond and has been a huge help with childcare. Last, my son, Kwado, has pushed me to finish with his frequent questioning about whether this book was done yet.

Tailoring Identities

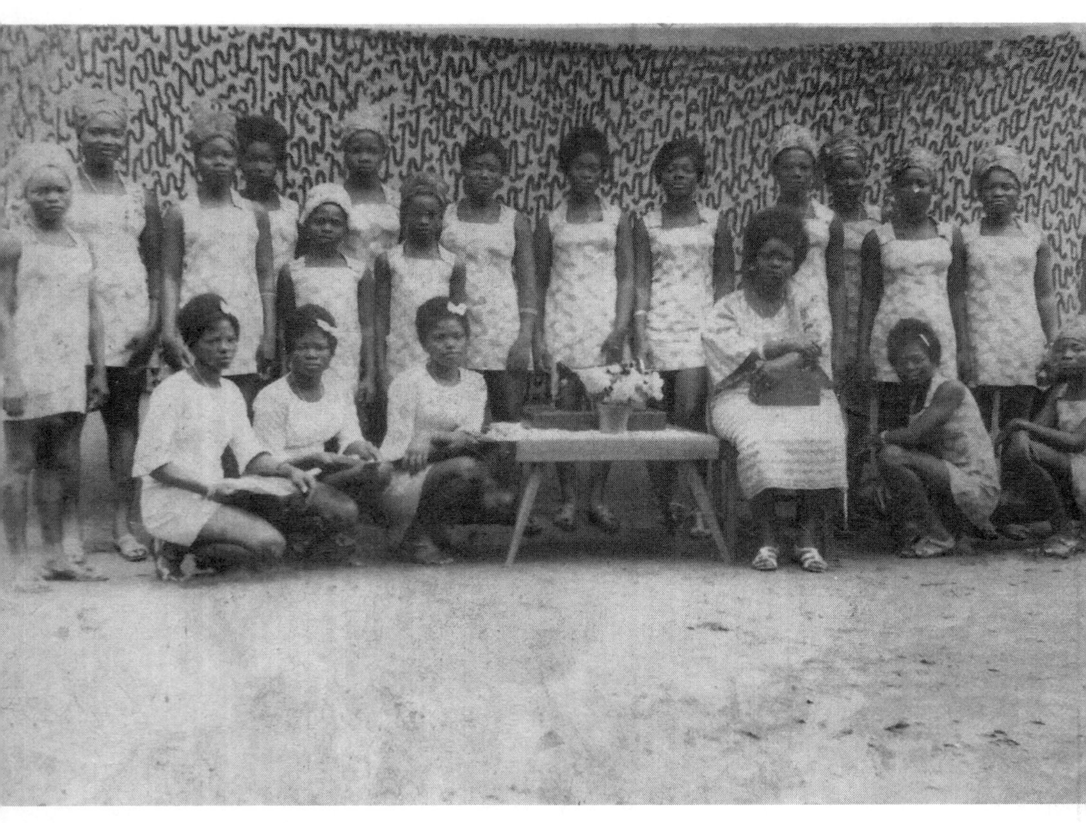

Figure 0.1. Elisabeth Alikpanou and her apprentices, Abomey, 1970. Courtesy of Sodokpa.

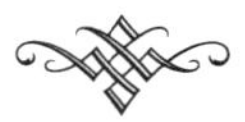

Introduction

Tailoring Identities

In Abomey, Bénin, on September 5, 1970, master seamstress Madame Elisa-beth Alikpanou (née Sodokpa) and nineteen of her apprentices posed for a group photograph in front of a piece of fabric pulled taut (fig. 0.1).[1] A handwrit-ten note on the back of the photograph indicates that it was commissioned to commemorate the *libération* (liberation) or release of three young women from their multiyear apprenticeship with the master seamstress. In the image, the three "liberated" apprentices crouch in the lower left and wear identical trendy minidresses with fabric, sleeves, necklines, and hair bows that dis-tinguish them from the other girls and women. Their outfits materialized a changed status—that morning they woke as apprentices but spent the day un-dergoing a series of rituals that transformed them from dependents of a master seamstress to full craftspeople within the community of Béninois artisans. Libération was also an occasion to share food and drink with the larger com-munity, and during the day's public moments the three women promenaded in the clothes they had made, providing an opportunity to put their technical competencies and command of style on display to potential clients. Most of the girls and young women in the photograph would eventually finish their apprenticeships and open their own workshops in the small town of Abomey while others would return to their natal villages or marry and move before they opened a workshop and began to teach their own apprentices. During their careers as masters, Madame Alikpanou's former apprentices would each train dozens of girls, forming a network of craft knowledge that linked the many seamstresses' workshops that dotted the landscape of late twentieth-century Bénin. As their fancy dress in the photograph suggests, these young needleworkers were also important trendsetters in their communities, using their own bodies and those of their clients to model style and comportment in a growing city and new nation.

By the time the photograph was taken in 1970, artisanal tailoring was well established in the towns and villages of southern Bénin, and Madame Alikpanou was one of many tailors and seamstresses at work. But the craft knowledge of these clothes-makers and the mass popularity of their products—sewn clothes—have relatively recent histories within the Republic of Bénin. Indeed, the form-fitting clothes in bright, colorful wax prints prevalent in today's Bénin and prominent within global imaginaries of West and West Central Africa are a creation of the twentieth century. But they are also the product of a long series of encounters between the Fon-speaking people of southern Bénin and the sartorial practices of groups as varied as the Yorùbá, Hausa, Portuguese, and French.

Tailoring Identities traces the development of artisanal tailoring in southern Bénin from the wrapped and draped fashions of the Dahomey kingdom (c. 1600–1894) to the extensive and tailored wardrobes of the past few decades to reveal the entanglements of craftspeople, materials, technologies, and sartorial meaning in the making of modern Bénin. Textiles and clothing are the most ubiquitous form of material culture and, as a "social skin," humans have used them to construct identities and to help them develop categories of being and belonging as well as political, social, and cultural affiliations.[2] Economies of dress bring together local and globally sourced materials with technical know-how and systems of labor. This book explores the history of clothes-making—inclusive of craft knowledge, craftspeople, and finished products—to bring together, in a single frame, economies of textiles and clothing with the social and political meanings around dress. In doing so, it shows how the gendered and occupational identities of ordinary clothes-makers like Madame Alikpanou and their mastery over the material world positioned them as experts on style and leaders within conversations on the uses and meanings of clothing. These craftspeople were important cultural and technological agents, combining and repurposing tools, techniques, and material inputs from African and non-African sources and refining their craft knowledge through innovation and collaboration with each other and clients. Using thread and needle, tailors materialized notions of gendered expertise and experiences of identity and affinity for the larger community, helping to give form and expression to the political and social changes of modernity,

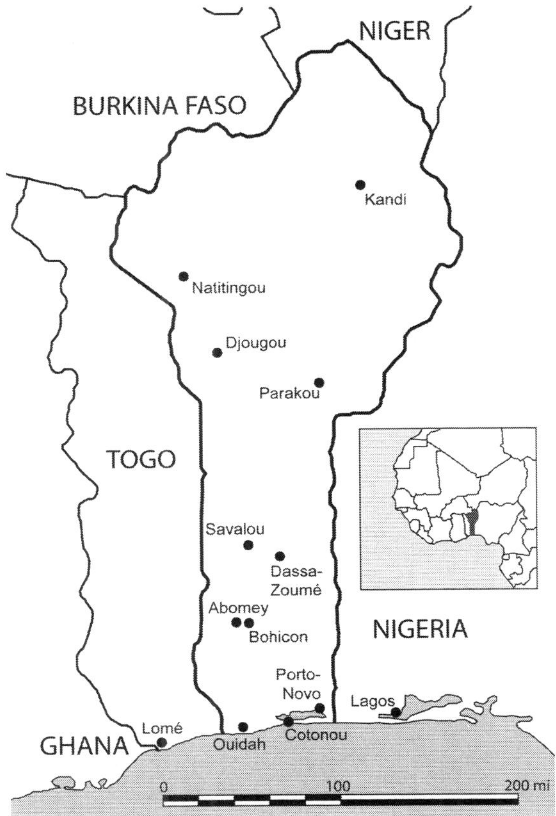

Map 0.1. Republic of Bénin.

decolonization, and urbanization. In other words, as tailors made clothes, they also crafted new ideas and experiences of status, identity, and power, helping give form to selves, cities, and nations in twentieth-century Bénin.

Before the spread of tailored clothing in the twentieth century, Fon speakers mostly wore cloth wrapped and draped on the body as *avɔ* or *pagne* (wrappers), a form of dress that remains popular, especially among women. By the fourteenth or fifteenth century, the region's inhabitants acquired avɔ through networks of trade that stretched far into the West African interior, and by the early eighteenth century the centralized Fon-speaking Dahomey kingdom began to trade textiles directly with Europeans, often in exchange for captives. Imported textiles supplemented the work of local clothes-makers like weavers and dyers who regularly domesticated forms and technologies from these same African and Atlantic networks. Fon speakers used this cloth—usually wrapped around bodies but also ritually displayed and occasionally sewn into tailored items—to create notions of social distinction and political authority in the precolonial kingdom. In 1894, the French conquered the Dahomey kingdom and incorporated it into their overseas empire, leading to new colonial markets that shifted the types and availability of textiles and clothing. Missions and colonial administrators also introduced programs to train needleworkers and sought to generate new social meanings around styles like suits and jackets, forms long familiar to Fon elites already integrated into global networks of consumption and prestige.[3] This book shows how precolonial practices of dress, craft production, and domestication, as well as changes under colonialism, laid the foundation for a twentieth-century shift from wrapped avɔ to tailored dress.

By the 1940s, young men in interior southern Bénin began to refine a system of artisanal tailoring, and by the final decade of the century a visit to the tailor had become the dominant way that Béninois assembled their vast wardrobes. These young tailors drew upon some of the lessons taught in missions and colonial schools, but they also created a body of knowledge rooted in earlier formations of craftsmanship and a repertoire of forms and silhouettes that reflected the Fon's deep history of sartorial encounter and incorporation. Following Bénin's 1960 independence, a client who wanted a new outfit might first purchase fabric in a central market or from an ambulant trader and then take the cloth to a tailor's stall, often in that same market. While a client usually had an idea in mind or arrived with a sample garment, they also relied on the tailor's stylistic knowledge and technical know-how when choosing a design. Tailors made recommendations based on the garment's intended use, recent trends, their strengths as designers, and their assessment of the client's body. In oral histories, tailors often claimed to have an innate aesthetic appreciation that fed their creativity, although most also acknowledged that their sense of taste and technical know-how matured through apprenticeship, additional training, travel, and media consumption. Indeed, Béninois tailoring was a learned skill as well as an embodied process in the sense that making clothes relied on a swiftness of hand, the physical manipulation of tools and inputs, and the creative transformation of materials through techniques honed during years of professional practice. Tailors deployed this craft knowledge to create Western styles such as wool trousers, polyester suits, cotton shirts, and dresses as well as more African or Pan-African forms like *bounba* made from wax print or *agbada*, both of which have roots in Yorùbáland.[4] Béninois sported these tailor-made styles in offices, churches, and *buvettes* (open-air bars), at weddings, funerals, and political rallies, and as they negotiated their daily lives.

The role of dress and fashion in the construction of identity in twentieth-century Africa has been well established, although scholars have usually approached clothing as finished objects given meaning by elite fashion designers or consumers.[5] In contrast, *Tailoring Identities* is a history of clothes-making, shifting from the "object biography" approach of understanding extant garments to their "textility."[6] Doing so permits a deeper exploration of the entanglements among technologies, materials, and sartorial meaning and the role of ordinary tailors and their craft knowledge within West African clothing cultures. As anthropologist Tim Ingold argues, making "is a question not of imposing preconceived forms on inert matter but of intervening in the fields of force and currents of material wherein forms are generated." In this way makers, like tailors, are best conceived of as "wanderers, wayfarers" who use their craft knowledge to "find the grain" and "follow its course while bending it to their evolving purpose."[7] Clothes-makers' command over the properties of textiles as different as raffia, homespun cotton, industrial wax prints, and polyester, and their ability to acquire these fabrics, affected the dress worn in everyday life. Likewise, the electric lights, glass storefronts, and roadside placement of workshops shaped how makers and clients used and gave meaning to the garments produced inside. Considering Béninois clothing through its making also reveals local styles' deep roots in craft and aesthetic practices that predated the colonial period.

By focusing on the making of garments and the development of craft knowledge, this book steers us aways from scholarly approaches reliant on dominant Western conceptions of technological diffusion, fashion design, consumption, craft, and labor and opens new artisanal paths into the history of technology, the interdisciplinary literature on style, and Africanist social and cultural history.[8] Tailoring in Bénin was not just a process of creatively stitching together fabrics and other elements from diverse sources; it was also a material, imaginative, and interpretive world-making process spearheaded by ordinary men and women. The history of tailoring reveals how Béninois' lived experiences and conceptions of self, city, and nation in the twentieth century were in part *made* through the work, expertise, and finished products of men and women like Madame Alikpanou and her apprentices.

Craft, Labor, Gender, and Occupational Identity in Bénin

Despite the ubiquity of bespoke clothing and artisanal tailoring in West and West Central Africa, there are no book-length studies of the important craftspeople involved.[9] In part, this has to do with the methodological issues that emerge in a study of tailors, which will be addressed later in this introduction. But *tailor* itself has also proved to be a slippery social and occupational category. In recent decades, the community of Béninois tailors has included women like Madame Alikpanou as well as men, who together are called *Nutɔtɔ*, a gender-neutral term that captures the common practices of cutting, designing, and sewing clothing for clients and the fact that both men and women collaborate together as clothes-makers. Men might also call themselves *tailleur* (French: tailor), *tayɛɛ* (Fon: tailor), or, if skilled in making high-end ensembles, a *couturier* (French: fashion designer). Women often self-identify as *couturière* (French: seamstress, dressmaker, or fashion designer). Nutɔtɔ, in contrast, refers directly to the work of sewing clothes and shares Fon roots with other tools of the craft, such as *Nùtomò* (sewing machine) and *Nùtɔnú* (needle). In this book, I generally refer to both men and women as tailors, admittedly an imperfect translation of Nutɔtɔ, unless I am describing specifically gendered aspects of production and identity for which *seamstress* provides a better fit. In bringing both men and women together in a single history, this book reflects a local Fon conception of the craft as opposed to Western approaches that tend to emphasize needlework, craft, and labor as gendered first and foremost.[10] However, as the multiple terms for describing tailors suggest, categories of gender, labor, and craft were historically fraught and shaped by outsiders as well as craftspeople themselves.

Craftspeople and their social status were prominent themes within early academic writing about West Africa. In the first few decades after colonization, French ethnologists and anthropologists wrote extensively about *l'artisanat africain* (African artisanship or artisanal sector) in a place far to the north of Bénin, the Mande-speaking areas of the Sahel. These colonial writers were keenly interested in the handmade and artisanal and how Mande people made things like pots, saddles, and hoes, but they were especially attuned to the relationship between making and social identity, introducing the idea of the "casted artisan" into the colonial lexicon of West Africa.[11] While these colonial sources correctly identified how some Mande artisanal production was the purview of hereditary, endogamous craftsmen, they also assumed that artisans were lowly or scorned members of society, a misapprehension corrected in more recent literature. Patrick McNaughton, in his seminal work on Mande blacksmiths, showed how smiths served as guardians of the driving force behind social transformation through their mastery over *nyama*, the power to transform raw material into useful forms. Blacksmiths' practical metal productions and spiritual powers put them at the center of social relations, not the outside.[12] While most of the scholarship on West African craft production has focused on men and male crafts, more recent work by historians and art historians has examined the social worlds of craftswomen, exploring complexity and change in the techniques, forms, and gendered identities of dyers, potters, and other makers.[13]

In contrast to the idea of the "casted artisan," craft practice and identity in precolonial Dahomey were fluid and relied on the domestication of forms, techniques, and individual artisans. During the kingdom era, the powerful Dahomean central palace sought out individual craftspeople skilled in textile production and other crafts like smithing and woodcarving, incorporating their knowledge and products into the kingdom's material culture through bondage or marriage.[14] As *Tailoring Identities* shows, occupation did not coincide with other forms of social status and identity in the kingdom, and weavers, woodcarvers, and other craftspeople included individuals across distinctions of free and enslaved and of gender, language group, and race. In the countryside as well, ordinary people increased their local economic power by incorporating skilled migrants into communities. Béninois scholars Alexis Adandé and Goudjinou Metinhoué traced how the economy of the Mono village of Sè reoriented around pottery production in the late eighteenth century as it incorporated pottery-producing migrants.[15] Indeed, the Fon word for craftsperson (àlɔnúzɔwàtɔ) is a compound of àlɔ (hand), nú (thing), and zɔwàtɔ (worker) and has no other social connotation—hand-thing workers were simply engaged in the labor of making, whether man or woman, king or enslaved. Yet the dynamism of precolonial Dahomean craft was ignored by the French colonial state, which conceived of a generalized category of "African artisan" based on assumptions of craftspeople's status and gender that drew directly on ideas about the low-status "casted artisan" developed by colonial experts on the Mande world. As explored in chapter 4, through a homogenous policy approach to the entirety of French West Africa, the colonial state imported conceptions of a male, low-status, endogamous artisanat from one part of the empire (French Soudan/Mali) to another (Dahomey/Bénin).

The French also drew on their own histories of craftsmanship to try to understand craft production and its social organization in West Africa. In doing so, they constructed African craft as a relic of a premodern past, providing justification for colonial interventions through the *mission civilsatrice* (civilizing mission). French observers delineated social organizations around West African craft, regularly describing them as "guilds" and equating them to prerevolutionary French organizations. Well into the nineteenth century, and long after the end of the guild system, French politics and labor periodically revived the idea of corporatism in hopes of returning to the perceived order and moral codes of prerevolutionary labor.[16] French conceptions of artisans in Africa being outside "modernity" drew not only on misunderstandings of their social organization but also on disparaging assessments of their tools and inputs. To Europeans, craft technologies such as handlooms and mud furnaces served as further evidence of African, but also more specifically African artisanal and technological, "backwardness."[17] Somewhat paradoxically, the "traditions" of the artisanat africain were also forwarded as worthy of preservation due to a burgeoning interest in African art in Europe and the paternalist tendencies of the mission civilsatrice. In 1930s Morocco and Mali, French colonial educational programs hired local artisans to teach young men crafts to preserve the "authenticity" of African techniques and forms while French oversight and good taste were put to work "improving" them.[18] In drawing on their own histories and social formations of craft, the French also introduced new concepts of gendered craft by drawing a rigid gendered distinction between men's productions for the market and women's domestic crafts. For example, needlework was reimagined as feminine and as a household activity as opposed to an economic one. French Catholic missions in Bénin taught "domestic" sewing to mixed-race girls and young women, a local iteration of a practice established elsewhere on the West African coast.[19]

While craftspeople in West Africa have long been interpreted through comparisons with premodern European "guilds," their use of nonindustrial tools reinforced perceptions of most artisans as outside or beyond capitalism or as cultural producers as opposed to labor. With a few exceptions, such as Judith Byfield's *The Bluest Hands*, craftspeople have been left out of African histories of work and economy and their tools, products, and social worlds relegated to the study of art history and anthropology.[20] But as the case of tailors shows, craftspeople were both cultural and economic producers who conceived of themselves as a skilled labor force despite being cast as part of an informal economy in the latter half of the twentieth century. Frederick Cooper points out that *informal economy* represented a "new term for an old anxiety" and that "the informal sector is what was left out in the process of defining a bounded working class and integrating that into a process of regulation and surveillance by a state."[21] Histories of labor and work in Africa have largely elided studies of informal or nonwage labor, instead focusing on wage-earning men working on docks, railways, mining, or government service and the consolidation of their class consciousness and labor movements.[22] In contrast, feminist scholars in the 1980s began to use life histories to reveal the complexity of women's economic experiences in the so-called informal economy. Rural to urban migration and independent trading created new opportunities for women denied work as wage earners, even as these women became the objects of state and elite derision.[23] Even more recently, government and NGO approaches to Béninois tailors and other artisans have shifted slightly, and craftspeople are often reimagined as small businesses to be partnered with in development programs that organize trainings for at-risk youth, orphans, and rural dwellers. The relatively low costs of entry into most crafts and misperceptions of them as easily teachable have made craft a continued focus—a low-hanging fruit—of such projects. However, unlike in the similarly constructed colonial-era interventions, today's artisans are not reimbursed for their labor or expertise, a reflection of the contemporary logic of "sustainable development."[24] Viewing tailoring through the lens of economic and labor history provides new insights into the social organization and self-identification of tailors as workers and how these social identities impacted their processes of making and their final products.

Despite ongoing misrepresentations of craftspeople as marginalized, precapitalist atavisms, nonlabor, or informal, this book reveals how Béninois artisans have repeatedly sought to define themselves and their work in ways that emphasize their roles as political, economic, and cultural actors. Tailors solidified their own identity beginning in the mid-twentieth century by first innovating a body of craft knowledge that was uniquely Béninois but pulled on multiple traditions. Next, they created systems of credentialing and rituals, such as the libération commemorated in the photograph at the beginning of this introduction, that instituted controls over craft knowledge and defined membership in the community of craftspeople. By 1970, when Madame Alikpanou liberated her apprentices, she could call upon her fellow needleworkers, both male and female, to attend (*assister*) the ceremony and to lend their prestige to the new master craftswomen. Tailors and other artisans formalized these horizontal ties at the national level in 1994 with the Fédération nationale des artisans du Bénin (FENAB). Since then, most Béninois artisans—including tailors but also weavers, masons, carpenters, mechanics, and others—are card-carrying members of artisans' associations, which include craft-specific groups and pan-artisan bodies organized at all levels of government.[25] Artisans regularly meet in these associations to resolve disputes among masters or between masters and apprentices, organize courses on new techniques, and articulate the concerns of the artisanat within formal politics. As part of an artisanat, Béninois tailors conceive of themselves as a category of labor and an economic sector, and they have attained a political voice in Bénin that rivals those of other groups of workers historically active in West African politics such as union members and civil servants.[26] This book traces these transformations in the gendered, social, and political identities of tailors and how they have helped shape craft knowledge and ultimately the clothes these artisans created.

Africanizing Technologies and the Expertise of Craftspeople

Craftspeople in West Africa have long been innovating and incorporating new technologies into their production methods. Material evidence and oral traditions attest that weavers, appliqué makers, and smiths in precolonial Dahomey embraced new forms and techniques from the Yorùbá kingdom of Oyo and elsewhere.[27] Tailors continued this tradition, and in the mid-twentieth century they brought together ways of making from a vast array of sources to develop and refine their craft knowledge. At various times, tailors adopted tools such as sewing and embroidery machines, metal needles, measuring tapes, photographs, mass-produced catalogues, and scissors, and their primary inputs, textiles, included everything from local weaves made on a variety of looms to manufactured cottons and industrial synthetics. Tailors also incorporated into their production methods new techniques of measuring, mathematics, recordkeeping, and marketing, alongside the more specialized skills of designing, cutting, and sewing. Addressing the multiple ways that tailors innovated, used, and maintained technologies complicates narratives of technological diffusion and places tailors alongside such previously identified groups as food preparers, mechanics, hunters, traditional healers, and scientists as African technological agents.[28]

This book argues that tailors "Africanized" technological things from the West, re-creating them as African technologies.[29] Imported things achieved different symbolic and material functions depending on local contexts.[30] For example, the history of tailoring complicates understandings of industrial objects like the sewing machine that emphasize their innovation and impacts in the West.[31] The modern sewing machine began to be mass produced and marketed by the US Singer company in the 1850s and quickly changed fashion in Europe and the United States—making ready-to-wear cheaper and more accessible and allowing women home producers to quickly alter clothes to keep up with the latest styles.[32] In late nineteenth-century Africa, sewing machines appeared first in missions and colonial outposts but were also adopted into elite material culture as status symbols.[33] Ordinary people in the colonized world often embraced these "small technologies" when they could acquire them, changing how they made clothes and notions around gendered labor, but in ways that diverged greatly from the use of these technologies in Europe.[34] As this book will show, tailors put sewing machines to work beyond just using them to stitch together fabric. In independence-era Bénin, young men in the interior regularly strapped sewing machines behind bikes to travel between towns and villages, making clothes and spreading notions of what constituted new men and women amid the changes of urbanization and decolonization. Tailors used drawings and stamps of the machine as a pictogram to communicate their occupation to publics who did not read French or Fon. Seamstresses like Madame Alikpanou (discussed at the beginning of this introduction) commissioned photographs next to them to assert their expertise about modern fashions to clients on urban peripheries and to invoke notions of female respectability.[35] In an even more specifically local use, tailors relied on the metallic properties of sewing machines to integrate themselves into the emerging community of artisanat alongside more established craftspeople like blacksmiths through a common reverence to the Gu, the *vodun* (deity, spirit) of metallurgy. The sewing machine took on all these meanings and uses in Bénin as tailors Africanized it.

But the case of the sewing machine also underscores the limitations of perspectives that might fully divorce certain technological things from their associations with Western-centric modernity. As objects they might achieve new uses and meanings, but their properties and their associated meanings might remain unchanged. For example, the *clack clack clack* of a treadle sewing machine should be considered like the *rat-a-tat* or the *tip tip tip* of the typewriter as one of "the auralities of mass modernity."[36] Hearing the sound of the treadle, seeing the whir of the needle, and touching the steel machine with its industrial origins fomented associations between its users, the tailors, and the wealth and privilege of the faraway places where the machines were produced. These associations were not effaced through domestication, but rather tailors deployed the machines to craft themselves as men, women, and artisans in ways that acknowledged and often amplified the cachet of their tools' and techniques' suggestions of modernity, industrialization, and Christianity. Indeed, while from the perspective of academic historians and scholars of science and technology studies (STS) it is overwhelmingly clear that tailors and other West Africans were technological agents, it is likewise apparent that among ordinary Béninois science and technology remain categories associated with non-African peoples and places, impacting Béninois engagement with certain technologies and their local symbolic and material uses. In part this is a colonial legacy, since European imperialism relied on the notion of the scientific and technological superiority of Europe and proliferated racial hierarchies based in part on groups' supposed technological aptitudes.[37] But these associations also emerged out of the region's ambiguous precolonial relationships with imported technological things and bodies of knowledge such as writing and accounting.[38] Anthropologist Douglas J. Falen noted in recent fieldwork that Fon speakers might describe "the creation of airplanes, automobiles, cell phones, and computers" as *yovo àzě* (white witchcraft), a contested term to be sure but one that reveals the ambivalence of these technologies as "tools or instruments of power that are guided by the moral disposition of those who wield them" and as visible evidence of global inequality and the marginalization of Béninois.[39] Tailors' adoptions and adaptations of technologies that might have been conceived of as yovo àzě were not a mimicry of Europeans; rather, tailors as a subaltern group within Bénin manipulated and repurposed the power of these materials and techniques to their own ends.[40]

Alongside Africanizing technologies from Europe and elsewhere, Béninois tailors also localized technologies from other groups of Africans. Tailoring is a body of knowledge and know-how that complicates perceptions of what might be considered local versus foreign as well as African versus European.

In *Endogenous Knowledge*, edited by the philosopher Paulin Hountondji, Béninois scholars provided case studies of indigenous techniques, including metallurgy, rain-making, mathematics, and pharmacopeia, both to push back against the idea of the West as having a monopoly over science and to lay the foundation for a development program rooted in African epistemologies.[41] Béninois tailoring, however, was not endogenous to the extent that there were not long-standing cultures of sewing in the region—as recently as a century ago, Fon speakers mostly wrapped cloth as dress. Instead, tailoring developed over a centuries-long series of encounters between the people of southern Bénin and different groups of Africans and Europeans. Historian Clapperton Chakanetsa Mavhunga detailed a series of "*kusangana kweruzivo* (knowledge encounters)" in the case of southern African knowledge of the tsetse fly in which knowledge systems were "fundamentally shaped, altered, diverted, or ended because of the encounter."[42] In the case of tailoring, multiple knowledge systems encountered each other within a single craft that tended to expand and grow during times of increased mobility and to languish during moments when political and economic changes limited the movements of bodies and things.

The craft knowledge of tailoring grew out of these encounters but was refined through collective and embodied innovation and transmission, the hallmarks of West African artisanal practice and ways of knowing. The cooperative labor of needleworkers and their efforts to share techniques and styles through mobile networks of apprenticeship and *cours de perfectionnement* (improvement courses) meant that tailoring was not just "embodied" but a "knowledge-made-in-common," or one emerging from the collective as opposed to the individual innovator.[43] In Bénin, the techniques for making a particular article of clothing were almost never transferred from one tailor to another through written instructions or abstracted technical drawings such as patternmaking. To be sure, tailors developed a sort of "knowing-in-practice" in which forms emerged not out of written plans but rather the craftsperson's own concept of space, their personal aesthetics, and their relationship to the material spaces of the client.[44] Apprentice tailors learned by observing, doing, and repeating small-scale skills (holding a needle, sewing a button, etc.), with the master there not to instruct but to "guide entry" into the discrete tasks that collectively make the craft of tailoring. After months or even years, they began to bring these skills together to construct a garment and later practice cutting.[45] Apprentices also learned other skills of management, marketing, and honing good taste that, along with the processes of design, cutting, and sewing, constituted the collective, embodied craft knowledge of tailors.

The expertise of tailors over matters of style and technologies of production is a subject of material history not just because making is a physical process but also because tailors created a system in which the invisibility of their craft knowledge became visible through rituals and material display.[46] Historian Joshua Grace described an "infrastructure of expertise" in the case of Tanzanian mechanics in which "the material places and spaces, things, and bodies . . . shaped learning, innovation, and assessments of a knowledge's credibility and desirability."[47] For the mechanics at the center of his study, this expertise was coded as masculine and developed in the garage. In contrast, young wives in 1940s Mali communicated their feminine mastery of cooking through their control over metal pots, whether soundlessly stirring them during the preparation of food or bringing them into the home upon marriage.[48] Historian Abena Dove Osseo-Asare provides a very different case of materializing expertise in which Ghanaian "traditional" healers used written documents such as pharmacopeia and math exams "to assert medical authority" amid the rise of biomedicine and its denigration of their know-how.[49] Tailors and other Béninois craftspeople delineated their expertise by actively combining discourses, practices, and ritual objects from "traditions" as varied as Vodun, Ifá (Fa), Christianity, and modern science.[50] They communicated their expertise through the physical spaces of market stalls and workshops, the things within them, and their own dressed bodies, but they, and other Béninois artisans, also concretized their status as experts through adherence to the vodun Gu and strategic displays of handmade diplomas modeled on those given by missions and colonial schools. Yet tailors' acts of rendering their expertise visible also had the unintended consequence of permitting them to be "seen" by the state and subjected them to new forms of governmentality.[51] Their legibility within the modern state culminated in 2013 when the Béninois government, assisted by European NGOs, nationalized artisan credentialing systems with the Certificat de Qualification aux Métiers (CQM) and made liberation ceremonies, such as the one captured in the photograph of Madame Alikpanou and her apprentices, extralegal occasions.

Vodun Aesthetics and Style beyond the Colonial Capital

In the introduction to the influential edited volume *Fashioning Africa*, Jean Allman argued that "power is represented, constituted, articulated, and contested through dress" and that dress and fashion served as a "political language capable of unifying, differentiating, challenging, contesting, and dominating" in colonial and postcolonial Africa.[52] Scholars in the past two decades have developed and refined her point, producing numerous studies exploring the relationship between clothing consumption and colonialism, nationalism, and party politics in Africa. They have consistently shown that Africans entered political debates and expressed discontent through their dressed bodies. Much of this literature has centered African women to trace how they deployed the language of clothing to negotiate gendered power.[53] *Tailoring Identities* takes this rich body of literature as a starting point and shifts the focus from consumption to clothes-making to reveal how this political language came into being through crafting as well as consumption and the complexity of gender within this process. By addressing the history of clothes-making in the *longue durée*, from the era of the Dahomey kingdom, this book reveals the deep roots of this political language and how local aesthetic traditions manifested in twentieth- and twenty-first-century Béninois dress and fashion.[54]

The styles of Béninois clothing and dress were not just "global," "cosmopolitan," or facsimiles of colonial urban cultures elsewhere in Africa but were deeply rooted in precolonial Fon aesthetic and craft practices. In the case of southern Bénin, a "Vodun aesthetic," associated with the material culture of the Fon religion of Vodun, informed clothing practices. In her work on Fon ceremonial staffs (*asen*), historian Edna Bay underscored the "Fon propensity to embrace and adopt influences from many directions" resulting in a "Fon eclecticism" in "items of material culture, technologies, deities, and principles of state organization."[55] Art historian Dana Rush took this a step further, noting that Vodun—as both a religion and a material culture—is "unfinished" and "engages newly arriving components as *already* having been part of the system."[56] Because of this openness, new elements arrived not through "assimilation" but because they were already of the world, and thus of Vodun. Vodun things such as *bociɔ* (power objects), shrines, and other ritual objects materialized the vastness of the spirit world, making it tangible, accessible, and even marketable to followers and potential followers.[57] These Vodun things required an ongoing relationship between the practitioner and the object through the regular application of sacrificial materials, and these interactions activated the thing's power (*bo*).[58] While the everyday dress of Béninois was not usually related to the practice of Vodun, this Vodun approach to the material world affected nonspiritual things as well.[59] Fon speakers sported a layered and draped look that openly embraced fabrics and adornments from elsewhere. Wrappers required adjustment and retucking throughout the day, and ensembles changed from moment to moment as bodies moved under fabric, even as the fabric's thickness, elasticity, and other properties influenced the wearer's intentional tucking, draping, and bodily movement. Extending the approach of seeing clothing as "unfinished" from the obvious case of wrapped fabric to tailored garments might seem counterintuitive, yet it opens the analytical purview from use to questions of (re)tailoring, wear, maintenance, and recycling and grounds them in a local worldview.

Fon values of incorporation and adaptation meant that over time Fon speakers combined tailored items with wrapped fabric as a local aesthetic practice and that these garments were not generally imposed on Fon speakers. The global spread of clothing like men's business suits, trousers, and certain styles of women's dresses has been described as a trend toward "uniformity," or the standardization of bodily practice that accompanied the imperial and commercial expansions that began at the advent of the early modern period.[60] Others have characterized these forms of dress as "world fashions" linked to the rise of cities, as urban dwellers the world over sported sewn clothes in similar silhouettes.[61] Scholars have also focused on modes of self-fashioning that subverted or diverged from imperial and capitalist systems, even as they relied on silhouettes associated with Europe. For example, Black dandies on both sides of the Atlantic donned fancy tailored dress to promote "pride, positivity, and self-worth."[62] In twentieth-century Lagos, people began to wear uniforms (*aso ebi*) of the same fabric tailored into different styles for special occasions and to express solidarity and friendship.[63] The twentieth-century expansion of the tailored silhouette in Bénin is best characterized as a spread of "fittedness," or clothing that formed to the body and conformed to fashion norms (whether Parisian or Lagosian). Ordinary people began to incorporate more tailored garments into their wardrobes not as a colonial imposition but as a gradual stylistic change grounded in a Vodun aesthetic and conception of the material world.

Approaching a clothing regime through the deep history of a local aesthetic opens new possibilities for understanding the spatiality of creativity and clothing design in West Africa. In his 2022 study of five Accra designers, art historian Christopher Brewer argued, "The culture of seamstresses and tailors, found throughout the African continent, is important to acknowledge, as it allows for a more democratic engagement with designer fashions and a given country's fashion culture, albeit through the act of mimicry."[64]

Yet this position assumes a one-way trajectory of African urban artists designing and artisans "mimicking," a model in which style trickles down and design is narrowly conceived along Western standards. Theories and histories of African fashion overwhelmingly center the city, and in Africa this almost always translates into capital cities like Kinshasa, Accra, or Lagos, the former centers of colonial power. Recent literature on African fashion has even occasionally moved the locus of creativity entirely off the continent to diasporic or "Afropolitan" designers and fashion houses in Euro-American locales.[65] On the rare occasion that dress in rural or semi-urban Africa is considered, it is often framed as something imposed by European colonizers or elite African urbanites.[66] But this scholarly emphasis on capitals as drivers of change threatens to render derivative the clothing practices and sartorial experiences of the many West Africans who lived in small cities like Abomey and Bohicon and the villages around them. Being open to the possibility of small towns and villages as generative spaces, as opposed to derivative, permits an exploration of how multiple regimes of style came into play within the realm of Béninois clothing and how the fashions made by an individual tailor emerged from their own creativity and craft knowledge.

Just as the designs of tailors were not simple copies of those developed in European or African capitals, the clothes they made were put to different uses within networks of migration and urbanization in the interior. AbdouMaliq Simone argues that, in the absence of real and meaningful programs in urban planning and local governance, African cities are a "frontier for a wide range of diffuse experimentation with the reconfiguration of bodies, territories, and social arrangements necessary to recalibrate technologies of control."[67] Amid the political and social upheavals of twentieth-century Africa, clothing became a way for people to experiment and embody new notions of self and community, forming the networks that sustain the city. In the small cities of interior Bénin, wax prints and other cloth tailored into a women's top with a matching skirt or pagne (*complet*) allowed women to create new urban personas that called on notions of Christian middle-class respectability while in the 1970s men began to wear polyester *détè* (similar to leisure suits) to express themselves as Béninois citizens and to reject both the traditionalism of Fon wrapping and the perceived elitism of the three-piece suit. Focusing on the making of this clothing shows not just how people used clothing to construct political and social relations but also how specific styles achieved their meaning through tailoring.

Methods and Sources

Tailoring sits at the confluence of various material, social, political, economic, and often very personal processes, and so writing its history requires a methodology that stitches together a diverse array of sources and ways of approaching them. Formal research for this book began with a summer-long apprenticeship with a master seamstress in Bohicon. Years earlier, during the mid-2000s, I had been an avid consumer of Béninois tailored clothing during a twenty-seven-month stint as a Peace Corps volunteer partnered with artisans in Toviklin, a small Adja-speaking community fifty kilometers southeast of Abomey. When I returned to Bénin for research, I sought out an apprenticeship because I wanted to grasp how tailors worked through replication and reenactment, a method of writing material culture history.[68] Anthropologists and historians of Africa have also shown the value of apprenticeship as a method particularly attuned to writing histories of makers and their technologies.[69] When I began the apprenticeship, I already had rudimentary sewing skills, acquired as a teenager employed in Las Vegas shops that rented bridal gowns and tuxedos, and my experiences ironing, reattaching buttons, and performing quick hems aligned rather well with the skills that Béninois boys and girls learn during their first year of apprenticeship. The techniques of cutting and design are much more advanced, and sadly I never became proficient. My master, a seamstress in Bohicon, also introduced me to the everyday experience of running a shop, interacting with clients, and managing the small retail trades that today's seamstresses often do to make ends meet. Chatting with her and other tailors, watching her work, and the repetitions of the treadle drove the elaboration of the research questions at the center of this book.

The book's arguments were further developed over the course of ninety-five oral histories collected from tailors, seamstresses, and their clients in the French and Fon languages and during participant-observation in craft-specific ceremonies, association meetings, and workshops in 2012, 2014–15, and 2021. During both oral historical and ethnographic work, most people were forthcoming, and many spoke proudly of their designs and their careers. Oral histories provided evidence on styles and production methods but also the shifting subjectivities of the artisans themselves. Tailors and clients occasionally kept personal archives, and many of these individuals were kind enough to open them up to me and to permit me to touch, photograph, and document objects as they explained their purposes and histories. Sewing machines and scissors were the most common tools presented, but other things like ceremonial paddles used to playfully smack apprentices, shrines to the vodun Gu, mannequins, and the spaces of workshops were introduced as items necessary to the craft. Articles of clothing proved a much rarer source since only a few people preserved these artifacts due to recycling—individuals refashioned old clothes into new ones for dependents or cut them up for use as diapers, rags, and eventually kindling. In their homes and workshops, tailors also kept documents such as tax receipts, craft association membership cards, accounting logs, old catalogues, agendas from trainings, copies of apprenticeship contracts, and, most important to them, their diplomas, which were often framed and mounted on the walls of the workshops. Finally, most tailors maintained extensive archives of images produced by Béninois photographers. Photographs in albums and on walls were part of a tailor's repertoire of tools since they used them to discuss and market styles, and tailors frequently commissioned images of their masterworks. They also used photographs to manage their identities as artisans by capturing ceremonies specific to craftspeople and affixing headshots to handmade documents.[70] Tailors oftentimes played a significant role in the staging of individual photos, working closely with photographers, and photographic collections in personal archives speak to the priorities and self-fashioning of the individual tailor.[71] These images, like the one of Madame Alikpanou and her apprentices at the beginning of this introduction, form a significant body of evidence for this book's final three chapters. In sum, this project emerged out of sources produced or archived by tailors and began with their interpretations of the limits and possibilities of their craft.

Apprenticeship and conversations with tailors led to where evidence on tailoring might be present in state archives and published sources. In archives in the United States, France, Senegal, and Bénin, I unfortunately never encountered a file labeled "tailors," but sources on tailors and tailored clothing could be found in colonial and national contexts ranging from craft fairs and expositions to programs in technical and artisanal education and within concerns about child labor, "familial production," and rural development. The tools and material inputs of tailoring, such as sewing machines but especially textiles, were also of concern to states that sought to regulate them and harness their power, leaving a hefty archival footprint. Songs recorded by the Herskovitses in the 1930s illuminate the more intimate relationships between wearers and their clothes while European photographic collections, engravings, and illustrations also provide insight into dress and society. As scholars have shown, European-produced visual sources are as problematic as written texts and cannot be read as representative of African experience; rather, these images both generated and reflected colonialist and racist imagery of Africans.[72] Additional published sources included precolonial travelers' accounts, colonial ethnographies, Béninois newspapers, and reports of international NGOs working in the domain of "informal economy." Yet almost all of these archival and published sources presented tailors, and Bénin's artisanat more generally, as a "problem"—as either evidence of African backwardness, a corruption of tradition, or an exploitative labor system. Indeed, tailoring has rarely been understood on its own terms, although tailors and tailored clothing have often been used as an example to illuminate economic or social issues deemed more pertinent. But, by reading these visual and written texts against the grain and through the words and archives of the tailors themselves, one can glean specifics about the development of the craft and the important role of tailoring in giving form and meaning to identity in twentieth-century Bénin.

Tailoring Identities reconstructs the history of tailoring over five chapters and a conclusion. Chapter 1 traces the history of clothing and craft in the precolonial Kingdom of Dahomey to show the deep roots of Béninois acts of sartorial and technological domestication and how textiles and dress helped solidify political authority and social difference. Chapter 2 argues that the expansion of fitted clothing—or clothing that formed to the body and conformed to notions of fashion—was linked to the early twentieth-century development of a sartorial economy in which clothing producers, states, missions, and consumers came into conflict over textile-based dress. The third chapter follows how tailoring developed as a craft in the decades after the Second World War and posits that tailors promoted their products through self-fashioning as masters of modern technology and experts in style, linking processes of craft knowledge formation to mobility and innovation and to the creation of popular new men's styles. Chapter 4 shifts focus from the formation of craft knowledge to the institutionalization of tailors' controls over their expertise through everyday innovations in systems of credentialing and associated rituals, resulting in an assemblage of things that rendered their skill visible and concretized their identity as artisanat. The fifth chapter argues that since the 1970s women have recrafted materials, workshop space, and styles to create new notions of embodied labor and prestige, feminizing both craft and fashion, and fundamentally changing how clothes are made and worn in Bénin. The book concludes with an exploration of tailoring in the twenty-first century and how shifting trade patterns, new media, and changing forms of governance have impacted the work and products of the craft. Béninois clothing culture has undergone profound changes over the past two centuries. The history of tailoring reveals the entanglements of materials, artisanal know-how, and sartorial meaning and how craftspeople were leaders and mediators, giving form and meaning to clothing and guiding how Béninois used it to express and transform identities.

1

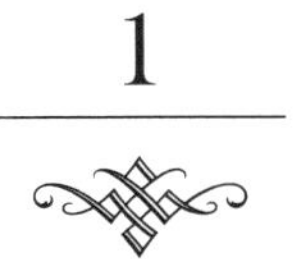

Wrapped and Draped

Making Clothing in the Dahomey Kingdom
(c. 1600–1890s)

War is our great friend; without it there is no cloth,
no armlets, let us to war, and conquer or die.
—Song of the "Amazons," recorded by Frederick Forbes, 1851[1]

Again we remarked amongst this people [Dahomeans] the in-
ordinate hankering after change, novelty, and originality, even
in the most trivial matters, and the failure which results from
their poverty of, or rather their deficiency in, invention.
—Richard Burton, 1864[2]

In 1850, the Dahomean *agojie*, an elite brigade of women warriors, sang to their king (*dadá*), Gezo (1818–58), about the relationship between warfare and cloth. The man who recorded the song, British naval officer Frederick Forbes, was in Dahomey to convince Gezo to abandon participation in the transatlantic slave trade, and like many other European visitors to Dahomey, Forbes was especially intrigued by what he called the *Amazons*, or women warriors. In their song, the agojie suggested that Dahomey's frequent campaigns against neighboring kingdoms and communities led to sartorial riches.[3] Soldiers pillaged locally woven or imported wrappers (avɔ or pagne) from other Africans. Dahomeans also captured artisan weavers, tailors, and needleworkers, bringing their know-how and technologies of avɔ production back to the royal palace. Warriors captured other people, whom Dahomeans sold directly into the transatlantic slave trade, often in exchange for cloth and other adornments.

In the decade after Forbes's visit, another Briton, the explorer Richard Burton, criticized Dahomeans for their interest in "change, novelty, and originality" in "trivial matters," which was in part a condemnation of how the kingdom's elite used cloth and accessories to create elaborate dress.[4] Burton had received a less than cordial welcome from King Glèlè (1858–89) during his 1863 visit, and Burton's disparaging tone hints at both his cold reception and prevailing British biases regarding race, gender, and fashion.[5] But by reading between the lines of Burton's and other Europeans' criticisms, one finds a palace and an urban elite rich in style and elegance. Dress within the kingdom differentiated men from women, rural inhabitants from urban elites, and Dahomeans from outsiders. Dahomean urban elites crafted styles to impress and to inspire reverence from the masses, and their individual outfits also spoke to the ability of the wearer (or one of their servants) to create beautiful outfits out of disparate items. Men and women wrapped copious lengths of fabric around their bodies, but they also sported cloth that had been transformed through cutting and sewing into tailored, fitted items and often enhanced their cloth-based dress by adding arrays of hats, jewelry, and other adornments.

By the time that mid-nineteenth-century British visitors like Forbes and Burton made their observations, a complex and varied Dahomean sartorial system had been in development since the kingdom's founding in the early seventeenth century.[6] This chapter explores how clothes were made and worn in the Dahomey kingdom and shows the deep roots of sartorial and technological domestication and the central role of textiles and clothes-making in the construction and enactment of power, authority, and social identity in the precolonial kingdom. In Dahomey, the palace exerted and maintained control over subjects and foreigners alike through the production and distribution of textiles and through norms and regulations on dress.[7] Although the palace complex of urban Abomey held an inordinate amount of power over dress through sumptuary law and control over artisan labor, it also encouraged innovation and incorporation in style and in techniques of production.[8] Indeed, what Burton dismissed as an "inordinate hankering after change, novelty, and originality" was a manifestation of a Fon worldview and a Vodun aesthetic that valued cultural borrowing and material layering. This propensity to incorporate new styles and techniques led to an array of vestiary configurations that Dahomeans used to express group affinities and personal attributes. While direct state control over clothes-making and textile consumption would slip into decline after the French conquered the kingdom in the 1890s, Fon interest in innovative and incorporative dress endured and even grew into the twentieth century, later flourishing under the skilled and knowledgeable hands of tailors.

Although Burton charged that Dahomeans were incapable of invention, sartorial practices shifted dramatically from the kingdom's founding in the seventeenth century to its colonization by the French in the 1890s. This chapter explores these changes and builds upon the significant historiography of the Dahomey kingdom with sources as varied as texts and images created by European visitors, Dahomean oral traditions and songs, and artifacts collected in Bénin and elsewhere. The accounts of travelers like Burton, Forbes, and other Europeans were shaped by the politics of the slave trade, contained clear exaggerations and misunderstandings, and contributed to the formation of nineteenth-century racism, but scholars have nevertheless used these problematic sources to reconstruct the kingdom's history. This chapter explores change over time from various perspectives, beginning with how Dahomeans made clothing and including the technologies, knowledge, and social formations around the production of avɔ, from fiber cultivation and spinning to weaving and finishing. It continues by tracing the importance of textiles to internal and external markets and the exchange and display of this fabric in social and political life, particularly during the annual festival of Hwetanu. After acquiring cloth, Dahomeans transformed it into dress that connotated status and identity as well as distinction and taste, helping delineate between those in the *tò* (town) and those in the *glètà* (country or bush). Dahomeans likewise used dress to materialize evolving notions of gender, ethnicity, and race and tailor them to the political and social changes of the eighteenth and nineteenth centuries. The history of textiles and dress in Dahomey reveals not only the important role of sartorial culture to political, economic, and social life in the precolonial kingdom but also how artisanal tailoring—a twentieth-century innovation—has deep roots within Fon craft and aesthetic practices.

Making Avɔ: From Fiber to Textile

According to an oral tradition, in around 1600, Dakodonou, an exiled Fon prince of the nearby Kingdom of Allada, migrated with a band of followers to the area around today's Abomey, where they encountered the region's original inhabitants, the Gedevi, and their leader, Dan. After killing Dan, Dakodonou built his palace on top of the entrails of his vanquished enemy and founded

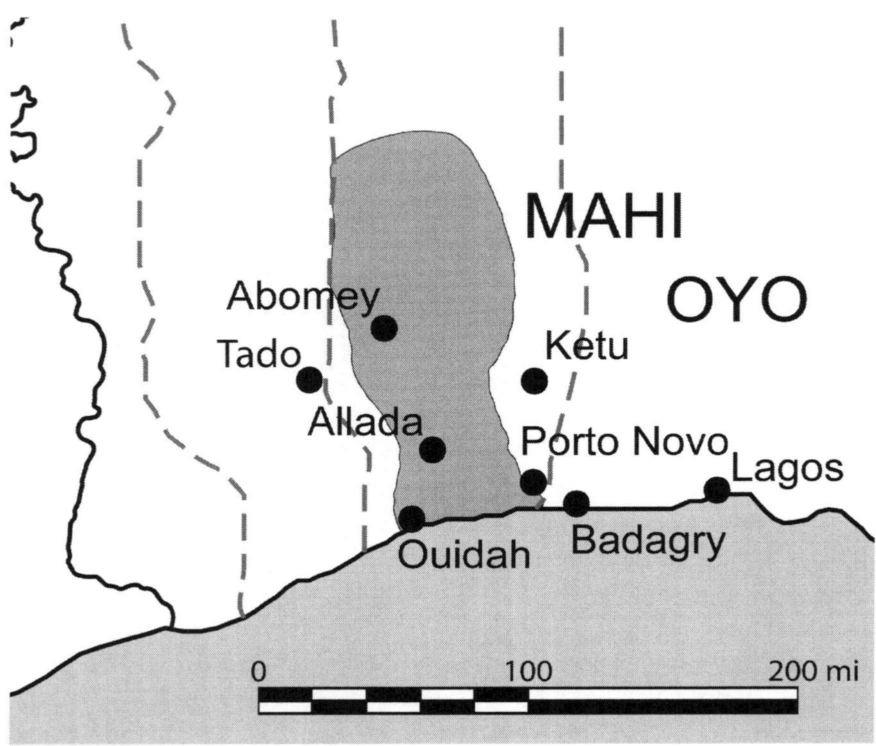

Map 1.1. Dahomey kingdom in the nineteenth century.

the Kingdom of Dahomey.[9] Under the reigns of Wegbaja (1650–80) and Akaba (1680–1716), the kingdom centralized and developed the beginnings of a complex bureaucracy. During the reign of Agaja (1716–40), Dahomey conquered the kingdoms of Allada and Hueda, which integrated Dahomey directly into Atlantic trade networks, although the capital remained at Abomey, a walled city about one hundred kilometers inland. Over the next century, the slave-trading polity raided for captives in communities to the southeast (Adja) and the north (Mahi) and periodically waged war against the Yorùbá kingdoms to the west, becoming at times a tributary state to the Oyo kingdom. These encounters, whether through migration, trade, or warfare, shaped and were shaped by Fon clothing culture and affected the ways that men and women in Dahomey both made cloth and used it as dress.

Throughout West Africa, cloth-making has a long and rich history with significant local variation in materials, techniques, and preferred colors.[10]

The unit of fabric is usually the wrapper, which wearers transform into dress by wrapping or draping it across the shoulder, chest, or waist. Fon commonly refer to wrappers as either *pagne*, a word with French and Dutch roots, or *avɔ*, a Fon term that captures textiles of different materials and origins. Over the course of their many encounters with Europeans along the coast and other groups of Africans, Fon speakers added innovations and techniques to their methods for producing fabric, creating a local textile tradition that was highly complex and varied and that drew upon the skills, knowledge, and labor of several farmers and craftspeople.

The diversity of Fon textiles began within the first step in producing avɔ— growing and harvesting fibers. Farmers cultivated raffia palms (*Raphia vinifera*) for palm wine and for fibers used in the production of mats, baskets, and textiles. Raffia fibers were also important to Vodun, a Fon spiritual practice, and followers twisted and knotted (*bla*) raffia fibers to create strong cords that adorned "power objects" (*bociɔ*) used to ward off "danger and discord."[11] To harvest raffia, women stripped the fronds from the trees, leaving the rest of the palm intact, although they also gathered fibers from trees felled to make palm wine.[12] According to the oral traditions of Abomean palace weavers, their ancestors sourced raffia from wild groves in areas to the north of Abomey as opposed to cultivating fields.[13] Along with raffia, cotton was another important fiber source for textile production. Old World cotton (*Gossypium arboreum* and *Gossypium herbaceum*) was grown in the semiarid regions of the Sahel by the tenth century and likely reached more coastal areas not long after.[14] The area around Abomey is an ecological anomaly in West Africa, which geographers call the Dahomey Gap because the forest-savannah of the interior extends to the ocean, whereas the coastlines to the east and west are covered by tropical rainforest. The relative dryness of the Dahomey Gap made it particularly suited to cotton, and cultivators continued to grow both old-world cotton, often intercropped with yams or maize, and new-world varieties of cotton (*Gossypium hirsutum*) introduced via the Atlantic.[15] By the nineteenth century, the work of gathering or cultivating fibers was done mostly by women and, increasingly, captive outsiders.

Processing both raffia and cotton fibers into thread was another process dominated by women and a key step in the production of cloth. Between harvest and weaving, raffia fibers had to be washed, dried, and sorted. But cotton was even more labor intensive because it needed to be ginned, a time-consuming process of removing the seeds that was done by hand until well into the colonial period. As in fiber cultivation, women did most of the work transforming the ginned cotton into thread.[16] In 1874, J. A. Skertchly, a British naturalist who spent eight months in the kingdom, described the technologies and methods of Dahomean spinning:

> The instrument for this purpose is a thin slip of "bamboo" about a foot long, stuck through a heavy round piece of clay which acts as a fly, and the whole is then twisted by the fingers, the weight of the fly generating sufficient momentum to keep it in motion for a considerable time. The end of the thread twisted from the bundle of cotton on the distaff is attached to this, and as it twirls round the cotton is disengaged with the right hand, and when a thread of sufficient length to allow the spinner to touch the ground has been spun, it is wound round the spindle-stick hitched over its top, and the operation continued. A small quantity of wood ashes is placed near the operator, who from time to time takes a little on her fingers to prevent them adhering to the cotton fibers. The thread is very uneven, and as thick as crochet cotton.[17]

An engraving portraying the tools of the spinners accompanies Skertchly's description (fig. 1.1). The spindle is shown attached to the circular clay fly, or spindle whorl, that weights the tool and increases its speed and efficiency. The spinner at the right of the image holds a distaff of unspun cotton in her left hand while operating the spindle whorl with her right hand.[18] Spinners often did their work with a finished product in mind, since threads intended for the warp (the lengthwise threads of the loom) needed to be stronger than those used for the weft (the crosswise threads).[19] But spinning was a slow process, and generating enough yarn for a single pagne (wrapper) took much more time than weaving it.[20]

Along with portraying the tools and methods of spinning, the engraving also hints at the social construction of spinning as women's domestic labor. The engraving's depiction of the women reflects a long history of European imagery that sexualized and racialized Black women along the West African coast and elsewhere in the Atlantic.[21] Yet, amid its problematic portrayals of women and their bodies, it also provides basic insight into how spinners practiced their craft in a social setting and not necessarily in a workshop or atelier dedicated to thread production. Three of the women in the image are not spinning and seem to be sleeping, lounging, or chatting, suggesting that women spun cotton during breaks from farming, crafts, and other domestic work.[22] Juliette Kanlihano, an Abomey resident born in the 1920s, described a lifetime of spinning and how the work kept empty hands busy while waiting for stews

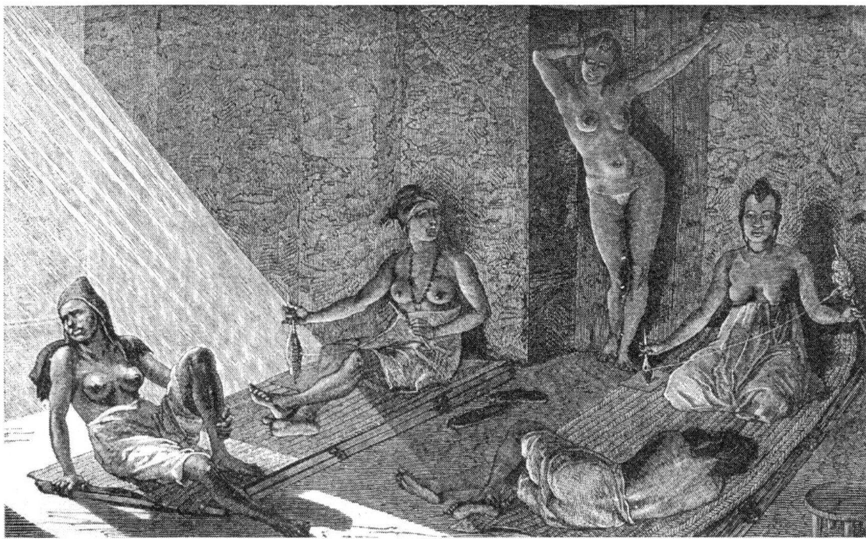

Figure 1.1. "Dahoman Women Spinning Cotton." From J. A. Skertchly, *Dahomey as It Is* (1874). Courtesy of HaithiTrust.

to cook, while selling in the market, or during pauses from other endeavors seen as more profitable or important.[23] Among the Dendi, who occupy an area well to the north of Dahomey on the south banks of the Niger, there was a similar social dynamic around spinning. Dendi women spun cotton "without distinction of status or wealth," and "it was also a time for socializing," with women coming together to craft and chat until well into the night.[24] The lack of designated spinners, the relegation of the work to women's "free time," and the slower pace of spinning versus weaving created a bottleneck in production, and the demand for cloth likely exceeded local availability. As the following section will show, imported cloth, first from interior West Africa and then from the Atlantic trade, supplemented the work of local weavers from the earliest periods of the kingdom's history and probably well before the consolidation of Dahomey in the early seventeenth century.

In contrast to farming and spinning, which were practiced widely, other textile crafts such as weaving were more specialized and less ubiquitous, although weavers worked both within and outside the royal palace. Unlike their counterparts in other parts of West Africa, weavers, spinners, and other craftspeople in Dahomey were not born into endogamous castes or considered a low-status group: The occupation did not confer any type of singular social status. Likewise, there were no guild-like institutions that restricted membership or set craft-specific regulations. Men and women usually took up a craft due to individual preferences and aptitudes, not because of the expectations of society or kinship systems. Craftspeople might be members of royal lineages, farmers, traders, or captive outsiders, as long as they had the desire to do the work. As an example, according to the oral traditions of palace artisans, Agaja encouraged his many children to learn crafts such as smithing, weaving, pottery, and woodcarving. He created a palace training center (*yokpo yokpo xwé*) where young princes could learn such skills. Agonglo (1789–97), one of his great-grandsons, received training in the royal workshop, and oral tradition remembers Agonglo as both a weaver and a woodcarver.[25] Some accounts contend that he even carved his own wooden throne.[26] Craftspeople in Dahomey were not considered socially inferior at all; in fact, they often occupied important positions of power.

In the absence of guilds or castes for managing training and participation in the arts, new craftspeople and their expertise and technologies were regularly incorporated into the kingdom's material culture. The king's forces captured artisans during raids against neighboring societies and wars with nearby kingdoms. In part, Dahomey instigated these wars to meet the demand for captives on the coast.[27] But the palace also profited from warfare by integrating skilled individuals into its productive workforce. Highly skilled craftspeople were separated out from captives bound for the transatlantic slave trade or human sacrifice, and these newly arrived artisans and their methods became part of the kingdom's artistic heritage. Specific lineages, including those who worked with avɔ, like palace weavers and needleworkers, trace their origins to Yorùbá kingdoms.[28] Historian Edna Bay has shown how a talented male artisan might be incorporated into the kingdom as an *ahosi* or "wife of the king." Through the idiom of marriage, the artisan became a subordinate of the king and his children came under royal control. Though a male artisan might gain an exalted position as an ahosi, he also lost power over his own family, and the artisan was unable to move as he wanted or contract marriages for his children.[29] Surely craftspeople throughout West Africa benefited from technological and formal borrowing from neighboring communities. But in Dahomey, innovations within material culture came at the cost of the forced incorporation of individual artisans, their families, and their craft knowledge.

Weaving provides a prime example of how craftspeople fused the technologies of multiple traditions into their own. Weavers worked in both raffia and cotton fibers and transformed them into avɔ using one of two different types of wooden looms—vertical looms used in the Yorùbá kingdoms to the west and horizontal looms similar to those used in the east, most famously in the production of Akan kente cloth. Weavers made both cotton cloth (*kanvɔ*) and raffia cloth (*dévɔ*) on vertical looms but wove only cotton fabrics on horizontal looms, since raffia fibers were too short for the machines. According to Alphonse Ahouado, the official spokesman for Béninois weavers, the Gedevi, the original inhabitants of Abomey, used vertical looms like the various groups of Yorùbá. But when the Gbe-speaking ancestors of the Fon arrived from Tado (present-day Togo) via Allada, they brought the horizontal loom.[30] European visitors to eighteenth- and nineteenth-century Dahomey dismissed horizontal looms as dubious tools, calling them "extremely rude," "artless," and, hyperbolically, "the most awkward machines imaginable," but weavers deftly operated these complex machines by foot, relying on a complex system of pulleys and counterweights to produce high-quality fabric.[31] That weavers in Dahomey employed two very different types of West African looms points to them being at a technological crossroads.[32] But it also underscores the underlying Fon Vodun worldview that privileged incorporation and the diversity of Fon sartorial culture.

While both men and women wove fabric, looms were gendered tools, and their products were destined for different uses. Like weavers in Yorùbá-speaking communities, men and women in Dahomey wove on vertical looms to make either cotton or raffia cloth for the general public.[33] Craftspeople also made avɔ by interweaving both raffia and cotton fibers. The cloth in figure 1.2 is a more recent production held in a private collection in Abomey, but fabric like this—in which raffia and cotton were intricately woven together—often served as one of the highest valued locally sewn cloths.[34] The evenly spaced holes in the fabric resulted from a technique called openwork and reflected the skill of a master weaver.[35] In contrast to vertical looms, only men worked on horizontal looms to weave cotton cloth, and these machines figured prominently in workshops serving the palace and the Dahomean elites. A few families, housed at Gbèkon-Houégbo in the royal palace of Agonglo, the artisan king, formed a weaver lineage that specialized in cloth for royals and their entourages.[36] Despite their disparaging descriptions of horizonal looms, European visitors also highly valued the textiles made on these machines, which they purchased and resold elsewhere along Atlantic trade routes.[37]

Much of the natural-colored cotton cloth that weavers produced went directly to wearers, although dyers, appliqué makers, and tailors occasionally

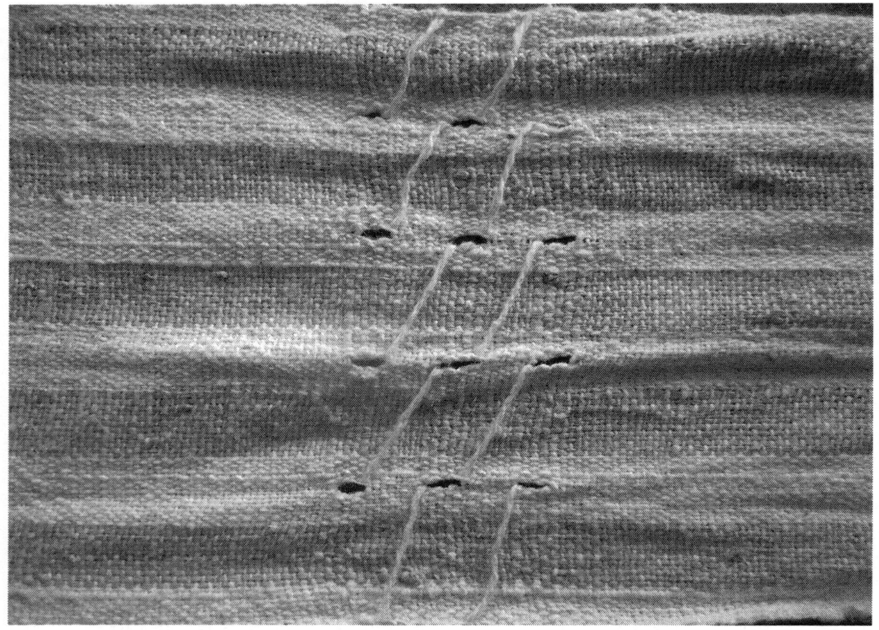

Figure 1.2. Raffia and cotton cloth, 2015. From the personal collection of master weaver Alphonse Ahouado. Photo by author.

worked avɔ into finished products. Craftswomen dyed lengths of cotton or raffia textiles various colors.[38] Dyers also colored locally spun cotton yarn before it was woven. Weavers used this thread, along with imported dyed thread, to create patterns or images on pagne, often the royal symbols of the various Dahomean kings.[39] Indigo grew locally and was "sold in cakes" in local markets, and the rich blue color was prominent in woven and dyed avɔ.[40] Dahomeans and Europeans alike appreciated indigo-dyed cloth as it could "stand washing very well."[41] But indigo was not the only color available to Dahomeans who also dyed cloth shades of red, yellow, and pink.[42] Other craftspeople decorated cloth through appliqué. According to oral tradition, unlike spinning, dyeing, or even weaving, appliqué was a specialized craft practiced by a single lineage, the Yemandjè. Like other artisans who migrated to the Dahomey kingdom, the ancestor of the Yemandjè arrived during the eighteenth century when he was "made to come," in the words of a descendant, to Abomey to serve Agonglo.[43] This appliqué maker and his male descendants decorated avɔ, hats, parasols, and banners with images of animals and inanimate objects. By cutting out shapes with symbolic meaning from an assortment of different colored fabrics and sewing them onto a single base piece, appliqué makers layered cloth with symbolic or spiritual value. Craftsmen of the Yemandjè lineage gained a relatively exalted position within the court of Dahomey through their work in creating regalia and embellished textiles for the palace and *vodunsi* (adherents to a vodun).

In the eighteenth and nineteenth centuries, tailors occasionally served in the palace sewing fabric into tunics, robes, and other voluminous clothing. With preferences skewed to wrapped and draped avɔ, there was little demand for tailoring in the kingdom, and most tailors were also weavers who had picked up methods of hand-stitching clothing using imported needles.[44] The Yemandjè maintain that their ancestors clothed the king by translating their needleworking skills to garment making. With their Yorùbá origins, they hailed from a part of West Africa with an established tradition of tailoring; this was not true in Dahomey and areas farther to the east, where wrapping served as the primary mode of dress. The Yemandjè's expertise in multiple forms of needlework made them important figures in sustaining the regalia and wardrobes of the palace. Along with making new articles of clothing, palace tailors also repaired both new and secondhand ready-to-wear items imported from Europe (*acouta*). Unlike the artisanal tailors of the twentieth century, most precolonial tailors did not use tapes or string to take measurements and either estimated size or determined cuts through bodily measurements such as their elbow to the end of their index finger.[45] Voluminous tunics and trousers did not require precise measurements, and that, along with a small and exclusive clientele, forestalled the practices of measuring and recordkeeping that would prove important to the craft knowledge of later forms of tailoring.

Along with African tailors who traced their origins to Yorùbáland, at least one mixed-race tailor served the king and his court. Bulfinch Lambe, a slave trader and the first European to record his observations of Abomey, described a tailor living in the palace in the 1720s during the reign of Agaja. According to Lambe, there was "an old mulatto Portuguese, which he [King Agaja] bought of the Popoe people . . . and though this white man is his slave, yet he keeps him like a great caboceroe [political merchant elite], and has given him two houses, and a heap of wives and servants. . . . Once in two or three months, he mends . . . some trifle or other for his majesty."[46] The presence of the old tailor led Lambe to conclude that "if any tailor, carpenter, smith, or any sort of white man that is free, be willing to come here, he will find very good encouragement, and be much caressed, and get money if he can be contented with this life for a time, his majesty [pays] every body extravagantly that works for him."[47] Similar to an African artisan incorporated into the palace complex as ahosi, this tailor received wealth and wives from Agaja, and the craftsman enjoyed a relatively exalted position despite his bonded status. Clearly, Agaja highly valued the labor of this tailor and his ability to transform pagne and maintain his wardrobe. However, Lambe's description also makes it clear that there was little work for a palace tailor. The man "mend[ed]" only "once in two or three months," showing just how little sewn clothing the dadá and others wore on a day-to-day basis.

The farmers and craftspeople who worked the different stages of avɔ production crosscut distinctions of status, gender, ethnicity, and even race. While this speaks to the general weakness of these categories during the precolonial era, it also hints that success in clothes-making was associated more with the skill of the individual than with the constraints of social identity.[48] This aspect of craft in Dahomey formed an important difference between Dahomean craftspeople and the well-known casted artisans elsewhere in West Africa. Yet, like the Mandinka *nyamakalaw* (craftsperson) who translated their occult powers to amulet-making, some artisans in Dahomey were able to harness their unique relationships to the spiritual world to create products imbued with additional value.[49] Dahomeans might call upon the artist's individual relationships to a vodun (deity or spirit) to instill objects with religious and spiritual meaning during acts of making.[50] For example, while many women spun cotton in their downtime, only vodunsi (devotees of a vodun) produced "the sacred yarn that is used to thread the beads which encircle the various fetiche deities."[51] Artisans who arrived in the kingdom as captives or through other means also brought their own vodun. In the royal workshops of Gbèkon-Houégbo, weavers crafted certain cloths according to notions of purity and secrecy—in the nude in the dead of night—and weavers intended this cloth for the royal body or for vodun ceremonies.[52] The spiritual qualities of these things were not simply activated through ritual or sacrifices over completed lengths of cloth; rather, they had to be worked by appropriate and knowledgeable artisan hands during each step of the production process in order to attain their power. But whether avɔ was intended for spiritual use or everyday dress, textiles passed through many skilled hands, and the diversity of the workers, their tools, and their craft knowledge created a rich and dynamic textile culture in the Dahomey kingdom.

Textile Transactions, Social Relations, and Political Authority

The slow pace of cloth production, especially the spinning of cotton, meant that demand for avɔ in Dahomey likely exceeded local artisanal production, and Dahomeans looked elsewhere to meet their sartorial needs. But understanding the trade and exchange of textiles solely in terms of market forces or as part of a fashion system ignores the complexity of Fon textile transactions within local social and cultural systems.[53] Approaching textile markets through the lens of consumer demand also mischaracterizes the motivations behind Dahomeans' propensity to trade for cloth, especially as they built one of the most formidable slaving states in Africa. Dahomeans sought new textiles not simply to amass wealth or to express prestige; the exchange and display of cloth in many instances helped constitute social relations and political authority in the Fon kingdom.

Even before the consolidation of the Dahomey kingdom, the region's inhabitants supplemented textiles made and finished locally with imported cloth and clothing items. Archeological sites in southern Bénin suggest that people there produced goods for market trade as early as the fifteenth and late sixteenth centuries and that there was "both intra- and interregional exchange" to other parts of West Africa.[54] Individuals and households produced commodities in exchange for foodstuffs and "textiles, basketry, calabashes, and wooden and ceramic vessels."[55] From the sixteenth to the early eighteenth centuries, neighboring Allada, a densely populated center about halfway between Abomey and the coast, was the most powerful kingdom in the region and an early textile exporter in the Atlantic trade. At the Alladan port of Offra, Portuguese, Dutch, and Swedish merchants purchased slaves, ivory, and "Allada" or "Ardra" cloth to resell in the Gold Coast and São Tomé.[56] Historian Colleen Kriger suggests that the seventeenth-century European moniker "Allada cloth" included textiles woven on both vertical and horizontal looms and may have come from Edo and Yorùbá sources.[57] Labeling cloth as "Allada" did not refer to a single production method or place of origin but rather to the region where Europeans purchased the cloth, and hints at a well-developed network of cloth trade that stretched into the West African interior.

Dahomey conquered Allada in the 1720s, and the kingdom absorbed this textile trade into its market system, although this likely supplemented a pre-existing market for imported African textiles within Dahomey itself. European travelers' accounts confirmed that Dahomeans avidly consumed textiles produced by and associated with other groups of Africans, hinting at the longevity of these interior West African textile markets. In the eighteenth century, the slaver Robert Norris noted the presence of "Eyo" cloth from Oyo in Abomey.[58] A century later, Burton described "a group of fifty Nago or captive Egba women in dark indigo dresses," perhaps wearing *adire*, an indigo resist-dyed cloth from Yorùbáland.[59] There was also a small Muslim population in urban Abomey, and these migrants forwent raffia cloth to wear tailored cotton fabrics imported from the interior.[60] Hausa traders who exported black shiny cloth from Kano also likely sold their textiles as far south as Dahomey.[61] Although evidence of internal African markets is scarce, Dahomey's known integration within the larger political and economic systems of West Africa suggests that textiles imported from other African groups were probably familiar and even widespread throughout the period in which the kingdom existed.

Dahomey conquered the Hueda kingdom and its port city of Ouidah in 1727, giving the interior kingdom direct access to the transatlantic trade in African captives, cloth, clothing, and other adornments. The Portuguese, Dutch, English, and French had established trading forts in Ouidah, and by the end of the transatlantic slave trade, Ouidah would have the dubious distinction of exporting the third highest number of captives by volume. One of the most exchanged items for these enslaved individuals was, of course, cloth. Some of the most popular types of cloth traded to Africans included calicos, chintz, and Indian-made Guinea cloth, as well as linens, silesias, silks, and velvets from Europe.[62] The European forts also traded in new and secondhand clothing (acouta) including gowns, shirts, jackets, and, most commonly, "kerchiefs" or hemmed, usually small, square pieces of cloth that consumers used as head coverings, neckerchiefs, or loincloths.[63] Imported hats, caps, beads, and jewelry of all sorts were also exchanged for captives in Ouidah and other points of coastal trade.

Dahomeans purchased both local and imported cloth in periodic regional markets (*ahi*), although proximity to the urban centers of Ouidah, Abomey, and Cana often determined availability. Kings often established these periodic markets after military conquests. By capturing a conquered enemy's vodun protector of a market, the king was able to absorb the commercial power of the vanquished into the kingdom. For example, Gezo founded Houndjroto, the primary ahi in Abomey, after his 1830–32 conquest of Mahi, and it remains the site where most fabric is traded in the former capital city.[64] In coastal Ouidah, European traders sold fabric directly to African clients.[65] The "drapery department" of the Ouidah market was incredibly varied and consisted of local weaves and imported textiles including "country cloths, either of cotton woven in narrow strips and sewn side by side, or of twisted grass, dyed in various colours; prints." According to Skertchly, "The more gaudy the pattern the more saleable."[66] Alongside these lengths of cloth, market traders sold accessories and necessities for finishing cloth into clothing such as "grass hats, tapes of all colours, fringes, ribbons, thread and cotton, bundles of cotton yarn and other articles."[67] While an array of textiles were available within the markets of southern Dahomey, the further one traveled north of Abomey, the more raffia cloth replaced imported fabrics and labor-intensive local cotton weaves.[68] Markets throughout the region were connected, but proximity to coastal trade facilitated a greater variety of textile products, likely at a lower cost.

Cloth was not just a good traded on the market; it also facilitated the exchange of other trade goods in the interior and on the coast by acting as one of the kingdom's primary currencies. The divisibility of strip cloth led it to be an early form of currency in the Sahel and Hausaland before the arrival of cowries.[69] Toby Green has argued that cloth, along with cowries, gold, and enslaved people, was one of the many currencies within the trading networks across the Sahara and later the Atlantic.[70] By the eighteenth century, Dahomey was a fully monetized economy with cowries as its primary currency, but cloth still circulated as a means of paying taxes and tribute alongside cowries.[71] For example, canoemen in 1850s Ouidah received cowries and rum as regular pay during their employment transporting goods and captives to ocean-going vessels, but they received a bonus of ten pieces of cloth at the end of their two-year contract.[72] These textile transactions meant that cloth circulated widely, and there were many ways that an individual might acquire it other than as an outright purchase in a market.

The origins, color, and fibers of cloth affected how Dahomeans utilized them in rites of passage and other social relations. By the nineteenth century, a respectable Fon burial required an expensive funeral shroud, and Dahomeans buried their dead with cowries, rum, and small rolls of cloth.[73] Tradition holds that cloth gifted to the dead must be a local weave dyed dark blue-black with indigo.[74] In a 1931 recording of a Fon song, singers recalled how "silk (cloth) one puts it in the grave. / This will go into grave with the other cloth (this) cloth one puts in the grave."[75] Along with burying bodies with bolts of cloth, lengths of cloth were layered on the body of the deceased. Once removed from the face of the dead, these clothes contained important powers when layered on objects, keeping others from death.[76] Dahomeans also gave cloth as a part of bridewealth to solidify the bonds of marriage, binding lineages and expanding kin networks. The quality and amount of cloth determined the type of marriage and whether the lineage of the bride or the groom held rights over children born from the union.[77] In both death and marriage, Dahomeans used cloth to assert social and kin relations.

The colors of textiles played key roles in communication, the facilitation of commerce, and relations between Dahomey, foreigners, and other African polities. Skertchly retold how when traveling from Ouidah to the court of Abomey, "passage beneath the *joji* [entrance to a village or town] was secured by [a] stick, which, being wrapped in a white cloth, indicated our being upon state business."[78] The white cloth showed passersby and local authorities that the travelers were on an official mission for the king and should not be harassed. Cudjoe Lewis, or Kossula, a man captured in Dahomey and transported to the United States in 1861, also observed different colored clothes communicating intentions during his forced march from his natal village to Abomey. Villages flew white flags to signify that they "pay to Dahomey whut dey astee dem."[79] Kossula's description of the signal for a tribute-paying polity is similar to Skertchly's assertion that white flags conveyed "state business" and peaceful relations. Kossula noted that red flags indicated that a village "ain' goin' pay no tax to de Dahomey" and that war was inevitable while black flags designated that a ruler had recently died and "dey doan bother [them]."[80] While these descriptions do not indicate whether the cloth was locally woven or imported, they do show how cloth, once affixed to a pole, served as a system of symbols relaying the intentions of the flyer. The white-red-black distinction described by Kossula mirrors the descriptions of twentieth-century scholars, implying deeper roots to more contemporary uses of colored cloth. In her work of Fon power objects, art historian Suzanne Blier noted that white cloth implied "protection and abundance," red was a dangerous color worn only by vodunsi or royalty, and black referenced "strength, family, ancestors, mourning, death, nighttime, and fertile earth."[81] Cloth flags printed in black, white, and red continue to be incorporated into vodun shrines throughout southern Bénin.

Beyond their importance to trade and communities, lengths of cloth also had important uses within the formal politics of the kingdom. Dahomean dadá materialized their power and authority over their subjects and others by gifting, receiving, and displaying fabric during public ceremonies, most importantly at the festival of Hwetanu, which Europeans called "Annual Customs." This monthlong ceremony celebrated the ancestors and showcased Dahomean military, material, and royal might. Agaja first held Hwetanu around 1710, and Dahomeans continued the ceremony until the French conquest in the 1890s.[82] European narratives of Hwetanu tended to focus on its more gruesome aspects, such as the ritual sacrifice of dozens to thousands of men, women, and children and the display of the skulls of enemy combatants.[83] During the transatlantic slave trade, proslavery Europeans used these accounts to argue that those destined for sacrifice were better served by being sold into slavery and transported to the Americas. Abolitionists wrote salacious accounts of the kingdom to provide evidence of the amoral effects of slaving on African society. Although the intentions of their European authors make these accounts problematic sources for historians, Robin Law has argued that these characterizations of Dahomey as a "militaristic and despotic state" largely replicated the Dahomean regime's own self-representations.[84] The kingdom sought to portray itself as an oppressor to instill fear, respect, and order among Africans and Europeans alike. The distribution and display of cloth, while marginalized in contemporary and scholarly accounts of Hwetanu, was instrumental in the processes of establishing the powerful persona of the king and maintaining allegiance to him.

Cloth flowed from subjects and outsiders to the monarch and from the king back to them, solidifying the relationship between the two. The quality of this exchanged cloth reflected the rank of the person and their proximity to royal power. The slave trader Robert Norris, an observer of Hwetanu during the reign of Tegbesu, provided one of the most detailed descriptions of the ceremony. In 1772, Tegbesu demanded that the governors of the French, British, and Portuguese trading forts at Ouidah travel to the interior to attend the festival. He required European invitees to "make a present on the occasion" to include "at least one piece of Indian damask, or some other handsome silk," while African merchants paid their tributes in cowries.[85] Other attendees included "the vice-roy [sic] of Whydah [Yovogan], and the governors of the different towns and provinces," and each of these local administrators came with presents and "an account of their conduct, and of every circumstance which the king wishes to be informed of."[86] Norris wrote that local administrators "who acquit[ed] themselves to [the king's] satisfaction" received "a large cotton cloth, manufactured in the Eyo country, of excellent workmanship, which they afterwards wear for an upper garment."[87] The finely made cloth from Yorùbáland signified the king's approval of the administrator, and when the recipient wrapped the Eyo fabric around his body he made the royal endorsement public. The king's distribution of cloth materialized bureaucratic hierarchies and the "Prime Minister" received the first choice of fabric with "the rest following his example, according to their rank."[88] These men confirmed their status through the types of gifts given to the king while the king redistributed the textiles to reaffirm administrative categorizations and social position.

The king also distributed cloth as part of "a profusion of presents" to ordinary people to show his authority over and benevolence to his subjects.[89] Francis Chesham's engraving "Last day of the Annual Customs for Watering the Graves of the King's Ancestors" portrays royal gift giving and makes clear its relationship to monarchial authority (fig. 1.3). In the far left of the engraving, a large pile of fabric sits on a platform that holds the king, his entourage, and visiting dignitaries. A man underneath the platform seems to be inspecting a newly acquired pagne. In the right of the image, a piece of cloth whizzes through the air from the platform toward the masses, who hold their hands up in anticipation. Although Chesham likely did not witness Hwetanu, his engraving reflected eighteenth-century descriptions of the ceremony and the platform from which the king distributed textile wealth. Norris described the platform as covered with "piled heaps of silesias, checks, calicoes, and a variety of other European and Indian goods; a great many fine cotton cloths that are manufactured in the Eyo country; and a prodigious quantity of cowries."[90] The king distributed these goods, with the highest-ranking person getting first choice of the Yorùbá "Eyo cloth" or the rich silks.[91] While human sacrifice may have been important in instilling fear in Dahomean subjects, African neighbors, and Europeans, the gifting of cloth and other goods also served to foster loyalty to the monarch.

The dadá and court also relied on the grandeur of the king's textile holdings to convey power and to delineate prestige. Attendants held up fabric around the king to protect him from the popular gaze when he ate or drank.[92] Lengths of cloth also served to literally separate the king's procession from the masses

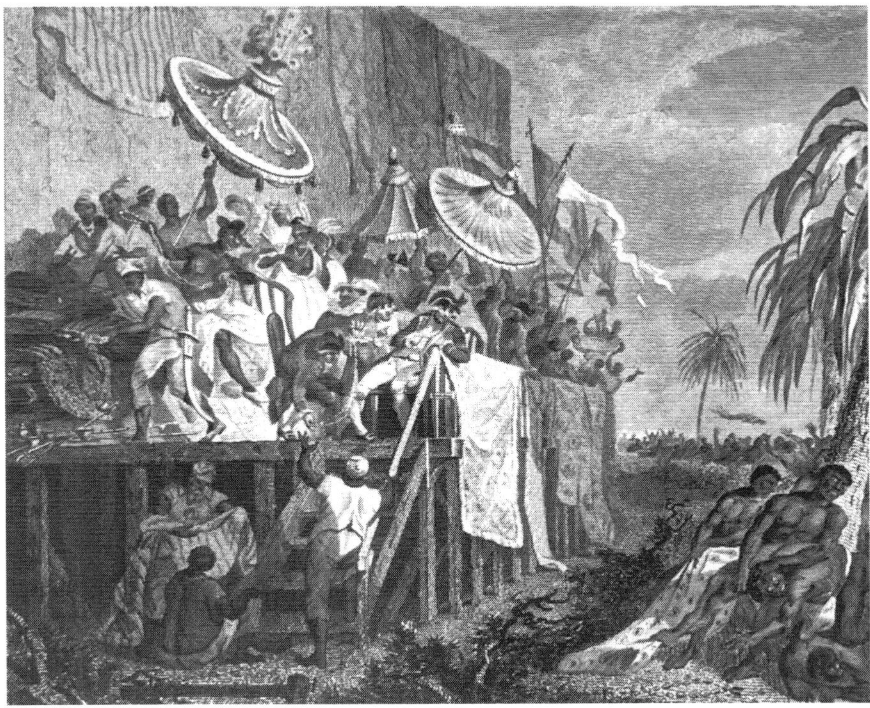

Figure 1.3. Francis Chesham, "Last Day of the Annual Customs for Watering the Graves of the King's Ancestors." From Archibald Dalzel, *The History of Dahomey* (1793).

during Hwetanu, with the king staying behind a "higher enclosure of finer cloth" while lesser-quality cloth created a barrier between other members of the court and the public.[93] These barriers of cloth mirrored the earthen barriers or wall-and-ditch systems (*agbogbo*) that encircled the region's towns, including Abomey, and served not to fortify an urban area but to create a "socially distinct space."[94] "Crimson velvet cloth" laid horizontally on the ground created a carpet where the king's subjects prostrated themselves before his throne.[95] Finally, the kingdom's regalia, at least in its final century, was often textile-based and included appliqué banners, flags, and umbrellas sewn by the Yemandjé.

In the 1870s, Skertchly observed an "enormous" patchwork textile called the *Nunupweto* at the center of a political and religious ritual. According to Skertchly, Gezo had created the Nunupweto, and Glèlè planned to wrap himself in the massive cloth after Dahomey emerged victorious in the campaign against Abeokuta, although Glèlè's armies would eventually lose that war. The Nunupwweto, or "'omnipotent' cloth," as Skertchly translated, was a large quilt-like object stitched together from "samples of every kind of textile fabric that is imported into the kingdom," including various-sized pieces of "denhams, chintzes, silks, vento-pullams, velvets, &c." This cloth was "an enormous length of four hundred yards and a breadth of about ten feet."[96] Although patchwork techniques like appliqué were practiced in the kingdom, the Nunupweto had no particular pattern, and the various textiles that made up the whole were "arranged hap-hazard, and of every hue and design that can be imagined."[97] Attendants hoisted the unwrapped cloth over the heads of a cheering crowd by attaching it to long poles. Not long after the raising of the Nunupweto, court servants piled other cloths into great heaps, "until the accumulation formed a wall of gorgeous-coloured fabrics nearly six feet high, the grandest silks being selected as the uppermost cloths."[98] The sheer size of the Nunupweto and the abundance of fabric displayed by being pulled taut or stacked high shows how Fon valuations of fabric exceeded its practical use or aesthetic qualities. Dahomeans used cloth to intimidate and impress at the same time that its exchange and distribution fostered allegiances and reaffirmed social and political identities. Cloth was not just a symbol of prestige or an allusion to royal wealth; control over the circulation and display of textiles directly constituted the wealth and power of the monarch.[99] In sum, Dahomeans used textiles, one of the most important and widespread materials in the kingdom, for all kinds of social, economic, and political purposes, and their color, texture, origin, and size were associated with different meanings and uses. Cloth, in other words, was not just the stuff of clothing.

Cloth Transformed: Dress and Style in the Tò

As previously shown, the making of cloth relied on the labor, craft knowledge, and material expertise of multiple farmers and artisans, and Dahomeans exchanged and displayed this fabric to concretize economic, social, and political relations. The distribution of both locally made and imported textiles during Hwetanu helped generate distinctions among elite and non-elite Dahomeans, but these differences became even more salient when cloth adorned bodies as dress. The king, inhabitants of the palace, and other elites used dress to display their power and prestige, regulate social categorizations, and foster new notions of taste. Elite dress was part of a uniquely urban material culture and helped to delineate difference between those who lived in the tò (town) versus the glètà (country or bush).[100] Textiles flowed from the two anchors of Dahomean urban life—the market (ahi) and the palace—and the palace communicated style to the rest of society during public spectacles such as Hwetanu. Dress distinguished elites at least by the early eighteenth century, but elite dress became progressively more complex over the course of the nineteenth. Similar to the transformations within technologies and forms of pagne production, elite dress reveals how Fon valued incorporation and innovation, although the palace guided these changes.

The royal body served as the ultimate arbiter of taste, setting sartorial standards for the tòvi ("children of the town" or citizens). Although depicting the clothing of "nobles" and "wives of the king" in Ouidah, not the inland Fon kingdom, an engraving included in French Captain Des Marchais's account of the Slave Coast gives insight into regional elite dress during the early eighteenth century (fig. 1.4). Their dress included wrapped cloth of domestic and foreign origins as well as articles of clothing tailored locally or imported as ready-made from Europe, and elaborate accessorizing complemented these fabric coverings. In the earliest European description of the Dahomean king, dating from the 1727 Hwetanu, William Snelgrave described Agaja has having "a Gown on, flowered with Gold, which reached as low as his Ancles; an European embroidered Hat on his Head; with Sandals on his Feet."[101] A hundred years later, Forbes described Gezo as wearing "a white silk flowing robe, flowered in blue, and a gold-laced hat" for the procession of the king's wealth but "dressed in an old black waistcoat, a white night-cap, and a cloth round his loins" while seated on the royal platform where he witnessed offerings and distributed gifts.[102] The "old black waistcoat" worn with a wrapper instead of trousers represented a common practice of juxtaposing imported items with local methods of wrapping and draping. At another point, Gezo met the crowd "plainly dressed, in a loose robe of yellow silk slashed with satin stars and half-moons, Mandingo sandals, and a Spanish hat trimmed with gold lace; the only ornament being a small gold chain of European manufacture."[103] Lacking any sort of official royal costume, kings from at least Agaja to Béhanzin wore complex amalgamations of different styles and adornments that Europeans considered "Mandingo" or "Spanish," creating Dahomean outfits that were a bricolage of items and hinted at the far reaches of the kingdom's influence and contacts.

The deep-seated practice of incorporating forms associated with outsiders into the king's dress is best exemplified through the story of Tegbesu's 1732

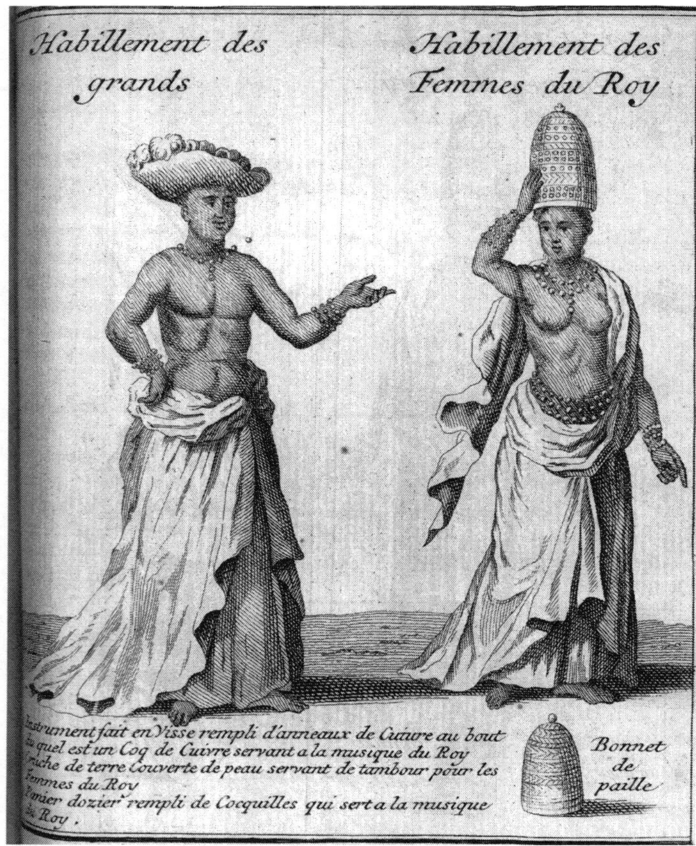

Figure 1.4. Clothing of nobles and the king's wives. From Jean-Baptiste Labat, *Voyage du Chevalier des Marchais en Guinée* (1730).

accession to the throne and his royal symbol, the tunic-wearing buffalo (fig. 1.5). According to oral tradition, Agaja sent one of his young sons, Tegbesu, as tribute to the Yorùbá Kingdom of Oyo, where he was raised as a ward of the court. Eventually, Tegbesu returned to Dahomey and took the throne, but his years abroad had left him with a taste for Oyo style, including clothing, hats, and sandals. The official history of the kingdom explains Tegbesu's royal symbol, the buffalo wearing the tunic, as representative of his struggles to ascend the throne. After Agaja's death, political factions proceeded to vie over who became the new king, and during this period Tegbesu had to wear Agaja's tunic for a full day. But there was a conspiracy against his claim, and

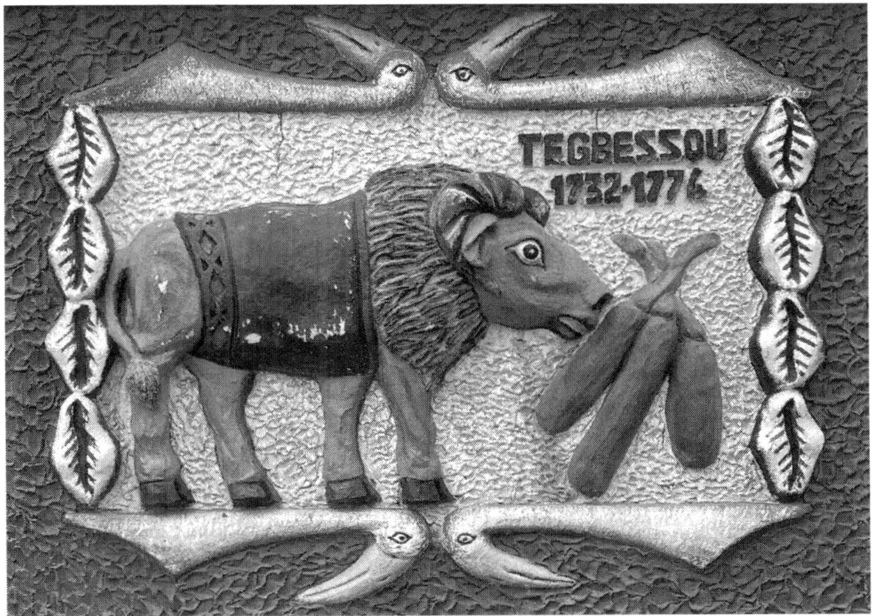

Figure 1.5. Bas-relief of the royal symbol of Tegbesu on an Abomean wall, June 2021. Photo by author.

a plotter, hoping to appoint a different royal to be king, filled the shirt with nettles. The tale emphasized Tegbesu's perseverance and strength since he wore the uncomfortable shirt to eventually become king, but the account also hinted at the role of clothing in forming ideas about who was fit to rule. Perhaps returning from Oyo clad in Yorùbá wear, the king had to prove his ability to lead Dahomey by literally wearing the shirt of the previous king. Once he was king, Tegbesu successfully incorporated Yorùbá styles from his youth into Dahomean courtly dress. He also brought Yorùbá artisans into the Dahomean palace and encouraged Fon-speaking artisans to replicate Yorùbá-made textiles and adornments.[104] Tegbesu's reign and incorporation of Yorùbá forms into the material culture of the Fon kingdom approaches an early revolution in Dahomean style, at least within the confines of the palace.

Similar to the king, elites wore dress that was incredibly complex and varied. These men included ministers of the court, local administrators, *caboceers* (political and merchant elite), and *ahisinon* (private traders) and although they dressed in the cloth gifted from the king, they also undoubtedly acquired their own fabric in local markets or from European merchants.[105] European descriptions of these elite men reveal a system of distinction that relied on differences in color, fabric, and ornamentation. A longer length of avɔ indicated a higher-status man, with greater value placed on certain fabrics such as Eyo cloth, silks, velvets, and brocades. Slave trader Archibald Dalzel, who spent four years in Ouidah in the 1760s, described Dahomean men's dress:

> The dress of the men, in *Dahomey*, consists of a pair of striped or white cotton drawers, of the manufactory of the country, over which they wear a large square cloth of the same, or of European manufacture. This cloath [*sic*] is about the size of a common counterpane, for the middling class; but much larger for the Grandees. It is wrapped about the loins and tied on the left side by two of the corners, the others hanging down, and sometimes trailing on the ground. A piece of silk or velvet, of fifteen or eighteen yards, makes a cloth for a *Caboceer*.... The arms and upper part of the body remain naked, except when the party travels or performs some piece of work, when the large cloth is laid aside, and the body is covered with a sort of frock or tunic, without sleeves.[106]

While a wealthy caboceer might wrap his torso in "silk" or "velvet" up to fifteen or eighteen yards (*grande pagne*), most men wore cloth that was "about three yards long."[107] They wrapped the cloth in a certain way, usually leaving the right arm free to permit movement. If needed, men might exchange the upper-body wrapper to sport a tunic made from a folded-over piece of cloth sewn together on the sides with neck hole along the folded edge. Tunics covered the upper body but freed the arms from the constant adjustments of wearing a wrapper.[108] Elite men's dress was a strategic display of wealth and privilege, and wrapped fabric required a certain bodily comportment that slowed movement and prevented physical labor.

Elite men who wore a grand pagne, or tunic, over their upper body wore either another wrapper around their waist or a pair of tailored baggy shorts (*chokoto* and *tchanka*) on the lower part of their body. Often, the wearer selected a pagne of a different fabric for the lower part of the body, creating a contrast with the wrapper covering the torso. In a French postcard image (fig. 1.6), the last independent king, Béhanzin (1890–94), sits at the center flanked by his family, who are dressed in wrapped pagne on both the upper and lower parts of their bodies. Both pieces of Béhanzin's fabric were strip cloth, with the seams visible on the solid upper wrapper, while the under wrapper was

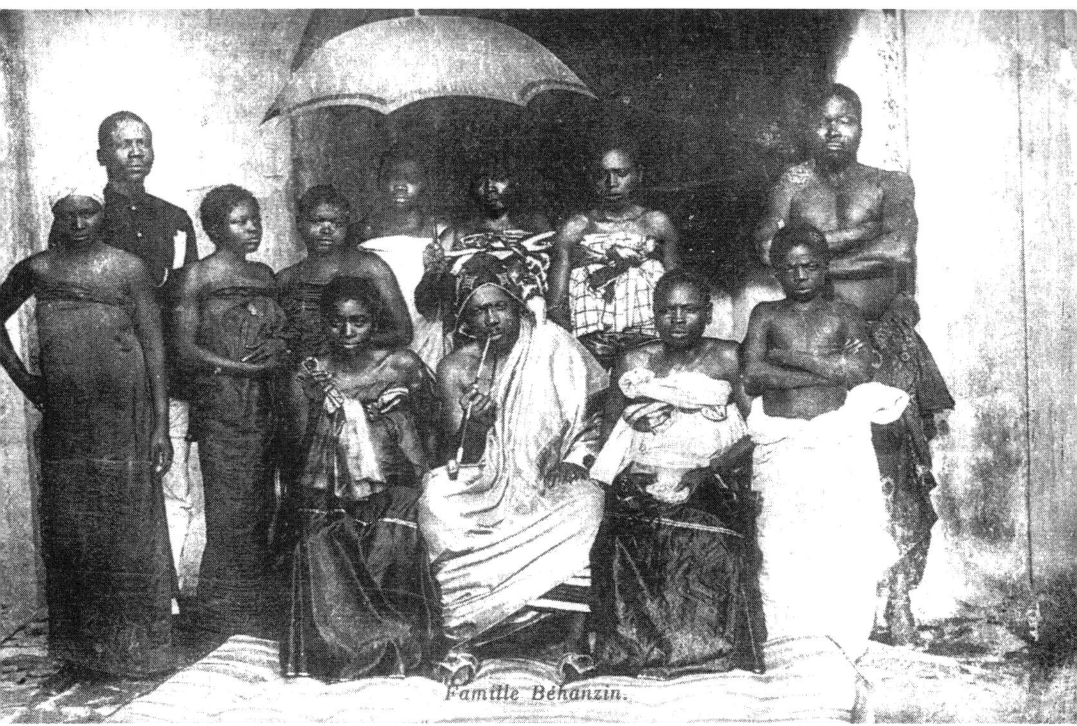

Figure 1.6. "Béhanzin Family," late nineteenth century. Postcard 4F1-1398, Colonial Postcard Collection, National Archives of Senegal.

striped, probably woven of white and indigo yarn, although the black-and-white image makes it impossible to tell. Although some elite men wore this style of over and under wrappers, others wore fabric tailored into a pair of baggy shorts, called *chokoto*, either under the lower avɔ or as a visible garment. Dalzel described chokoto as "a pair of striped or white cotton drawers of the manufactory of the country" while Norris characterizes "country dress" as "a pair of wide drawers."[109] According to local tradition, this short pant with a panel in between the two legs, also called the *tchanka*, is original to Dahomey, unlike most tailored styles, which are admittedly based on European and other African garments.

Apart from wrapped and tailored cloth, accessories and other adornments constituted the dress of the king and other elite men in Dahomey. The king often wore fancy European- and Yorùbá-style hats, and he also held exclusive rights over footwear.[110] Sandal makers supported by the palace produced the king's footwear during a secretive ritual, and their descendants attributed the style and its manufacture to one of Tegbesu's imports from Oyo.[111] Men also wore necklaces made of coral or other local and imported beads, and high-ranking men carried clubs and staffs (*recade*), with the lower-ranking caboceers carrying ornamental blunt sabers.[112] Local artisans made these objects or they were imported from elsewhere in Africa or through Atlantic trade, and their use was but one aspect of a complex culture of male adornment where rank and status materialized on the body.

In general, elite women's clothing consisted of fewer tailored items and accessories than elite men, but, similar to men, avɔ was the basic unit of dress. In 1724, Lambe, in a letter written while a captive of the court, described the wives of the king as wearing uniforms of wrapped cloth. The king, "having at least 2,000 wives . . . when 160 or 200 of them go with small pots for water, they one day wear rich silk waist cloths, called **** [*sic*]; another day they all wear scarlet clothes, with three or four large strings of coral round their necks, and their leaders sometimes in crimson, sometimes in green, and sometimes blue velvet clothes, with silver gilt staffs in their hands, like golden canes."[113] The women wrapped their "rich silk waist cloths" differently from men. Instead of the masculine style of throwing one end of the upper cloth over their shoulder, women "simply wound [it] round their persons above the breasts."[114] Again, gendered distinctions of wrapping pagne are evident in figure 1.4, as the women to the left of Béhanzin wear pagne tied horizontally above their breasts. Younger women might wear one wrapper covering the waist to the floor or mid-calf and a second covering from above the breasts to above the knee. Married women might cover these wrappers with a third pagne, wrapped about the waist and occasionally removed and retied to strap a baby on their backs. In the image, the knotted cloth of the women holding the umbrella and the woman to her right suggest baby-wearing. Pins or other means did not fix wrapped cloth, and women moved their pagnes throughout the day, reattaching and shifting the fabric, which covered and revealed certain parts of their bodies. The loose-fitting fabric did not mold women's bodies into regular forms, such as a corset might for European women.[115] When wearing wrappers, women and men alike had an intimate and ongoing process of managing their bodily coverings. The properties of pagne, including the thickness, stiffness, and roughness of the fabric, affected the way it molded to the body and the longevity or durability of knots and ties.

As the kingdom became more integrated into Atlantic trade in the eighteenth century, palace women (*kposi*) who worked in political, military, or ritual functions also wore tailored items, including elaborate dresses imported from Europe. Chesham's engraving (fig. 1.3) of Hwetanu portrays palace women wearing fancy fitted costumes of European origin. Although Chesham undoubtedly incorporated his own understanding what entails "fancy" clothes in his depiction of the festival, his rendering again is closely aligned with the accounts of other African and European observers. A Yorùbá woman who served as a servant to a kposi recalled how "on the day of the sacrifice [Hwetanu], the wives of the king dressed in very fine clothes, because it was a celebration; and the servants in fine clothes."[116] Forbes characterized kposi gowns as in the style of "Charles II."[117] His reference to the reign of the English monarch (1660–85) alluded to a style of women's dress characterized by voluminous skirts, low necklines, bright colors, and a general disheveled appearance, which would have been familiar to someone like Forbes from Restoration-era paintings.[118] Skertchly described Glèlè's wives as being dressed *à la polonaise*, a style of European women's dress popular in late eighteenth-century Britain. He wrote, "the leopardesses [kposi] were dressed in white waistcoats, bound with scarlet velvet, and a long petticoat of violet and green figured silk descended to the ankles. Above this a 'polonaise' of dark blue velvet reached half way down the petticoat."[119] Referencing forms of dress from their own history, European travelers sought to convey the excesses of the Dahomean court to their readers. But the kposi's dress of heavy velvet overskirts draped over silk underskirts more than likely came to Dahomey secondhand from Europe and thus also represents a direct link between European and Dahomean courtly costume. Imported accessories designed specifically for European men such as "Charles II's hat" and "gilt helmets" completed kposi dress.[120] Agojie, the female military force, similarly wore clothing and accessories that Europeans associated with men, and uniforms and insignia distinguished regiment and rank.[121] Indeed, imported clothing and accessories were familiar to Dahomean men and women long before colonization, although these items were used in very different ways than within European sartorial systems.

Clothing preferences were informed not only by a Vodun aesthetic of layering and incorporation but also through more direct interventions from the palace. The king used his own clothed body to promote taste and to convey to elites and others the desirability of specific types of clothing and accessories. Skertchly described a sort of royal fashion show (*Avo-use-gbe*) wherein Glèlè, aided by his wives, changed into numerous different outfits, some in the style worn in enemy kingdoms or in neighboring communities. After each change of clothes, Glèlè danced before the crowds while servants held an umbrella over him.[122] The display of the clothed body of the king served a similar ritual purpose to the Nunupweto, or omnipotent cloth, since both were a tribute to the ancestors done to ensure victory in the forthcoming march against Abeokuta. During the *Avo-use-gbe*, the agojie sang, "Gelelé has changed his cloth for his father and has danced many times for Gézu; / Gézu will therefore remember his son and will prosper his arms against Abeokeuta."[123] While this ritual changing of clothes was intended to show respect to the ancestors and ensure victory in the upcoming war, it also made an impression on the living as they saw the king's wealth through his clothing and, in doing so, learned what constituted valued cloth, clothing, and accessories as well as the identifiable dress of the enemy others.

Alongside the kingdom's political and economic elite, *vodunon* (mother of vodun), the "priests" and "priestesses," and vodunsi (followers), were other groups of Dahomeans distinguished by dress. Vodunon were exempt from sumptuary law as one of their "privileges" and "both sexes [of vodunon], for instance, may wear dresses forbidden to the commonalty." The exceptional status of these women and men permitted them to pursue styles according to their "personal vanity," or their own preferences and their relationship to their vodun.[124] Many vodunsi also forwent imports and cotton weaves to wear raffia textiles (dévɔ).[125] Similar to the bindings around power objects, using raffia as opposed to cotton to cover bodies invoked the power (*bo*) of their vodun. But vodun are numerous, and these people, places, and things took various forms, leading to different relationships between textiles, dress, and Vodun practice. Skertchly described a "fetish-woman" (vodunon) who he called "The Eahweh, or English landlady," who "appeared dressed in profusion of cloths, as though her whole wardrobe was on her back."[126] The bo of this woman was embodied in her performance of foreignness as the "English landlady" and was materialized through the abundance of (probably imported) cloths layered on her body. Like the wives of the king and agojie, the dress of the vodunsi indicated their unique status within society, and the use of cloth was not just symbolic but materialized their relationship to the vodun and their place within the sociopolitical order.

Alongside delineating differences among tòvì, elites, and vodunon, clothing also helped Dahomeans negotiate and manage other forms of identity, including gender, ethnicity, and race. Travelers' accounts and more recent scholarly work note how Dahomeans used dress to invert gender categories. Male soldiers and agojie alike dressed in "a tunic, short trowsers [*sic*], and skull-cap," collapsing the gendered distinction between the two groups even as regiments were formed around sexual difference.[127] The uniforms of the agojie, along with their reported claims that "we are men," led Forbes to conclude that "they have changed their sex."[128] Other masculine women and feminine men likewise occupied politically important positions. A late nineteenth-century visitor noted that the palace recruited sons of prominent families and raised them as women to guard the palace and for other roles.[129] These men, elsewhere identified as eunuchs, entered the palace—a political domain of women—wearing women's clothing. Historian Edna Bay details that "women whose function was to oversee the male ministers of state wore *agbada*, men's gowns in Yorùbá style," reinforcing their status as part of the "male" political world beyond the palace walls.[130] These sartorial inversions of gender and the alterity of Yorùbá-style outfits reaffirmed politically substantive conceptions of different roles for men and women and gendered divisions of power, even as they disassociated them from sex.

By the mid-nineteenth century, Dahomeans also consciously used the careful manipulation of clothing and style to invert ethnic difference and to make these differences politically meaningful. In Cana, at the opening of Hwetanu, Gezo had people destined for sacrifice "made to personate in dress and avocation Oyos."[131] While perhaps not from Oyo, victims of sacrifice were dressed like the kingdom's enemy before their ritual deaths. Muslims from areas to the north traded in the kingdom and sported turbans and sewn cotton robes common in the Sahel, making them an outwardly recognizable minority population.[132] In the 1850 "Procession of the King's Wealth," Forbes noted the presence of "16 malams (Mohomedan priests from Haussa)," but he argued, "I much doubt, except in dress and some outward show, that these priests are Mahomedans; the very fact of their prostrating to the king would go far to prove them not."[133] While the actual origins and backgrounds of the sixteen men remain unclear, their appearance at the procession dressed as Muslim Hausa religious leaders helped convey the monarch's authority over even the Muslim fringes of the kingdom. The association of specific forms of dress with ethnic and religious identities reinforced these differences while it also allowed the court to manipulate them for performances of power.

Men of African descent who came to Dahomey from across the Atlantic region to work in the trade or settle wore European fitted styles and, in doing so, adopted a European persona (*yovo*) within Fon society.[134] At the 1850 procession, there were also "14 liberated 'Bahia' Africans, in the European costume," possibly men from Brazil who had been recaptured and forced to serve the king.[135] Similar to the men dressed as Muslim Hausa, the costume of these men reinforced their outsider persona and, in this case, their associations with Atlantic culture. Elsewhere, Forbes claimed that "any native who leaves his country, even as a slave, and returns, if he wears the dress of a foreigner, is termed ee a voo [yovo], a white man."[136] The Aguda, or Afro-Brazilians, were a coastal community of Atlantic returnees and their descendants. In Ouidah, the community practiced Catholicism and adhered to other aspects of Atlantic town culture, including dress.[137] Trousers, jackets, and shirts associated coastal peoples with Aguda identity and Catholic practice, but in the Dahomean heartland, their connections to white Atlantic culture reached the point in which they too became white foreigners or yovo unless they reverted into outward appearances of Dahomean-ness by wearing wrappers.

The king and other elites occasionally sported European articles of clothing like suit jackets but made them Fon dress by layering them with wrapped avɔ or Yorùbá hats. But articles of imported clothing worn together according to the dictates of world fashion could upset individual claims to Fon identity and even invert racial distinctions, helping make even a Dahomean man into a white outsider. As explored earlier, the gifting of cloth helped foster racial distinctions since European and African merchants had different textile obligations to the monarch. But there were also "black white men" within the kingdom, or Fon men who gained the rights and privileges of yovo. In his 1820 account, John M'Leod noted that "the king occasionally confers the title of white man on some of his subjects, which authorizes them to assume the European dress, to carry an English umbrella, wear shoes, and in short to play the parts of white men in all respects."[138] Most of these men likely entered into this status by learning Portuguese or another European language and working as secretaries.[139] But this persona also had its limitations. In 1863, two such men were "dressed in trowsers [*sic*] and blouses, but shoeless, walking under ragged parasols." While identified as "black white men" they received a parasol, an accessory reserved for the king, dignitaries, or visitors, even if "ragged," but their lack of shoes marked them as "natives" constricted by sumptuary law that gave the king exclusive rights over footwear.[140]

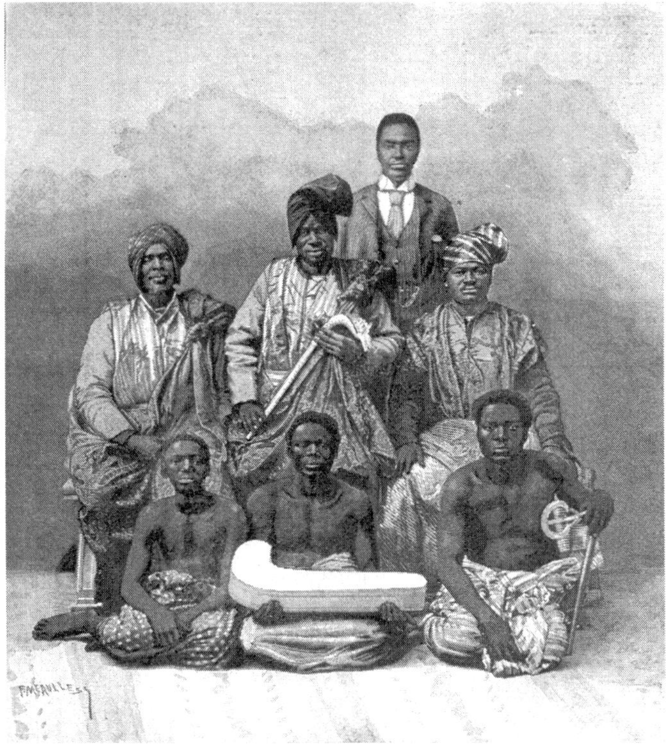

Figure 1.7. "The Mission of King Béhanzin to Paris." From *Supplément illustré du Le Petit Journal* 158 (1893).

An image in the French magazine *Le Petit Journal* underscores how dress materialized complex identities and statuses in the waning days of the kingdom. In 1893, Béhanzin sent an envoy to Paris hoping to broker a peace deal during the Second Franco-Dahomean War (1892–94), and even though the French government refused to meet with the envoy, the visit was documented in the French press (fig. 1.7). The caption identified the man seated in the center as Chedingen, the "chief of mission," while the "king's secretary" Dosso stands behind, dressed in a three-piece suit, likely a reference to his role within the kingdom's administration. Sitting on the floor were men identified as "slaves." Their single wrapped pagne stood in contrast against the multilayered ensembles of the higher-ranking men seated above them. The "slave" in the middle clutched a box used to transport the ceremonial cane (recade) held by Cheding-en.[141] The image portrays how social difference manifested on the bodies of Dahomeans and hints at how the palace used dress to manage distinctions. Bodily coverings were imbued with enough power to remake women as men, Fon as Yorùbá, or African men into having European privileges. Yet even within this strict system of vestiary difference, the incorporation of new elements and the exercise of creativity was encouraged. However, by the time that this image was made in the late nineteenth century, the vast majority of people living in Dahomey were not tovì and did not have elaborate wardrobes of grand pagne, chokoto, or imported fitted items.

Farmers, Captives, and Undress in Dahomey

Elaborate elite dress was part of a town (tò) material culture, but dress in the glètà was inexpensive and better suited to laboring in fields. Archeologist Cameron Monroe estimates that 29 to 66 percent of the precolonial population of Dahomey lived in rural areas as opposed to major urban centers like Abomey and Cana, which were distinguished from the countryside both politically and spatially.[142] In the early years of the kingdom, the rural population was mostly commoners (anato) working in agriculture, but the composition of the countryside changed over the course of the nineteenth century from an overwhelmingly commoner populace to more outsider captives. Dahomey's military conquests against the Mahi to the north and Yorùbá kingdoms continued even after the abolition of slavery in the Americas led to collapse in the coastal Atlantic market for captives. As the export market shifted from captives to palm products, captives from conquests and raids began to work the labor-intensive process of palm oil production within Dahomey. With a growing domestic population of captives, the increasing complexity of dress in the nineteenth-century tò, shown through accounts of cloth-based spectacles and sartorial inversions, likely helped create differences between Dahomean and captive populations.[143] The people of the glètà, both commoner and bonded, were distinguished sartorially from the citizens of the town.

Both men and women in the countryside wore a gòdó, or loincloth, on an everyday basis, saving pagne, if they had it, for special occasions.[144] The gòdó was a smallish piece of cotton or raffia cloth covering the genitalia, draped between the legs, and attached at the waist with a cord or belt. Early in the eighteenth century, Dalzel identified how differences in status and wealth affected women's clothing, contrasting the dress of the "poor" and "young girls" as "a zone of beads, supporting a bandage beneath the do'vo [gòdó], or scanty loin-cloth," while "the upper classes" wore cloth "covering all from the bosom to the ancles."[145] Nineteenth century observers noted that the gòdó served as an undergarment for Dahomean elites while it became outerwear for the majority.[146] As these accounts attest, minimal textile-based clothing concretized the lower social status of the wearer, yet it also freed their movement. In contrast to elites who needed to carefully move and constantly adjust their multiple lengths of fabric, men and women in a secured gòdó could easily move while farming and during other forms of labor. They were not bound by wrapped avɔ's discipline on bodily movements.

Despite their lack of textiles, people in the glètà used other forms of adornment as outward markers of identity. European visitors often focused on the "nakedness" of men and women in Dahomey and other colonial contexts, equating minimal textiles as a lack of dress and evidence of their shameful "uncivilized" state.[147] But local ideas on what constituted being undressed were mutable and unaligned with European discourses.[148] In Dahomey, non-textile forms of adornment complicated the very idea that rural men and women were mostly "naked." For example, along with their gòdó, hunters layered other things on their bodies, including "a cartouch-box of their own manufacture, a power-flask of callabash, with many grotesque ornaments and fetishes."[149] Their tools and power objects marked their status, and they were not "naked" even if they wore little in terms of textiles.

By the mid-nineteenth century, political and economic transformations altered the landscape of rural Dahomey to create more opportunity for men and women in the glètà to purchase and wrap avɔ even as new forms of inequality became entrenched. As the economy changed from its orientation around exports of captives to palm products produced by captive labor, the economic center of the kingdom shifted from the markets of the tò to the countryside. Politically, this involved the construction of a series of satellite palaces spread across central Dahomey.[150] These new palaces brought a greater familiarity of tò textile culture to people in the glètà, likely contributing to more interest in wrapping and draping. Countryfolk also had more opportunity to acquire textiles as the economy shifted to palm products. Bonded laborers might work on elite-owned and royal plantations, although palm production, especially after the opening of the market for palm kernels, favored small producers over centrally run enterprises.[151] With new opportunities for a regular income stream, commoner small producers had greater purchasing power in the second half of the nineteenth century, and given that textile imports remained strong, more people in the glètà were able to purchase and wrap avɔ than ever before. While commoners and captives had less access to textiles than Dahomeans in the tò, they likely had more access than earlier generations living in rural Dahomey.

The history of clothing in the Dahomey kingdom reveals how Fon speakers have long used textile materials to communicate, occupy, and upset social identities and notions of difference. The Dahomean palace largely directed engagement with sartorial culture through spectacles of power and inversions as tools of social control. Incorporation of outsiders and their vodun, craft knowledge, markets, and material culture was a political strategy for expanding Dahomean power over territories and people, but it also was a practice rooted in a Fon Vodun worldview of incorporation, one that multiplied vestiary possibility. The body of the king, artfully displayed during Hwetanu and other ceremonies, encouraged the layering of styles with diverse origins at the same time that the capture of artisans and technologies invigorated Fon textile production. But the importance of avɔ extended beyond dress, since exchanged and displayed textiles materialized political and social relationships, and the demand for these strategic goods encouraged Dahomey's intense participation in regional and Atlantic trade. The production of textiles from thread to fabric and the ways they were put to work on and off bodies reveal long-standing practices of Fon people bringing together elements of different origins to create single ensembles. However, the French, after their conquest in the 1890s, would attempt to create very different relationships between craft, technology, and style in colonial Dahomey. While French administrators strived to harness the social, economic, and political potential of dress, new groups of Dahomeans began to gain control over the meanings and circulation of textiles and clothing.

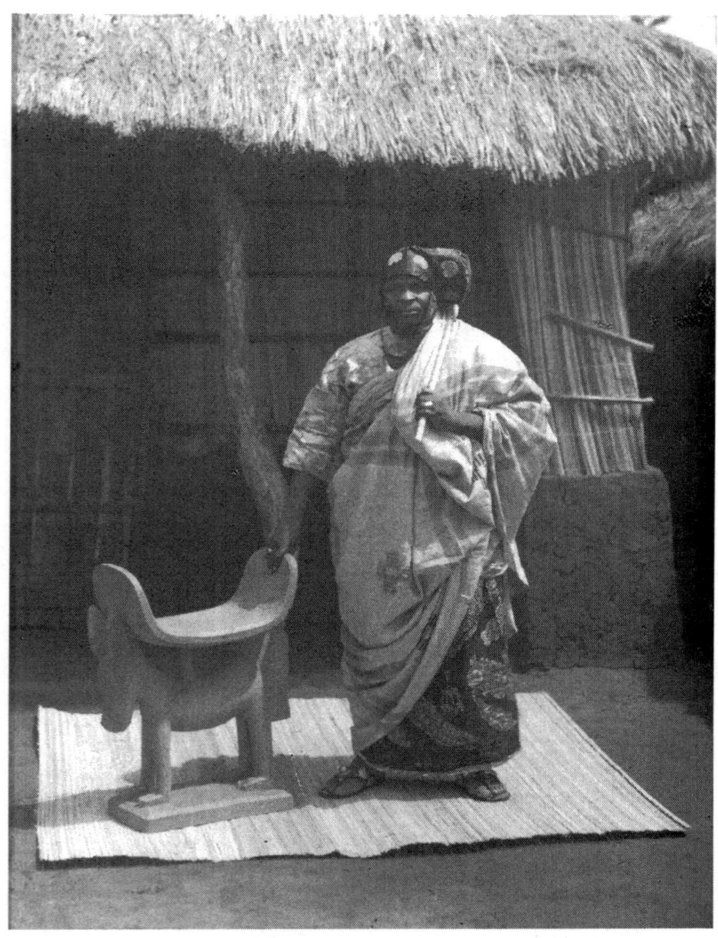

Figure 2.1. Frédéric Gadmer, "Dahomey, Abomey, Chief Justin Aho, Nephew of Béhanzin," 1930. No. A63636. Musée départemental Albert-Kahn, Département de Hauts-de-Seine, Boulogne-Billancourt, France. CC-BY-4.0.

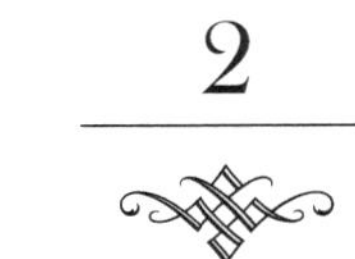

2

Fitting Changes

The Sartorial Economy and the Tailored Silhouette

On March 8, 1930, the *chef de canton* of Abomey, Justin Aho, a grandson of King Glèlè, wrapped himself in fabric, donned the sandals of his ancestors, and posed for a photograph next to a symbolic stool (fig. 2.1). A wealthy French banker had commissioned the photographer to travel to the French colony of Dahomey and liaise with Francis Aupiais, a missionary with the Société des missions africaines de Lyon (SMA), and the two men toured the colony, taking ethnographic photographs and films of traditional customs and rituals. In Abomey, they, along with other tourists and ethnographers of the era, approached Justin Aho as an expert on cultural life in the former kingdom's capital.[1] Although an important contact for European visitors, Aho's local position in Abomey was more tenuous. Aho became chef de canton in 1929 and afterward used his position to amass large tracts of land and establish palm oil plantations.[2] Over the next decade, local farmers brought multiple suits against Aho and other local chefs for their land grabs while some residents made even more insidious complaints and accusations against Aho.[3] Faced with these challenges to his position, Aho fashioned himself as the heir to the throne of Dahomey, a claim he maintained well after Bénin's 1960 independence from France.[4] As a part of his performance of Dahomean heritage, Aho wore appliqué hats sporting a lion, the symbol of Glèlè, and, as seen in the image, a grande pagne likely with a chokoto underneath. He wrapped pagne to dance in festivals in public squares, imprinting on the community's memory how, in his role as a chef de canton, Aho "wore local."[5] Styles associated with the Fon kingdom became a way for Aho to enact his "traditional" authority for foreign visitors and Béninois alike.

Justin Aho seems to have been equally comfortable donning a European-style three-piece suit and living the life of the educated African colonial elite. Aho had attended secondary school and traveled extensively in Europe, including a three-year stay in France, before becoming chef de canton.[6] A French administrator commended him as a good example of the success of the *mission civilisatrice*, writing that Aho had "come closer and closer to our [French] civilization."[7] Aho had good relations with French officials in the colony. For example, in 1935 he invited them to a cocktail party, sending out engraved invitations on fancy cardstock to the colony's French community.[8] As someone who not only had lived in France but had also traveled there multiple times during the 1930s, often as an interpreter at colonial exhibitions, Aho would have been familiar with European men's fashion and likely sported evening wear during his cocktail party hosting duties and at other social events. Abomeans too encountered him in his fitted clothes. One retired cabinetmaker in Abomey, Pascal Adouhouncla, remembered Aho as an early wearer of trousers and jackets in the community.[9] For many Fon speakers in the interior like Adouhouncla, styles like trousers and jackets seemed a natural choice for Aho since it was the garb of the formally educated "intellectuals" or the *hunnukún* (Fon: eyes [*nukún*] open [*hun*]), and wearing it represented wealth and education. Aho's stylistic choices show how, from the early part of the twentieth century, Béninois actively used clothing to negotiate power structures, invoking the authority of their ancestors through tradition at times and adopting fitted ensembles to make claims as modern subjects and urban citizens.

Aho's daily decision to either wrap a pagne or wear a three-piece suit also reflected a colonial context wherein the uses and meanings of dress differed greatly from the precolonial order. This chapter explores the interplay between changing fashion preferences, particularly the slow expansion of fittedness, or tailored dress that formed to the body and conformed to European fashions, and the development of a sartorial economy in the French colony of Dahomey, an area that corresponds to the present-day country of Bénin. Sartorial economy describes how, during the first half of the twentieth century, the production and consumption of clothing became central to the functioning of agriculture, labor, and markets in Bénin. This clothing-focused economic order emerged from the common concerns of Béninois and the colonial state, who at times shared a vision on the potential power of clothing to generate profits and express power but whose visions diverged greatly on who should benefit from this system and whose values it should represent.

The entanglements of European and Béninois systems of technology, knowledge, and stylistic meaning gave form to the Béninois sartorial economy.

Béninois acquired cloth, domesticated technologies, and donned styles in ways that undermined colonial authority, even as they occasionally reified colonial categories of class, gender, and ethnicity. From promoting new technologies for cotton production and controlling the circulation of cotton and other textiles to training children and young people in needle crafts, the colonial administration sought to intervene in how Béninois made and wore clothes. Institutions like missions, schools, and offices were at the forefront of garbing new social classes and categories of labor into tailored styles, extending precolonial associations between fitted styles, wealth, and literacy in European languages. But Béninois confounded French efforts to control the sartorial economy. Farmers pushed back against French plans for a "cotton colony" by choosing different crops, selling their cotton in unsanctioned markets, or keeping cotton for domestic spinning. Consumers preferred textiles manufactured by France's imperial rivals over ones made in France, and traders illicitly trafficked fabric from British colonies to acquire more desirable cloth at a lower cost. Students took certain skills and technologies from colonial education programs—sewing and writing, for example—while rejecting other aspects of Western domesticity and colonial employment. Finally, while fittedness spread through the ranks of colonial employees and dependents, its meaning did not always translate into allegiance to the colonial order. To be a well-suited hunnukún often meant active anti-colonial resistance, and the colony of Dahomey was noted for the outspokenness of its elite in the 1920s and 1930s. As the case of Aho shows, the growing linkages between tailored clothing and colonial modernity also helped to contribute to a reinscription of "tradition" onto unfitted fashions like wrapped and draped cloth.

The multifaceted relationship between markets, technologies, and the meanings of clothing became particularly apparent during the market disruptions of the Second World War. Amid shortages of imported goods, Béninois turned to reviving spinning and weaving cotton. The fabric that was produced, *botoyi*, was a rough cloth, and its name is used to reference scarcity and deprivation, a stark contrast to both earlier and later periods when locally made fabrics were some of the most highly valued. Indeed, the interconnectedness of the various aspects of the sartorial economy meant that changes within cloth and machinery imports affected agriculture, artisanal production, knowledge transmission, and even the semiotics of dress. In sum, they reveal the formation of a sartorial economy and the new ways that clothes were made and worn between 1900 and 1950. This period created an important rupture in Fon clothing culture, although older notions of aesthetics and craft work did not disappear and would contribute to the creation of an independence-era culture of tailoring.

Fibers and Textiles in a Cotton Colony

> Béhanzin is of medium height, taller rather than short. . . . His head was covered by a blue silk Dahomean cap, he walked proudly draped in a splendid satin *pagne* 'Loïe Fuller,' and leaned on the shoulder a favorite wife who kept fanning him. In his mouth, he had a pipe with a disproportionate stem that hindered his movement obliging him to use his hands to climb the bank.[10]
>
> —Description of Béhanzin during his surrender, Commander Léonce Grandin, 1895

A French officer described Béhanzin (1889–94), the last independent Dahomean king, during his surrender to the French as wearing a blue cap and a "splendid" satin grande pagne. The officer's observation foreshadows the ambiguous relationship that the French would have with both the former members of the Fon royal families and Fon material culture. On the one hand, the officer described the dress as impressive, and he made a striking comparison to the costume designs of Loïe Fuller, a US dancer whose experiments in flowing cloth and lighting intrigued French audiences and proved foundational to modernism. On the other hand, the officer characterizes the ensemble as impractical; the pipe's stem was "disproportionate," and the robes hampered Béhanzin's movements as he surrendered to the French. In January 1895, Béhanzin turned himself over to the French only a few months after their army occupied the walled town of Abomey, conquering the Dahomey kingdom. As the French had marched on Abomey, Béhanzin had ordered the burning of the royal palaces and the rest of the town before he fled north with only a few members of his immediate family. After his surrender, the French military exiled Béhanzin and negotiated with a cousin, Agoli-Agbo, to succeed the throne. But in 1900, the kingdom was dissolved and incorporated into the larger colony with its capital in Porto-Novo and as a part of French West Africa (AOF), administered from Dakar (map 2.1). In the new colony of Dahomey, the French hoped to generate profits and taxes in an economy oriented around markets in textiles and clothing.

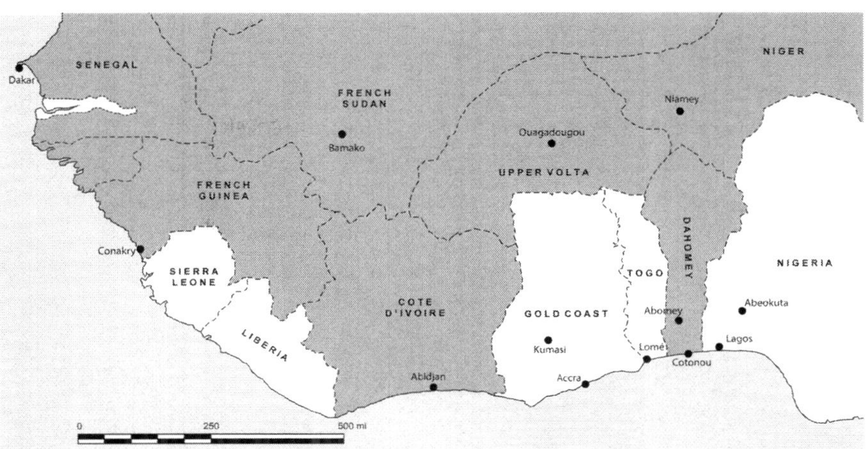

Map 2.1. Map of French West Africa.

In the first decade after conquest, administrators set forth a program of transforming Bénin from a palm oil exporter into a cotton colony, setting a precedent for state interest and investment in cotton production that continues into the present. By the nineteenth century, cotton had become the most important fiber in global textile production and linked factories in Europe with growers in the Americas, Asia, and Africa.[11] But France's cotton textile industry lagged behind other European countries such as Britain and Holland. In order to be more competitive, some European states, including France, turned to a policy of "cotton imperialism," hoping to transform certain West African colonies into cotton exporters that would supply textile manufacturers in the metropole and reduce manufacturing costs to make a product that was more competitive on the world market. The African peasant farmers who sold the cotton would then have the cash to buy industrial cotton cloth.[12] The French proposed Dahomey as a prime location for cotton because, unlike its other major cotton colony in Africa, the French Soudan (Mali), Dahomey had a coastline and a growing port in Cotonou, which would cut transportation costs when exporting the crop to France.[13] To the colonial state, Dahomey held enormous potential as a cotton colony.

Dahomeans had cultivated cotton to supply local spinners long before colonization, although it was not grown as an exportable cash crop. Colonial administrators hoped to reorient rural economies to cotton production by exploiting preexisting structures of power to avoid directly forcing labor.

Auguste Le Herissé, the commandant in Abomey, proposed that precolonial officeholders might be co-opted into aiding cotton cultivation. He suggested reviving the precolonial position of the "Topo[,] a bona fide minister of agriculture" who, under colonialism, "would order the intensive cultivation of cotton, maize, [and] groundnut, as we desire."[14] Despite Le Herissé's proposal to use indigenous institutions to meet colonial goals, commercial cotton cultivation began in earnest only when a French agent hired by the French Cotton Association arrived in colonial Dahomey in 1905. The representative of metropolitan cotton interests distributed seeds to local chiefs in the central and southern regions of the colony, and these chiefs, in turn, hired laborers to work their fields.[15] The French Cotton Association also built cotton gins in Savalou, Bohicon, and Cotonou to prepare the crop for export.[16] As a result of these early efforts, cotton exports more than tripled from less than 50 tons in 1905 to over 160 in 1913.[17] Local sources also point to the growing importance of cotton to colonial economies and society. In one "song of ridicule" recorded by Melville and Frances Herskovits in 1931, the singers mock a thief who "has eaten money, and he took the bicycle (of his patron and) ran away and he took cotton / And went to the commandant, his friend, his friend, his friend."[18] Cotton, while not a new crop to the region, relied on the "friendly" interventions of the French to create a larger export market.

The "song of ridicule" also underscores how French efforts to market cotton for export faced multiple challenges. The singers called the man bringing the cotton to the commandant a thief likely because peasant producers could usually sell their crops at higher prices outside the official purchasing framework. As early as 1909, French officials noted that Fon speakers trafficked cotton to German Togo, where it fetched a higher price than from French colonial purchasing agents.[19] After 1919 and the mandate system in French Togo, administrators claimed that producers were still trafficking cotton to Lomé because transport and port fees were 50 percent lower there than in Cotonou.[20] Occasionally growers hoarded their crops, as in Abomey in 1928, when farmers attempted to wait out low prices until the state raised the official purchase price.[21] But cotton also ended up in the local market for purchase by spinners. Historian Richard Roberts identified a parallel "two worlds of cotton" in the French Soudan in which price differences between the French textile industry and Soudanais handicraft cloth producers led growers to sell to local spinners and weavers at higher prices than those offered by official export firms.[22] In Bénin, weavers colluded with growers and spinners to acquire local cotton, resulting in a complex system of pricing for both cotton and finished products.[23]

Even when the cotton market functioned according to colonial aspirations, increased investment in cotton created unintended benefits for artisan spinners and weavers. Traders occasionally deemed a cotton harvest unfit for exportation, usually because the fibers were too short for mechanized spinning. Undoubtedly, growers did not burn or otherwise dispose of these harvests, and they made their way into hands of local spinners who were used to working with short fibers of local varietals. Abomean spinner Juliette Kanlihano described how in Houndjroto, Abomey's central market, spinners could purchase so-called "waste" cotton from the export trade to make yarn or thread.[24] Even cotton that made it to the port created a byproduct used in local production. After harvests, women and children combed fields to gather cotton that cash crop farmers had missed. As it was baled and transported by train and later truck, pieces of cotton tended to become detached and fly off onto the ground.[25] Small amounts of cotton gathered in harvested fields or on the side of the road could also be spun and woven, although on a very small scale.

Local spinners and weavers continued to practice their craft because Béninois still demanded their products, continuing a long-standing Fon practice of consuming both local and imported textiles. Multiple qualities of domestic weaves circulated; some were made from local yarn and others with imported thread. There were low-quality weaves that fetched corresponding prices, but other local weaves were some of the most expensive fabrics on the market, with prices rivaling those of imported luxury fabrics such as velvet.[26] At the same time, the quantity of imported textiles grew significantly in the first three decades after conquest. Unbleached cottons were deemed the least desirable, followed by cotton prints, bleached cottons, and velvet, the most expensive and highest-valued imported textile. According to historian Patrick Manning, bleached cotton served as a substitute for cotton print while unbleached cottons complemented prints.[27] Vodunsi (adherents to a vodun) wore vibrant white bleached cottons, wrapping them for participation in ceremonies.[28] At other times, women dyed bleached cottons, and images and oral accounts are rife with women wearing imported wrappers locally dyed with indigo.[29] Wax prints also became widespread in the early nineteenth century, and these textiles, easily recognizable as West African today, were produced in European factories after the creation of a mechanized process of imitating

Indonesian batiks. Consumers bought all this imported fabric locally from vendors, some of whom traveled as far away as the markets of Lomé. In the Togolese capital, women wholesalers purchased wax prints directly from European companies and, after the 1930s, began to influence their design.[30] While much of this cloth was used as wrappers, its tight weave, elasticity, and lower prices also made industrially produced textiles ideal for cutting and sewing into fitted clothes.

The vast quantities of cloth consumed made the textile trade a particular concern of French administrators responsible for the overall functioning of the colony's economy. Traders acquired British textiles and other cloth by traveling to the nearby British colonies of Gold Coast and Nigeria, where they purchased more desirable fabrics. As early as 1904, French administrators recognized the problem created by the colony's long land borders with other empires where textiles were cheaper and the available fabrics were more suited to local tastes.[31] By the mid-1930s, border controls limited the amount of fabric that Béninois could legally bring into the colony to ten meters per person.[32] But men and women found ways to evade these quotas. Abomean resident Amadou Adamou remembers how traders walked the over two hundred miles to Accra, Gold Coast, in order to trade goats for fabric. The journey was difficult, and travelers took special care to evade colonial officials who tried to capture returnees, impound their cloth, and send them to prison.[33] This black market in fabric panicked administrators, who feared that the large quantities of trafficked goods threatened the colony's currency holdings as more and more francs crossed borders into British territories. Bankers considered the black market as augmenting a preexisting shortage of cash in the colony since West Africa was alleged to "hoard" metal currency.[34] Local demand for cloth and the French inability to meet Béninois sartorial needs threatened the economic and financial stability of the colony.

Control over the circulation of textiles also became important to colonial practices of managing local conflicts. In the lowest level of colonial civil courts (*tribunal de premier degré*), a European judge and African assessors resolved conflicts, and textiles occasionally became embroiled in these disputes. For example, when Cotonou resident Berthe Durand, a Senegalese widow, tried to leave the house of her mother-in-law, a Fon woman named Toussi, the older woman refused to let Durand leave the house with her clothes and furniture, which Toussi claimed should be hers according to custom. The court intervened to declare that because it was a civil marriage and not subject to local custom, the objects legally belonged to Durand, and the widow was permitted to take her cloth and clothing with her.[35] Other complainants accused people of stealing cloth from them, hoping the court would award them damages.[36] Upon divorce, families often demanded the return of bridewealth (*dot*) which sometimes included fabric, although judges usually settled by assessing a cash value for the fabric and ordering that to be repaid.[37] While the French colony did not pursue the sorts of direct interventions of redistribution and sumptuary law favored during the kingdom era, they were nevertheless keenly interested in controlling the production and exchange of cotton and textiles as part of their larger efforts to create a colonial economic and social order, even as the actions of Béninois unwove their plans for a profitable colonial sartorial economy.

Gendering Craft Knowledge and Technology

In the first few decades of the twentieth century, elite Béninois like Justin Aho increasingly turned from wrapping fabrics to wearing tailored clothing. One of the factors that contributed to the spread of tailored dress was the establishment of mission and colonial programs that trained needleworkers and promoted clothes-making technologies. While never successful in convincing most Fon to abandon Vodun and adopt Catholicism, Catholic missions played an important role in spreading new notions of domesticity, dress, and needlework. Missions, along with state educational policies designed to promote rural development or to domesticate women, led to an expanding pool of clothes-makers while also regendering needle craft labor and tools and fixing them into categories of "traditional" and "modern." In the kingdom period, women spun cotton and worked as dyers both inside and outside the palace while men sewed clothes, wove, and made appliqué. But the gendered dynamics of clothing production shifted during the colonial era, when missions and later state schools encouraged competencies in sewing as an integral part of a girl's domestic education. In contrast, rural manual and urban technical education programs steered boys and young men into crafts deemed more physical and masculine such as masonry and electrical, although for a short while in the late 1920s and 1930s the state taught tailoring and weaving to young men.

Catholic orphanages and schools were the earliest institutions to promote domestic education as part of their "civilizing mission." In nineteenth-century urban Senegal, the heart of France's African empire, missions taught mixed-race girls (*métisse*) music, dance, and sewing and needlework, or the skills of a middle-class French women. Colonial educators hoped that this curriculum would lay the foundation for a mixed-race community with middle-class values whose members would serve as useful colonial allies.[38] In coastal Bénin, Catholics built similar institutions for métisse children. By 1912, there was a small school in Ouidah serving young girls, including ten "abandoned" métisses. The school separated the girls into two classes, and each week the girls spent an hour on basic sewing, supplementing their lessons in reading, writing, and domestic skills.[39] By the early 1920s, the colonial state began to operate similar institutions. In a Porto-Novo orphanage for mixed-race children, girls spent each Thursday from eight a.m. to eleven a.m. and two p.m. to four p.m. learning sewing, mending, ironing, and other housework; nearly a full day of their studies was devoted to learning to maintain a home.[40] These orphanages were the first in the colony to promote sewing as a feminine skill and a necessary one for the wives of a burgeoning African colonial elite.

In the following decade, missions and colonial educators extended programs in domestic education from institutions serving métisses to those designed for the rest of the colony's African population. By 1931, there were 845 girls enrolled in secular schools in the colony, including 54 in Abomey and 27 in nearby Zagnanado. That same year, there were 1,287 girls in Catholic institutions serving both métisse and African girls in Porto-Novo, Cotonou, Ouidah, Agoué, and Calavi.[41] Many of the educators in the Catholic institutions were mixed-race women who had finished their education at the Porto-Novo orphanage.[42] But state schools consistently struggled to staff their programs with qualified female teachers, and the numbers of girls and young women enrolled in state-run schools remained small relative to mission schools. It was only in 1955 that the administration built a secondary school in Côte d'Ivoire for training women as domestic education teachers, with the hope of ending the chronic teacher shortage.[43] Overall, the numbers of girls trained in these programs was relatively small, yet they had a disproportionate impact on fashion in Bénin.

Although missions and administrators designed these domestic education programs to train wives and mothers based on French middle-class values, girls and young women derailed these plans by sewing bespoke clothing for the market. When a girl's school opened in Abomey in 1935, an unnamed administrator remarked that while the school would teach sewing, "the school will not and should not be a workshop offering apprenticeship for lucrative industry."[44] Colonial administrators lamented the tendency of girls and young women to use their needleworking skills for profit as opposed to household projects. When an administrator despairingly wrote of the messy dress of female students at the Abomey School, he accused students of using their "sewing hour" to work on other people's clothing instead of repairing their own outfits.[45] Evidence from oral histories also supports the contention that girls and women who followed colonial and mission courses in sewing later opened up shops and trained their own apprentices. Seamstresses who had done apprenticeships under women could almost always directly trace the origin of their craft knowledge to religious or colonial-era formal education. By listing their master, their master's master, and so on, women showed the important role of colonial-era schooling in creating a cadre of women needleworkers who would translate their "domestic" skills in sewing into profit-generating ventures. Colonial programs intending to train housewives unintentionally laid the foundation for craft knowledge of making women's fitted clothes (*couture dame*), a topic more fully explored in chapter 5.

Girls might have learned domestic sewing at schools and missions, but boys and young men were directed to trades and crafts deemed more masculine at workshops and technical schools. The Apprenticeship School opened in Porto-Novo in 1913, and by the next year, boys and young men could follow courses in cabinetmaking and smithing. But the small program suffered from mismanagement; its French director described the African teachers, or "master craftsmen," as "a little too spoiled" since they often demanded longer breaks and refused to work five days a week.[46] The first school closed after a few years, but another institution that focused on teaching technical competencies later opened as an annex to Victor Ballot School, the École primaire supérieur of Dahomey. Administrators planned for the annex to focus on "training workers to meet local needs," including positions with the colonial state and in French "commerce and industry."[47] One of the technical competencies offered was tailoring. In the academic year 1929–30, students in the program sewed "white canvas or khaki" uniforms for different groups in Porto-Novo connected to the colonial state, including the métis children at the orphanage, the students at Victor Ballot School, and the "native" employees of the Post Office.[48] A newspaper photograph (fig. 2.2) from a few years later shows the likely design for these uniforms, although it was taken after the colony moved its technical program to Cotonou. These technical programs

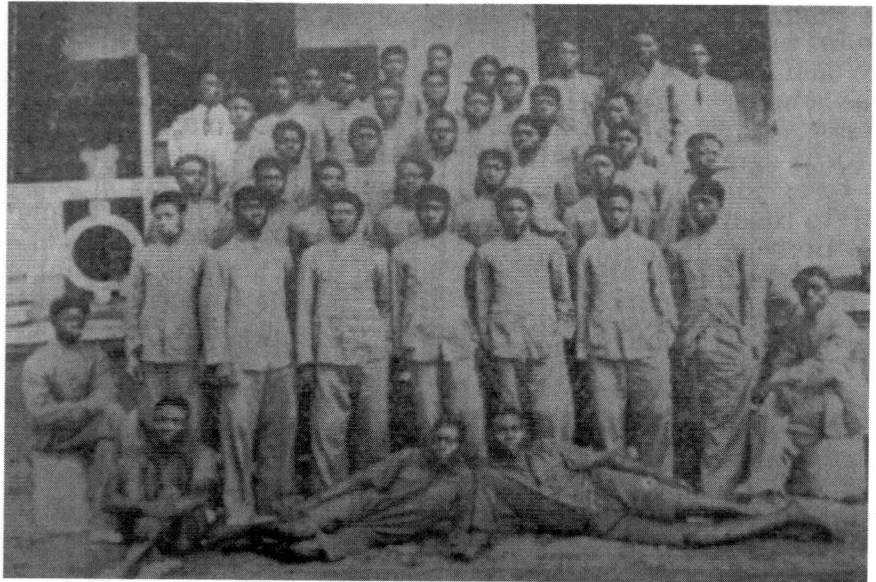

Figure 2.2. Students at the Professional School in Cotonou. From *Le Phare du Dahomey*, September–October 1935.

instructed young men in trades and crafts that supported the creation and maintenance of colonial infrastructures, from building roads and offices to clothing the men who occupied them.

However, Béninois had fewer opportunities for pursing structured courses in tailoring after the colony retreated from interventions in clothes-making to focus on construction trades. In the academic term 1931–32, the year after the technical program moved to Cotonou, there were 115 apprentices enrolled, including 40 metal workers, 28 cabinetmakers, and 39 masons. But during the move, the sections in tailoring and shoemaking were left in Porto-Novo as an annex to the Ballot school and served only four shoemakers and four tailors.[49] The following academic year, the annex closed, and the administration sent home the two apprentice shoemakers who had not yet completed the program.[50] Apparently, colonial administrators decided that they did not need state-trained tailors and shoemakers to make the outfits of Africans affiliated with the state. Perhaps they recognized that tailors and shoemakers trained in private workshops or mission schools could meet the colony's clothing demands while requiring less state investment. The colony continued to invest in technical education right up until independence in 1960, but it never again offered programs for male students in designing, cutting, and sewing clothing.

Alongside with studying construction trades in cities, boys and men could pursue courses as clothes-makers in "rural" weaving and needle crafts within a parallel set of institutions under the umbrella of "artisan education." In the mid-1930s, the state opened a *Maison des artisans* in Abomey where boys and young men could learn the "traditional" crafts of the Dahomey kingdom. The maison replicated a similar institution in Bamako, French Soudan, which was designed as "at the same time, a workshop, school, conservatory, [and] craft fair."[51] In 1935, Jules Brévié, governor of the AOF, requested that the governor of Dahomey open an Abomey Maison built according to the model of the Bamako one. He justified the school's location because of the town's "history and the existence of the Museum [at the Abomey royal palaces]."[52] Located within the museum complex (where Justin Aho happened to be the director), the maison served as a center of production and learning, focusing on the royal arts of the precolonial kingdom. It was also an art market where tourists and other colonial travelers could acquire traditional African craft objects.

But the Abomey maison did not treat all precolonial craft traditions equally, and administrators selected the crafts that they deemed worthy of promotion and protection, which did not include needlework. Administrators selected plastic arts in wood and metal as opposed to textiles and clothing for promotion. The 1936 judgment that created the maison interpreted l'artisanat (artisan sector) broadly, and while it listed some crafts that might be taught at the maison, it did not specify exactly which crafts administrators should choose.[53] In 1939, the governor of Dahomey requested a report on artisans from M. Cosson, a Cotonou administrator and the president of the Artistic Society of Dahomey, an organization of Frenchmen who had taken an interest in local arts and artisanal objects. Cosson concentrated on artisans in the southern and central regions of the colony to identify the crafts worthy of state encouragement. For example, he deemed the carved calabashes and "poor quality" appliqués of Abomey as well as the basket weaving of Porto-Novo as three crafts unworthy of colonial support and protection. But, he argued, Abomean sculpture, hatmaking (done by appliqué makers), and shoemaking deserved "encouragement."[54] Cosson's assessments, a result of his personal tastes and the priorities of the mid-1930s art market, selected masculine crafts over ones done by women (basketmaking and pottery) for support and preserved specific crafts as traditions. Yet despite his recommendation that the maison not support appliqué makers, these needleworkers would continue to operate out of the museum workshops, sewing for tourists and the local community alike.

Weavers, especially those descended from the royal palace weavers who worked on horizontal looms, were also subject to French interventions, although like appliqué making, the craft endured despite colonial meddling. In 1939, Jean Le Gall, the creator of the Bamako Maison and the inspector of technical and artisanal education of the AOF, contributed to the colonial assessment of crafts in the colony. Similar to European observers in the eighteenth and nineteenth centuries, Le Gall was unimpressed with local weaving, especially the use of the horizontal loom. He recommended that Béninois artisans go to the Bamako Maison to learn "improved" techniques of weaving and carpet making using Soudanais-style tools.[55] Le Gall hoped that the introduction of new techniques would revolutionize weaving in the colony of Dahomey by making it more efficient and by resulting in a product that was more desirable for foreign consumers.[56] While his plan may have influenced designs and techniques, local weavers continued to use both Akan-style horizontal looms and Yorùbá-style vertical looms to make cloth, showing the limitations of colonial intervention in artisanal production methods.

In contrast, Béninois embraced other clothes-making technologies such as the sewing machine, which would help fundamentally change how clothes were made and worn. Along with looms, colonial agents interpreted the sewing machine as a technology that would modernize craft production methods and society in general. Metropolitan and colonial discourses on sewing machines had associated them with civilization and modernity since the nineteenth century. Sewing machine companies, such as Singer, used imagery of the civilizing effects of sewing machines to sell their products to a French public interested in empire. For example, one advertisement portrayed "a white sewing machine salesman" being carried into a forest above the slogan "Singer, harbinger of civilization."[57] French consumers would have recognized the familiar colonial imagery of a dark "jungle" with the salesman serving as a vanguard of civilization in an "untouched" wilderness. In the AOF, colonial administrators deployed a similar discourse and promoted the practical and potential civilizing effects of the sewing machine. As early as 1916, tax collectors tried to assess a tax on tailors by charging them by machine, using machinery to quantify a tailor's success and integrate them into the colonial economy.[58] Albert Charton, inspector general of education in the AOF and a supporter of artisan education, argued that African artisans, whom he interpreted as unable to "evolve" because of their attachment to traditional methods of production, were beginning to "open themselves to progress, be attentive to change." For Charton, one of the clearest examples of this was the shift from hand sewing to the sewing machine in urban centers. Charton claimed, "Instead of seeing the disintegration of the artisanat as we thought, an evolution is beginning. The sewing machine, in all the shops in Senegal, in most of the markets of Dahomey and Soudan, is becoming a new tool of indigenous tailors."[59] Tailoring was one of the first African crafts to become mechanized, and for colonial administrators who doubted African ability to engage in industry, the adoption of sewing machines showed them that African artisans were capable of mechanization and modernization.

While administrators promoted the sewing machine and saw its use as an index for civilization, mission and colonial programs also gendered models, creating different opportunities for men and women within the sartorial economy. Men used foot-operated treadle machines while missions and schools required women to use hand crank machines due to widespread misconceptions about the treadle's impacts on female reproductivity. Colonial states in Africa were keenly interested in women's bodies and the effects of miscarriage, abortion, and breastfeeding on the reproduction of labor.[60] Controlling the use of treadle sewing machines was another aspect of this larger effort to manage African women's reproduction, even as it relied on a false understanding of the treadle's impact on the body. For example, a 1937 law in Guinea made it illegal to employ pregnant women and children under fifteen to operate pedal sewing machines even in "familial work," a term that administrators used to describe African artisanal industries.[61] A proposed law in the French Soudan specifically prohibited girls under sixteen from using pedal-operated machines, although it made no mention of their use by boys or pregnant women.[62] Oral histories attest that women learned in missions and schools to avoid pedal-operated machines because their operation caused infertility and miscarriage. Pregnant women were seen as especially at risk, and anecdotes linked pregnancy loss to the repetitive motion of the legs as they moved up and down on the treadle.[63] These assumptions about the machine's effects on women's bodies were transferred from artisan to artisan long after the end of colonization, gendering tools and production methods until the end of the twentieth century.

Norms around the labor and technology of needlework changed significantly in the decades after French conquest. Bodies of craft knowledge and tools were gendered in new ways by colonial and mission programs that attempted to recast tailoring and other needle crafts according to an idealized European standard in which a few men produced for the market, but the majority of sewing was done by women in the home. But Béninois took what they wanted from these programs. Girls used domestic education sewing hours to make repairs for others while weavers and appliqué makers established themselves in state-sponsored workshops, even as their work was decried by colonial tastemakers. Tools also achieved new associations, and looms and sewing machines were seen both as an index of modernity and as having material impacts on bodies. Although missions and schools trained perhaps only a few hundred needleworkers before independence, over the next few decades the graduates of these programs would have a disproportionate influence on the content and transmission of the craft knowledge of tailoring.

Fitted Dress and Social Distinction

> I ask you not to be poor Fa, I receive you
> I ask you again not be poor-o
> If I have no wife, then I am poor
> If I have no money, then I am poor
> If my cloth is torn, then I am poor . . .
> —"Fa Song (with a Gong)," recorded by Melville and Frances
> Herskovits, 1931[64]

When calling on the Fa divination spirit, the singer of the song had to correctly identify his problem in order to have it properly analyzed. The singer's problem was his poverty, which he identified as having no wife, no money, and a torn cloth. Indeed, as the previous chapter showed, textiles were not just symbolic of wealth in the kingdom era, but they also constituted a currency and a store of wealth. When worn on bodies in the kingdom and into the present, the types and qualities of textiles materialized status and social distinction. Tailoring added additional layers of complexity to clothing's ability to communicate and construct difference. Fitted clothing became more popular over the course of the first half of the twentieth century as individuals and groups sought to tap into the possibilities of the sartorial economy for negotiating shifting conceptions of class, race, and gender.

Of course, fittedness was not an entirely new phenomenon of colonization. Tailored dress had circulated long before Béhanzin's surrender. Dahomean elites in the kingdom occasionally wore form-fitting articles of clothing that they layered with pagne and accessories, although these ensembles reflected a local Fon aesthetic of Vodun and did not correspond to global fashion norms. However, during the nineteenth century, another privileged group, the coastal communities of Fon-speaking Aguda (Afro-Brazilians or Brazilians) wore tailored items in very different ways from their contemporaries in Abomey and the interior of the kingdom. Formerly enslaved people and their descendants from Brazil and elsewhere had settled on the coast, re-creating urban centers in Ouidah and Agoué. As elsewhere on the Bight of Bénin, the Aguda Afro-Brazilian community practiced Catholicism and other aspects of European town culture, leading one French administrator to describe how Ouidah's Brazilian community "dress[ed] as Europeans."[65] In a 1936 series of photographs, French photographer and ethnographer Pierre Verger captured images of Aguda community members holding up large paintings of their ancestors. Both the man next to the frame and the man in the portrait wore three-piece suits, although in very different styles, pointing to continuities within Aguda desires to follow trends in global men's fashions even as the fashions changed (fig. 2.3).[66] Their style of fittedness became more widespread with the expansion of the sartorial economy as Fon-speaking elites embraced a tailored silhouette along the lines of the Aguda and the colony's white residents.

Although many Fon-speaking Béninois started wearing fitted styles by choice, in the years following the French occupation of Abomey in the 1890s, colonial officials attempted to create order with uniforms for local populations. After the conquest, the French quickly established a local police force (*guarde indigène*) to keep the order and to compel Fon workers to build colonial infrastructures. Clothing this colonial workforce was a priority. In 1899, the head of the colonial authority in Abomey juxtaposed his description of weapons training for the guardes with an acknowledgment that their clothing had recently been replaced, since it had "left much to be desired."[67] Properly armed and uniformed, the local police force was ready to do its job, and the prison population began to grow. But prison officials in Abomey struggled to clothe prisoners and sent word to Porto-Novo that the imprisoned men were "naked," leading the colony to supply funds.[68] Grants were also issued to buy clothes for deportees removed from other parts of the AOF and forcibly

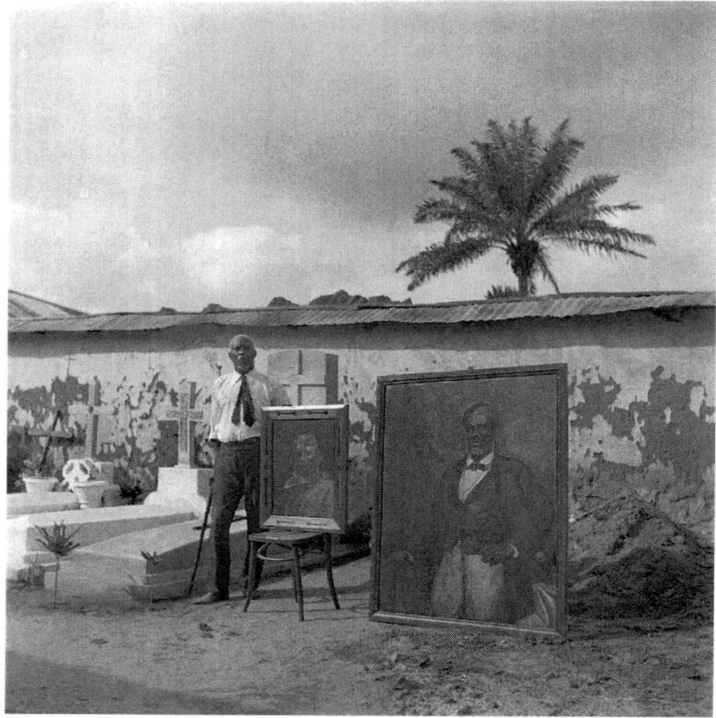

Figure 2.3. Pierre Verger, De Souza, Ouidah, Bénin. Fotos Pierre Verger © Fundação Pierre Verger.

resettled in the former Fon capital.[69] Colonial officials in Abomey repeatedly requested clothing for employees and other dependents of the state, and provisioning them proved difficult and expensive. Much of the colony's European population, from priests and nuns to certain segments of the administration, also wore uniforms, and while uniforms were not unfamiliar in the kingdom—colors and insignia delineated ranks and units within its well-organized military—the colonial administration used them to expand the local repertoire of sartorially distinguished occupations and statuses.

In the early twentieth century, French rule also created a new social category of men—the *évolué*, who, like the Aguda, embraced fitted styles according to the dictates of global men's fashion. The évolué were men who had assimilated into French civilization through education and the adoption of

Christianity and French culture. In Bénin, the majority of the évolué lived in the urban centers of Porto-Novo and Ouidah and the new port city of Cotonou. There was also significant overlap between Aguda and évolué as the Aguda had found a cultural ally and a valuable partner in the French.[70] Compared to other parts of the AOF, Bénin also had a disproportionate number of subjects working in the colonial administration; these civil servants staffed offices and served as secretaries locally and in other colonies such as Senegal and Côte d'Ivoire.[71] Contemporaries referred to the colony of Dahomey as the AOF's "Latin Quarter" due to the relatively high numbers of Béninois men educated in French and mission schools and working in colonial employment. Despite French plans to make Dahomey a cotton colony, these civil servants became one of Bénin's most valuable contributions to France's imperial project. Their regular salaries and mobility set them apart from the majority of the population, and by the 1920s Béninois évolués created a particularly active print culture. In the pages of their newspapers, these men debated the merits of local colonial policies and administrators, becoming one of the most vibrant circles of colonial criticism in pre–World War II Africa, even as their privileged positions within the local community were closely tied to the operation of colonialism.

Wealth and educational attainment both found expression when évolués wore global fashions, part of a worldwide phenomenon in which twentieth-century urbanites increasingly wore the same styles.[72] Locally, to dress "*comme les grands*" ("like big men") was to wear business suits, ties, and dress shoes of a hunnukún, or the "intellectuals." Associations between fitted fashions and literacy in European languages existed long before formal colonization, with the kingdom's secretaires and Aguda communities abandoning the pagne and adopting the three-piece suit. Colonization expedited the spread of this practice as more Béninois men followed a course of formal schooling. Néstor Dako-Wegbe, a traditional healer and the spokesman for the Dakodonnou lineage, described seeing formally schooled men wearing fitted dress when he was a young man: "When we saw someone, a Béninois dressed like Europeans, we realized that this man really was 'evolved' in order to imitate the Europeans like that. These men who barely had their CEPE [primary school certificate]! They just finished primary school and they became like the Europeans, we saw that they now were intellectuals. When we saw them dressed like that, they were happy that we considered them like someone who came from Europe even though they were a Béninois."[73] For Dako-Wegbe, part of his surprise was that men had to have only a few years of primary school before they could enter into the rank of intellectual (hunnukún), a contrast to more recent times when many students were expected to finish secondary school and continue to university. But these men, even after a relatively short period of formal education, wore their suits as symbols of their literacy and intimate knowledge of French culture. Amid colonization, attaining wealth became inextricably tied to entering the realm of the lettered, and each of these materialized on the body through a global symbol of masculine achievement—the three-piece suit.[74]

Elite men embraced global men's fashions in the decades before the Second World War. But their adoption of the three-piece suit and other fashions were not usually political acts signaling their approval of the colonial state. Indeed, clothing was much more important to emerging systems of status and distinction than as a sign of political affiliation, a significant change from the precolonial era. In a 1937 photograph (fig. 2.4) printed in the weekly newspaper *Phare du Dahomey*, Augustin Nicoué, a Porto-Novo évolué and the editor of the paper, wore a nearly identical suit to the French colonial administrator who stood to his right.[75] Outfits like Nicoué's were either imported from Europe as ready-to-wear and altered locally or sewn by tailors within the coastal cities. Coastal tailors, such as the ones trained in the Porto-Novo technical school, used fabrics including imported drill (a durable cotton-fiber fabric from Europe) khaki or poplin to make the shirts, trousers, and other clothes of the évolué. Yet, despite his adoption of a suit so similar to the colonial agent, Nicoué, like many of colonial Dahomey's intelligentsia in 1930s, was a vocal critic of colonial policies and individual administrators. His choice to wear the suit, have himself photographed in it, and then publish the photograph in his newspaper speaks more to his self-fashioning than a specific political agenda.[76] Indeed, unlike the precolonial era when dress signified one's position relative to the king and whether the wearer was in the dadá (king)'s favor, fitted clothing did not necessarily coincide with political allegiance, although it did suggest familiarity with colonial institutions and inclusion within the literate world.

Students and wage laborers also wore sewn clothes, but not the three-piece suit. One local administrator referred to these boys and men as the *demi-évolué* (half evolved)—a problematic term, of course, but one that made sense to an observer of the semi-fittedness of their sartorial practices.[77] A retired civil servant from Abomey, Gabin Akouêdenoudjè explained how he acquired his

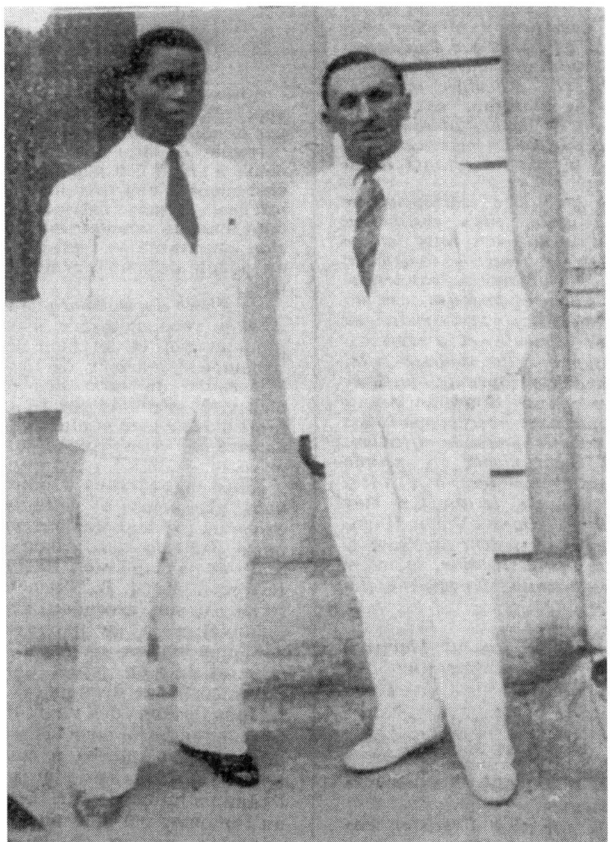

Figure 2.4. Aimé Quinsou and Augustin Nicoué. From *Le Phare du Dahomey*, No. 144, May 1937.

first outfit of tailored clothing as a primary school student. Akouêdenoudjè dressed in a pagne wrapped around his body with the two ends tied behind his neck to attend school in the 1930s and 1940s. But when the time arrived to take his exam at the end of primary school (CEP), Akouêdenoudjè's family bought imported cloth and had it tailored into his first shirt and pair of shorts. He justified his family's outlay for cloth and its tailoring as an investment in his education, explaining that "the whites came to administer the exam. . . . You could not wear a pagne around your neck to go to the exam."[78] In large cities, students were expected to don more fitted items. A newspaper photograph of the student-apprentices at the Cotonou technical school in 1936 depicts students each wearing a cap and a long-sleeved shirt with a small collar (fig. 2.2). Some of the boys and men wore shorts, but presumably the upperclassmen wore trousers sewn from a light-colored sturdy fabric, probably a cotton percale or khaki. Wage laborers, employed on the colonial railroad or other construction projects, wore similar ensembles. Although they had to make purchases out of their own pockets, laborers on the railway and other colonial construction projects reported wearing shorts and tunics during work.[79] Indeed, missions, colonial offices, and businesses encouraged or required tailored clothing, leading a gradually expanding number of men and a small number of women to wear it. As they adopted it, this led others in the community—those hoping to either mimic the wealth of their regular salaries or attain it themselves—to become more interested in fitted clothing as an object embodying what was, to many, an aspirational status.

As business suits and trousers entered local semiotic systems as indicators of education and wealth, the meanings of other garments shifted even as forms remained the same. For example, the place of short pants within society changed drastically from the precolonial era to the 1930s. In the kingdom, elite men wore the chokoto (short baggy pants) with a tunic and a grand pagne covering their torso. Under colonialism, short pants became the uniform of the primary school student and the wage laborer and a physical manifestation of the wearer's subservient status to the wearers of long pants—the French, the secondary student, and the évolué. While a very few men, like Aho in this chapter's opening vignette, might use the chokoto as a reference to precolonial authority, for most men, the short pant became a reference to a lack of power. As this example shows, shifting demands within the sartorial economy did not rely on an introduction of new sartorial forms, since jackets, trousers, shorts, and dresses had already circulated before French rule. Rather, there was a reconfiguration of wearing these forms based on new notions of proper dress and the meanings embedded within these objects.

Aho's chokoto and grande pagne also show how wrapping and draping fabric was reimagined as traditional amid the spread of fittedness and its associations with economic advancement and opportunity. Aho successfully drew upon colonial and traditional sources of authority to enrich himself and increase his influence, and he changed his clothing to fit the occasion— wearing suits in a colonial capacity and pagne when performing his role as a community leader, a role he was able to maintain even after the French state ended the system of chef de canton after the Second World War. For Aho, the strength of his performance of tradition was its perceived authenticity by outsiders and Fon alike. Unlike his grandfather King Glèlè, who had ruled Dahomey at the height of its power and global significance, Aho did not mix pagne with a suit coat or a Spanish hat and instead constructed an imagined idea of royal power that existed apart from the rest of the world and its influence. Perhaps he drew upon the ideas of the anthropologists and ethnologists he regularly worked with, who would have had a very rigid idea of an unchanging African tradition, or perhaps he was influenced by the demands of the community who mythologized a past in stark contrast to their colonized present. Like Aho, other groups of Fon speakers also drew upon traditional notions of power through dress, particularly wrapped pagne.[80] Female vodunsi and male Fá diviners continued to wrap cloth and to wear other adornments associated with their power, completely rejecting fitted forms as a top layer. As one Fá priest explained, "You can wear pants underneath, or shorts underneath . . . [but] one must always use a pagne as a wrapper."[81] In his estimation, the performance of wearing pagne was weighted more than the reality of wearing other garments.

As the pagne came to be associated with tradition, men found fewer opportunities to wear it. Most women continued to wear pagne on a daily basis, and men such as Aho, Fá diviners, or Dáa (heads of clans) wore it for ceremonial purposes. Indeed, as "tradition" became a more rigid category during the colonial period, social restrictions limited which men could wear certain articles of clothing in public. Ordinary men might wear a pagne lounging around their house or working in the fields, but if they were not Dáa, then wearing tchanka or Fon hats associated with royal families as they circulated through town could warrant public humiliation or even a beating by community members supportive of their Dáa.[82] Furthermore, many ordinary men identified as Fon but recognized the enslavement and subsequent forced migration of a recent Yorùbá or Mahi ancestor during the kingdom era, creating a measure of unease if wearing articles of clothing promoted as Dahomean heritage. By the 1930s the Royal Palace of Abomey became a center of performing Dahomean tradition and a tourist attraction in a city otherwise marginalized in the Béninois political and social realm. As wrapped cloth on men became the norm during periodic performances of the kingdom's traditions, fitted dress became a desirable alternative for ordinary men looking either to mimic the wealth and mobility of the colonial African elite or to escape an oppressive traditional and colonial social order that continued to place power in the hands of descendants of the royal family.

Notions of what constituted traditional Fon garments shifted dramatically during colonization, and new systems of meanings emerged around specific clothing items and fittedness more generally. Ideas about "tradition" and "modern" dress emerged in tandem and were replicated on many levels within colonial society, as both colonists and Béninois used the terms to describe everything from craftspeople and clothing to forms of knowledge. Within the sartorial economy, wrapped and draped textiles deployed the symbols of the precolonial dynasty and spirituality to legitimate authority while trousers, shirts, suits, and other fitted garments were associated with literacy, wealth, and masculine economic opportunity.

Sartorial Economy in Turmoil:
War and the Time of Botoyi

The Second World War and its aftermath caused a break in what had been a gradual, decades-long transformation in the sartorial economy and the expansion of fittedness.[83] The ruptures of the war reveal how closely cotton and textile markets, skills and technologies, and systems of distinction were linked within Bénin's sartorial economy and how deeply this economy was integrated within the larger global economy. The war exacerbated preexisting textile shortages and caused Béninois to turn to other methods of cloth production that exploited locally grown cotton. While the population of the colony had doubled between 1910 and 1950, the quantity of imported textiles did not grow significantly from the mid-twenties to the early fifties. Depression in the metropole during the 1930s had led French politicians to pursue protectionist economic policies for industry and workers in mainland France, and these same policies often made it more difficult for consumers in the colonies to access goods like textiles.[84] British cloth also became very expensive, but French textiles did not meet the needs and tastes of African consumers. The wartime disruption to markets exacerbated these preexisting shortages and there were severe textile shortages throughout the colony during the 1940s.[85] Cotton fabric imported to all of the African colonies decreased from 42,485 tons in 1938 to 28,081 tons in 1948, with the AOF receiving about half of these imported textiles.[86] The inability of markets to keep up with demand disproportionately affected Béninois living in interior areas like Abomey, which had once been the epicenter of the region's textile wealth. Wealthier urban dwellers on the coast had much more access to fabric than people in the countryside and colonial officials suspected that urban dwellers hoarded fabric and exacerbated a rural-urban divide in access.[87] Colonial officials feared that fabric shortages might affect the day-to-day operation of the colony, since Béninois would be unwilling to work for wages if the items that they wished to purchase, namely cloth and petrol, were unavailable.[88]

Along with textiles, wartime imports plummeted in other goods important to clothing production. Most sewing machine factories in the United States and Europe shifted to producing armaments, although some continued to produce at reduced levels. As the Singer Company pointed out, "the sewing machine [was] a critical item urgently required in large quantities in time of war to repair uniforms, gas masks, parachutes, and the like."[89] Indeed, with some factories shifting their production and the remaining machines being sold for war purposes, almost no machines were imported to the AOF during the Second World War.[90] The dearth of imported textiles and machines for processing them meant that clothes-makers and consumers had to look for other ways to meet their sartorial needs.

Rural Béninois, faced with rampant shortages, turned to spinning and weaving botoyi, a coarse cloth woven from thick handspun cotton thread. In a 1943 letter to the governor of the AOF, a colonial administrator noted that locals overcame "the problem of native clothing" by using primary materials to make "basic but usable clothing."[91] Local spinning experienced a revival when women gathered cotton from harvested fields or purchased the cotton directly from growers in order to make it into yarn.[92] Their means of accessing cotton further complicated France's plans for a cotton economy in Bénin and elsewhere in the AOF, and in 1944–45 exportable cotton was one-third of what was expected. While pests and drought contributed to reduced production, administrations also attributed the shortage to "the insufficient quantity and high prices of imported fabric." They continued that "cotton is reserved for familial spinning and weaving; or it is the object of illicit transactions between natives," since the price on the wartime "lateral market" (artisanal market) was "five times higher" than the export market.[93] Although the governor of the AOF used the word *illicit* to describe the local trade in cotton, in reality wartime AOF-wide regulations prohibited peasant producers from selling their cotton to commercial enterprises outside of official markets but made an exception for "transactions [in cotton] between natives for the sole use of the local artisanat."[94] Long-standing colonial investments in cotton, acute shortages of imported textiles, and a developed craft knowledge of spinning and weaving led the production of botoyi to flourish during the war and in its aftermath.

Local weaves such as kanvɔ, dévɔ, and interweaves fetched high prices before and after the war, but Béninois do not remember botoyi as a particularly desirable cloth. Artisan weavers wove the thick yarn into a coarse, heavy fabric that they sold to consumers or to local sellers who resold it in the regional markets.[95] Although it circulated on the market, the fabric might be better framed as homespun rather than the product of master weavers, even if some trained weavers undoubtedly produced it during the shortages. As shown in the previous chapter, Bénin lauded local weaves for their material and spiritual uses, but not botoyi, which served as a material reminder of acute deprivation suffered during the war and its aftermath. Unlike other cases where people in the colonial Americas or India embraced homespun for political, often anti-imperial reasons, the turn to botoyi was not a choice but a failure of the sartorial economy.[96] While most oral historical descriptions of botoyi focused on the negatives of the fabric, narrators occasionally described botoyi as more durable than imported cloth or finer weaves, and, as a thicker weave, as better suited to the cold season. These few positive assessments aside, botoyi was generally disdained, considered low quality, and associated with impoverished people waiting for better days.

Even if sewing machines had been available, the thickness and dense internal structure of botoyi made it a poor fabric for tailoring into fitted styles. At the debut of WWII, the colonial office in France had suggested using West African strip cloths such as botoyi for wartime bandages, but the governor of the AOF rightly pointed out that it was about four times the price of French cotton textiles and more difficult to cut.[97] Cutting strip cloth led to fraying, and the cloth needed an additional seam before it could be sewn into clothing. Strip cloth was also thicker and less flexible than its industrial counterparts, and if sewn into a garment that hugged the body, these properties restricted the movement of the wearer. Botoyi's propensity for unraveling and inelasticity made the fabric a particularly poor choice for fitted styles. In sum, botoyi served as a material manifestation of wartime shortages, the global economic downturn, and the misguided policies of the French colonial state. Since it could not be easily sewn into fitted styles, the production of botoyi and the contraction of the market of imported textiles created a rupture in what had been a decades-long gradual expansion of fittedness.

This chapter has explored how Béninois makers and consumers and French colonialism shaped the emergence of a sartorial economy. Available materials, skills, and sartorial meaning shifted dramatically in the decades following the conquest of the Dahomey kingdom. The French administration attempted to promote cotton cultivation, control textile trades, train craftspeople, and delineate status through fittedness in order to make a profitable colony and the well-ordered society that would support it. In rural areas, the French encouraged cotton cultivation, hoping to make the colony an exporter to metropolitan textile manufacturers, while also repeatedly trying to manage the textile market to protect French metropolitan interests and the fiscal security of the colony. At the same time, administrators were interested in shaping who was making clothing and for which consumers. Missions had long promoted sewing as a part of women's domesticity, and by the late 1920s and 1930s state education too started training girls as housewives for a growing African colonial elite and, in small numbers, boys as tailors to clothe them. Men who worked for the colony or were otherwise associated with it would be distinguished by their dress, from the three-piece suits of the évolué to the short pants and button-down shirts of schoolboys and workers.

Béninois, however, thwarted French efforts, instead selectively integrating knowledge and materials from these programs into their own sartorial system. Cotton was never as successful as hoped, since cultivators chose other crops and cotton producers trafficked their crops to markets with higher prices, whether in other colonies or among spinners and weavers. Men and women purchased textiles according to their own tastes, which often meant illegal or non-French fabric. Students and apprentices took the skills that they wanted from programs in domestic, technical, and artisanal education while African colonial elites used fitted ensembles to express wealth and educational attainment instead of colonial accommodation. Ultimately, changes to the global economy and global war crushed French ambitions for a colonial sartorial economy, and Béninois turned to their own older forms of clothing production, albeit hastily adapted to the circumstances, to make botoyi and meet basic clothing needs. As the next chapter will show, in the wake of this rupture, new groups of Béninois embraced fittedness and an ambitious group of young men turned to artisanal tailoring to clothe them.

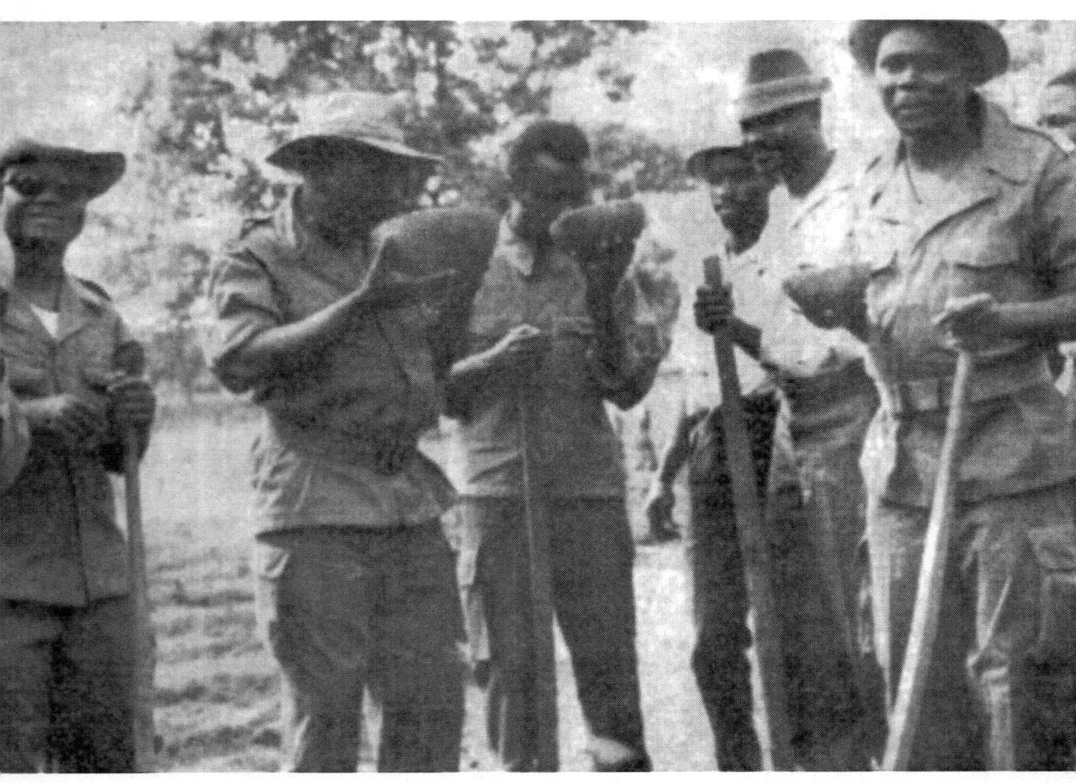

Figure 3.1. The president and his cabinet in the national costume. From *L'aube nouvelle*, June 5, 1966. Courtesy of National Archives of Bénin.

3

Tailoring Men

*Mobility, Modernity, and Men's Fashions
in the Era of Independence*

In 1966 a newly installed military regime led by Colonel Christophe Soglo began to require ministers and other high-level bureaucrats to wear official "military style" dress, complete with long pants and a long-sleeved shirt sewn from a tough khaki. *L'aube nouvelle*, the state newspaper, promoted the outfit through images of ministers working the fields and drinking from calabashes, emphasizing how the national costume might help break down the distinctions that divided the nation socially and politically (fig. 3.1). An editorial in the newspaper, written under the pseudonym E. Cayode, suggested that the costume might quell poor Béninois men's aspirations to the luxurious life of the political elite. According to Cayode, "The citizen of Karimama or Segbana [both poor and very remote northern villages] will take notice of the fact that the '*grands*' [big men] are dressed as they also can be." Cayode also promoted the new form of dress for practical reasons since he deemed that the wool and many layers of the three-piece suits usually associated with grands were unfit for the "tropics." He also characterized wrapped "African dress" as a mismatch for a modernizing country and its development priorities, since one "cannot imagine that a nurse, a driver, a schoolteacher or a worker could juggle all these skirts and overhanging parts." Cayode continued by asking, "How can a man drowning in ten meters of cloth happen to do something serious?"[1] The state newspaper promoted the 1966 national costume in "military style" as a pragmatic alternative to both the perceived pretention and foreign origins of the three-piece suit and the impracticality of wrapped pagne. However, the push for adopting this ensemble ended up as short-lived as the regime behind it, which was overthrown by a younger group of military officers the following year.

Debates over national culture, similar to Bénin's state-sanctioned costume in "military style," took on multiple forms in independence-era Africa, in the realms of both formal politics and the everyday. The 1950s and the 1960s were a period of "possibility and constraint" when political thinkers at the highest levels engaged in acts of "worldmaking," or reimagining how African states and societies might be constituted in a postimperial world.[2] Newly independent states across the continent attempted to consolidate their power over fragmented populations through nation-building efforts that regulated and promoted specific cultural practices in institutions like art schools and government-sponsored spectacles such as festivals and fairs, and later with restrictive laws such as *authenticité* in Mobutu's Congo.[3] At the same time, prominent African men, such as Kwame Nkrumah, Léopold Sédar Senghor, and Nnamdi Azikiwe, used their dressed bodies to move between political worlds and project their agendas.[4]

However, there was no dominant political personality in Bénin, and the Soglo regime's push to create a men's costume was exceptional in Béninois history. Coup d'états led to twelve different governments between 1960 and 1972, and amid this political instability, there were few top-down programs to consolidate a Béninois national culture. As a result, tailors and other clothesmakers, both as cultural producers (this chapter) and as artisanal labor (chap. 4), were largely left to fend for themselves and were not regularly subjected to interventions in their styles or their businesses. This chapter shifts the focus on style in postcolonial Africa from the cultural policies of states and the dressed bodies of elites to how ordinary people like tailors drove sartorial change by innovating new uses for technologies and by generating new styles and motifs. Through their work, tailors became important leaders in materializing Béninois men's everyday experiences of urbanization and decolonization, helping to articulate what it meant for ordinary, nonelite men to be "modern," Béninois, Fon, and city dwellers during a period of great uncertainty.

The new forms of artisanal tailoring that developed between the Second World War and the 1970s were largely within the realm of male labor and men's fashion. The exception, of course, was middle-class women, usually the wives of civil servants and missionaries who ascribed to Christian notions of female respectability and dressed bodies. But these women were a small minority, and Christian missions, churches, and their ideas on female modesty and covered bodies made few inroads into central Bénin, where most farmers, craftspeople, and traders continued to practice Vodun. Women's demand for tailored ensembles was also shaped by economic changes. With the growth of the colonial economy, male wage earners became reimagined as "breadwinners," and the wives of wage earners were better placed to make claims on the salaries of their husbands.[5] As the housewives of civil servants, middle-class women might use some of their husbands' salaries to purchase tailored skirts, blouses, and dresses. But the vast majority of Fon-speaking women were neither Christian nor the wives of wage-earning civil servants, and the accounts of husbands and wives usually remained separate, although complex systems of exchange and credit existed within households. Without access to their spouse's wages and systematically left out of the late colonial and postcolonial economy, most Fon women simply had less opportunity than men to finance clothing purchases and tailoring. Indeed, in the final decade of French colonialism and the first few decades after independence, the expansion of fitted fashions in the interior and of the craft of tailoring in general was heavily gendered as male. Men had more opportunities to make the money to support fancy wardrobes, and they were also more invested in the emerging masculine nation and city. Men were relatively better placed to dabble in new forms of self-expression; however, as chapter 5 explores, religious and economic change and the aspirations of women would contribute to the feminization of tailoring and fashion in the late twentieth century.[6]

This chapter explores how the men's styles that tailors made in the era of independence were the product of a locally generated craft knowledge that drew upon older aesthetic and craft practices shaped by the emergence of a sartorial economy. Growing demand for fitted clothing, especially the three-piece suit, attracted ambitious young men to tailoring in the decade after the Second World War. Tailors became important wearers of these suits, spreading new notions of masculinity at the same time they marketed their individual skill. They also tapped into additional opportunities for promoting their creations to an aspirational clientele through associations with and strategic use of technologies of production, which positioned tailors as experts on urban life, capable of projecting their own visions of a locally grounded Béninois modernity.[7] Men's tailoring flourished in the era of independence—not just because it was a political moment ripe for the generation of new social imaginaries but also because it was a time of relatively unfettered mobility of people, technologies, and materials.[8] By using clothing and other materials to promote their craft and by integrating global, local, and ethnic styles through media consumption, imported goods, and "adventuring" (*aventurer*), or travel, within West Africa, tailors refined their processes of making and styles within the "mobile workshops" of the craft.[9]

The chapter ends by exploring how tailors created two Béninois men's styles—the bounba and the dété, which provided new opportunities for self-expression and identity formation among ordinary Béninois men. Like Colonel Soglo's "national costume," these styles were designed to embody the supposed values and aspirations of a newly independent people. Yet unlike Soglo's national costume, bounba and dété achieved mass popularity and became Béninois dress, worn regularly up until the present. This popularity was due to the work of tailors, whose mastery over materials, technologies, and style put them at the forefront of creating social meaning around clothing in post-independence Bénin. By wearing fancy suits, using and displaying sewing machines, photographs, and other tools, and traveling extensively, tailors fashioned themselves as experts on how ordinary Béninois men should act and look in a new city and nation, driving new associations between specific clothing styles, sartorial meaning, and social change.

The Tailored Body: Aspirational Clothing and the "Modern" Silhouette

In 1960, Bohicon resident Lékolihoui Djibidisse started his career as an independent tailor. At twenty-seven, Djibidisse was much older than the average craftsperson first venturing out on their own, since he had initially sought to become a photographer.[10] In the early 1950s, Djibidisse moved to Kumasi, then in the Gold Coast, to train as one. Upon his return to Bohicon, he realized that he could not afford a quality camera or the costs of building the sets and darkroom of a proper studio photographer and went in search of a new career. An older relative had just set up shop as one of the few men professionally making bespoke fitted clothing in the small town. The man sewed all kinds of outfits, but the most high-end ensembles produced by the tailor were three-piece suits. In an interview, Djibidisse explained that "it was not just anybody who sewed suits at this time; only the good people, the rich people ordered them."[11] Djibidisse associated the suits with wealth and even the goodness of the clients but he also noted how few tailors had the skills to make the suits. To Djibidisse, the three-piece suit, and the tailored silhouette more generally, reflected a certain level of wealth and prestige that was available to only a few.

As previous chapters have shown, associations between the three-piece suit and wealth, prestige, and education existed in the Dahomey kingdom but became reified and more widespread between conquest in the 1890s and the Second World War. Yet it was during the postwar period that this "modern silhouette" of fitted clothing was embraced by men, like Djibidisse, who were not usually considered part of the évolué or hunnukún (intellectuals). Along with tailors, who regularly wore three-piece suits, other wearers included war veterans and a new cadre of Fon businessmen. Collectively, these tailors, veterans, and businessmen of the 1950s and 1960s should be considered a small-town version of the Atlantic-wide practice of Black dandyism.[12] As men who "threatened the existing class structure by dressing up," Black dandies could "transcend circumstances, as well as societal perceptions."[13] In this way, the Black dandy stood in contrast to previous generations of African elites who at times mimicked European culture, replicating its distinctions of power and privilege. These Black dandies also differed from Franz Fanon's "colonized intellectual" whose embrace of static "customs, traditions, and costumes" served as a performance of "cultural authenticity." As Fanon pointed out, the colonized intellectual's "mummified fragments" of dress, dialect, or other aspects of culture "are in no way related to the daily lot of the men and women of his country" who have experienced massive transformations.[14] The fancy dress of men like tailors, veterans, and businessmen represented a reality in which Bénin was already part of the world and had been for quite a while, not an imagined traditional space.[15] At the same time, tailors subverted more local societal norms that linked their corporeal presentations to wealth, formal education, and social prestige in Bénin's sartorial economy.

As more men embraced dandyism and the meanings around these styles changed, the independence-era demand for the work of tailors also grew. One of the groups driving the adoption of suits for ordinary men was veterans recently returned from the Second World War. Fitted uniforms worn during the war, especially after the liberation from German prisoner of war camps, served as symbols of these men's service to the Allied effort but also, more intimately, their equality with servicemen of equal rank, whatever their background.[16] Memories of elder relatives collected in Bénin echoed that war veterans returned with a new sense of style and preferences for a fitted silhouette. A Béninois retired tailor and *chef du village*, Lêgbânon Bénoit Djezandé, made this relationship explicit when he claimed, "Because [his] father was a veteran, he liked to always wear shorts or pants."[17] War veterans usually lacked the resources of the older colonial elite explored in chapter 2, but their experiences and perspectives in a world beyond Bénin nonetheless found expression as they abandoned pagne in favor of more fitted ensembles. Returning to the interior, they circulated these designs and helped foster a taste for the fitted among ordinary men. Fitted clothes, including button-down shirts and trousers, became a part of veteran status, helping make them an identifiable group of non-elite men in the interior.[18] Their clothing hinted at the worldliness of the wearer while also allowing veterans to make claims on colonial (and national) states and upset local social organization.[19]

At the same time, a growing cadre of Fon-speaking merchants also carved out a new social position by dressing well in tailored outfits. Small-scale commerce in the interior had traditionally been the domain of women or itinerant Muslim traders while large firms on the coast were dominated by coastal groups such as the Aguda or Afro-Brazilians. However, with the wartime and postwar restructuring of the colonial order and the decline of official power of former *chefs de canton* like Justin Aho, "a new aristocracy" of Fon businessmen took hold.[20] The old guard of merchants felt the pressures of change within the local economy, and in 1944 coastal Aguda textile traders petitioned the state to curtail the activities of these emergent businessmen.[21] One of these new businessmen was Frédéric Sodokpa, an Abomean who moved to the area north of Cotonou in the 1940s to open a small retail shop, a type of petty commerce that Fon men had previously avoided. Yet his business quickly expanded, and he opened other shops in the towns and cities in the southern part of the colony, frequently returning to Abomey, where his wives and children lived. In Abomey and elsewhere, Sodokpa passed out his business card, which contained a photograph of him wearing a suit jacket and tie (fig. 3.2).[22] In this sense, Sodokpa represented a new type of Béninois man. He made significant profits in retail, tapping into a domain that in the small scale had been the work of women and in coastal cities was the domain of Agudas and other coastal elites. Sodokpa used his profits to buy fancy dress, build a home, and send his sons and daughters to school. As a man embodying the new possibilities of the era, Sodokpa adopted the dress of the colonial African elite, a masculine style that referenced his new status and distanced him from the traditional Abomean authorities like Aho in his grande pagne.

Despite the growing demand for fitted fashions among men like veterans and businessmen, there were not enough qualified craftspeople to make these garments. These consumers, as well as the more established wearers of the

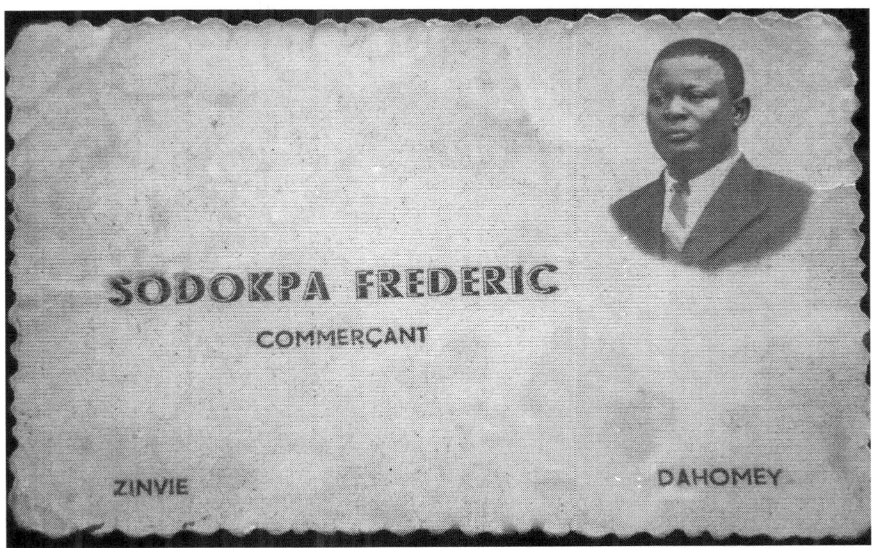

Figure 3.2. Card for Frédéric Sodokpa, businessman. Photo by author. Courtesy of Elisabeth Sodokpa.

three-piece suit—the colonial civil servant and the húnnukun—usually had to travel to the coast to find a shop capable of meeting their demands. For veterans, shopping trips and fitting sessions often occurred when they made the trek to the coast every three months to pick up their pensions. In the flourishing port city of Cotonou, they purchased fabric and commissioned a tailor to sew it into the newest style.[23] But Béninois were not just moving to coastal cities like Cotonou; they also migrated to regional towns like Abomey and Bohicon, the latter of which had grown significantly since the French constructed a railroad in the early 1900s.[24] For many Béninois, Abomey represented the past, a place with reconstructed palace walls where Dáa and men like Justin Aho wrapped grand pagne and, even after the ending of the chef de canton system, ruled informally through tradition. Bohicon, in contrast, held some of the same opportunities as other African "colonial cities" where men and women might escape some of the confines of traditional hierarchies and take part in a growing number of activities like traveling cinema or live concerts.[25] Yet in these growing urban spaces in 1960, there were few tailors; there were allegedly only four working in Bohicon's market and about a half dozen more in the Abomey, serving a community of tens of thousands of people.[26] By the 1970s, there would be hundreds of male tailors in the two towns and the surrounding villages.

The appeal of fitted clothes to makers and consumers drove this rapid expansion in tailoring. While ambitious young men were interested in making suits in order to turn a profit and become independent artisans, they were especially intrigued by tailoring because it provided new opportunities for dressing well and self-expression. The allure of suits—both making and wearing them or becoming one of the "good" and "rich" who wore them—drew young men like Djibidisse to the craft. Most of the tailors who started setting up shop in the 1950s and 1960s were the sons of peasant farmers and had never attended school, or at most had attended the first year or two of primary school. Suits appealed to them as men interested in social mobility, travel, and acquiring the look of the well-off húnnukun. Abomey tailor Maurice Béhanzin told how he "had an uncle who was a teacher and the way he dressed led [him] to sewing."[27] The teacher's standard of *la tenue pique* (machine-stitched dress) and the style of tucking a long-sleeved shirt into a pair of trousers inspired Béhanzin to abandon the wrapped pagne of his royal ancestors in favor of the sewn dress of an uncle.[28] While his uncle took a more standard path of acquiring an education, getting a formal sector job, and purchasing a wardrobe of fitted clothes, Béhanzin sought to change his outward appearance through making the clothes himself.

The dirt-free body of a tailor also drew many men to take up the craft. Before colonization, wrapping one's body in many yards of expensive, pristine cloth and constraining it from performing physical labor was a sign of the king's favor and wealth. Later, European businesses and colonial institutions invested in linking ideas about "civilization" and "cleanliness" in colonized Africa.[29] Sitting at machines in the shade or indoors, the body of a tailor more closely resembled that of a teacher or a civil servant than the dusty or muddy body of a farmer or most other craftsmen. As a fifteen-year-old boy, Anago Yobode chose tailoring over other artisan trades because, as he said, tailors "live cleanly." Yobode contrasted the tailor's body with mechanics', which he saw as "always dirty."[30] Despite both crafts being mechanized and associated with global modernity, men who fixed cars became covered in grease and grime over the course of a day's work. Most Béninois labored in fields, returning home each day sweaty and dusty. In contrast, a tailor resembled a grand or a hunnukún in his office and minimized sweating by removing his jacket and artfully draping it on the back of his chair. Men opted into the craft to avoid the muck, grease, and grime of most manual labor and its associations with subservience and poverty, which had existed in the kingdom era and were amplified under colonialism.

Young men and their families also interpreted tailoring as a "safe" profession because the body of a tailor was relatively immune from work-related accidents, unlike many of the other crafts open to rural men with few connections and little education. After the death of his father, Agbaignzoun tailor Pierrot Akpako's mother encouraged him to look for work that might support him and his family. Taxi driving and car repair were viable careers for young men of a similar social background, and they were also jobs that allowed young men to self-fashion as "modern."[31] Like many men, Akpako wavered between working as a bush taxi driver or tailor, but his mother ended up selecting tailoring since she feared the very real possibility of a car accident.[32] Bohicon tailor Alain Baba, who would later be instrumental in the development of tailoring associations, fell into the craft for a similar reason. His uncle had been entrusted with helping him select a craft after Baba made it clear he was not interested in farming. Baba wanted to train as a mechanic, but his uncle associated repairing cars with accidents. Rumors of victims of car accidents being "buried next to the road" meant that a mechanic's body might even be mistreated after death, creating more opportunity for body snatchers who might use his corpse for nefarious means.[33] Another man, who had first trained as a master mason, changed careers and began to learn tailoring after an on-the-job accident at a construction site in which he fell and "broke his kidneys."[34] In contrast to the real threats posed by other careers like driving, car repair, or construction, the primary occupational risk to a tailor was eye strain, which often led to vision problems as tailors aged, a concern that seemed too distant for young men and their families who looked to preserve clean, whole bodies in the present.

The idea of the clean, safe body and its association with upward mobility were furthered by the fancy dress of tailors whose sartorial practices served as an embodiment of their ambition as well as their most effective means of marketing. A Bohicon tailor, Clotaire Blenon, recalled how he was initially drawn to the craft: "I wanted to sew something so I went to the tailor's, I saw that he was clean, he made money, when I saw these things, it started . . . that was when I made my choice."[35] For Blenon, the tailor's pristine, well-dressed body was inextricably related to the profits of the craft. Throughout their careers, tailors like Blenon sought to dress well as a means of attracting a similarly aspirational clientele. During an interview, Blenon described a recent outing to Sunday mass dressed in an all-white suit of trousers, vest, and a matching jacket. Upon welcoming Blenon to church, the priest joked, "Ah, Monsieur Clotaire, you know we are in Bohicon here?"—suggesting that his ensemble would be a better fit for a larger, more cosmopolitan city, not the regional center of Bohicon. The town had few paved roads then, and perhaps the priest was referring to the difficulty of keeping white clothes pristine amid the red mud of the rainy season or the thick red dust of the dry season, both of which dirtied clothing when thrown up by the wheels of Bohicon's many moto-taxis. But Blenon took the priest's remark seriously, responding to him, "Yes, I am in Bohicon, but I have to wear this." He continued his justification in an interview: "People look at us [fashion designers] . . . you become the man-nequin . . . that is why us fashion designers, normally we cannot dress messy, we cannot dress like good-for-nothings [*la voyoucratie*] even at home."[36] Dressing well and circulating within the city's public spaces had become es-sential parts of Blenon's and other tailors' work of designing, marketing, and making clothing. The mobile tailor-mannequin not only displayed his skills and fashion sense for potential clients to see but also, in doing so, embodied his expertise in matters of masculine style and disrupted notions of what kinds of men wore three-piece suits.

Bodies remained the most important place to display sartorial creations, even more than hangers or mannequins, because movement allowed clients to discern the quality of their work. At the beginning of this chapter, the editorial by Cayode took the position that wrapped and draped avɔ was not "serious" enough for men in the new nation. Indeed, hanging and tucking fabric disciplined bodies into intentional, slow movements while a well-fitted ensemble opened new possibilities. Blenon continued by emphasizing the importance of movement: "When you get out of a vehicle, you have to get out and walk a little [gestured] so people can see you, your pants, your shirt, and how when you are walking how it gives. We call that a pose. He is going to say, 'Look at that gentleman there, his pants sure are a success.' Because there are people who sew pants and it does that [not lay correctly]; it is a defect."[37] Poorly tailored trousers might wrinkle in odd places during movement, but a well-tailored piece continued to lay correctly even during quick or awkward bodily movements. These might include actions like getting into and exiting a car or working at one of the few factories in Bohicon, places where a wrapped avɔ might unintentionally snag and tear. While men might continue to wear

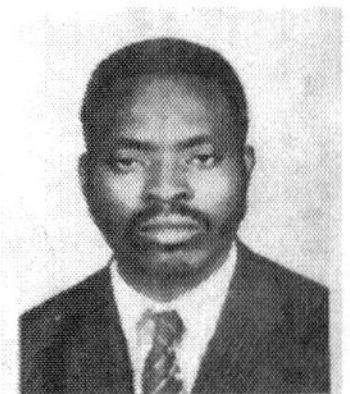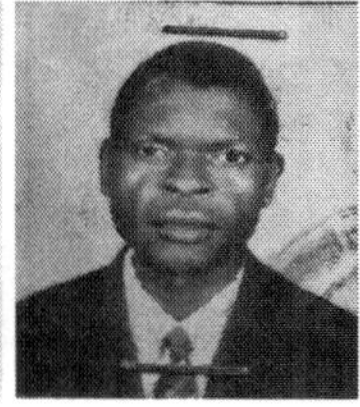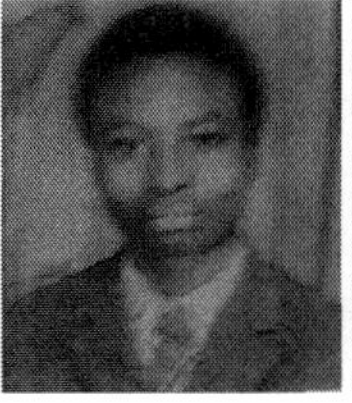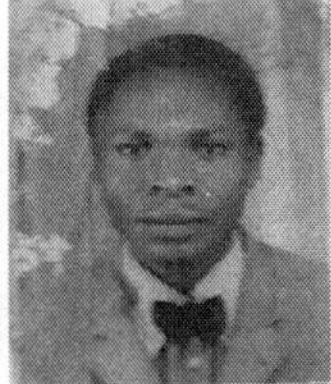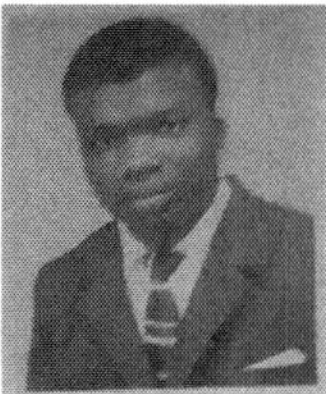

Figure 3.3. Headshots of Bohicon and Abomey tailors in suits, 1950s–1970s. Photo by author.

avɔ in the home, well-fitted clothes became necessary for men hoping to take advantage of new opportunities in Bénin's changing economy.

Although movement through the growing city might be the best way to promote one's shop and skill, tailors also used photography to project their personas as part of the larger world of suited men. Although Lékolihoui Djibidisse, the tailor who had trained as a photographer in the Gold Coast, had been unable to open a studio after his apprenticeship, photography became more widespread in the years around independence.[38] Wearing a fancy three-piece suit and commissioning a photograph were widespread and longstanding practices of tailors, dating to the earliest expansion of the craft. Tailors kept passport-sized prints safely on identification cards and apprenticeship diplomas that they displayed in their shops.[39] Tailors also enlarged and framed versions of these images on the walls of homes and workshops. Figure 3.3 includes examples of images found on tailors' cards, diplomas, and framed pictures. The men wore jackets, although all slightly different because the photographs date from the 1950s to the 1970s. But the basic form—the three-piece suit—remained the same. The tailored silhouette attracted to the craft young men who aspired to the wealth and prestige of fellow suit-wearers like businessmen and hunnukún; it also created new meanings around the accessibility of world fashion and global inclusion for ordinary Béninois men. Capturing these images on film allowed men like Alain Baba and Lékolihoui Djibidisse to create enduring images of themselves in their finery, inspiring others to dress well and to visit their shops to have the clothes made.

But the business suit was not the only form of expressing achievement and aspiration in Bénin. West Africans named waxes, status fabrics imported from Europe and consumed throughout the region, to communicate and commemorate specific events. Tailored wax fabrics also expressed wealth and

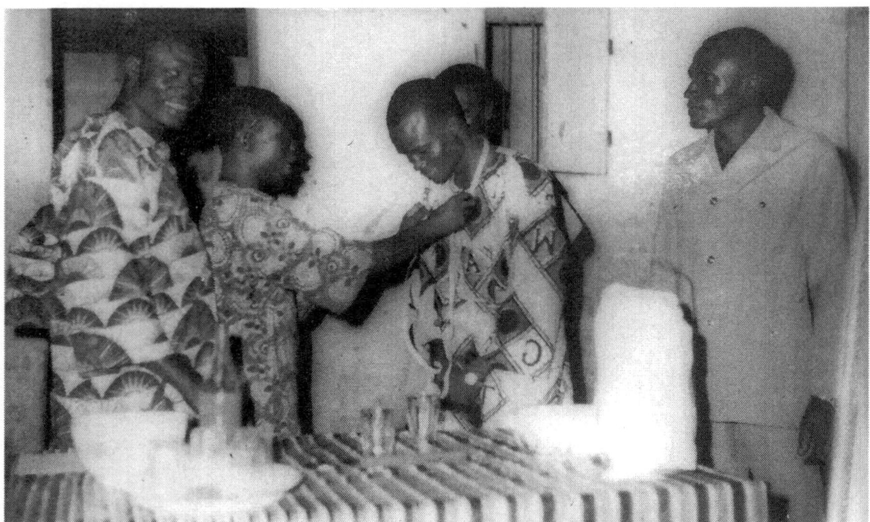

Figure 3.4. Celestin Godou Kpodo at his libération, Abomey, 1970s. Courtesy of
Celestin Godou Kpodo.

literacy as well as their wearer's participation in global economies of style and
fashion. For example, in figure 3.4, Godou Kpodo does not wear a suit but uses
a different celebration of educational achievement—the wax print commonly
called ABC, originally designed and produced by the Dutch fabric company
Vlisco.[40] The design features letters from the Latin alphabet organized into a
diamond shape "to illustrate that knowledge is precious." The fabric's design
was originally created by a missionary around 1904, but West Africans have
used the fabric "as a symbol of social advancement ever since."[41] That Godou
Kpodo chose ABC fabric to make the outfit for the day that he officially became a tailor was not a coincidence. Often worn by students or their parents
to celebrate educational attainments, Vlisco's ABC fabric conveyed an equivalency between Kpodo, the new master tailor, and the students who, upon
finishing school, entered into lucrative jobs as suit-wearing civil servants. As
Bohicon tailor Sébastien Djokpe described it, "In those times [tailors] were
well respected because everyone went to the field to work. If someone did not
go to the field, if he went to his apprenticeship and he did tailoring, he was
well respected because he was like an intellectual."[42]

Men's aspirational clothing took on many forms in independence-era Bénin, from ABC fabric tailored into a bounba to the three-piece suit, a global symbol of urban prestige. While the 1966 image of ministers toiling in the fields wearing fatigue-like uniforms was a radical anti-colonial statement and a rejection of colonial elite masculinity, it was not a masculine type that spoke to the aspirations of ordinary men like Djokpe, Djibidissé, and Blenon. Instead, the sons of peasants sought to transcend their circumstances and become part of the modern world even as they defined what that meant in very local or even individual ways. Tailoring was bound up in these aspirations on multiple fronts. Craftsmen produced so-called modern things like three-piece suits, but the besuited, clean, and safe bodies of makers provided a mode of inclusion in a global urban world. These Black dandies hinted that wealth and social mobility were accessible to ordinary men, not just the besuited ministers encountered in the pages of newspapers and through the windows of motorcades. The fact that tailors were both makers and wearers of these fine clothes attracted ambitious young men to take up the craft, expanding men's sartorial possibilities in interior Bénin.

Mobile Things as Technologies of Self and Production

> I kept this [indicates sewing machine] after retirement so that maybe my children will talk about it. That this is the craft that I studied. That they were born from this. I keep it here because of my children, for history.
> —Bohicon tailor Alain Baba on his sewing machine, June 5, 2021

Between interviews collected in 2014 and 2021, Alain Baba's eyesight became progressively worse, a condition that he attributed to years working behind a sewing machine in dimly lit spaces where he made stylish *costume* (suits) for himself and clients. Although he was no longer able to work on his sewing machine, Baba kept it carefully guarded in the corner of his living room. The artifact, he declared, was kept for "[his] children, for history" so that they might understand how "they were born from this" and that their existence and ability to flourish came from work done on the machine.

A few kilometers away, another retired tailor named Donatien Dansi had kept his machine in a similar space in the corner of a living room before his death. Like Baba, Dansi had given up tailoring, although Dansi had remade himself as a traditional healer, providing remedies to clients from as far away as Côte d'Ivoire. While his sewing machine sat unused, someone had prominently written the entire receipt for the machine on the wall of his living room. He had purchased it on June 3, 1976, and the receipt, written in chalk, had faded away and been traced over many times.[43] Both Baba's and Dansi's machines were conspicuous in rooms otherwise almost devoid of collected or displayed items. Their preservation was notable in semi-urban, relatively poor households like theirs where recycling, reuse, or reselling dominated. Although now immobile, unused, and preserved for "history," these machines helped the men remember earlier times when machines were particularly mobile—produced in factories continents away and then sold to tailors who carried them throughout the countryside—and how the cachet of their mobility helped tailors self-fashion as "modern" men.

Tailors like Baba and Dansi dressed in suits to position themselves as vanguards of urban life and culture, but clothing was not the only material that tailors used in their self-fashioning. These men also had command over and creatively used mobile things like machinery, measuring tapes, and synthetic fabrics to promote their skills and shops. Before colonization, a few tailors in Dahomey had incorporated sewing machines into their production methods, and as the previous chapter showed, the early colonial state promoted sewing machines as a necessity of "civilized" life. Even amid the postwar rhetorical shift from the colonial civilizing mission to development, sewing machines maintained an important place in French approaches to modernizing individuals and societies. For example, in 1948, amid postwar shortages and economic uncertainty, the French set aside a significant amount of foreign currency to import sewing machines and justified this seemingly excessive expense because sewing machines were necessary for "domestic and artisanal needs" and "African social evolution." Other small portable devices, such as typewriters, record players, and cameras, were imported for "private needs" or "various needs" or as "objects in high demand by évolués," but only the sewing machine could initiate a societal "evolution," hinting at a colonial belief that subjects might be transformed from the outside in.[44]

With the colonial state prioritizing imports, sewing machines became more available than ever to tailors. In oral histories, nearly all tailors identified Singer as their preferred brand, due to perceptions of their higher quality, efficiency, and portability. The Singer machines available in Bénin were designed as "household" models for domestic users.[45] Flourishes and "artistic touches" added to the machines and tables made the objects into decorative items suitable as furnishings for middle-class interiors.[46] Despite Singer's designs and marketing of these machines for households, tailors opted for small versions over large industrial models because of their lower prices and because they were easily repaired and transported.[47] Colonial administrators agreed that these machines were better suited to the African colonies because of the use of "lightweight fabrics" in warm-weather areas.[48] However, machines were a costly investment. By the early 1950s, French treadle machines were imported at 24.000f and English machines at 20.000f, a significant outlay when the price of a cotton Ecru fabric was 64f per meter and a machete or a small metal basin cost 150f.[49] If tailors were able to raise the funds, they could easily find a machine at an official retailer in the coastal city of Cotonou. Later, machines would be sold directly to consumers in Bohicon where a yovo (white person or foreigner, probably French or Lebanese) opened a shop next to the central market.[50] This shop eventually closed, and Davakan, a Béninois-owned company, replaced it and sold Singers and other brands to the local community of needleworkers. A sewing machine became a widely available, if costly, investment for a young man starting his career.

Tailors sought out high-quality machines like Singer not just because they were the most efficient for clothes-making but also because branded machines served as symbolic objects promoting the success of the shop, and by extension the men who wore clothes from it. Machinery such as automobiles, bicycles, and tractors served as prestige items throughout mid-century Africa.[51] But the allure of machinery was not reducible to its cost, rarity, or even productivity. Béninois Philosopher Paulin Hountondji points to how industrial-produced objects like sewing machines had obscured origins for ordinary people in colonial Bénin who knew little about how and where they were made. He writes that people encountered them as "surreal artefacts, beyond their understanding, magically dumped into their daily lives."[52] As men able to control and manipulate these "surreal" objects to make beautiful clothing, tailors possessed a unique knowledge and mastery over an unfamiliar and almost magical object.[53] In many ways, the control of tailors over the objects of modernity calls to mind the vast literature on the West African blacksmith and how their power over the seemingly magical transformation of metals through fire made them feared and respected members of society.[54] In Bénin, the knowledge of craftspeople such as tailors regarding the more intangible aspects of the material world was expressed through their common adherence to *Gu*, the Fon vodun of metallurgy. Through the Gu cult and ritual sacrifice, craftspeople like tailors maintained their relationship to material knowledge, seeking protection from Gu.[55] The sewing machine's transformative power, encapsulated in its decorated metal head and whirring needle, and the tailor's ability to put this power to use made it an especially important object for men carving out a new social role for themselves.

Tailors prominently placed sewing machines front and center in their market stalls and private workshops. While this placement was partly a strategy to take advantage of natural light, it also helped to attract clients. The tool caught the eyes of people passing in the street, including new arrivals from rural areas, and indicated to them that a tailor worked out of the space.[56] The whirring and clicking noises (*clack clack clack*) of a treadle machine might draw people to take a second look even if they did not initially see the tailor. With few cars and a minimal electric grid, this *clack clack clack* was a unique sound that drew attention from curious people, suggesting something modern and different was going on in the space. Sewing machines also appeared in photographs, and paintings of them communicated occupational identity when they appeared on signs in front of workshops, on diplomas, and, much later, on membership cards in craft organizations. The image of the sewing machine became almost a pictogram for the word *tailor* and communicated one's craft to people unable to read French or Fon.

Behind the machines, there were usually colorful stacks of outfits ready to be picked up and piles of untailored fabric waiting to be sewn, hinting at the demand for a tailor's skill. The growth of tailored menswear in the postwar era coincided with significant changes to the types of fabric available in the market and new ways of marketing fabric through its industrial origins. In the wake of wartime disruptions to the sartorial economy, the colonial state moved to liberalize textile markets to increase legal imports and reduce local reliance on the black market.[57] Previously restricted fabrics from non-French manufacturers, along with other valued goods such as enamels and bicycles, could now enter through the port of Cotonou instead of via the British colonies.[58] However, Béninois continued to traffic fabric from Lagos and Accra, where prices remained much lower.[59] With a robust postwar black market, manufacturers and colonial officials hoped to increase Béninois demand for French textiles through new modes of market research and marketing.[60] In 1951, the General Union of the French Cotton Industry (Syndicat Général de l'Industrie Cotonnière Française), an association of French textile producers, launched an overland exposition in French West and West Central Africa to promote their products and gather data on preferences. In Abomey and other "centers deprived of a cinema," the exposition set up portable screens to show a documentary, *The Beautiful Fabrics of France* (*Les Beaux Tissus de France*).[61] The Syndicat Général likely sought to replicate the excitement surrounding mobile cinemas, the traveling film shows that served as early forms of urban leisure in West Africa and attracted a diverse audience.[62] During *The Beautiful Fabrics of France*, viewers in Abomey watched footage of the machines and factories where fabric was made, learning about the industrial processes behind it. French observers deemed the film a "real triumph," claiming that it sparked local interest in textiles and their production.[63]

New ways of marketing fabric, especially with the spread of synthetics by the 1960s, encouraged tailors and consumers to consider the properties of these textiles by using senses beyond just sight. Along with promoting their fabric through a film that emphasized its industrial origins, the Syndicat Général also traveled with displays of fabric. But one French observer noted a problem with their displays: "The Africans could not touch the cloth," which, they argued, gave the exhibition "a spirit more artistic than commercial."[64] Pierre Verger's 1959 photograph of Abomey's main market, Houndjroto, captured how market women displayed textiles for consumers, permitting them to touch and assess the cloth in many ways. Women wrapped the fabric into a cone, creating different angles for tailors and other consumers to judge its type, quality, and print (fig. 3.5). Consumers could touch the cloth or use their other senses such as taste and smell to determine its desirability.[65] These ways of evaluating textiles became increasingly important as new types of fabric beyond cotton prints, such as synthetics, entered the market. While chemical companies in the United States, Germany, Japan, and elsewhere spearheaded the development of synthetic fibers and their use in fashion, the qualities of these textiles appealed to tailors in Bénin, who began to use them to make men's clothing.[66] Synthetic fabrics offered certain benefits to wearers, since they lasted longer than cotton and kept their color despite repeated washings.[67] Tailors and their clients appreciated this durability along with the fabric's malleability, which allowed tailors to transform synthetics into fitted items such as suits, trousers, and dresses. Amid the burgeoning interest in modernization, the industrial origins of synthetics made them seem especially suited to men wanting clothes with a contemporary look.

Tailors adopted another tool—the measuring tape—into their production methods to make synthetics and other fabrics into fitted ensembles. Tailors

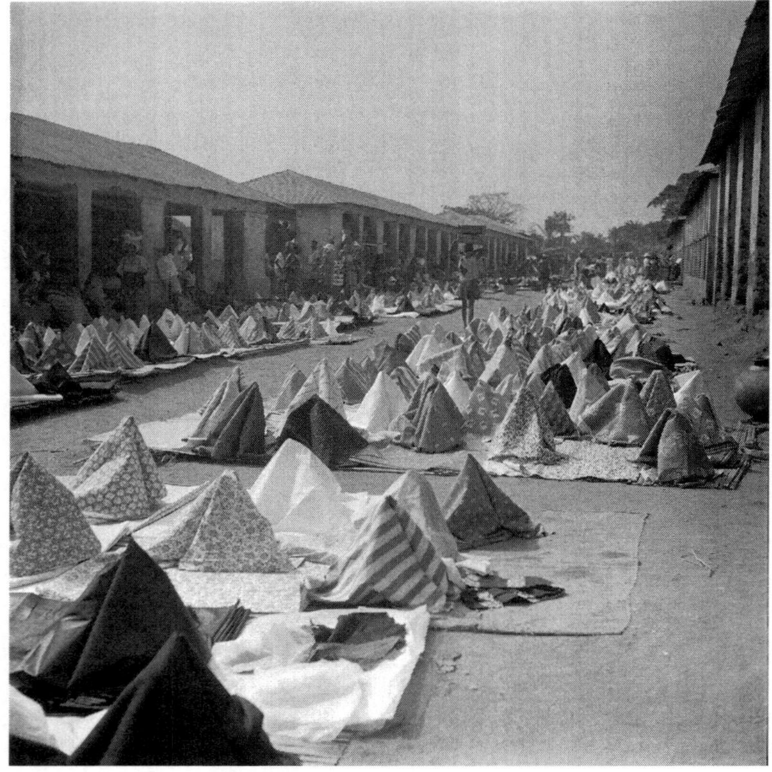

Figure 3.5. Pierre Verger, "Abomey Market," 1959. Fotos Pierre Verger © Fundação Pierre Verger.

who made voluminous ensembles prominent in earlier periods either estimated sizes by sight or used parts of their bodies, like lengths of hands or arms, to measure a client's body. While these methods worked well for generous outfits, they did not allow tailors to make the precise cuts necessary to sew suits, trousers, and the like. For these styles, a tailor needed to use a string or measuring tape to record the exact size of the client's body. When a client wanted a suit, for example, the tailor had to measure chest, arm length, torso length, shoulder, waist, back, inseam, and so on to make a quality garment. Most Béninois tailors used the metric system and recorded measurements in centimeters; however, with the proximity to Nigeria, which used the imperial system under British rule, other tailors kept notes in inches. The adoption of either system of measurement required the acquisition or development of recordkeeping and other "paper tools" for the craft.[68] Tailors wrote down information in a notebook, writing measurements alongside names, which allowed them to work on multiple projects at the same time and easily delegate to apprentices. Others went so far as to adopt accounting methods so that clients could make purchases in installments. But these "paper tools" also required levels of literacy and numeracy that most young Béninois men did not have. Boys and men interested in becoming tailors often sought out alternative paths to learning how to read and write. In some cases, family members who had attended primary school informally taught basic literacy to apprentice tailors.[69] The growing importance of measurement to the craft compelled young men to learn to read and write if they wanted to be successful, and these competencies often permitted them to take part in other forms of literacy.

Tailors often chose to be photographed with their measuring tape draped from their neck on the day of their libération, the celebration at the end of an apprenticeship. While the histories of apprenticeship and libération are the subject of the following chapter, tailors' use of measuring tapes on this day reinforced their image as socially mobile men. In figure 3.4, Abomean tailor Celestin Godou Kpodo is shown receiving a measuring tape on the day of his liberation in the early 1970s, after his master hung the tape around his neck to acknowledge his former apprentice's entrance into the profession as a full member. The tape also suggested Godou Kpodo's computational and record-keeping skills, which made it easier for him to plan, accumulate a roster of clients, and increase his efficiency and profits. However, Godou Kpodo had never attended school, and his ability to write numbers and letters as well as the few phrases he knew in French were all learned during apprenticeship. In our interview with him, Godou Kpodo presented himself as a cosmopolitan whose worldliness manifested in his command over letters and numbers, his marriage to a secretary, and his travels and familiarity with communities beyond his own. For him, the measuring tape was a symbol not just of his ability to transform cloth into fitted clothing but also of another process of transformation in which he, an outsider due to his rural origins, poverty, and lack of formal education, became a part of the new nations' urban society through tailoring. Indeed, the use and display of globally mobile things, like measuring tapes, synthetic fabrics, and sewing machines as well as the three-piece suit, helped tailors position themselves as men at the forefront of modernity, making them local leaders in the articulation of what that might look like in an independent Bénin. Tailors' strategies of self-fashioning as modern and successful attracted young men to the craft. However, looking the part was only one aspect of being successful; a tailor also had to be able to put these modern tools to work and master the craft knowledge of clothes-making.

The Market and *L'aventure*: Space, Movement, and Innovation in Craft Knowledge

By the late 1950s, there were about five or six men already sewing clothes in Bohicon's central market. These tailors rented stalls in the covered portion of the Bohicon market, Ganhi, which was built by the French and was adjacent to the market Sèhi, where women sold produce.[70] The colonial-era market operated alongside older commercial centers like Houndjroto, founded during the reign of Gezo (1818–58), where another half dozen tailors worked alongside the fabric vendors photographed by Verger (fig. 3.5).[71] Markets, whatever their origin, occurred every fourth day in southern Bénin and brought together vendors and buyers from surrounding towns and villages, ultimately shaping how rural inhabitants experienced the growing towns.

Jules Wimêllo, a tailor in Tindji-Kponzou, a village a few kilometers north of Bohicon, described how in his youth, his family and friends acquired sewn clothing from tailors like Djibidisse and his peers. Wimêllo walked two hours along a single-track trail into Bohicon to visit a Ganhi tailor. There, customers ordered a shirt or pants, and the tailor told them to return in two to twenty-four hours, giving clients like Wimêllo the opportunity to walk around town, do some shopping, or visit transplants from the village. Then they returned to the market to pick up their outfits, make any alterations, and continue back home.[72] The waiting period was a unique opportunity to spend time aimlessly wandering and experiencing the new city. Newly tailored clothing served as the material remnants of Wimêllo's recent encounter with the city, which he could display on his body for the other people in his village.

Visiting a tailor was an exciting experience for Wimêllo and others because there were new fashions to see, discuss, and order. Tailors were able to constantly change their offerings because of their proximity to fabric vendors and the burgeoning market in acouta, or secondhand goods. In Ganhi, Wimêllo would have ordered from tailors who learned new styles through improvisation and experimentation with acouta and a sewing machine. The tailors

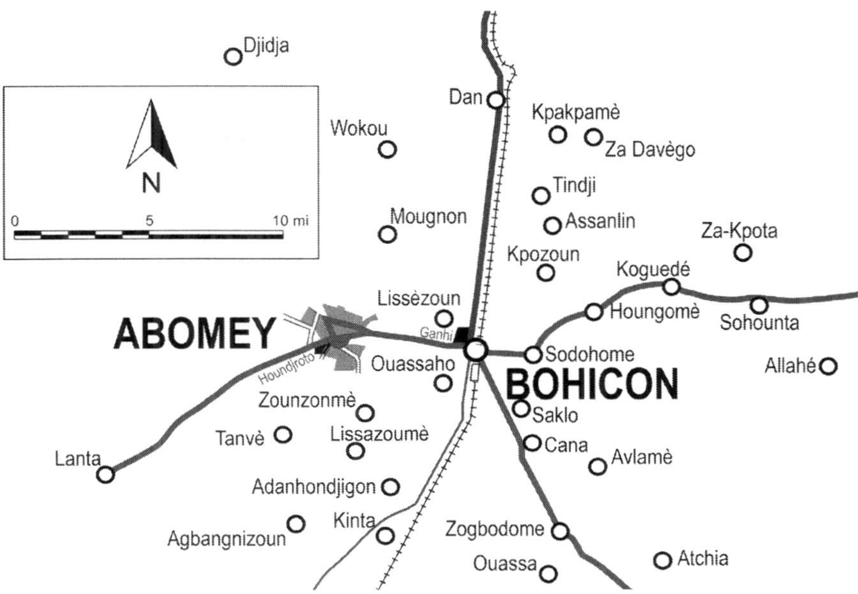

Map 3.1. Abomey, Bohicon, and surrounding areas.

purchased secondhand items and carefully took them apart the seams. They practiced sewing a new jacket, pants, or a neckline by using the disassembled garment as a pattern.[73] Tailors combined these new elements with forms they were already familiar with to create something wholly new. Creations that failed or that did not meet the tailors' aesthetic standards were taken apart and sewn into something else, reducing the cost for the tailor. Their creative process, rooted in trial and error, relied on the quick stitching of a machine to sew seams or hems.[74] The same machine that allowed tailors to broadcast their global inclusion to an aspirational clientele also opened new possibilities for technical innovation, improvisation, and experimentation with fabrics and styles. Working out of the same spaces as other tailors and fabric and secondhand vendors, tailors often collaborated and improvised to generate new fashions. Their creative processes drew on regional practices used in other crafts, from pottery to blacksmithing, and not Western-derived fashion design with its use of croquis and abstracted patterns.

Not only did acouta provide inspiration for designs, but tailors also worked to refashion extant garments into new styles. Similar to imported fabrics, secondhand materials had a long history in the region, arriving via Atlantic trade during the kingdom era and when missionaries distributed items to converts, but they took on new meaning after independence. In the wake of the Second World War, the global market in secondhand clothing expanded rapidly due to surplus military uniforms and women's clothing. Charitable organizations in the United States and Europe also received more donations due to lower clothing prices and new niche markets, such as leisure wear or clothes for teens, which created a huge wearable surplus.[75] In Bénin, women bought bales of acouta in Cotonou and resold it to clients in regional markets. But wearing acouta was fraught with social and political meaning in the post-independence era. In 1968, a newspaper commentator claimed that 95 percent of Béninois wearers of secondhand were "illiterates and semi-illiterates," reflecting a reformulation between wearing secondhand clothes, status, and education.[76] A student in Porto-Novo summed up the consequences of wearing acouta and argued that the government "must abolish the sale of these clothes" and "block the imperialists who want to sell us everything." He foresaw the consequences of Béninois wearing secondhand clothes: "In the next few years, we will be powerless against the sale of the leftovers from meals already served in European restaurants."[77] Célestine Agassounon, an acouta trader, proposed another argument on the unpopularity of acouta when she recalled that "they said [acouta] was dead people's clothing," and followers of vodun refused to wear it.[78] While re-wearing actual used garments might have been dismissed as embracing neocolonial dependency or spiritually risky, tailors were able to remake the clothes and add value to otherwise undesirable garments.

Tailors influenced final forms not just through design and tailoring but also by working with clients to select the best type of fabric for their outfit. Within the market, a tailor might leave his stall to assist a client in a fabric purchase or visit an acouta vendor to discuss new styles and motifs. Tailors occasionally served as direct intermediaries between clients and European textile manufacturers, especially for fabric intended for high-end menswear, like the wool or a high-quality synthetic blend for a suit.[79] Tailors ordered fabric for individual clients through the mail by visiting the post office, where the artisans, most of whom could not read, would pay a small fee to the postman to help them fill out fabric order forms. European companies sent the fabric along with catalogues showcasing new textiles and clothing made from them. The mail order textiles were important inputs for suits, but the catalogues became especially useful aids for discussing styles with clients, and the images provided new ideas for forms that might be combined into a new design.[80] Tailors passed the catalogues among themselves or even sold them to each other to provide inspiration for their creations.

While the influx of materials and images from Europe and elsewhere inspired creative appropriations and combinations, tailors also relied on physically moving from the market to hone their skills and stylistic knowledge. Often tailors referred to these travels as *"l'aventure"* (adventure). In Mali, *aventuriers* (adventurers or *tunga* in Bambara) began to self-identify as such during the colonial period, when laborers migrated in search of profits far from their natal homes. When returning home, these men relied on the cachet of their gained knowledge to position themselves as *"civilisés* or *évolués."*[81] For tailors, being aventuriers became part of their worldly personas, complementing their suits, sewing machines, and measuring tapes in their self-fashioning. But their travels also helped tailors hone their techniques and fashion sense through encounters with other tailors and dressed bodies.

The ability of tailors to aventure stemmed from the portability of their tools. Chalk, sewing machines, and measuring tapes were light, and unlike mechanics, plumbers, or electricians, tailors' work sites were not constrained by urban electrical grids or sewage systems. This portable workspace meant that a tailor could move to any well-lit area simply by tying their machine on the back of a bicycle or carrying it on their head. Bicycles became increasingly common in independence-era Bénin, and a man who saved up enough money to purchase one used it to engage in trade and accumulate wealth.[82] This flexibility allowed tailors to move between town and countryside on a regular basis. Residents of villages invited tailors to their towns for "three or four days" to sew for multiple families for special events like a wedding or funeral.[83] A marriage celebration might be particularly profitable, since brideprice almost always included cloth, although attendees at a funeral also commissioned new outfits. Bohicon tailor Antoine Zohou described how he regularly tied his machine to the back of his bike and rode out to a village where he might stay for a few hours to a few days. For Zohou, these short stints were more profitable than renting a stall and working out of the central market.[84] Bicycles, along with sewing machines and portable flourmills, became some of the few industrially produced machines to circulate in small villages. In oral histories, tailors often described their experiences traveling from small towns to surrounding villages and how the rapidly moving needles of their machines still surprised and delighted the unaccustomed *villageois* (villagers) even as late as the 1970s.[85] Crowds of children and adults might gather to watch a tailor work to see the newest clothing styles or even to get a glimpse of an unfamiliar machine.

Tailors' attempts to associate themselves with urban culture were largely successful, and Béninois equated cities with superior craft knowledge—the bigger the city, the more skilled the craftsman. In the early 1970s, Za-Kpota tailor Lêgbânon Bénoit Djezandé decided to pursue an apprenticeship in tailoring, but his father insisted that he move to Bohicon to learn the craft even though there were already a handful of tailors in the village of Za-Kpota whom he could work under. Djezandé's father considered himself an expert in clothing and world style, since he was a tailor who had learned his craft while serving in Indochina during the Second World War.[86] When it came time to select a master tailor to teach his son, Djezandé's father selected one who had trained in Cotonou. Djezandé summed up his master's claim on expertise: "The tailors here [in the village] did not understand the work like him, the gentlemen learned tailoring in Cotonou. . . . The way that he made clothes [was] different than the tailors here."[87] The Cotonou apprenticeship of Djezandé's master meant that he was perceived as more skilled than his counterparts in Abomey and Bohicon and much more skilled than those in rural Za-Kpota.

Other parents sent their children to the coast for apprenticeship. Dáa Ganmanssô-Ahéko went to Cotonou for his six-year apprenticeship, and he returned to Abomey claiming to have a sartorial know-how unrivaled by his locally trained counterparts. He explained his expertise: "The [tailors] who learned their craft in Cotonou, they work better than those who learned in Abomey, for example. That said, there is also a difference between those who studied in Paris, for example, and those who studied here in Africa."[88] Ganmanssô-Ahéko and others constructed a hierarchy of craft knowledge that reflected proximity to the métropole and then the coastal cities. It was in sprawling urban centers that tailors had the most opportunity for encountering fashions of all sorts and the men who made them.

Tailors enhanced their cosmopolitan profiles and stylistic know-how by traveling to the coastal cities to follow "improvement courses" (cours de perfectionnement) with other master tailors. Often these short-term trainings were geared toward specific skills—learning women's fashions, specific styles of suits, sport jackets, or embroidery.[89] For example, tailor Pierrot Akpako

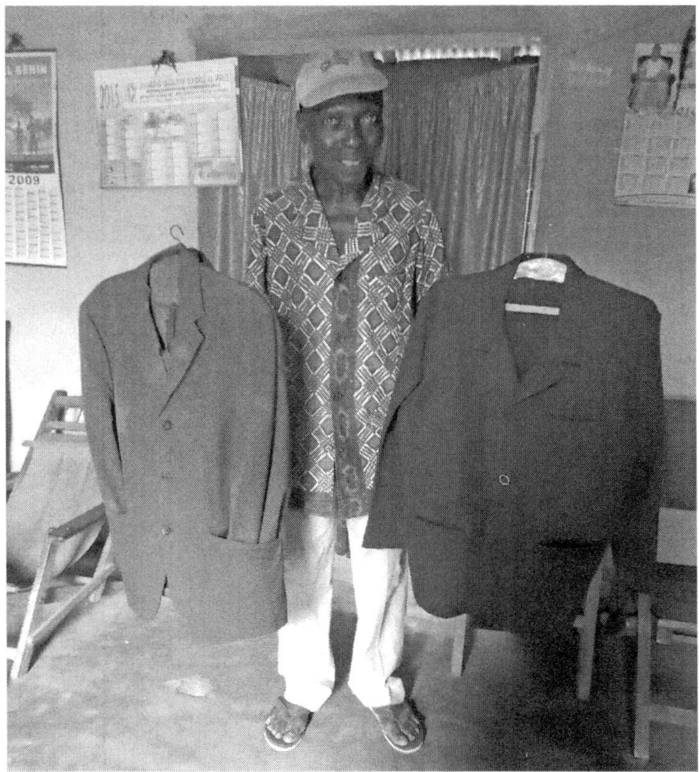

Figure 3.6. Agbaignzoun tailor Pierrot Akpako and his coats, August 2015. Photo by author.

was from Agbaignzoun, a small village fifteen kilometers from Abomey. After finishing his Abomean apprenticeship in 1964, he was eager to broaden his repertoire. Trained only in women's styles and men's tunics and shorts, he negotiated with an uncle to let him go to Cotonou for an additional year of perfectionnement. There, he learned how to embroider and to make suit jackets and pants.[90] In figure 3.6, Akpako holds up two of his creations, jackets that he learned how to make in Cotonou. The three-button light blue coat on the left, which Akpako pulled out from a dusty trunk, dated from the late 1970s while the one on the right was a more recent creation. One of the styles that tailors fondly remembered traveling to the city to learn was *pantalons bas d'eph* (bell-bottoms). Antoine Zohou claimed that he had traveled to Cotonou to learn how to make bell-bottoms and then, returning to Bohicon, was repeatedly consulted by the twenty or so tailors there who also wanted to learn how to make them.[91] While most tailors like Akpako and Zohou traveled to cities to learn new techniques, some tailors also went to cities to diversify their skills by learning sewing machine repair, for example, which supplemented income from clothing production.[92] The adventuring of tailors linked the villages, towns, and cities of southern Bénin in a network of craft knowledge, creating opportunities for exchange and then innovation as tailors brought together techniques and styles with diverse origins.

Tailors were also able to create new modes of dress because they encountered both urban world fashions and African styles—"ethnic" or "traditional" dress—over the course of aventure. Porto-Novo, unlike Ouidah, Cotonou, and Bohicon, was not a Fon-majority area, and the Gun and Yorùbá speakers who lived there had their own ethnic styles. Fon tailors acquired skill in making the region's traditional dress, commonly known as the *agbada* or *trois pièces* (three piece). The agbada is a type of boubou that consists of pants, a long tunic, and an overshirt. President Sourou-Migan Apithy (1964–65), a Gun speaker from Porto-Novo, wore the agbada in most official photographs and during political activities. Apithy's political base was in the southeast of the country, and his dress underscored his powerful position among the Gun and Yorùbá speakers in the region. His status as a grand was reinforced by his dress, since agbadas were particularly expensive and required a significant outlay of fabric, often locally woven and intricately embroidered. Fon tailors who pursued apprenticeship or perfectionnement in Bénin's capital of Porto-Novo might become experts in the three-piece suits of the political elite as well as the agbada worn by the local Gun elites. Tailors also traveled north to learn other styles, especially embroidery from Hausa clothes-makers in northern Bénin and Nigeria.[93]

Tailoring also brought young men from interior Bénin to beyond the country's borders to places like Ghana, Nigeria, Algeria, or other Francophone West African countries. Similar to the way Fon tailors learned new styles such as the agbada in Porto-Novo, tailors there picked up new techniques and forms. During the ten years that Goudou Kpodo spent working in Côte d'Ivoire, he was able to learn several Ivoirian styles, especially in women's wear. He explained, "Ethnicities are different there, there are Djoula, there are Bété, there are Monsi [Burkinabe immigrants]. Monsi wears different styles than the others, that is how it is, that is the difference."[94] When he returned to Abomey, Godou Kpodo incorporated these ethnic flourishes into his craft, and this, he felt, differentiated him among the other tailors in town. For those men who were unwilling or unable to travel, collecting samples or images of styles was important, and a good tailor made an effort to reach out to visiting foreigners, both African and European, so that they could observe their clothes and even acquire sample garments.[95] For some, foreigners made excellent clients because they often asked for new styles and provided samples, and they paid higher prices.[96] Tailors were able to negotiate these differences, bringing together styles and ethnic flourishes from multiple sources in their creations.

A common yet perhaps unexpected effect of their adventuring was that some tailors used their profits and knowledge of local and regional networks to invest in transportation. A few tailors bought cars and then used them to work in other parts of West Africa.[97] Others' wanderings led them to become full-time bush taxi drivers.[98] Za-Kpota tailor Jules Wimêllo purchased flour-mills and vehicles to transport his mills between villages, where his employees ground the grain produced by locals for a small fee. A few years into the business, he had eight cars. Later, he bought a truck to do long-haul transport. By the time he was in his seventies, he had five wives and a sprawling compound that served as a home to his many children and grandchildren.[99] Buying cars and trucks and investing in dependents became a way for tailors to store and augment their wealth, reinforced their personas as aventuriers, and integrated them into larger transnational networks.

While most tailors' migrations were voluntary and part of developing their craft knowledge, personal and political reasons occasionally curtailed aventure. For example, Goudou Kpodo returned to Abomey from Côte d'Ivoire after receiving a pleading letter from his mother. His younger brother had moved to Canada, leaving her without any nearby sons.[100] Many tailors were also forced to return to Bénin because of nationalist policies in other African countries. One woman described the career of her father, a master tailor for the French military in Niamey, Niger. A native of Porto-Novo, her father moved the family to Niamey when he received a contract sewing uniforms for the colonial military. But independence forced the family to move back to Bénin since the newly minted Nigerien army wanted to hire its own Nigerien craftsmen as tailors.[101] Post-independence states facing economic woes forcibly repatriated foreign workers, and many tailors had the experience of packing up and fleeing on a moment's notice. These abrupt moves could result in painful losses, for tailors sometimes departed with such haste that they had to leave behind their machines, diplomas, and caches of photos and catalogues.[102] As the 1970s and 1980s progressed, forced repatriations from places like Gabon, Nigeria, and Ghana limited tailors' ability to learn new styles when their movement was restricted. Unable to observe other clothing practices, they had to rely on the importation of images and secondhand clothing from Europe and the United States for inspiration and innovation, which, until the turn of the twenty-first century, overwhelmingly provided images of world fashions and rarely gave any insight into the ethnic dress of other Africans.

Whether for apprenticeship or perfectionnement or in search of profit, tailors used aventure to become knowledgeable about urban fashions in coastal cities and other African capitals. Adventuring also brought Fon-speaking tailors into contact with the ethnic dress of other groups of Béninois and West Africans. These men brought their expertise back to the markets and workshops of central Bénin where they worked in partnership with their fellow masters and to make outfits that met local demands for new and exciting clothing. But the mobility of tailors, clients, technologies, and styles between towns and countryside also led to more local processes of differentiation between tailors trained in towns versus villages. The craft knowledge of tailoring formed through encounter, improvisation, and informal collaboration, hinting at its deep roots in West African craft practice. The styles that tailors created and that gained popularity in postcolonial Bénin were a product of this unique system of designing, sewing, and marketing clothing.

National Dress, Local Costumes, and Men's Style in Postcolonial Bénin

A 1962 article in the state-run newspaper *L'aube nouvelle* brought the fashions of Paris runways to Béninois audiences.[103] The article presented multiple images of fashionable women's dress but contained only a single photograph of men's fashion (*la mode masculine*): a safari suit. This style, with its belted coat and cuff-free pants, offered male consumers a casual look that, combined with light-colored fabric, prepared them for the intense heat of the tropics. The newspaper's promotion of the safari suit was a rare official commentary on men's fashion in post-independence Bénin. As noted at the beginning of this chapter, that situation changed, however, in 1965, when General Christophe Soglo took power through his second military coup (his first was in 1963) and his new government took aim at menswear (fig. 3.1).[104] Commentators defended the "military style" costume as a move toward equality and democratization—instead of a small elite wearing three-piece suits while farmers struggled to purchase fabric—all men would wear the same outfit. General Soglo also required ministers to work the fields, at least in front of photographers, forwarding his goals of increasing domestic economic production while encouraging Béninois to de-emphasize, or decolonize, from its intellectual colonial past as French West Africa's Latin Quarter. Yet these top-down attempts to create a form of dress that materialized the values of an independent Bénin were fleeting. Indeed, the birth of a Béninois national costume did not take place within the pages of the national newspaper or in the halls of the legislature but rather within the networks and market stalls of tailors.

Male tailors often characterized themselves as experts in either *tenue française* (literally, "French dress," but a signifier for world fashions) or *tenue locale* (local dress). Tailors in the first category were especially skilled in the production of suits, trousers, and jackets and, by the 1960s and 1970s, began to make an outfit called *détè*. The détè (from the French *chemise d'été*, or a short-sleeved button-down) consisted of pants and a matching short-sleeved jacket, usually worn with no undershirt or at most a thin T-shirt. In figure 3.7, the man second from the right wears a typical détè, although the boxiness of its ample silhouette reflects the preferences of the decade—the 1990s—when the photograph was taken. Béninois also called the détè *trois poches* (three pocket) because of two large patch pockets at waist level and a third at chest level. The pockets provided an ideal place for men to store their pens, identification cards, and other documents—the stuff of modern urban life.

Tailors drew inspiration for the détè from the safari suits and leisure suits that gained global popularity in the 1960s and 1970s. In the United States and Europe, collarless suit coats, usually without a visible undershirt, entered the realm of high fashion in the late 1960s as counterculture or hippie style became mainstream. These coats had their origins in India and China, especially the Nehru coat, modeled after the Hindi *achkan* or Muslim *sherwani*, and the Mao suit (*Zhongshan zhuang*).[105] In the following decade, leisure and safari suits became immensely popular, and these ensembles, made of breathable fabrics with lots of pockets, hinted at armchair adventuring.[106] But in the Global South, jacket styles such as the Nehru coat, Congolese *abacost*, Zambian Kaunda suits, and Jamaican Kariba suit entered the formal workplace as the garb of the political elite.[107] The lack of layers and the occasional use of short sleeves made these outfits better suited to the high humidity and

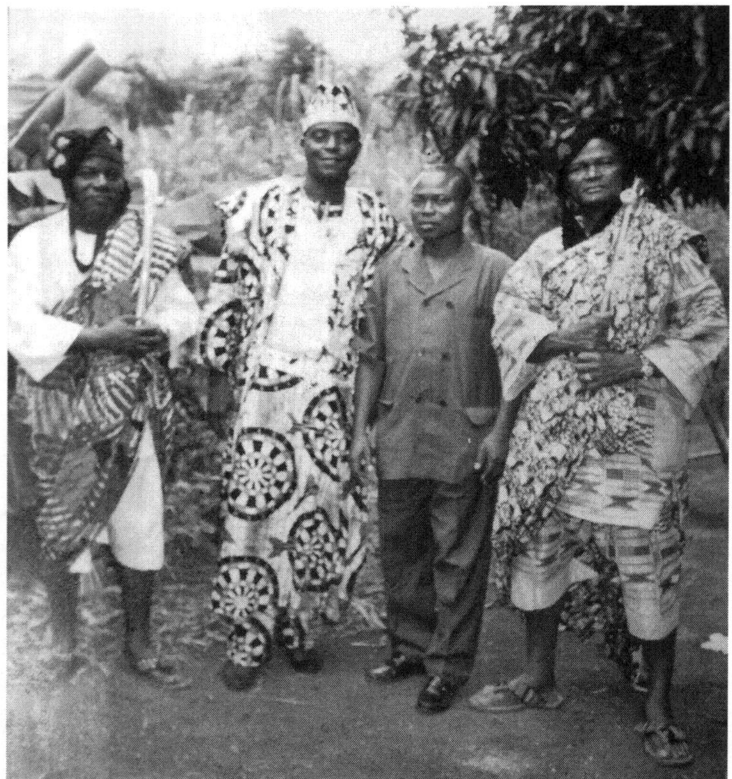

Figure 3.7. Men dressed for Saturday ceremonies, circa 1990. Courtesy of Fidel Ouèdjo. In photo: the men to the far left and far right wear tchanka and pagne, second to the left wears an agbada, and second from the right wears a détè.

intense heat of the tropics, meeting the standards of someone like Cayode, who viewed the three-piece suit as a mismatch for "tropical" locales. But the forms of the abacost, Kaunda suit, Kareeba suit, and détè represented more than just a practicality. They were also a symbol of decolonization and served as an embodied rejection of the constraints of the shirt and tie and their Western origins. Over the next few decades and into the 1990s, these decolonial fashions became less popular among elite men, particularly in countries like Congo, where the abacost became symbolic of a dictatorial regime. But the fad did not fade in Bénin, and the détè remained one of the most popular Béninois men's styles worn by men of all social classes.[108]

Béninois tailors kept the dété fresh and fashionable by embracing new fabrics and promoting the ensembles to men as accessible and local while still part of a larger global fashion trend. For many tailors, the origins of the dété were obscured. One Bohicon tailor, Célestin Kokossou, recalled the newness and popularity of the dété when he finished his training in 1975 and how, although he referred to it as abacost (even going so far as to define it as "down with the suit," *à bas costume*), he "did not know where it was brought from."[109] Another tailor recalled an especially popular early '70s style of a collarless dété with three buttons, which Béninois called *nous les jeunes togolais* (we young Togolese), hinting at that particular version's origins in nearby Togo.[110] For tailors, sewing a dété was more profitable than most other outfits since it required more hours of work and more could be charged as a complete ensemble.[111] But the dété was also a localization of the three-piece business suit; it was the business suit made available and useful to ordinary men in a society that often conflated education, wealth, and prestige.

The fabrics of dété were as important as their form in spreading ideas of global inclusion and a socially mobile masculinity. Tailors preferred to sew these outfits from tergal, a type of polyester imported from France or ordered through the mail; it is no longer available, though fondly remembered. Bohicon tailor Rene Allaga argued that the price of tergal was a significant outlay but still within reach for most Béninois, unlike the expensive wool of a three-piece suit. Allaga explained, "Even farmers who sell their harvest, they order [tergal], those who are workers who find a little money order too and those who are civil servants and are permanent state employees, they order too."[112] Tergal did not fray when cut and could be sewn quickly on machines. For wearers, it was a good fit for the hustle and bustle of everyday life since it was easy to keep pressed and "if you ironed it one time, it's done, you did not need to iron it again."[113] If the cost of wool barred certain Béninois from purchasing fabric, a dété made of a polyester blend was well within reach for most ordinary Béninois and was still associated with global modernity. The differences between higher-end and lower-end garments rested beneath the surface of the ensemble, since tailors might make the outfit unlined (*non doublée*), reducing the fabric and labor costs for clients with less means.

Tailors' work of establishing and spreading a globally inspired style like the dété in Bénin also accompanied an expansion and reinterpretation of local dress among Fon speakers. In the editorial where he defends the 1966 national costume, the writer, E. Cayode characterized "African dress" as not suited to the demands of the new nation and city due to "all these skirts and overhanging parts."[114] Yet his assessment reveals a very specific understanding of "African dress" as something akin to the wrapped fashions of Fon speakers or the flowing robes of agbadas, the Yorùbá style worn by Apithy and popular in Porto-Novo. But how did ordinary Fon-speaking men begin to reimagine their local or ethnic dress?

In the early twentieth century, traditional authorities, like chef de canton Justin Aho, helped establish "Fon dress" as avɔ and tchanka. In figure 3.7, the enthroned Dáa on both the far left and far right wear grande pagne and tchanka and hold the ceremonial canes (recade) of their clan. However, for most men in postcolonial Abomey these styles remained outside their reach since local traditional authorities, including the Dahomean king and Dáa, declared exclusive rights over wearing the Fon traditional ensembles. This created a situation where ordinary Fon-speaking men lacked an ethnic style. For example, President Justin Ahomadégbé-Tomêtin (prime minister 1964–65; president 1972), although Fon, did not have any customary rights to wear tchanka since he was not an enthroned Dáa and had married into the Abomean royal families. Ahomadégbé-Tomêtin regularly wore suit coats, trousers, and button-down shirts on national and international stages, unlike other African leaders who often either appeared in military garb or, like his predecessor Apithy, sported their ethnic styles for official occasions.[115] Presumably, Ahomadégbé-Tomêtin deemed wrapping a pagne as unacceptable because photographs and informants attest that he usually wore a business suit or casual fitted styles. Indeed, most Fon-speaking men lacked a wearable ethnic dress even as ethnic markers were becoming increasingly important within postcolonial African and international politics.

Béninois men turned to men's bounba (figs. 3.4 and 3.8) as a form of local or traditional dress, although many of these same men openly acknowledged the outfit's recent foreign origins. Alain Baba, the former head of the Bohicon tailors' association, claimed that Fon men began to wear bounba in the 1930s.[116] Consisting of a long tunic and drawstring pants, the bounba style originated among the Yorùbá of western Nigeria and eastern Bénin. Today, it is a style especially popular among Togolese, Béninois, and Nigerians. When Godou Kpodou opened a workshop in Abidjan, Côte d'Ivoire, he specialized in sewing the bounba, which Ivoirians called *anago* (also their term for Yorùbá speakers).[117] While traditional authorities in central Bénin might still wear the tchanka and pagne at a ceremony, the bounba became *the* local dress in Bénin for Fon speakers and other men. It united men under a common

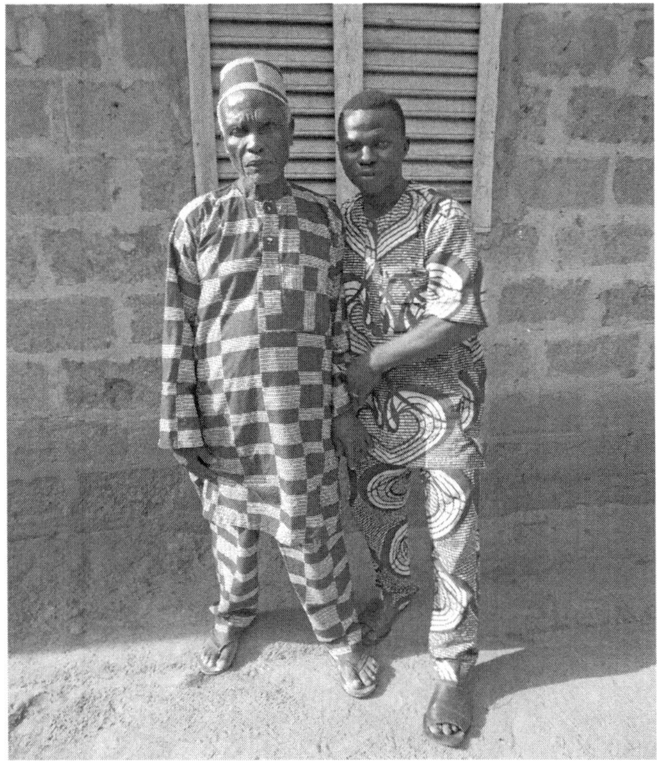

Figure 3.8. Marc Esse and Pascal Adouhouncla wearing bounbas,
Abomey, July 2015. Photo by author.

sartorial regime as Béninois, even if more subtle distinctions such as scarifica-
tion differentiated the population.[118]

The general form of the bounba has changed little over time, although
tailors have adjusted necklines, embellishments, fittedness, and fabric in
line with fashion trends and through their own craft knowledge. Originally
the neck was wide enough to be pulled over the head, but necklines became
tighter by adding buttons, snaps, or short zippers down the front.[119] The neckline could also have additional embellishments, such as piping or embroidery
in a style reminiscent of the Hausa. In figure 3.8, research assistant Marc Esse
and his former patron wear bounbas in the style of the mid-2010s, with tight
necklines that include two buttons to permit the removal of the garment over

the head. Esse's pants are fitted and tapered, a nod to the global trend for younger men to wear tight-fitting pants like the skinny jean, while his patron wears an older style with a baggier fit. The photograph also shows how the hem of the shirt often changed, hitting anywhere from the upper thigh to right above the kneecap. The bounba could, at times, be roomy or tight. Fabrics also changed over time. In the 1960s, tailors made bounbas with inexpensive percale or poplins and occasionally more expensive local fabrics that they heavily embroidered.[120] Bounbas made from wax prints or imitation waxes, such as those worn by Esse and his patron, are a more recent trend, dating from the 1970s. Tailors could make bounbas very cheaply, for as little as two hundred or three hundred fcfa in earlier decades, though they might charge exorbitant amounts for a bounba with fancy finishes or embroidery.

These slight changes in bounbas resulted from the creativity and know-how of tailors. Tailors incorporated flourishes learned in other cities, colonies, and countries into their creations. They culled knowledge gained from catalogues and disassembled secondhand clothing to add embellishments that attracted clients in search of new and exciting fashions. Instead of being a Yorùbá style that had a fleeting popularity during late colonialism, the bounba became Béninois local dress because tailors kept it fresh and new with their constantly evolving craft knowledge. In styling the bounba as a local tradition, tailors also showed ordinary men what it meant to be an African and how to incorporate non-African and other ethnic markers into one's own self-fashioning.

The popularity of the bounba and the détè can be understood as the result of similar desires among Béninois. The bounba was local and African but not quite Fon or even Dahomean. In contrast, the détè was a version of a global urban style but localized and accessible to ordinary men. While leisure suits and shirt jacks fell out of favor elsewhere in the Global South, they remain incredibly common in Bénin. Blenon explained why Béninois still like the détè: "When you wear détè, you are wearing French dress and regular dress [*tenue ordinaire*], the two, you are wearing the two."[121] To wear the détè allowed men to perform their multiple identities as members of the modern world and as locally grounded in Béninois particularities. To wear the bounba reflected a sense of pride in being Béninois or African. Both were a manifestation of the Vodun aesthetic and worldview of incorporation. Tailors' skill and ability to make these forms and keep them popular were grounded in their trainings gained over the courses of adventure and their expertise, which became recognizable through their own dressed bodies and their command over mobile things. The creativity of tailors sustained these two styles for much of the twentieth century as they were constantly redesigned and remade.

The tailors of interior Bénin positioned themselves as experts on men's fashion through their own dressed bodies, their mastery over technology and materials, and the knowledge they gained through travel and collecting. For a few of the first generation of tailors, projections of wealth and prosperity occasionally translated to real social mobility for them and their families when they made significant profits from bounba, détè, and other designs. While many of these tailors lacked formal schooling, they often sent their children to school and some on to university. For example, Akpako declared, "I live in poverty now but my children are intellectuals ... one is a doctor ... a teacher ... construction engineer."[122] If tailors performed wealth and global inclusion, many invested the profits of this performance in their children's education and future financial stability.

The personal trajectories of tailors speak to how they sought to improve their own lives and those of their families while also making beautiful things, and how their craft led to them to be at the forefront of multiple social changes. With veterans and emergent businessmen, tailors in the post-WWII era were some of the first non-elite wearers of three-piece suits, showing ordinary men that their inclusion in the wider world was possible and even desirable. Tailors domesticated a wide range of technologies including synthetic fabrics, machinery, measuring tapes, and photography, using them in innovative ways that changed both how clothes were made and the local perceptions of their users. Tailors were also travelers, and their training and work brought them to cities, towns, and villages where they encountered new styles, which they brought back to their home communities. Although tailors were often avid wearers of the three-piece suit, helping to make it a Béninois look as well as a modern look, they were also fundamental to establishing the many alternatives to it. Their styles allowed Béninois men to create new affinities that stretched beyond Bénin's borders, even as they remained resolutely grounded in local craft and aesthetic traditions.

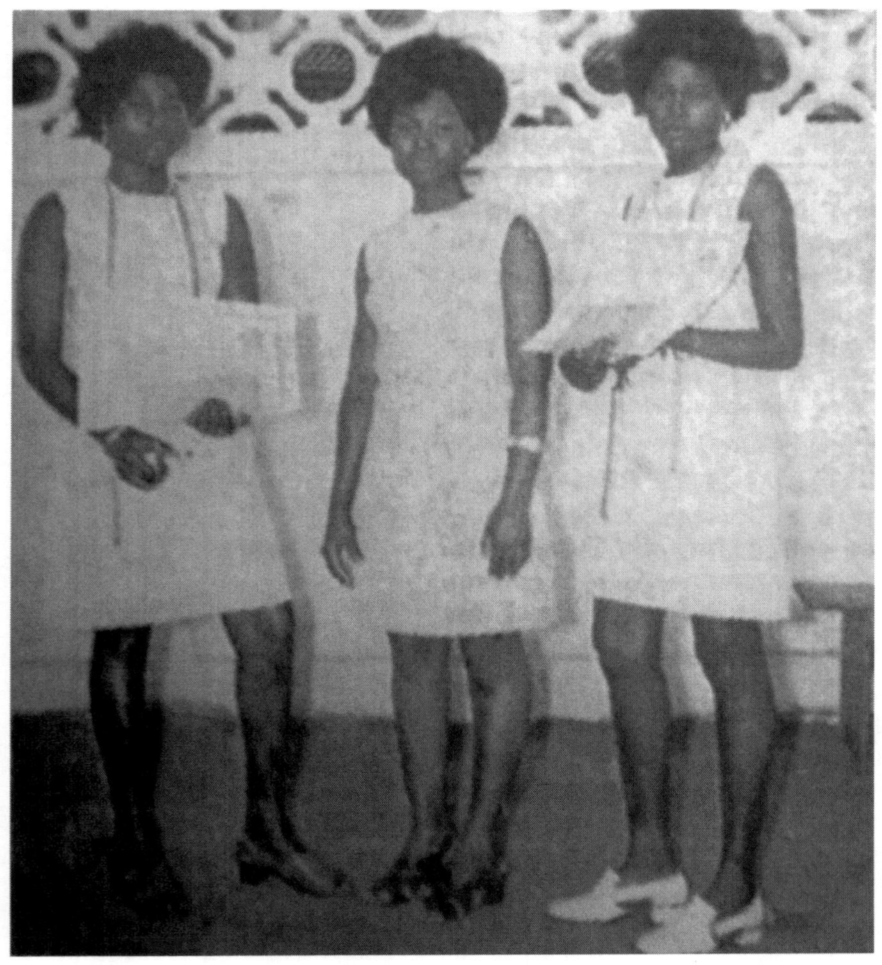

Figure 4.1. "Madame Aplogan Between Misses Lucienne Glin (*left*) and Claire Dassi." From *Daho Express*, August 28, 1971.

4

The Material Culture of Expertise

Artisanal Ways of Knowing, Apprenticeship,
and the Professionalization of Craft

In "Under the Sign of the Tape Measure," a 1971 article in the women's section of the Bénin state daily newspaper *Daho Express*, Béninois readers were introduced to libération, or liberation ceremony. The article explained, "If you hear someone say, 'I am going to assist in a liberation,' you would be wrong to conclude that they are going to be at the release of a prisoner or the return home of a soldier. In fact, a 'liberation' is a symbolic and pleasant ceremony that marks the end of an apprenticeship . . . for tailors and seamstresses, cabinetmakers, jewelers, etc." The reporter continued by narrating the libérations of two cohorts of young apprentice seamstresses in Porto-Novo, focusing on the various steps of the ceremony, which included "timed technical tests and mock corporal punishment . . . speeches, handing out diplomas, advice, sketches, [and] more recently, but no less traditional, a reception with dancing." Two photographs accompanied the article, including one of master seamstress Madame Aplogan flanked by two young women, each with a tape measure draped around her neck and holding a newly acquired diploma (fig. 4.1). The young women had received the blessed tape measure, one of "the tools symbolic of the perfect seamstress," from their former master.[1] The diploma certified their competencies as seamstresses, and the whole ceremony served as a rite of passage as the young women now joined the community of master seamstresses and artisans.[2]

Although the reporter described libération as "traditional," her account also revealed that it was a tradition with recent origins.[3] The purpose of the article was to introduce a seemingly unfamiliar reading public to the ceremony. The newness of libération is confirmed by the oral accounts of Béninois craftspeople who consistently described how master artisans did not undergo formal ceremonies to mark the end of apprenticeship before the mid-twentieth century. Indeed, libération and its associated material culture were firmly rooted in the technologies of the twentieth century. The ceremony included the exchange of documents modeled off diplomas and awards, timed technical tests, gifts of imported industrial tools, photography, consumption of mass-produced beverages, and, later, sound systems and DJs.

This chapter argues that tailors and other artisans developed libération as a way to solve the challenges of regulating their identity and expertise as craftspeople in an era of increased urbanization and growing numbers of craftspeople. As demonstrated in the previous chapter, craft knowledge was mutable, learned, improvised, and ultimately invisible. So how did tailors—as craftspeople interested in translating their skill into profit—communicate their mastery of the craft to each other and to potential clients? The most straightforward answer is through their finished products—craftspeople made things that appealed to the eye and that worked well. Consumers approached them with commissions because they had seen or heard of an individual artisan's skill. But by the mid-twentieth century, with increasing urbanization and anonymity, these sorts of direct encounters between client and made thing, or even word-of-mouth marketing strategies, faced challenges. In response, Béninois craftspeople sought other ways to professionalize or to make known they possessed the skills and knowledge to make beautiful and well-functioning things.

This chapter argues that craftspeople turned to materials other than their finished products to verify their expertise as makers and that this had far-reaching political and social ramifications. In considering tailors alongside other craftspeople such as weavers, aluminum pot casters, masons, carpenters, automotive mechanics, and plumbers, this chapter takes a broader and more inclusive view of l'artisanat Béninois [the Béninois artisanal sector] to show how categories of labor and craftsmanship were redefined by artisans themselves as they generated and then demarcated new ways of knowing. As particularly mobile craftspeople, Béninois tailors were leaders in these efforts to reimagine a pan-artisan community through a common material culture. Tailors and other artisans brought together material and ritual aspects of different traditions, like modern science and Vodun, to create innovate new ways of asserting knowledge and knowhow. Artisanal diplomas were awarded during libération ceremonies, bringing artisans into a common material and ritual practice that helped mitigate distinctions of craft, gender, ethnicity, and class and solidified occupational identities. West African craftspeople, whom scholars often depict as marginal to colonial and postcolonial states and societies, reshaped local notions of expertise and ways of assessing and identifying skill in postcolonial Bénin.[4]

The chapter begins by returning to the colonial period, when European "experts" tried to pin down exactly what was meant by *African artisans* as a social and occupational identity and traces how these assumptions informed colonial policy. Colonial programs in education and economic development, later replicated by national governments, introduced new ways of thinking about the traditionalism and informality of artisans while also helping spread new practices of transmitting knowledge and ways of assessing and certifying skill. Béninois craftspeople borrowed and applied state modes of managing expertise into preexisting, precolonial forms of apprenticeship, even as they rejected notions of "authentic" craft materials and aesthetics. In the decades surrounding independence, craftspeople began to draw upon the symbols and practices of formal institutions and integrate them into rituals of display and performance rooted in Vodun cosmology to create libération. By the 1970s, craftspeople used diplomas, membership cards, photographs, and libération to manage the ranks of l'artisanat and created economic cooperatives that traversed distinctions of craft, gender, ethnicity, and class. With these associations, artisans have taken on a particularly active role in Béninois politics. Tailors were important leaders in helping to build this distinctly Béninois artisanat, and their shifting access to political, social, and material opportunities would ultimately shape the content of their work and products, a topic continued in the following chapter.

Colonial Experts on Artisans and Artisanal Know-How

Indigenous society, as we still observe it in most peoples of the AOF, is a closed and complete organism, providing the essential elements necessary for its traditional life. The artisan, rural or urban, has a marked place and places an important role within it. . . . In every village, an *artisanat* develops, particularly vivacious, firmly rooted in traditions and indigenous mentality, an integral part of the social structure. The "blacksmith," locked in his hereditary caste, is the technician of this uncomplicated world. The blacksmith works iron and wood and his wife is often a potter. He knows the secrets and mysteries and has the know-how of a sort of magician.

He makes the "*dabas*" (hoes) and polishes jewelry. This is one of the most vivid characters in indigenous villages.
— Albert Charton, AOF Education Inspector, 1931[5]

Artisans, their technologies, and their social identities were of great interest to colonial agents in French West Africa. In the metropole, tools and machines were "measures of men," creating justifications for the imperial project and its *mission civilisatrice*.[6] In the colonies, French experts, administrators, and African informants sought to tease out the relationships among tools, production, and social formations as part of a larger goal of controlling and improving local economies. To observers like Albert Charton, the education inspector in French West Africa, the craft knowledge, or "secrets," "mysteries," and "know-how" of craftspeople in Africa, was "traditional," linked to the constraints of "social structures" that dictated which gender, lineage, or other group had access to it.[7] Charton's understanding of the individual knowhow of artisans as linked to their social identities drew upon a large body of work by early twentieth-century French ethnologists and other colonial administrators who interpreted African societies as "organisms."[8] In their vision of an "uncomplicated world," artisans like blacksmiths were bound by caste, blood, and marriage to produce things for the greater society.[9] Colonial ethnologists delineated African social groups such as artisans throughout the AOF but especially in the French Soudan, where they recorded multiple classification systems for Mande-speaking craftspeople that collectively characterized them as casted and often low-status members of society.[10]

Although they developed their ideas in the Sahel, colonial experts sought to find corollary hereditary and hierarchical social structures in coastal areas like Bénin. Yet in his 1938 ethnography, anthropologist Melville Herskovits noted, with surprise, that craft production in Bénin was not hereditary. Instead, he found that craftspeople were organized spatially, not by lineage. For example, blacksmiths were "organized into 'forges,' each group operating in a separate quarter of the city, or in a separate village," with residences around them.[11] Children of ironworking fathers might learn the craft, but they did not have an exclusive right to practice it. Herskovits also found competing ideas about the status of makers and their social hierarchies. An "upper-class Dahomean" contended that weavers ranked the highest as "their labor supplies the shrouds in which the dead are buried."[12] Following weavers, the informant listed smiths (specifically makers of ceremonial staffs [*asen*]), "cloth-sewers," calabash carvers, and finally palm-oil pressers as the most important craftsmen, no doubt a reflection of an elite man's purchasing power and preference for luxury and ceremonial goods.[13] A second informant posited that gravediggers were the highest status craftsmen while a third claimed woodworkers as the most respected and important craftsmen, since they made stools for sitting and figures for shrines. Herskovits argued that among "the women" there was disagreement whether potters held "first rank" or if spinners were the most valued since they made the primary input for marriage and death shrouds. A final informant, an ironworker, privileged his craft over others and argued that it held the highest status since ironworkers made the tools for other craftsmen.[14] Craft in Bénin did not seem to fit any of the Western anthropological models of craft production in a supposed organic African society.

Despite Herskovits's recognition of the spatial and fluid organization of craft in Bénin, colonial policymakers expanded education programs developed in the Sahel to an AOF-wide policy that understood "African artisans" as naturally casted, low status, and rural. By the late 1920s, many French experts and administrators, especially in education, saw themselves as particularly enlightened and wanted to understand African craft in order to create policies more rooted in the particularities of individual African societies.[15] In 1932, Bouyagui Fadiga, an *assimilé* (African assimilated into French culture) in French Soudan, submitted to Dakar a plan for artisanal education that urged the administration to incorporate craft education into general primary education. According to Fadiga, the need for cash to pay taxes and other expenses led to the corruption of indigenous production techniques as unqualified Soudanais entered into the "easier" professions like weaving, sandal making, and saddlery.[16] Fadiga proposed incorporating artisanal education into regional schools by recruiting students from "the sons of artisans or from volunteers."[17] The following year Dakar proposed an AOF-wide education policy that incorporated craft into rural primary education and created an upper-level system of "workshops of applied arts and craft schools, for the conservation and the reform of traditional native crafts."[18] While a 1930 law recognized that Bénin was "one of the rare regions of the AOF where the artisan is not considered as belonging to an inferior caste," administrators still sought to make craft hereditary in state workshops.[19] Officials extended this hereditary requirement from rural primary schools to urban centers through its flagship institutions of artisanal education called *Maison des artisans*, which sought to admit "as much as possible the sons of artisans."[20] In this way assumptions about the hereditary nature of African artisanship entered into the AOF's artisanal policy and eventually into the structures of technical education in trades like plumbing, electrical work, and cement masonry, as they developed over the course of the next few decades.[21]

Along with linking occupation to specific heritable identities, colonial experts also sought to "improve" the technologies and craft knowledge of artisans. The French rarely imagined improvement as analogous to modernization but rather as a codification of traditional or customary production methods and materials. French educator and former cabinetmaker Jean Le-Gall planned the Bamako Maison des artisans not only to train craftsmen but also to foster "authentic" tastes among Africans by reviving "local artistic themes and local materials."[22] He and others feared that the materials and technologies of African craft were naturally being displaced by "superior" ones from Europe, creating bastardized artisanal forms, neither authentically African nor European. Administrator Robert Delavignette later described Le Gall's impulses in creating the Maison as "attempting to return taste to his Africa. Without literature. By manual labor and in a country where artisan castes are despised."[23] Linking together the supposed inferiority of artisans within both local society and the global economic order portrayed them as a group doubly in need of colonial paternal protection. Colonial educators developed a practical solution to this by having European craftsmen teach generalized "African" production methods and forms to male craftsmen who, in turn, transferred this knowledge to young students in rural schools.[24] Historian John Warne Monroe argues that the Maisons des artisans "reflected the fundamental assumptions of French connoisseurs of *art nègre*."[25] Rooted in their belief that authentic precolonial statues and masks were true objets d'art and colonial-era creations were merely inauthentic copies, the goal of the Maisons was to teach Africans techniques and aesthetic principles that had been forgotten with the colonial occupation. Ideally, artisans trained and working in the Maison would create objects with high enough quality to be exported to France.[26] Maisons also had attached open-air markets to sell objects directly to European tourists and to foster taste for locally made products among African consumers.[27] At the Maison in Abomey, opened in 1935, the state issued permits for vendors' booths to families, many of which had been dependents of precolonial royal palaces, and not individuals—itself a reflection of the colonial interest in promoting authenticity and tying it to specific bloodlines.[28]

Colonial approaches to artisanship had a spatial component as well, and craftspeople were redefined as rural as well as low-status, hereditary, and in need of colonial protection. Craftspeople fell into two categories within colonial policy—modern and urban or traditional and rural. In one 1931 scheme, crafts deemed urban included cement masonry, plumbing, glazing, upholstering, bookbinding, and tailoring while rural crafts were weaving, shoemaking, basketmaking, jewelry making, and chair making.[29] Administrators hoped to keep rural crafts in rural areas and to prevent craftspeople from becoming "too urbanized" through the strategic locations of schools and state workshops.[30] As late as 1956, the French planned to build a workshop for cabinetmakers by placing it in a village a sufficient distance from Parakou so "that the apprentices are not subjected to the influence of the urban environment, but it is not so much as to prohibit easy communication with Parakou for resupplying."[31] The workshop was only six kilometers away from the largest city in northern Bénin, but this short distance appeased colonial fears that students would become overly urbanized and would resist returning to the rural areas. At the same time, the state might better control the materials supplied from Parakou and the furniture produced by the men. This state approach to artisanal education as a priority of rural development would continue after independence.[32]

Alongside educational policy, colonial experts also created new notions around African artisanship through programs such as fairs, exhibitions, and other competitions where panels passed judgment on the quality and authenticity of artisanal objects. Historians and others have shown how fairs and expositions in Europe shaped Western perceptions of race, gender, and the colonized other.[33] But these imperial tastemaking programs must have also impacted the perspectives of the colonized African participants who traveled to Europe to take part in them or who participated remotely by submitting their objects for sale and competition. Organizers of these exhibitions required colonial subjects on display to repetitively perform tasks such as cooking, smithing, and fishing with traditional technologies for Western audiences.[34] In 1931, local administrators in Abomey debated the tools and other objects, including clothing, that would accompany the twenty-one Abomeans for a display on Dahomean fishing and artisanal activities at the Colonial Exhibition.[35] Abomean *fondeur* (blacksmith) Zokpe Hountondji, along with thirty-two other artisans from the AOF, spent four months at the 1937 International Exhibition in Paris, where organizers managed every aspect of their stay, even designing diets for them based on their colony of origin.[36] But the stress of the exhibition must have taken its toll, as three of the artisans, including Hountondji, fell ill, resulting in the institutionalization of another blacksmith from Côte d'Ivoire who had suffered a *crise de folie* (attack of insanity). Other than the Ivoirian blacksmith, the artisans returned to the AOF by way of steamship, guarded by gendarmes.[37] Wearing clothes chosen by administrators and performing activities deemed authentically African must have shaped participants' perspectives of themselves and the other (in this case, the European spectators), although we do not have any firsthand accounts from the artisans.

While the number of African artisans who traveled to European exhibitions was small, many more participated by sending their objects for sale or competition. At the International Exhibition, organizers restricted the goods that "native shopkeepers," or vendors, could sell, forcing them to sell only products originating from their own colonies, since vendors had previously sold "objects of European fabrication and of very low quality," which "gravely harm[ed] the good name of our local [colonial] industries."[38] Most of the Béninois objects destined for sale came from Abomey, and they included pagnes woven by Abomean weavers as well as embroidered "chief's clothes."[39]

Beyond colonial fairs, craftspeople in the AOF also submitted objects to other French competitions such as the National Exhibition of Work, started in 1924.[40] French artisans might participate in categories such as cabinetmaking, pastry making, and clothing design, and by the time of the Third National Exposition in 1933, artisans in the AOF sent submissions.[41] But participation of colonial subjects in the AOF and Indochina created an unsettling situation for administrators and the French public alike when Indochinese or African artisans won the title "One of France's Best Craftsmen," upsetting the very foundation of the colonial project and the supposed technical superiority of Europeans.[42] Following the backlash, organizers created new categories for submissions from the colonies, codifying distinctions between European and African makers.[43] Four artisans from Zagnandado, sculptors Akéminou Donvidé and Saké Ghéto and metalworkers Dihoun Nicolas and Hountondji Jean, won the competition in these new categories.[44] This type of competition might have been marginal to the overall colonial project, but participation of a small number of craftspeople helped spread conceptual categories and notions of authenticity within Bénin.

Local administrators replicated these models of colonial and industrial exhibitions in the colony's towns and villages, providing sites where artisans could take on a bigger role in articulating what it meant to be an artisan and how to assess skill. Initially, these competitions were organized as a first round before sending objects to panels in France.[45] In 1948, the governor of Dahomey solicited submissions for the competition "to stimulate the professional zeal and consciousness of workers and artisans, to encourage their craft taste through affirmation of their personality and their spirit of initiative, and, finally, to give them a fair reward."[46] Despite the colony's claims to offer a "fair reward," artisans often protested the lack of reimbursement for their objects or demanded their restitution—requests that usually remained unfulfilled.[47] Over time, however, administrators recreated the National Exposition of Work as a stand-alone competition at the colony level and gave awards to the "Best Craftsmen in Dahomey" in categories such as Dressmaking, Clothing, Embroidery, Umbrellas and Parasols, and Weaves.[48] In the category of Clothing, a tailor from Porto-Novo sent in a one-button suit coat while another tailor submitted shirts, ties, and "Canadian jackets."[49] Unlike in other categories such as Building, Furniture, and so on, the Textile sector was open to "not only workers and professional workers, but equally all people . . . to make known the qualities and aptitudes of Dahomean labor."[50] In other words, needlework was exceptional as it was considered both a craft and domestic labor. As independence approached and local officials became more interested in rural development, they expanded the fair system into regional towns. A 1957 fair in Bohicon allowed farmers and artisans to rent booths to display their wares.[51] Along with displays by artisans and industry, the electrified fair included folkloric presentations, film screenings, drumming, soccer matches, and bars.[52] Mirroring the distinctions made in educational policy, the Bohicon fair displayed artisanal objects according to a system that "distinguished the modern artisanat and the customary artisanat, either functional or decorative."[53] The expanding practice of using fairs and exhibitions to shape Béninois tastes and promote industrial development linked the artisans participating in small-town fairs in late colonial Bénin to a much longer and more insidious history of colonial exhibitions.

The idea of an "African artisanat" formed during interactions between craftspeople and the colonial experts who designed and implemented educational programs and craft competitions. To French "experts," craft knowledge was bound by the social identities of ethnicity, gender, and caste, with specific individuals coming into knowing through birth and hereditary training. These experts considered themselves enlightened colonialists and reasoned that this primordial knowledge of African artisans was threatened by capitalism and subject to corruption. Under the guise of colonial paternalism, French administrators proposed to improve African techniques and forms while reining in innovations to maintain authenticity through a series of schools and workshops. Fairs and exhibitions became sites where this authenticity was judged and rewarded with cash and awards, contributing to the prestige of individual artisans. Little changed with independence, and postcolonial governments continued to embrace fairs, competitions, and artisanal workshops to promote a "national culture" that drew heavily upon ideas about "traditional craft."[54] These state programs sought to intervene in craft knowledge, often shaping it to meet development priorities. While these programs did help introduce new ways of thinking about craft knowledge and ways of managing who might access it, artisans like tailors continued longstanding precolonial practices of incorporating and innovating new forms and techniques whatever their origins, and Béninois craftspeople never fully embraced these characterizations of their knowledge as "primordial" and in need of "improvement."

Apprenticeship, Contracting, and Credentialing in the "Informal Economy"

In the precolonial Dahomey kingdom, craft easily incorporated people, technologies, and forms from outsiders, leading to a layered and eclectic material culture. This emphasis on domestication continued into the twentieth century, as evidenced by the innovative styles created by tailors through aventure and consuming media in the era of independence. But tailors also relied on emerging forms of apprenticeship that drew upon and expanded older ways of transferring knowledge from elders to juniors. The transmission of craft knowledge in precolonial and early colonial Bénin was not a particularly structured process outside of the *yokpo yokpo xwé* (palace workshops) established by Agaja in the eighteenth century. For most crafts, children with an interest and an aptitude might spend time learning from a relative or a neighbor. When they became sufficiently proficient, the master craftsperson would start to pay them or otherwise reimburse them for their work. Eventually, the young craftsperson could save up enough to buy the tools of the craft and build a forge or loom, for example. Occasionally a craftsperson inherited their tools. The newly established craftsperson might siphon off a few of their old master's clients, but they would also find clients among their peers or new community members.[55]

After colonization, the French made few attempts to create a framework for regulating apprenticeship, largely because of colonial assumptions about craft as "familial" or operating out of the household. In the 1930s, the French Popular Front government briefly attempted to intervene in apprenticeship due to worries about the exploitation of children, but ultimately the administration concluded that the Béninois "do not abuse [apprentices]" and that they "have adult laborers for the hard tasks."[56] Notions about the heritability of craft or that apprentices "take over from a master who has become too old" reinforced the idea that crafts were household activities as opposed to economic ones.[57] A 1938 law advanced this characterization by grouping "artisans of all categories" with other economic activities such as fishing and agriculture and "family work" such as cooking, gathering wood, transporting water, and cleaning.[58] By imagining that all apprentices were related to their masters and that their work fell under the realm of "household labor," the colonial administration could avoid enforcing other child labor laws that banned the employment of children under fourteen. The 1938 law fixed the minimum age of apprenticeship at twelve and made only one requirement of masters: that they provide sanitary living conditions to all apprentices residing in their homes.[59] However, it is unclear how the state enforced or attempted to enforce these restrictions, since children might start an apprenticeship as young as eight or nine. In this way, craftspeople became part of the "informal economy" or what was "left out" in the colonial creation of African regulatory frameworks.[60]

But the idea of an economy divided into informal and formal sectors obscured how many craftspeople moved between colonial and self-employment and how conceptual categories and practices of artisanship transferred between the formal and the informal. Artisans trained in the technical schools of Dakar and Cotonou experienced chronic unemployment in the so-called formal sector of colonial offices and French businesses.[61] The administration struggled to find trained instructors to teach manual studies in rural schools, since graduates of Cotonou technical programs often refused to return to rural areas to teach at the regional primary schools. The lack of qualified teachers led students to drop out of rural programs. For example, after a teacher left the Djougou school in 1948, six students were so "discouraged" that they left their state school apprenticeship, leaving only four students in the program.[62] State programs were designed to create skilled wage laborers and did not train students in other aspects of artisanship such as business and personnel management. Unable to find employment with the state or private enterprise or uncredentialed and relatively unprepared to open their own businesses, many of these state-trained craftsmen eventually became self-employed artisans, opened their own workshops, and began to train apprentices in the "informal economy."

Young people started apprenticeships with master craftspeople after negotiations and exchanges of goods with the master. Older tailors described how parents and guardians provided a master with maize, palm oil, or liquor upon acceptance into an apprenticeship. Often these products were used in a sacrifice before being consumed by the master and their dependents. Families also made regular cash payments to masters for their children's training, similar to school tuition. As one administrator wrote in the 1940s, "Apprentices are not, in principle, paid by those who employ them"; instead they paid a regular fee to a master, either monthly or yearly as in a case where a "tailor asks for 500 francs per year from his student for an apprenticeship that lasts 3 years."[63] Forms and types of payments depended on the master, who might adjust the price based on their perceptions of the skills of the apprentice—a master might be willing to take on a particularly promising youth for a lower price. A master might also lower his price for a family with fewer resources or allow them to pay over time. As these systems of exchange became more formalized after the Second World War, colonial administrators feared that cash payments for apprenticeship might lead to abuse or poorly trained artisans.[64] Some administrators suggested that the colony prevent this situation with a head tax on apprentices to limit the number that masters were willing to take on.[65] Another local administrator suggested solving the problem of exploited apprentices by setting a minimum wage.[66] The colonial and postcolonial states did, at times, pursue any or all of these strategies, but masters easily evaded taxes and minimum wage laws by keeping their apprentices home on days when tax collectors visited or bribing officials, and apprenticeship remained outside the purview of the state.

Artisans began to adopt practices, such as written contracts, from colonial institutions and French private enterprise to manage these increasingly complex and monetized forms of apprenticeship. Early apprenticeship negotiations were oral, although archival records indicate that by 1955, artisans in Porto-Novo were using written contracts and taking them to the local administration for notarization. For example, Ousson Fréjus, a woman in the Honuou neighborhood, agreed to take on a daughter of Fadaïro Heuri for a five-year apprenticeship in couture.[67] On the same day, Fadaïro also placed his son Raymond with another master tailor for a period of five years.[68]

While both of these contracts declared that no money was exchanged between Fadaïro and the tailors, other contracts show that apprenticeship could be a pricey option for a family looking to establish their son or daughter in a career. In January 1955, Jacques Montcho, a teacher from Adjohon, signed a five-year contract to apprentice his sister to a woman tailor, Rosaline d'Oliveira, in Porto-Novo. As a part of the contract Montcho agreed to pay one hundred francs per month to d'Oliveira to teach his sister how to sew.[69] Apprenticeship was a lengthy commitment and relied on family members to broker deals for their dependents.

These contracts provide insight into the concerns of parents and other relatives as they sent their children to work, and often live, in the care of another adult. In apprenticing his sister to d'Oliveira, Montcho also agreed to regularly check on his sister's progress and be ready to "denounce to his parents any observed irregularities" that might "compromise the morality of the apprentice."[70] As an elder brother, Montcho was responsible for ensuring that his sister avoid any immoral relationships that might reflect poorly on her family or her *patronne* (master). His sister, the apprentice, Jacqueline Montcho, also signed the contract and, in doing so, agreed to "submit to the discipline inside the establishment of her master during the length of the apprenticeship."[71] This clause prevented the young woman from ignoring the direction of her master or breaking her contract to open her own shop. Other tailors recalled how, during oral negotiations at the onset of an apprenticeship, masters and guardians discussed the offenses that would result in a beating versus being sent home, a condition that arrived when the master nullified the contract due to an apprentice's unruly behavior.[72] Masters perceived the difficulties of working with children and the opportunities it might present for the former to abuse the latter, but they also recognized that the situation might lead to bad conduct on the part of the apprentice.

Operating almost exclusively outside the realm of state control, master artisans and young apprentices shaped apprenticeship to best meet their needs. In contrast to state-run artisans' workshops and technical schools where young students learned only the competencies of their craft, masters in private workshops taught young artisans other skills for running a business and navigating life. Occasionally, apprentices lived in the homes of their masters, performing domestic duties such as fetching water, washing clothing and dishes, and cooking both before and after work. Masters also taught apprentices how to manage human relations. As the contract between d'Oliveira and Montcho illustrates, masters were also responsible for the morality of their young charges. When an unmarried young woman became pregnant or a young man indulged in too much *sodabi* (distilled palm wine), the community might blame the master as much as the parents. The *patron* became directly implicated in the former if he was the one who impregnated his apprentice, an issue that became more commonplace near the end of the twentieth century as more women and girls entered into crafts with male masters. Additionally, an individual apprentice might be a slow learner or not have an aptitude for a craft and become more of a burden than a help. Although additional apprentices could lead to higher profits as well as heightened prestige, the challenges of having multiple young people in their charge led artisans to self-limit their apprentices.

Despite the responsibilities and drawbacks of taking on multiple apprentices, the number of artisans, and tailors especially, steadily increased during the era of independence as masters trained young Béninois in craft. According to a survey conducted by the colonial state in 1936–37, there were 149 tailors in the eight *arrondissements* of Porto-Novo.[73] Nearly thirty years later, in 1964, a survey conducted by the International Labor Organization (ILO) found 219 tailors just in the city of Porto-Novo. Areas close to Porto-Novo, which were perhaps included in the first survey, also had relatively large numbers of tailors, including Adjohon (in between Cotonou and Porto-Novo) with 125 tailors; Sakete (north of Porto-Novo) with 94; and Pobe, which was even farther north, where there were 65 tailors.[74] The 1964 ILO survey also reported the presence of 44 tailors in the cities of Abomey and Bohicon, although it is unclear if this number includes apprentices and neighboring villages such as Za-Kpota and Agbainzoun. Overall, the survey found 357 artisans in Abomey-Bohicon compared with 895 artisans in Porto-Novo.[75] While these numbers are not entirely reliable, they provide a rough estimate of the number of artisans in Bénin at that time, and compared with earlier (and equally unreliable) data they show a substantial increase. Among these artisans, there were usually only two categories, master or apprentice, and very few or no waged employees of journeyman status. When apprentices finished their apprenticeship after four years on average, master artisans preferred not to keep them and pay them a wage but rather to find a new apprentice who would pay for a contract and provide free labor. The ILO interpreted this to mean that the "new worker [became] an unemployed person."[76] In contrast, Béninois did not interpret the young person who had just finished an apprenticeship as an "unemployed person" but rather as a new patron or master artisan.

It was during these years surrounding independence, when Béninois cities were growing and the numbers of artisans increased dramatically, that craftspeople began to create a new material culture to manage the distinction between masters and apprentices. The most significant change was the adoption of artisanal diplomas that drew upon colonial models from schools and fairs, which would have been familiar to informal sector artisans due to collaborations among them and the presence of artisans who straddled the two realms. Artisans in state-run workshops and schools received diplomas as early as 1929, and the colonial state created an official document in 1931.[77] A few decades later, the state conducted a survey of primary school manual education instructors to check their credentials, creating an archive of these documents and revealing how the state used them to credential graduates and manage information. For example, Cohoundé Adoula submitted a notarized copy of his certificate, which he received on September 2, 1929, when he was awarded a grade of *assez bien* at the completion of his apprenticeship in masonry.[78] To colonial educators, exams created the opportunity for "a serious consultation for apprentices and their employers."[79] A master carpenter, Valentin Gbaguidi, submitted his original certificate of apprenticeship, signed in 1930 by the colony's governor and school inspector (fig. 4.2).[80] The certificate contained an abundance of information on Gbaguidi—he was born in Savalou in 1911, received excellent marks, and formally finished his apprenticeship on September 7, 1930. The certificate also bore information about the state, including the laws that established the apprenticeship programs and the certificate's official registration number. Gbaguidi obviously carefully guarded his diploma in the two decades between when he received it and when he submitted it to the state, perhaps displaying it for others to see, as later artisans would do.

Many state and mission trained artisans participated in colonial competitions as well, providing other examples for how to assess skill. At the four-day 1930 Exposition-Fair in Porto-Novo, particularly good pieces received accolades, and organizers awarded winners a certificate of achievement and a cash prize. For example, Valentin Gbaguidi won "honorable mention" in "European furniture" and received an award that he later submitted to the state alongside his diploma.[81] At the Porto-Novo Craft Exposition of 1936 (Exposition de l'artisanat de Porto-Novo in 1936), the winners received an embossed certificate printed locally with blanks to fill in the name of the winner, their residence, and the prize.[82] At the 1937 International Exhibition in Paris, the Maison des Artisans de Dahomey earned a "commemorative diploma"

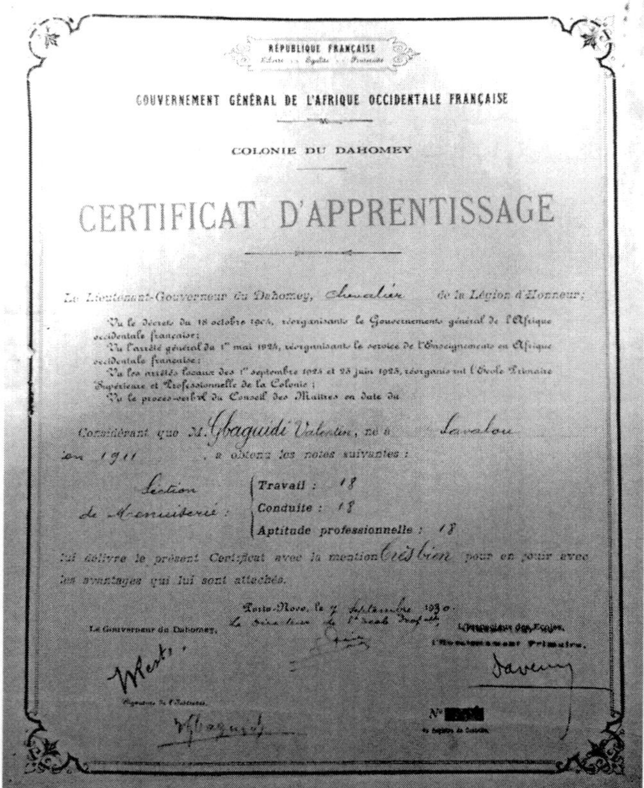

Figure 4.2. Apprenticeship certificate in carpentry, 1930. Box
1G/4/8. National Archives of Bénin.

for their submissions.[83] These certificates of achievement attested to the skill
of the artisan who won them, but they also provided examples to artisans on
how to create their own systems for measuring skill.

By the 1950s, artisans in the country's main metropolitan areas on the coast
were beginning to issue handmade diplomas and certificates to apprentices
trained in market stalls and private workshops. In the next decade, these
documents began to circulate in interior areas like Abomey and Bohicon that
had formerly been the center of the Dahomey kingdom. Artisanal diplomas
contained information similar to that on a diploma from a formal technical school: the names of the master (school) and apprentice (student), the
length of apprenticeship, the qualities of the apprentice (marks or grades),

and the signature of the issuer. While artisans likely modeled their documents off of ones issued by the state, a 1964 diploma issued to Pierrot Dakossi reveals an even closer connection between artisanal and state-issued versions of the document. At the very bottom of the certificate were the words "Designed at the Center of Technical Education—Abomey" (Dessiné au centre d'Enseignement Technique—Abomey) (fig. 4.3).[84] This meant that perhaps as a course assignment, a student at a local technical school had designed and drawn this certificate for an informally trained craftsman. This, in a sense, blurred the distinction between state schooling and private workshops and provided another mechanism for how practices of formal education began to be used by informal sector craftspeople. The men and women who issued these artisanal diplomas also undermined the ability of the state and other state-sanctioned organizations such as missions to define and regulate expertise through exclusive control over credentialing.

However, not just any master artisan could issue diplomas, and by the 1970s new norms emerged and standardized which artisans could give them out. The onset of systems of artisanal credentialing led tailors who had previously completed their apprenticeships to retroactively make diplomas by filling in a date from an earlier period. Like his patron, tailor Jules Wimêllo did not receive a diploma when he completed his apprenticeship in 1966. Wimêllo opened a shop in a small village and quickly became successful. Nearly a decade later, Wimêllo was ready to celebrate the completion of his first apprentice's contract. But by this time, diplomas had become a standard practice, and his apprentice expected one, so Wimêllo returned to his master, Appolinaire Lanteffo, to have a diploma made for himself (fig. 4.4) so that he too could start signing the documents for his apprentices. Lanteffo, who was unable to write, signed the document with his thumb print. This document, dated 1974 for an apprenticeship completed in 1966, gave Wimêllo the power to issue diplomas to the young men finishing apprenticeships in his own workshop.[85]

In contrast to colonial systems of credentialing, which emphasized the information written on the document, its veracity, and its references to specific people, laws, and institutions, the materiality of the artisanal diploma—its form and public display—often achieved greater power than the words written on it. For example, Alladassi Tavi was a tailor whose father taught him traditional methods of sewing in the 1950s. As a young man, he made large, voluminous robes and only learned the techniques for sewing fitted clothing much later in his life. Lacking a formal apprenticeship or contract, Tavi's father simply gave him a verbal blessing to start working for himself when

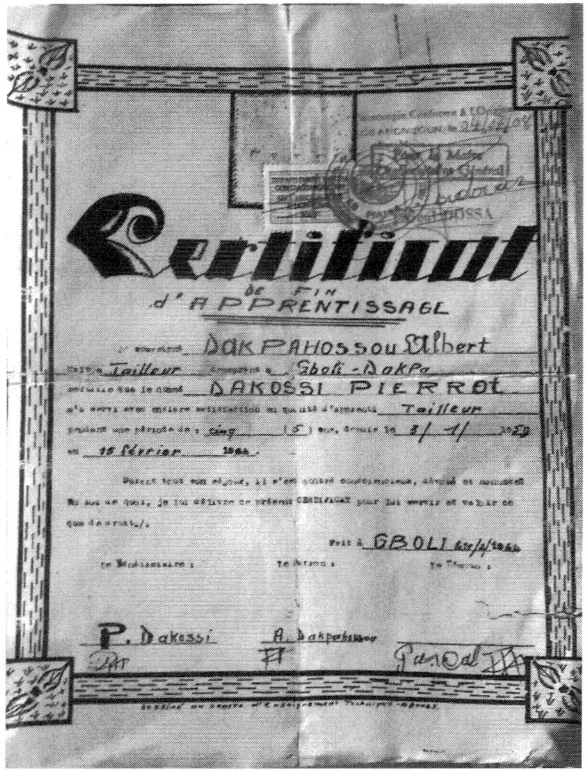

Figure 4.3. Certificate in tailoring, Gboli, dated 1964.
Photo by author. Courtesy of Pierrot Akpakpo.

he felt he had attained the skills necessary to open a tailor's shop. There was
neither a ceremony nor a written diploma to mark the occasion. For decades
Tavi made clothing for clients in his small village and the surrounding area.
Yet in semi-retirement, by 2015, he had a diploma hung on the wall of his
workshop. Based on the materials and style of the document and its signatories, it is clear that Tavi commissioned his diploma in the 2000s or 2010s. He
signed the document with his own thumbprint, since his father/master was
deceased, and retroactively dated the diploma 1958. While an outsider might
consider this document a forgery or a fake, Tavi nevertheless used it to prove
his status as a master tailor by having it framed and hung prominently in his
workshop.[86]

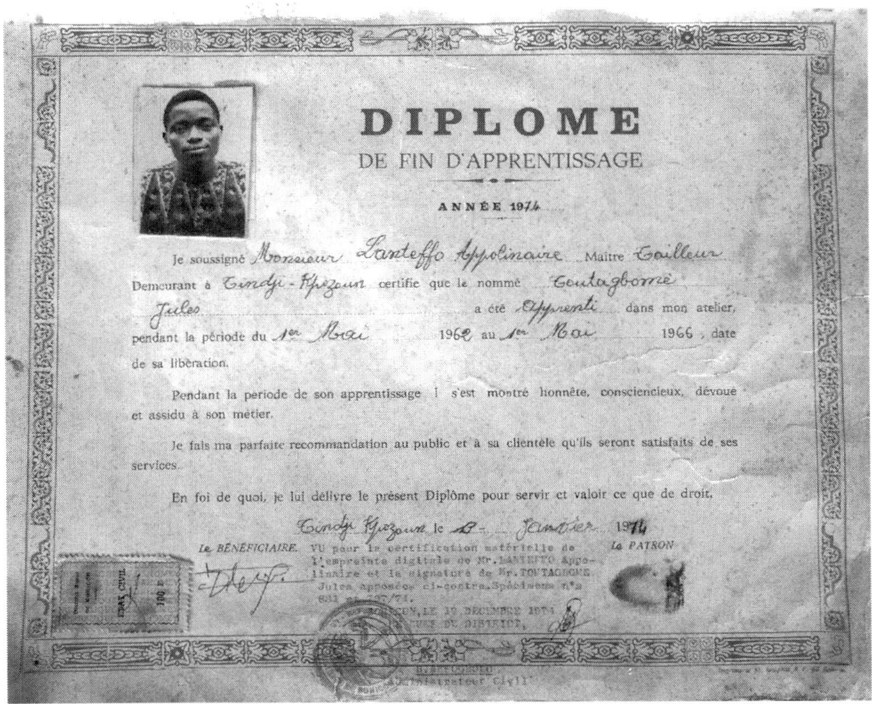

Figure 4.4. Diploma in tailoring, dated 1974. Photo by author. Courtesy of Jules Wimêllo.

Artisans created even more legitimacy around their documents by adding official stamps and other signatories, whether local administrators or artisans. About twelve months after Appolinaire issued a diploma to Wimêllo in 1974, it was taken to Bohicon's local administration (it was not a municipality at the time) to notarize Appolinaire's fingerprint for a cost of one hundred francs per stamp. Anagono Yobode took his 1977 diploma to the mayor's office in Abomey, paying twenty francs to have the signature notarized, although the official put the stamp on the diploma but did not actually fill it out. Tavi's diploma was signed by the president of the local artisan's association in the 2010s, which certified it under the system of artisans' associations explored at the end of this chapter. At the same time, other artisans did not take their diplomas to have them notarized or officiated, and the only signatures or fingerprints on them were those of the master and former apprentice. Indeed, diplomas, like contracts, did not have a standardized form among informal craftspeople, perhaps because many of the artisans who used and issued them did not read or write in French or Fon. Artisanal diplomas were made to be presented and displayed, not closely read or scrutinized as texts. However, while the documents themselves often looked very different from one another, libération, the ceremony that culminated in their awarding, would assume a more regular form, bringing together craftspeople to celebrate and define membership in the artisanat.

Libération Ceremonies and the Professionalization of Craft

"An overcrowded profession: SEWING" read a 1968 headline in the *L'aube nouvelle*. C. Elegbede, the author of the article, argued that tailoring in the administrative capital of Porto-Novo was in steep decline because too many young men "without any vocation, without any taste for the trade" took up tailoring. In his estimation, the craft had become "a place of refuge for school-boys flunked out of school who cannot find another future and who think that petty commerce equals belittling oneself to the rank of peasant"—a reflection of local norms that valued the hunnukún (intellectual) but saw trade and market commerce as women's work.[87] Elegbede guessed that there were over five hundred tailors, seamstresses, and apprentices in Porto-Novo, a number he deemed too large for the small city. He feared that this bloated number of practicing tailors meant that few apprentices would be able to establish work-shops, and they would slip further into poverty. Competition too was driving down prices to unsustainable levels, further destabilizing the profitability of the sector. Credentialing with practices like diplomas and the ceremonies around them were an internal artisanal answer to this dilemma. Libération in particular served to professionalize tailoring and other crafts, and at the same time these events brought together different types of craftspeople, helping to consolidate a pan-craft Béninois artisanat.

By the 1970s, libération ceremonies were widespread in southern Bénin, although it is impossible to pinpoint the exact moment when they started. Oral histories suggest that libération has origins on the coast, where there was more overlap between independent masters and craftspeople trained in state institutions. Most of the first generation of tailors who underwent liberation in the late 1960s and 1970s in the areas around Abomey had patrons from Porto-Novo and Cotonou.[88] A libération ceremony consisted of a series of rituals, some private but most public, that materialized a former apprentice as part of the community of masters. A master scheduled a libération only when they deemed that an apprentice had attained a level of expertise commensurate with their fellow masters. The master tailor watched the work of an apprentice and studied their finished products to make their determination. They also consulted with other master tailors about whether an individual apprentice had the requisite level of skill and taste. The attendance and participation of other masters, especially the master of the apprentice's master, was necessary in providing legitimacy to a ceremony. When the master decided that the time had come for a libération, the apprentice's family had to pay a significant sum for the ceremony, and financial considerations might delay or curtail plans for the formal end to an apprenticeship.

In its simplest form, libération required that apprentices put their best works on display to the public and that masters give them a diploma, tools, and advice. Before the main Saturday gathering, the tools of artisans underwent a private blessing, often the previous evening or morning. Using the blessed tools during a career would protect the artisan and promote their success. For a tailor, these tools included chalk, scissors, needles, and a measuring tape. A Catholic furniture maker in Abomey conveyed how he brought a hammer and nails to church, where he and the priest prayed to Saint Joseph, patron saint of woodworkers, and the priest blessed the tools and sprinkled holy water over them.[89] Every May 1, on International Workers' Day, the carpenter might bring his hammer and the tailor his scissors back to the church to reactivate the blessing.[90] The small Muslim community in the *zongos* of Abomey and Bohicon said a quick prayer before beginning a liberation.[91] However, until very recently, most craftspeople took their tools to Gu, the Fon vodun of metallurgy.

Gu or Ogun is a mutable and widespread deity who, in various forms, appears in religious and spiritual practices in Bénin, Yorùbá areas of Nigeria (as Ogun), and parts of the African diaspora.[92] Gu, kept in front of homes and workshops, took on many material forms, including holes dug into the ground and then filled with organic materials and metal objects, including *asen*, old car parts, and other pieces of scrap. A Gu, photographed in 2021 outside of an Abomey blacksmith's shop, provides an example of how these vodun combine multiple types and qualities of materials (fig. 4.5). Gu might also take the form of figural sculptures such as Akati Ekplékendo's famous nineteenth-century Gou, also made of scrap metal and displayed in the Louvre in Paris.[93] Masters took the tools of their respective crafts to the Gu to perform the sacrifices that would consecrate the artisans' relationship to the vodun and its protection of

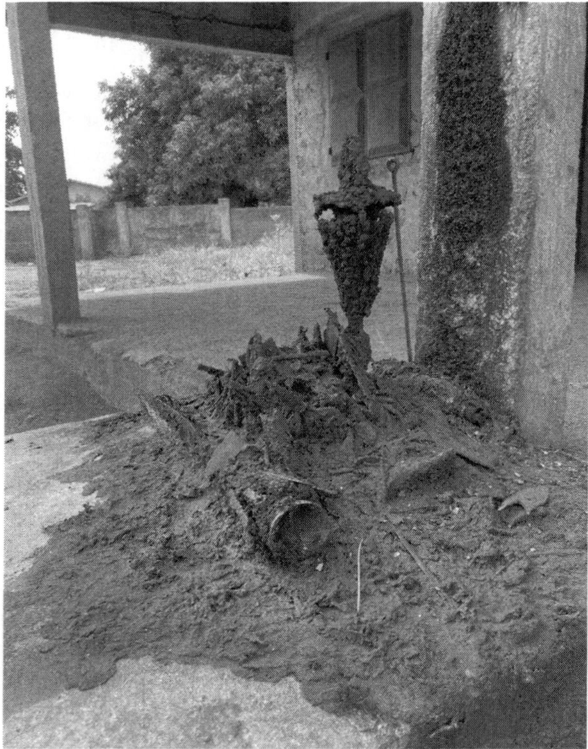

Figure 4.5. Gu in front of blacksmith's shop, Abomey,
June 2021. Photo by author.

their users, whether apprentice or master. Pre-liberation offerings to the Gu
might require roosters, chickens, palm oil, corn flour, greens and other leaves,
or alcohol. The common adherence to Gu among artisans as varied as blacksmiths, tailors, carpenters, mechanics, and plumbers, all of whom worked with
metal tools, helped to bring artisans into a common material and spiritual
identity and upset the caste, occupational, and modern/traditional distinctions promulgated in colonial and national policy.

Once consecrated, the tools were given to the apprentice in front of fellow
masters and community members invited to witness the ceremony. Advice
and blessings formed an important part of the public aspect of libération.
Returning to the vignette in this chapter's introduction, the reporter for *Daho
Express* recorded the counsel given by another master seamstress, Madame

Lebrun, to her apprentices: "Today it is your turn to enter into the line of artisans in the evolution of your country. / Above all, do not rest on your laurels, be curious to deepen and widen the little that you have learned during more than three years. Today's world is for you; it is up to you to discern elegance from the ridiculous within the diversity of fashion. / Have the spirit of invention; the spirit of beauty."[94] She advised the young women both to acknowledge their achievements—the "laurels," as evidenced by their diplomas and blessed tools—and to seek out possibilities to "deepen and widen" their skills and sense of "beauty." Madame Lebrun's counsel also revealed the complexity of a tailor's craft knowledge and that it was not just a command over the sewing machine or the ability to do a fine cut; a good artisan always sought to improve their ability to "discern" and be capable of "invention." By giving this speech in public and permitting a reporter to transcribe it, Madame Lebrun made a powerful assertion about what constituted a tailor's craft knowledge and how her apprentices should continue this tradition.

Masters tried to ensure that apprentices understood and absorbed the spoken word through acts of embodiment that drew upon Vodun. Public speeches were supplemented with more private forms of council, whispered in ears, under the watchful eyes of other masters. Afterward, masters spit or blew soft drinks, beer, or liquor like gin or sodabi on the apprentices' heads, helping them bring the words into their bodies and actions (figs. 4.6 and 4.7). As art historian Suzanne Preston Blier argued in her work on Fon bociɔ (power objects), vodun practitioners used *atan* (saliva) to activate the object's *bo* (power), and the atan served as a "glue which holds the words together on the object's surface" during offerings.[95] In this way, the saliva of the masters helped the advice permeate into the mind, body, and work of the new master, in the hopes of a successful career for the craftsperson. Further embodiment of advice was achieved through acts of ingestion, as masters offered sips of liquid to the apprentice, allowing the advice to fully permeate their bodies. Sharing beverages also conveyed a sense of trust among masters, even amid increasing anxieties about poisoning by *àzètɔ* (witches), which became more prevalent in the late twentieth century.[96] At the end of the ceremony, the former apprentice rose and took a drink as an equal partner in the community of masters (fig. 4.7).

Masters of different crafts came together to observe a reenactment of apprenticeship in a part of libération that a newspaper article described as a "mock corporal punishment (in which spectators rush to 'buy' to save the

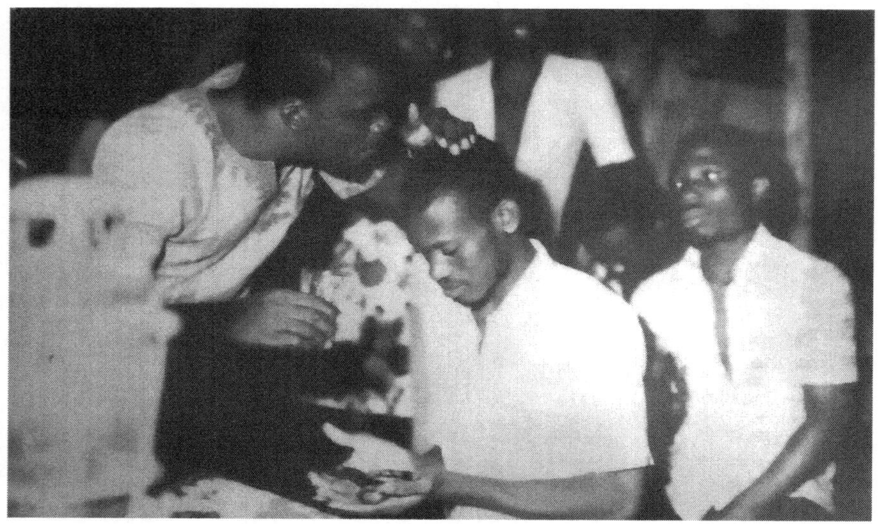

Figure 4.6. Alain Baba giving benedictions to his apprentice Célestin Nicolas Kokossou, Bohicon, 1975. Courtesy of Alain Baba.

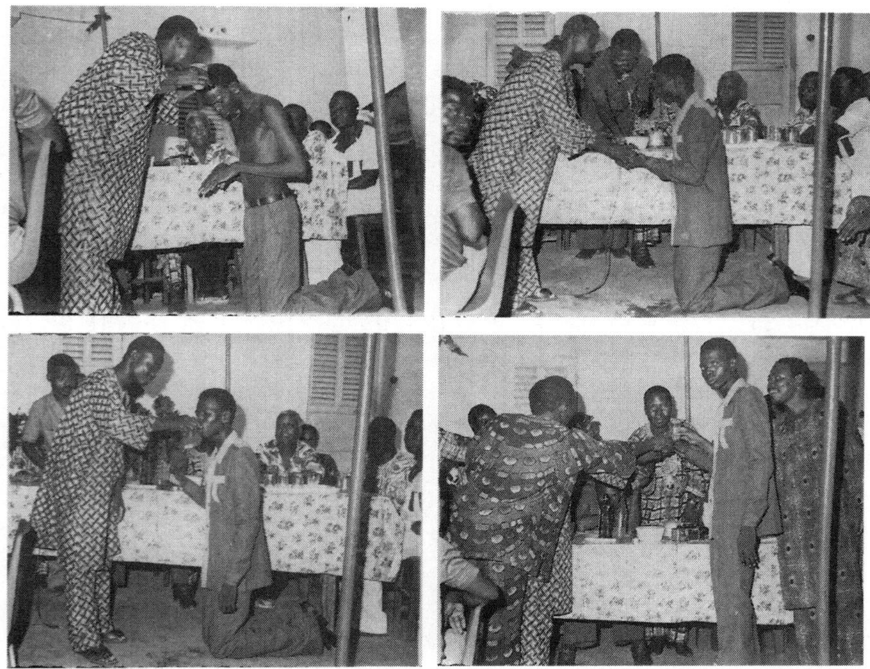

Figure 4.7. Libération of a photographer, June 4, 1983. Photographs courtesy of Chez Photo Deguenon.

apprentice)."[97] Masters used wooden paddles to playfully whack the hands of an apprentice during the *palmatoire* (fig. 4.8). The word *palmatoire* is uniquely used in Africa to describe the beating of hands with a wooden paddle and has origins in the colonial period. The French suffix *-oire* implies a place where something is done while the first part of the word might very well be the English word "palm" as opposed to its French equivalent (*la paume*). During the palmatoire, the apprentice stood stoically, trying not to flinch with their hands being hit, while audience members approached the master to give them money to stop the "punishment." Between the palmatoire and the direct monetary gifts from the apprentice's family to the master, master artisans might leave a libération with a tidy sum of money, which served as recognition for a job well done in training the apprentice. Tailor Célestin Kokossou told how the palmatoire signified the "last time" a master could hit an apprentice, even though a master might not "hit hard like before [during the apprenticeship]."[98] Corporal punishment was common in colonial Africa, and prisons, schools, and courts served as sites where colonial authorities inflicted bodily violence on African subjects.[99] Given this history and the violence done against apprentices, the playfulness of the palmatoire is striking. Indeed, the shape and materials of the paddle, its use in initiation, and its later ritual display have remarkable corollaries to fraternity or sports hazing rather than the canes and *chicote* (whips) often associated with colonial punishment. While palmatoire arrived in Bénin via an unknown route, it remains fundamental to understanding what libération meant to artisans. Apprentices were not just initiated into a community—they were also liberated from the suffering, drudgery, and occasional bodily harm of apprenticeship.

Libération was exceptionally visible; it often took place outside and usually in prominent spaces in front of workshops or compounds, as opposed to within their walls. In this way, an entire community could assess the skill of the newly minted craftsperson and observe their journey to master status. As we can see in the image of a libération in a small village outside Cana (fig. 4.9), the public part of the ceremony took place in a courtyard. In this image, a master seamstress spits a beverage onto the apprentice, activating her advice. Behind her, other masters supervise the ceremony, providing it legitimacy. In the upper right of the photograph, the audience observes. In this way, communities encountered new masters and also might assess their skill through their masterworks, which for tailors included the clothing that they had made and worn to their own ceremony. At the end of the ceremony, after the new master received

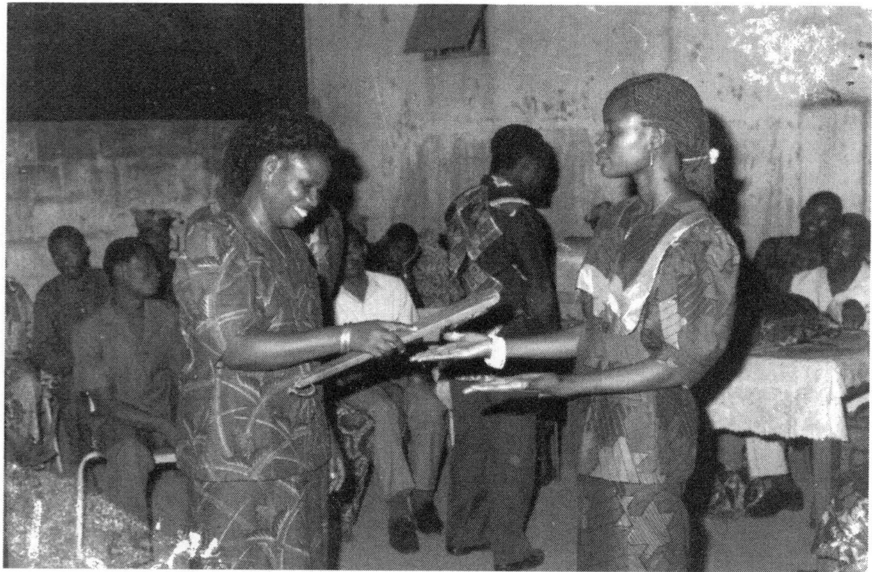

Figure 4.8. Marie Félicité Babagbéto and her apprentice during the palmatoire, Bohicon, circa 2000s. Courtesy of Babagbéto.

their diploma and shared a beverage with the other masters, the former apprentice's family served food and drinks to the masters and audience. Depending on the circumstances of the family, this might include multiple courses, bottles of beer and soda, and sometimes a *petite verre* (shot glass) of sodabi, gin, or whisky. At her liberation in 1980, seamstress Léocadie Zehounkpé's master asked her to bring eight bottles of liquor.[100] An apprentice's family often served multiple courses of meat, chicken, and fish in sauce with rice or *pâte* (a dense maize-based fufu), and each course was served with a new bottle of beer or soft drink. In recent years, families also rented party equipment and hired DJs to play music in the background, and masters would get up to lead the dancing before others joined in.

Libérations were meant to be documented, and families commissioned one of a growing number of photographers to capture images of the ceremony. Tailoring and photography overlapped in mid-century West Africa. Tailors often became photographers, tailors encountered new styles in images, and consumers recorded their latest fashions at the photographer's studio.[101] Béninois photographers, themselves artisans who had undergone libération, captured key

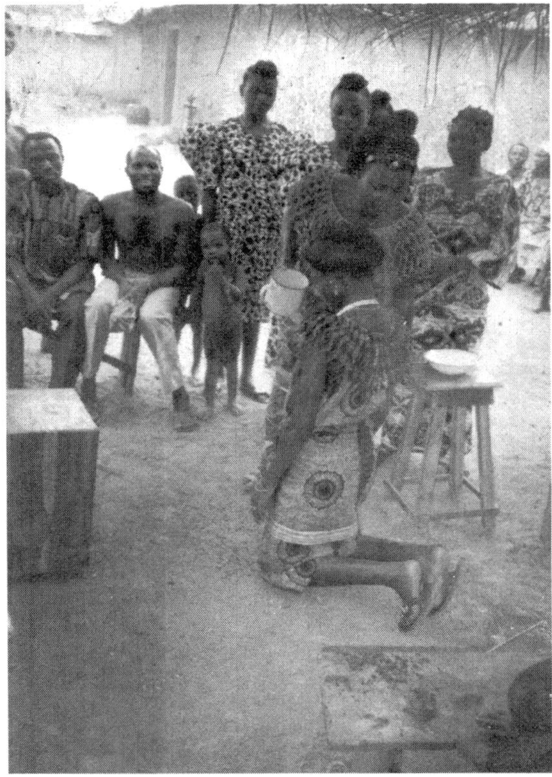

Figure 4.9. Libération ceremony, Atchia, Zogbodomey.
Courtesy of Christine Agbamandé.

moments of the ceremony such as speeches and the palmatoire. Candid shots were supplemented by staged photographs of new masters holding diplomas, shaking hands, or making toasts. Tailors were often posed with their measuring tape around their neck or standing next to a sewing machine, usually a gift from their parents. By holding their diploma for a photographer in front of a crowd of onlookers, new masters promoted their skills and changed social status. Prints of these images, amassed in albums or framed and mounted on walls, allowed artisans not only to reminisce about a key day in their own personal histories but to provide further documentation of their master status. Libération was a day that brought masters together but also left a rich material and visual archive that supported their claims to craft knowledge.

The Material Culture of Expertise and the Artisanat Béninois

Béninois artisans would use their common material culture to consolidate a pan-craft identity as artisanat in the final few decades of the twentieth century, and tailors were important leaders within these movements. The idea of artisans' associations has deep roots in Bénin. As early as the 1930s, colonial educators promoted associations and cooperatives as a way for artisans to increase productivity and cut costs by buying tools and primary materials at wholesale rates.[102] French proposals drew on their conceptions of the norms and roles of historic European guilds and modern-day trade unions. Tailors, as artisans who straddled the traditional/modern dichotomy imposed by the state and who heavily relied on international imports of thread, needles, machinery, and fabric, were some of the earliest proponents of these collective efforts. In the 1940s, tailors in Cotonou and Porto-Novo formed a union of seventy-six members. The Trade Union of Artisans in the Abomey Cercle (Syndicat des artisans du Cercle d'Abomey) had 216 members, although it is unclear who these members were and, as operators of small businesses, what kinds of collective efforts they pursued.[103] Indeed these groups quickly became inactive, leaving little imprint in the archive or popular memory and making it unclear if they ever existed as more than an association on paper.[104] By 1955, thirty-two tailors on the coast had formed the Union of Clothing Workers of Dahomey (Syndicat des travailleurs de l'habillement du Dahomey), although this single record of the group makes no mention of their activities.[105] After independence, the International Labor Organization (ILO) became invested in assisting the Béninois government and promoting artisans' associations. While the ILO did not find evidence of earlier associational efforts—these previous incarnations had been forgotten—it noted a tailors' collective launched in Parakou in March 1963 and one in Cotonou only in the process of being formed. The report stated that tailors were "particularly receptive to cooperative work" since, the researchers reasoned, tailors faced intense competition from imported clothing and that "tailors grouped into co-operatives" would be the only way to make the craft sustainable in a modernizing Bénin.[106] Perhaps tailors agreed, because they would continue to spearhead efforts to create artisans' associations.

Efforts to bring artisans together before independence and in the first few decades following it floundered. The state and international organizations assumed that associations failed due to lack of funding. For example, the ILO took the position that a 1961 pan-artisan collective of carpenters, masons, painters, and tailors dissolved because of a "lack of an appropriate funding mechanism."[107] Yet inconsistent revenue streams were characteristic of artisanship, since profits fluctuated regularly and entered long slumps after national and international economic downturns. Artisans often opted out of joining associations because of membership fees and because they did not want to register as businesses and pay taxes. The ILO estimated that only 25 percent of artisans paid the fees to have a licensed business by the mid-1960s, although even this low percentage was likely an overestimation.[108] What the state and ILO failed to grasp was that cooperatives and associations also floundered in Bénin because they relied on assumptions that occupation was a meaningful social identity, a relic of French experts' ideas about "African artisans." They imagined history unfolding as it had in France, where traditional modes of craft organization like guilds gave way to modern trade unions. In reality, artisans in Bénin did not have historical precedents for either craft-based or pan-craft cooperation. The common experience of occupation could not supersede other forms of difference, such as gender, generation, and class, in the formation of collective artisanal bodies.

However, the 1970s brought a renewed interest in cooperatives and associations among artisans, especially when faced with increasing tax burdens under the Kérékou government.[109] Uncoincidentally, the rise in associational life coincided with the increasing importance of libération, which created a common material culture of expertise among artisans and helped them to transcend other forms of social difference. New master craftspeople opened workshops or market stalls to make and sell their objects, and their ateliers also served as repositories and display spaces for the things of libération. In these workshops, tailors might hang the wooden paddle for the palmatoire neatly in the corner and let clients browse through albums of images of their styles next to photos of their libération.[110] One tailor in Abomey even had the scissors he received during his ceremony mounted on the wall. Nearly forty years after his ceremony, he did not use the rusted scissors anymore but still proudly displayed them.[111] But at the center of this material culture of expertise lay the diploma, which artisans of every craft began to adopt. Tailors used diplomas as tools to broadcast evidence of their status as master craftsmen and prominently displayed them on workshop walls where they might be seen from the street. These things provided evidence to other masters, potential clients, and parents of potential apprentices that a skilled master operated out of the space, which brought in new revenue streams but also changed local notions about what constituted expertise and who might have access to it.

Investment by state and nonstate entities supplemented this network of things and relations created by artisans, eventually leading to the creation of artisans' associations. In the early 1970s, the ILO returned to Bénin to supervise the construction of Maisons des artisans in towns and cities across the country.[112] Craftspeople booked the centers as spaces to conduct meetings, although young people, other residents, and nonprofits also used the maisons for community activities, such as skill-building classes and seminars. After President Kérékou officially adopted Marxism-Leninism in 1975, he revived interest in supporting pan-artisan cooperatives at the national level. As part of the Kérékou regime's drive to create a "revolutionary culture," his administration envisioned "cultural and artistic squads" of artists and artisans who would operate in "every village and every neighborhood" and teach Béninois proper revolutionary tastes.[113] In Abomey, the Kérékou government pursued a particularly invasive strategy and commissioned the National Office of Tourism and Hotel Management to reduce the number of artisans, especially those making objects for the tourist market, in order to make the sector both more manageable and profitable.[114] But, like most of the Kérékou government's attempts to create a centrally planned economy, state support for the artisan cooperatives floundered.

Indeed, amid the increasing financial and economic difficulties of Kérékou's Marxist-Leninist regime and international isolation in the 1980s, it was artisans themselves who organized the longest-lasting *collectifs des artisans* (artisans' collectives). Picosi, a Cotonou tailor, started an association in the 1970s and by the early 1980s had traveled to Bohicon to attend libérations and to help tailors organize among themselves and with other craftspeople. Picosi emphasized the role that associations needed to play in regulating libération, and he presided at a number of these events in the 1980s and 1990s.[115] Bohicon tailor Alain Baba remembered that at the time, tailors felt threatened by the tax collection practices of the local government, which would take their sewing machine heads and cause work stoppages if they failed to pay. Tailors were also interested in coming together to petition the local government for space for libération.[116] Bound by their common practices of libération and diplomas, Picosi's association of tailors worked with other artisans to organize a pan-artisan group in Bénin that they hoped would regulate contracts and apprenticeship and provide a means for artisans to present their collective concerns to the state. By the time of the National Conference in 1990, artisans' collectifs would be one of the main participants in the rewriting of the constitution and the move toward democratization.[117] After the fall of the Marxist-Leninist regime in Bénin and free elections in 1991, artisans from all over the country met in Cotonou to launch the National Federation of Béninois Artisans (Fédération nationale des artisans de Bénin [FENAB]) under the guidance of the new democratic government. The artisans elected an Abomean furniture maker, Georges Henri Ayadji, as their president, and its founders conceptualized the organization as explicitly political. FENAB would fight for the rights of artisans at the national level as opposed to earlier iterations of Béninois associational life where craftspeople designed cooperatives for mutual aid and assistance.[118]

According to Ayadji and Ernest Fiogbe, an Abomean master weaver, one of the most significant distinctions between FENAB and earlier groups of artisans was that FENAB was founded through "text"—it included an administrative structure and formalized set of documents—as opposed to the "word of mouth" organizational structure of earlier artisans' groups.[119] These texts legitimized the organization within the realm of formal politics, allowing for greater artisan participation at the various levels of government. FENAB had offices in every region and *commune* of Bénin. Local chapters were further divided into groups based on craft, creating a seemingly endless number of officeholders—presidents, vice presidents, secretaries, and treasurers—at each level of the association, including village, commune, region, and national. FENAB continued the work of creating new material practices that, like contracts and diplomas, were used as "paper tools" for refinement of craft knowledge and identity. To receive membership cards, young apprentices filled out an "information sheet" and submitted it to their local chapter, which then issued the cards.[120] Alain Baba, the former president of the Bohicon tailors, supplied his card, dated the year after the artisans founded FENAB. The card was valid for three years and signed by the president of the Zou as well as the national president Ayadji.[121] Card-carrying members gained access to trainings organized by the association, the state, and international NGOs, and associations increasingly played the role of gatekeeper after internationally funded sustainable development projects mushroomed in the years following democratization. After each training, a tailor might receive cash compensation or an *Attestation* certifying attendance in a short course with titles like "cutting and sewing layette" or "the patron in their role as trainer."[122] The association played important roles in bringing issues important to craftspeople into formal politics and in helping members access new resources and sources of revenue.

However, common material practices and associational life did not completely efface the challenges faced by earlier iterations of artisan groups. Collecting dues remained a particular problem. Although Baba was a ranked member, his FENAB membership card makes it clear that he paid his first year of dues but did not pay dues for the remainder of the card's validity. FENAB also never included all Béninois artisans—some opted out to avoid fees while others felt that the association had little to offer them based on gendered, generational, and class differences with other members. For example, Za-Kpota tailor Barthélemy Adjahouinou refused to join the local tailors' association because his younger brother, also a tailor, was a member. Membership in the same association would have put them on equal footing, undermining the authority that he held as an elder brother.[123] Finally, the internal structure of associations often elevated the voices of the most successful artisans while silencing those of less well-off members. As associations increasingly took on the role of gatekeeper between artisans and external resources, material inequalities were exacerbated. Presidents and vice presidents were often wealthy and literate in French. They invested profits in expensive machinery such as embroidery machines and grew their businesses and networks of former apprentices. On the other end of the spectrum, some tailors farmed or engaged in petty trade, and women began to sell soap, hard candies, or *klui klui* (fried peanut paste) to survive. Despite their diplomas, these *petit tailleurs* often felt shut out of associations, their leadership, and the access that the associations offered to trainings and financial support.

Artisans used libération to professionalize craft and to create new ways of assessing and identifying mastery over bodies of knowledge in post-independence Bénin. In the early twentieth century, colonial administrators and anthropologists had sought to link African craft knowledge to blood and tradition—artisans were born in Africa and their know-how was primordial, although subject to corruption. This conception of "African artisans" informed colonial and national policies that approached craftspeople as low status, hereditary, rural, and ultimately informal. However, schools and competitions also offered new models of certification that craftspeople would later adopt as they carved out their own path in a post-independence informal economy. Tailors and other artisans professionalized by localizing systems of credentialing and innovating libération as means of managing master status and craft knowledge. Libération became the moment in which artisanship was defined, and it was a craftspeople-run process beyond the reach of the state. Libération also led to the creation of a material culture of expertise that artisans used to prove their mastery to each other and to potential clients, bringing together craftspeople of all types into a common set of practices and experiences. This helped them to coalesce into politically active associations that intervened in local and national politics and attracted the resources of international nonprofits.

This chapter has focused on changing ideas and practices of craftsmanship in Bénin as material processes in which ordinary Béninois combined multiple ways of knowing to assert their expertise. The new emphasis on credentialing as a measure of craft knowledge would create lasting effects on how clothes were worn and made in Bénin. While earlier tailors had innovated styles like détè and bohunba through mobility, media proficiency, and honing creativity, the shift to more rigid forms of acquiring and measuring craft knowledge discouraged these more fluid ways of attaining and developing styles. Furthermore, an apprenticeship system in which families paid dues and libération served as an opportunity for profit encouraged quantity over quality in terms of apprentices trained by a master, which, as the next chapter will show, disproportionately impacted craftswomen and women's fashion. Associations created a collective voice for artisans while also introducing new hierarchies and systems of gatekeeping within the community of craftspeople. Finally, ordinary Béninois became increasingly frustrated with the costs of libération when it grew to include rented tents and chairs, DJs, multicourse meals, and large monetary gifts to master craftspeople. By the mid-2010s, a libération could cost upward of 250,000 fCFA, or about $500, a significant sum for most Béninois. The ceremony was recast as a tradition that promoted the exploitation of apprentices and that wasted scarce resources. Shifting conceptions of who and how one could become a tailor altered how people made and wore clothing in Bénin, particularly as tailoring and fashion became the domain of women.

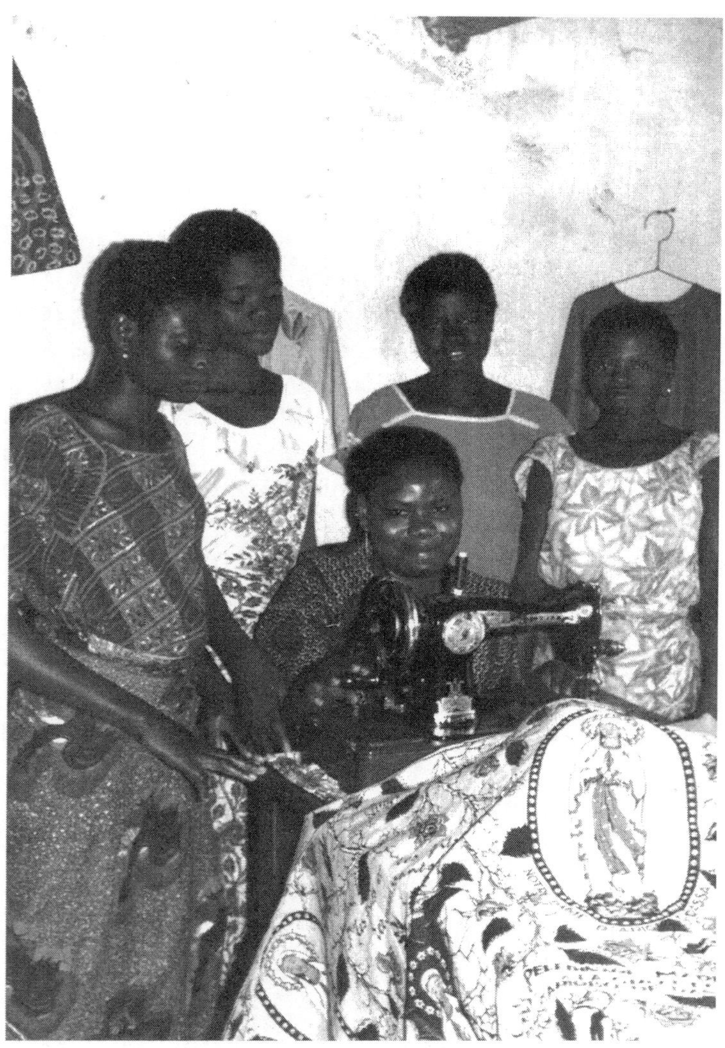

Figure 5.1. Marie Félicité Babagbéto and her apprentices, Bohicon, circa 1990s. Courtesy of Babagbéto.

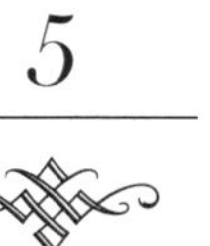

5

Feminizing the Craft

The Urban Workshop, Woman's Space, and Respectable Dress

In a photograph carefully kept in an album in a Bohicon workshop, master seamstress Marie Félicité Babagbéto sits behind a sewing machine surrounded by four of her apprentices. On a table in front of the machine, someone had carefully arranged a pagne (wrapper) printed with an image of the Virgin Mary, clearly displaying the design for the photographer. According to the text on the cloth, it was produced and sold to commemorate the annual pilgrimage to Our Lady of Agribo, a Marian shrine in Dassa-Zoumé, only eighty kilometers from Bohicon. Although a staged photograph, the image seems to capture an everyday moment in the seamstress's workshop—the apprentices were not wearing their finest and had dressed for an ordinary day of work. Clothing displayed on hangers surrounds the women and provides sample garments for discussing styles with customers and for attracting business from women walking by the shop. Two of the girls in the image look to their master, who was responsible for teaching them how to design, cut, and sew respectable fashions but also guided them in other facets of life such as negotiating relationships or comporting themselves in a growing city. Babagbéto looks toward the camera, smiling, claiming ownership over her craft knowledge, her workshop, and the futures of her apprentices.[1]

By the time the photograph was taken in the 1990s, the number of women working as clothes-makers had surpassed that of men in southern Bénin. Most of these women, like Babagbéto, ran workshops where they designed and sewed *couture dame,* or women's and children's clothing, only occasionally making men's clothing for male relatives. In recent decades, Béninois have delineated women-run couture dame workshops from those specializing in

159

haute couture, which usually have male masters, although they are sometimes run by women. Haute couture shops produce men's and women's garments that are more expensive and often perceived as higher quality than those produced in couture dame shops. A third category of Béninois tailoring, called *tailleurie simple*, includes the few men who remain in the market, working out of stalls, doing repairs, altering secondhand clothing (acouta), and sewing more basic ensembles like a simple bounba. While the craft knowledge of haute couture and even tailleurie simple draws on multiple registers of style honed through travel (aventure), apprenticeship, and frequent training, practitioners of couture dame typically trace their craft knowledge back to Catholic missions or state domestic education.

This chapter traces the development and expansion of women's workshop-based couture dame in Bénin from the decades following independence from France in 1960 to the twenty-first century. In the nineteenth century and during French colonization, Catholic mission programs emphasized sewing as women's household labor. Training for girls and young women was imbued with the politics of the civilizing mission and a focus on Christian respectability, modesty, and women's roles in the home. These colonial-era mission education programs and their successors, post-independence programs run by Béninois clergy and nongovernmental organizations, continued to shape how women made and acquired clothing. From seamstresses' self-fashioning to their tools, production sites, and practices of apprenticeship, couture dame was distinguished from male-dominated haute couture. Seamstresses in couture dame shops took on dozens of apprentices over the course of their careers, which quickly expanded the population of women clothes-makers, altered the gendered makeup of tailoring, and fundamentally changed notions around the craft and the clothes worn by Béninois consumers. By the final few decades of the twentieth century, tailors and seamstresses continued to work together to build craft associations and regularly met to celebrate their craft during the graduation, or libération, of their apprentices, yet both fashion and needlework were rapidly becoming the domain of women.

Girls were often drawn to an apprenticeship in clothes-making for different reasons from their male counterparts. While some seamstresses also used aventure to self-fashion "modern" personas, generate profits, or refine styles, for most women the appeal of the craft lay in the stability of the workshop and the respectability that the craft and its spaces—including the workshop—offered to women who faced limited economic opportunities in a rapidly growing city. Originally from a small community outside Ouidah, Babag-béto arrived in Bohicon for an apprenticeship and eventually settled down and opened a workshop. Indeed, she and many other Béninoise seamstresses are among the many women in colonial and postcolonial Africa who sought income, new opportunities, and freedom from kinship obligations in urban informal economies.[2] Seamstresses like Babagbéto were, similar to their male counterparts, migrants to the city and sought to re-create themselves in a new community. But women's relationship to the city, its spaces, and the technologies of the craft were gendered in ways that both created and curtailed personal and professional opportunities. Indeed, the craft and the workshop generated redemptive possibilities for women marginalized within families, politics, and the waged and cash crop economies. In oral histories, women often described their lives as a series of struggles against men, poverty, or a combination of the two and how workshop-based sewing brought them greater stability and respectability, allowing a woman to become a *grande dame* (important woman) within her community.[3]

This chapter traces how women tailored identities within the workshop by recrafting technologies and materials, including the space itself, to create new notions of embodied labor, prestige, and female respectability. It begins with the postcolonial politics around women's dress and how Béninois women's fashion was imagined within the pages of newspapers and in domestic education programs. Instead of looking to the past for Béninois women's styles, post-independence political elites promoted dress that included "modern" global fashions and, after the declaration of Marxism-Leninism as state ideology in 1975, homogenous "revolutionary" garb. But despite political rhetoric and formal policy changes, missions, churches, and even some secular nonprofits continued the work of encouraging modest garments for women.

The chapter then shifts to the development of cities in the interior of Bénin and how the infrastructural and material strategies pursued by governments, tailors, and seamstresses contributed to the development of the urban tailor's workshop. By the late 1970s, tailors and seamstresses used workshops as sites to put their expertise on display and as vibrant places where people, especially women, might come together. In doing so, seamstresses developed resilient gendered strategies of using the spaces of the workshop for personal uplift by taking on dependent apprentices and establishing themselves as independent and respectable businessowners and *mamans* (mothers). The final section explores how women's styles materialized desires for respectability and stability in an unstable economy around the turn of the century. Women's practices of tailoring and place-making differed from the "adventuring" men of the earlier independence-era generation, yet these women drove larger conceptual shifts around gendered labor, space, and sartorial meaning in late twentieth-century Bénin.

The Postcolonial Politics of Women's Fashion

The 1966 Soglo regime had proposed men's "military dress" to promote equality among men and to create an ensemble suited to a modernizing country, yet it did not attempt to mandate an equivalent dress for women.[4] Indeed, throughout the 1960s and 1970s there were no direct state policies or laws dictating women's dress in Bénin, although there were widely circulating and competing discourses on women's fashion. In the pages of the state-run newspaper, political elites emphasized the potential transformative qualities of dress and circulated new patterns and images of world fashions. The national government even occasionally sent garments to rural areas, attempting to influence fashion through samples. At the same time, mission programs in small towns and rural villages continued their work of teaching methods of sewing and female comportment. In doing so, they embroiled dressmaking and women's fashion in the politics of Christian respectability and modesty even in communities where most people practiced Vodun. Ultimately, seamstresses wove stylistic elements from both movements into their creations, creating fashions that spoke to ordinary Béninoise women's lived experiences in a new nation and city.

In the 1960s, politicians and popular movements in countries like Tanzania, Senegal, and Niger began to target global trends like miniskirts and form-fitting outfits as antithetical to African or national values.[5] Béninois political elites closely followed these debates on women's fashion happening elsewhere in the continent, yet they employed a different approach in Bénin by promoting world fashions for women and by not implementing any controls on women's dress.[6] Editors of the state-owned newspapers picked up stories from news wires that covered the high fashion scene in Paris while the women's page regularly described styles popular in Europe and provided miniatures of patterns to show readers how to sew trendy blouses, skirts, and dresses.[7] The postcolonial state even went so far as to spread new global women's styles in government-issued dress. For example, in a 1970 spread in *Daho Express* women police officers in Cotonou wore short-skirted uniforms during patrols.[8] In part, the political elite's embracing of a global look in women's dress was a manifestation of a local Vodun aesthetic of incorporation, which had, since the precolonial era, embraced new techniques, forms, and styles from elsewhere.

Promoting fitted women's styles, however, also reflected the modernizing interests of the various West-leaning governments that administered Bénin from 1960 to 1972. Despite five coup d'états and twelve governments during this twelve-year period, there were no substantive ideological differences among the different regimes, and they sought, in slightly varying degrees, to develop and prosper along the lines of the United States and Europe. As one man, Valentin Alagbe, wrote in the newspaper, "To condemn the revolution in clothing is also to condemn the actual progress of humanity. . . . Today the outfits in style during the reign of Louis XIV or during the dynasty of 'Ouegbadja' have disappeared."[9] His comparison between prerevolutionary France and precolonial Dahomey reveals how elite Dahomean styles such as tchanka (baggy shorts) and wrapped grande pagne (three meters of fabric) might be considered relics of a distant past and, like the ornamental ensembles of the court of Louis XIV, a mismatch for a modern present.

The national government and Cotonou philanthropic organizations also invested in "beauty diplomacy" by fostering a high-fashion scene in Cotonou and promoting individual female designers in their efforts to define and promote the Béninois nation as prosperous and globally oriented.[10] In 1969, customs officials staged a fashion show at their annual banquet (fig. 5.2). The women wore different long and short styles, mostly modeled after evening gowns or cocktail dresses in fashion in Europe. The author of the accompanying article described the dresses as successes with "one or two exceptions."[11] These failures were likely the styles modeled after men's tchanka and grand pagne, worn by the models who are fourth and fifth from the left, since these outfits both upset local gendered wear and failed to conform to the norms of global women's fashion. In 1970, the Cotonou Lion's Club staged another fashion show that made a few women-owned Cotonou fashion houses household names among the newspaper-reading public.[12] One of these, Cherita Couture, was featured prominently in the newspaper over the next few years. The designer promoted her styles by giving them names such as *Soleil* (Sun), *Présidence* (Presidency), and *Apollo*, evoking aspirational status and contemporary global events such as US missions to the moon. In an image in *Daho Express*, a photographer captured the women in motion, or at least in the appearance of motion, as they were staged in a runway walk along a street. The designs

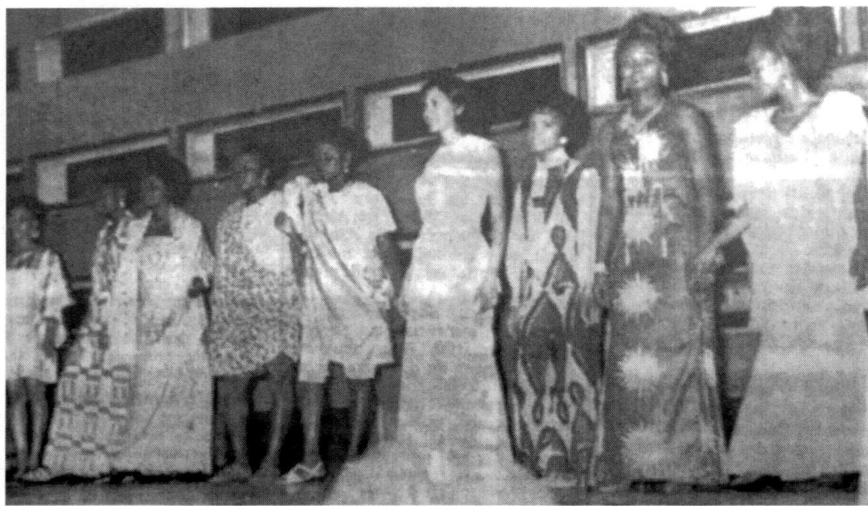

Figure 5.2. "The Models After the Fashion Show." From *Daho Express*, November 3, 1969.

represent an array of styles made from imported waxes and prints and sewn into forms increasingly common in West Africa. The women's branch of the national party also held fashion shows, giving out awards for clothing designs and hairdressing.[13] These programs brought attention to Cotonou women who designed the clothing and also to the new ways that familiar textiles and forms could be refashioned for the urban Béninoise. Alongside the political elite, many regular people also embraced modern urban styles. In peripheral areas like Abomey, girls and women wore trendy form-fitting outfits for both celebrations and work (fig. 0.1). Ultimately, styles like miniskirts or evening gowns were not an affront to the nationalist goals of the West-leaning state or to mainstream southern Béninois culture, in which most people practiced Vodun and, unlike the Catholic and Muslim minorities, did not prioritize concealed women's bodies as part of their religious observance.

However, state media coverage and promotion of elite women's fashion came to an abrupt end under the Kérékou regime. In 1972, Mathieu Kérékou seized power in Bénin's fifth and final coup d'état and, two years later, made the surprising move of declaring Marxism-Leninism state policy, which would last until 1989. The new orientation of the state introduced a communist aesthetic of uniformity and "imagined homogeneity" to Béninois sartorial culture.[14] Within this standardized look, male and female party loyalists wore shirt-jacks and pants, breaking down distinctions of gender. For example, Alladass Sodonou, a middle-aged woman at the time, wore the official dress of the People's Republic of Bénin during her work on behalf of Kérékou's government. An enlarged photograph framed and hung prominently in her living room showed her wearing an oversized shirt and cargo pants (fig. 5.3). She recalled how representatives brought the outfits from the capital and loaned them out to her and other Kérékou supporters who then went door to door informing the population that the president or some other official was visiting and encouraging them to attend the event. After the visit concluded, state employees took back the uniforms, and Sodonou changed back into her wrapper or bounba. When asked how people responded to this style, Sodonou replied, "Everybody congratulated me because it is a good woman who wears fatigues, who wears pants, and they knew that I am a fighting woman."[15] Of course, the chilling threat of Kérékou's notorious political prison in Ségbana may have led to people's positive comments about Sodonou's ensemble. Yet much like attempts to establish a men's military dress in the preceding decade, these styles failed to catch on as everyday wear, especially for women. Indeed, the loaned-out uniforms sported by Sodonou and others were indicative of the challenges facing the fledgling communist state. It was not able to supply all Béninois, or even party loyalists, with uniforms, and it could not rely on loyalists to proactively acquire the fabric and make the outfits themselves. Many initiatives of the communist regime floundered due to a lack of state resources and investment and everyday resistance from ordinary Béninois.

Missions and churches continued to play an important role in shaping sartorial culture after independence and even after the turn to Marxism-Leninism. Cash-strapped governments permitted and even relied on Catholic missions to provide services in poorer and more rural communities.[16] Local Catholic dioceses and Béninois priests invested in teaching women how to sew conservative-style clothing in ways very similar to the missions established by French and other European priests. Near the Our Lady of Agribo Grotto in Dassa-Zoumé, women could take a two-year course in domestic education, followed by a third year where they learned cutting fabric and sewing it into covering, loose-fitting ensembles. Practical education was supplemented with what one newspaper reporter called "civic and moral instruction (subjects taught by Abbot Okioh)," a type of education that he declared "they [did] not teach in the makeshift tailoring workshops situated here and there on the side of the road."[17] At the Foyer Sainte Monique in Abomey, Agbainzoun tailor Jeanette Agadame learned basic math and French along with making clothes.

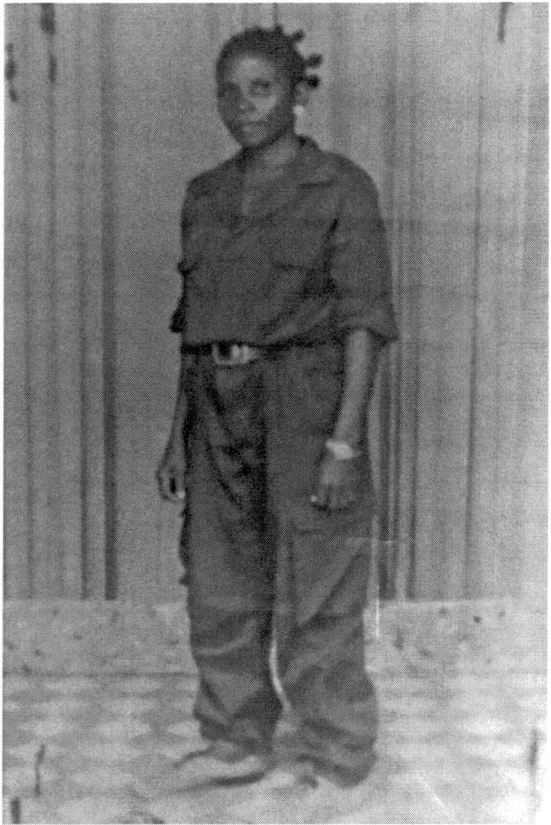

Figure 5.3. Framed photograph of Alladass Sodonou
in revolutionary dress, circa 1977. Photo by author.

Although men taught the academic subjects, female nuns of both Béninois
and French descent taught her couture dame and *layette* (children's and baby
clothes). Nuns also taught her European recipes for potato dishes, salads, and
French toast (*pain perdu*), all recipes that used ingredients that were rare and
expensive in Bénin. Later, when she finished a program and opened a shop,
she taught her own apprentices these same dishes along with the techniques
of couture dame.

Like apprentices liberated by master tailors in private shops, Agadame
received a diploma and ordered a photograph of the ceremony, complete
with measuring tape draped around her neck. In figure 5.4, the "bishop who
opened the center" blesses Agadame's diploma on the day of her libération

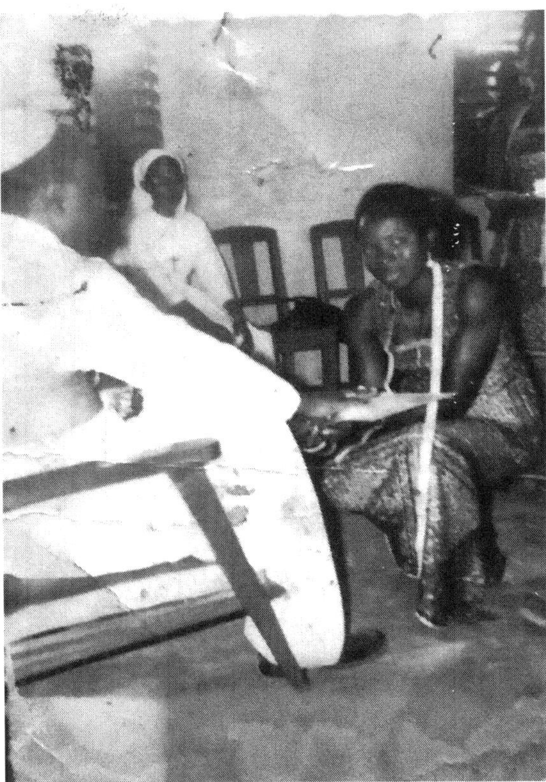

Figure 5.4. Jeanette Agadame on the day of the
libération, 1975. Courtesy of Agadame.

in July 1975.[18] Other seamstresses in the area traced their craft knowledge to
Davougon, a large Catholic mission with a hospital and a leprosy program,
just south of Abomey. Recounting their experience through oral histories,
they explained how graduates of domestic education programs specialized
in voluminous styles as opposed to form-fitting ensembles featured in newspapers or designed in high-end shops like Cherita Couture in Cotonou. Yet, in
mission programs, girls learned techniques like knitting, hand embroidery,
lace-making, and draping (pinning mannequins during the design process),
which many workshop-trained clothes-makers often did not know.[19] These
programs were some of the many Catholic missions and centers that trained
women in couture dame while providing "civic and moral instruction" on how
to be upstanding wives and mothers in their communities.

Along with their emphasis on sewing for the household and conservative women's dress, missions introduced two key aspects of couture dame that had significant effects on Béninois tailoring—the use of hand crank machines over treadle machines and the tendency to take on dozens of girls as apprentices. As chapter 2 showed, colonial-era missions and even some local colonial laws prohibited women's use of treadle machines over fears about their effects on female fertility. After independence, the belief that the vigorous movements needed to operate the treadle might cause miscarriage was still prevalent in both Béninois and foreign-run domestic education programs, and women continued to learn to sew on hand crank machines despite their inefficiency relative to treadle machines. Additionally, centers like those in Dassa, Abomey, and Davougon structured themselves as schools as opposed to workshops and admitted large classes of girls to learn domestic skills. Agadame recalled that during her time at Foyer Saint Monique in Abomey, she was one of forty-five students learning to sew.[20] At Davougon, one woman noted that incoming classes had up to thirty-five apprentices, although the number fell to almost half by the second year as girls left the program for personal reasons or because they (allegedly) did not like the work.[21] Girls often lived at these centers as "orphans," supported in part by charities, even though most of them had at least one living parent. Practically, these mission programs contributed to the femininization of the craft, as the number of girls trained in sewing rapidly increased. The mission origins of couture dame would also be key to seamstresses' refashioning themselves as respectable *Mesdames* when faced with increasing urban anonymity and a grim economy during the Kérékou years and into the twenty-first century. Although state and mission efforts to promote certain fashions and sewing practices influenced the craft knowledge of seamstresses, women's ability to retailor notions of embodied labor, prestige, and respectability was also tied to their control over a new urban space—the tailor's workshop.

Urbanization and the Expansion
of Workshop-Based Production

It's the *villageois* (countryfolk) who come from their villages to order
[clothing] in the market.
    —Emilienne Agbo, Adandokpodji Daxo, Abomey, June 8, 2015

In the era of independence, male tailors refined their craft in the open-air markets where they innovated new forms and collaborated with each other, clients, fabric sellers, and acouta vendors to make clothes for ordinary people. Yet even amid this system, there were a few independent workshops alongside throughfares and minor roads. In these workshops, men made high-end outfits for civil servants and wealthy traders, and a handful of middle-class women, often the wives of civil servants, made clothing for women of a similar social status. But by the 1970s, workshop-based production would eclipse market production as the site of tailoring moved from central markets to walled-in spaces, leaving only a few male tailors, those doing taillerie simple in the market. As Agbo makes clear in her statement, only "villageois," a term often used in a derogatory manner to describe rural residents and their ways, would order in the market. Popular opinion had shifted until no self-respecting urbanite would order an ensemble in a market, and market tailoring became the domain of basic repairs and inexpensive outfits for the community's most impoverished. In this way, workshops became entangled with the physical development of the city and changing notions around urban space. State development priorities, infrastructure projects, and the marketing strategies of tailors collided in creating the urban workshop.

Tailors and seamstresses served the growing populations of Abomey and Bohicon, two towns that were vastly different in terms of overall aesthetics and urban infrastructures. Abomey, as the regional capital of the Zou, was an administrative seat flush with civil servants receiving regular salaries while Bohicon had more industrial and commercial development. The Zou region was one of the most densely populated regions in Bénin, although most people lived in small towns and villages within a short distance of one another.[22] In fact, at independence, Bénin was one of the least urbanized coastal West African countries.[23] But cities were growing, especially in the years following the Kérékou revolution, and state planners hoped to slow the course of urbanization, or at least encourage migration to regional towns instead of the coastal cities, by investing in the infrastructure of towns like Abomey and Bohicon.[24] The national government estimated Abomey grew slightly at 2.2 percent and Bohicon at 3.2 percent between 1979 and 1983, and by 1983 the populations of the narrowly defined city centers were 42,021 and 25,840, respectively.[25] But these numbers are also misleading since the borders of Bohicon were in flux and the town rarely held the status of a municipality before the 1990s, often in an effort to appease both civil and traditional powers in Abomey.[26]

While the official position was that Bohicon had a smaller population, Abomey was a much sleepier town than its neighbor, and its historic buildings, festivals, and residents' clothing reinforced its image as unchanged since the precolonial era. Abomey, as the capital of the Dahomey kingdom, had mostly been burned down at conquest, but beginning in the 1930s domestic and international investors had helped reconstruct historic sites, which made up a large portion of central Abomey and gave the town its traditional feel of mudbrick palaces and public festival sites.[27] The palace and local heads of clan (Dáa) actively kept up a schedule of ceremonies and festivals and retained significant local authority in the town. Sartorially distinguished from other Abomey residents, Dáa sported tchanka and wrapped pagne as they presided over their families and local communities.

In part to counter the local power of Fon traditional authorities, the Kérékou government constructed Place Goho in the early 1970s. This public square, built on the periphery of Abomey and along the road to Bohicon, opened in a November 30, 1974, ceremony where President Kérékou declared Marxism-Leninism official state policy. Exactly a year later he returned to the same spot to announce that the country was renamed the People's Republic of Bénin. The choice to make both announcements in Abomey, the former seat of precolonial power, was intentional, and Kérékou argued that "[Béninois] must categorically reject all history founded on the magnificence of a dynasty" and that the history of the kingdom needed to be deemphasized in the contemporary political moment.[28] Kérékou's announcements, along with the urban construction project, were part of a larger effort to marginalize the Fon within Béninois politics (Kérékou was a northerner) and within the national history of the independent state. Designers planned the square as a community park, in contrast to Abomey's preexisting public spaces that were either tied to the precolonial palace complex or adjacent to the colonial-era houses and office buildings in the northwest of town. Somewhat paradoxically, the centerpiece of Place Goho was a large bronze statue of Béhanzin, who, with his two wars against the French, was revived as an anti-colonial and anti-imperial figure, mirroring Kérékou's own rejection of the West and liberal democracy.

Ancillary aspects of the Place Goho project expanded the urban infrastructure of the town, creating more public leisure sites where clothing designers might promote their styles and laying the networks of water and electricity that facilitated workshop construction. The project included a stadium and a hotel that a writer for *Daho Express* described as having "charm that one cannot find in the *cité* of the Kings."[29] Other improvements included paving five kilometers of Abomey streets, installing streetlights from Djimè to Abomey, and extending the electrical grid to "illuminate a larger part of the city," including the Houndjroto market and the police station.[30] The expansion of the electrical grid in particular allowed tailors to easily continue production into the night and avoid the poor lighting and danger of kerosene lamps. The highly publicized project was one of the first of a series of monuments and public squares that the Kérékou government built in cities and towns across the country over the next decade.[31] Like Goho, these sites were built on the periphery of rapidly urbanizing cities and towns, and most invoked the Kérékou Revolution with a vaguely Marxist-Leninist aesthetic. In Abomey, the Goho project provided an especially stark contrast to the center of town with its winding paths and mud buildings, although the two vastly different approaches to urban construction continued to coexist.

While tailors and seamstresses found clients among Abomey's many civil servants, Bohicon had a stronger local economy that created a growing market for tailored everyday wear. Abomey's physical growth was constrained by restrictions meant to preserve the historical town and, according to a retired civil servant, by traditional authorities who wielded significant power and resisted the construction of roads, industry, and other infrastructure.[32] Bohicon, in contrast, had no such restrictions and was a crossroads between Bénin's main north–south and east–west routes as well as an important stop on the railway. In the years following independence, Bohicon became the site of most industry, services, and utilities in the interior of the new country. The first bank in the region opened in Bohicon in 1970, and although there were only a handful of factories in Bénin, many of these were in Bohicon, including ones that processed cotton, palm oil, and jute sacks.[33] The jute factory employed dozens of tailors who worked round the clock on a three-shift schedule, and many of these men moonlighted sewing clothing for clients.[34] Utilities were also better developed in Bohicon than in Abomey. Even after the water lines were extended to Abomey as part of the 72 Goho project, the water "flowed abundant" in Bohicon, leading one writer of *Daho Express* to remark that "the inhabitants of Abomey cast envious looks at their neighbors in Bohicon."[35] As these two cities grew in very different ways, tailoring continued to expand, and people sought out new ways of ordering clothing without going to a central market.

Proximity to high-traffic areas and connection to water and especially electricity grids influenced where tailors and seamstresses chose to open workshops. The best locations were on thoroughfares to central markets, churches, and schools. After having a workshop in Cotonou for a few years, seamstress Célestine Dangbé moved back to Abomey to open a shop on the road from the Houndjroto market to the Adja-speaking regions to the southwest. This location appealed to her because, she remembered, "there were no artisans, but there were many people who passed by."[36] Thérèse Hountondji, another woman who also opened her shop next to Houndjroto, did so because "a lot of villageois passed by," and she anticipated tapping into the market of women traveling from rural areas to Houndjroto to trade. Her shop stayed open late to catch women leaving the market, hoping that some of their profits might be spent on fabric and left with a tailor.[37] The strategic placement of their workshops brought sewing from the central markets or the cloistered home production of middle-class wives into the street. When workshops like Hountondji's attracted clients and apprentices from the countryside, they also created new loci for the networks that connected city to village.

Tailors, both male and female, often built shops in spaces rented from relatives or in front of their families' compounds. Houses in interior Bénin were organized into compounds where multiple structures surrounded a central courtyard. A high wall, made either of mud brick or cinder block, encircled the compound, and a single wood or metal door provided entry. While residents of a compound were often related, in urban areas many of the homes were rentals, which meant that unrelated individuals shared common spaces for washing clothes and cooking as well as latrines. Owners occasionally built shops into the exterior walls of the compounds, which they rented out or used themselves as boutiques (small neighborhood stores) or as ateliers for tailors, barbers, photographers, and other artisans (fig. 5.5). Individual tailors and seamstresses often had access to shops on family land or they worked out a deal with a neighbor.[38] But these arrangements, based on personal relationships, sometimes went awry, and shops might be closed due to squabbles with families or landlords.[39]

Whether on a main thoroughfare or in front of a home, tailors and seamstresses sought new strategies to differentiate their shops from each other and other businesses in a changing urban landscape. They started to hang signs to promote their shops, altering the visual experience of people walking throughout the towns. Other than government offices, there were few signs in the Zou before artisans, bars, and shops began identifying their businesses to potential clients. Lékolihoui Djibidisse, featured prominently in chapter 3, was one of the four or five master tailors working out of Bohicon's Ganhi market in the 1950s. A few decades later, he moved his workshop to a storefront

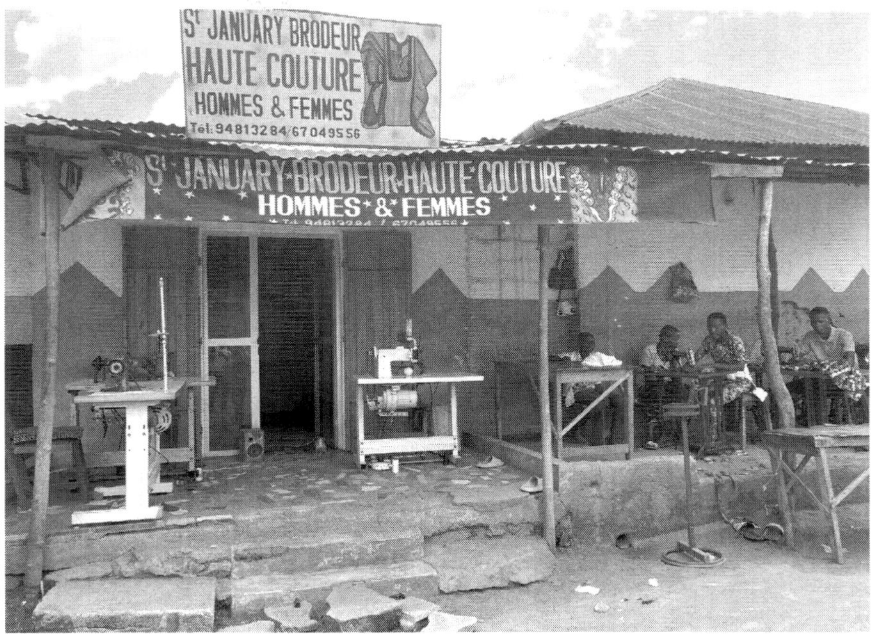

Figure 5.5. St. January Haute Couture Workshop, Bohicon, June 27, 2001. Photo by author.

outside his family compound in a neighborhood northwest of the Ganhi market. Although he was unable to read, Djibidisse ordered a metal sign to affix on his compound wall in hopes of attracting clients.[40] Djibidissé's sign contained basic information about him and his business, including his title, "Master Tailor," name, and address. Later, tailors and seamstresses ordered signs from local artists who painted images of clothing and the tailor's tools—the machine, the measuring tape, and scissors—alongside basic textual information about the tailor. Other artisans chose names for their workshops and wrote them on the sign, such as "St January" in figure 5.5, hoping that it might differentiate them from their competitors. Shop names might reference religious figures or, during the Kérékou years, Marxist symbols such as "Red Star" or "November Revolution," a reference to the date of Kérékou's declaration of Marxism-Leninism in Place Goho.

The most successful tailors and seamstresses installed glass windows and created storefront displays, allowing potential clients to absorb the newest styles and judge the skill of the craftsperson.[41] In Abomey, Olga Dokponou had finished her apprenticeship in men's and women's fashions in Cotonou and did not have a local base of clients. At first she tried to dress mannequins in front of her shop, but they would quickly become covered in the red dust that blanketed everything in the dry season. Dokponou saved up her profits to install glass windows and, behind them, strategically place lights to illuminate her mannequins.[42] These brightly lit windows filled with mannequins sporting colorful wax prints or the starched grays, browns, and blacks of polyester-blend suits created a rupture in the dust-covered landscapes of the towns. Storefronts also led to a new type of shopping experience for Béninois by fostering distance between seller and buyer. In the market, even a slight glance at a piece of fabric, pot, or tomato led the vendor to initiate bartering, but windows distanced the shopper at the same time that they helped remake the city.

In the interiors of their shops, tailors and seamstresses strategically displayed the material culture of their craft expertise. As chapter 4 showed, master artisans prominently hung their framed artisanal diplomas, often in plain view of the street when the door was open. These documents were supplemented with other things like scissors or the paddle from a palmatoire (humorous ceremonial paddling of an apprentice), serving as evidence of the artisan's master status. Machines sat at the front of workshops so that tailors and seamstresses could take advantage of natural light but also because the sight and sound of a machine drew the eyes and ears of potential clients. Behind the machines, there were colorful stacks of outfits ready to be picked up and piles of untailored fabric. Clients occasionally stored their fabric in their tailor's workshop while they saved up the money to pay the advance for zippers, buttons, and other flourishes so that the tailor could begin her work. If tailors and seamstresses could not afford three-dimensional imported mannequins, they hung locally crafted mannequins to display their styles. A photograph hanging on the wall in the workshop of Marié-Rose Kponsenon showed two mannequins dressed in her creations (fig. 5.6). While she used the mannequins to advertise her talents, she also used the photograph of the dressed mannequins to show these styles after refreshing her display.[43] As apprenticeship became more elaborate and as the numbers of clothes-makers increased, the workshop served as a depository and an exhibition space for the things that signified one's abilities in the craft.

However, moving production from central markets to workshops also created new challenges for tailors and seamstresses. In contrast to craftspeople

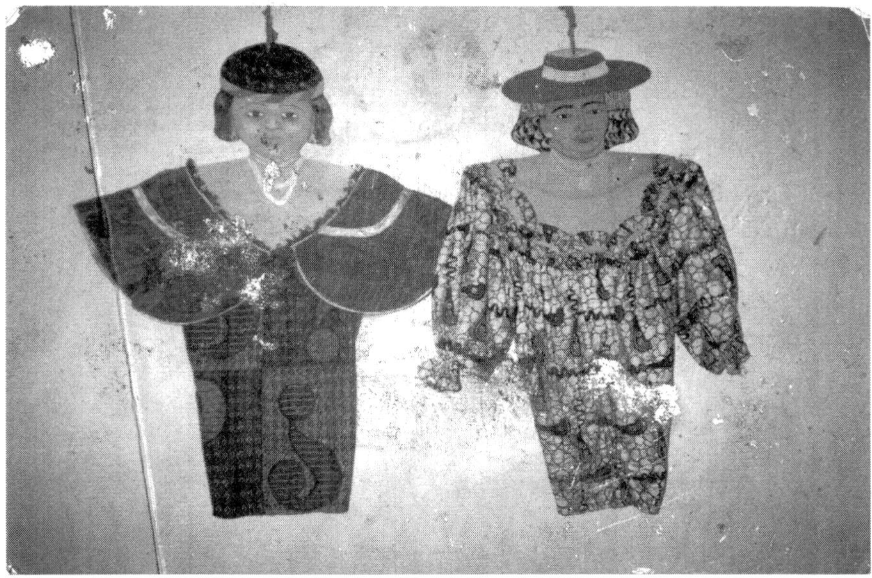

Figure 5.6. Photograph of mannequins on the wall in a workshop, Bohicon, circa 1990s. Courtesy of Marié-Rose Kponsenon.

who worked in their homes or brought their machines to market, tailors and seamstresses in workshops left all their tools, clothing, and unfinished products in the shop each night when they went home after work. Locked doors might be breached, and machines, fabric, and clothing might be stolen. Tailor Marc Agbandjaï described multiple break-ins at his shop in Abomey and how, during one incident, the thieves also took his diploma.[44] Shoddy electrical wiring might lead to fires that destroyed the livelihoods of tailors or seamstresses who lost all their tools and still had to reimburse clients for burnt or stolen fabric.[45] Neighborhood workshops also occasionally led to disagreements among clothes-makers, particularly when one moved into the territory of another. Edmonde Semassou chose the location of her Abomey workshop because she saw that there were no other seamstresses on the street, although it was relatively busy. When she first leased the shop, she noticed a new construction project next door and begged the landlord not to rent the space to another woman tailor. But he did, and the two women operated shops next door to each other for over twenty-five years. Although their apprentices had open fights that the two older women often had to resolve, they also developed strategies for avoiding direct conflict with each other. For example, if one of Semassou's neighbor's clients was unhappy with an outfit or felt like the tailor lacked the skill to make it, the client discreetly passed cloth through Semassou's window. Later, the seamstress and her new client would meet in the nearby mechanic's shop where Semassou took their measurements and discussed the outfit.[46] Workshops heightened competition among tailors and seamstresses, but they also allowed them to manage it.

The shift to workshop-based production also changed the relationships between craftspeople, fabric sellers, and the local government. In the market, tailors consulted with fabric and acouta vendors, but the move to workshops made this relationship untenable. Many tailors and seamstresses attempted to exert more influence over final designs and to increase their profits by selling fabric in their shops. Some seamstresses had carpenters outfit doors with racks where waxes and fancy prints might be displayed while others bought glass display cases. Workshop-based production also created more opportunity for state surveillance. When a man or woman worked within the home, they were able to avoid taxation.[47] In the central market, tailors paid authorities small sums on a regular basis, but in workshops, tax collectors assumed that makers had more resources and attempted to assess taxes by machine or apprentice. Master artisans successfully avoided paying their entire bill by sending apprentices home and hiding machines on tax day, but most paid something if they operated out of an identifiable roadside space, receiving a receipt in return.[48] Ultimately the move to workshops changed how people made clothes and interacted with each other, clients, and local authorities and altered how Bénin's cities looked and how Béninois experienced daily activities such as walking and shopping.

Most importantly, workshops were urban spaces where people came together to do more than just order clothes and do fittings. Both men and women met in workshops to gossip, to discuss politics, and to enact local and cosmopolitan cultures. Deciding on a style, taking measurements, and doing alterations was a long process; clients might spend an hour or more in a workshop, and an outfit might take form over multiple visits. Clothesmakers also occasionally called upon each other—usually men or women who apprenticed under the same master—in workshops and might work together on a large order or a tricky article of clothing. Neighbors also dropped into the workshop to chat with tailors, seamstresses, and clients, although adults usually ignored the presence of apprentices or talked around them.

The conversations among masters, clients, and passersby sometimes focused on clothing—the newest styles and their costs, who was wearing them, who was not, and what they said about the wearer. Béninois public spaces like parks or squares were tied to contentious political pasts whether precolonial, colonial, or revolutionary. Patriarchal institutions such as Dáa (heads of clan) and secret societies, especially the cult of Orò, monitored women's movements and circulation within the city. The communist state was also concerned with surveilling the population and used the threat of the political prison in the northern city of Ségbana to quell dissent. Workshops served as sites where small groups of Béninois could freely meet beyond the bounds of state, traditional, or religious authorities. Rooted in the development of the city and the expansion of urban infrastructures, workshops contributed to the remaking of the city and the experience of moving and living within it, but they were also sites of leisure, community, and connection. For women, this aspect of workshops was paramount, both drawing women to take up the craft and helping them to establish themselves as prominent and respectable women.

Seamstresses in the City: Couture Dame and Female Respectability

The world changed, there was development. Many women thought "I need to know how to do something before I marry." Before, it was not like that, your parents brought you to the field and you worked, you did fieldwork with them, but today, it is not like that.

—Marié-Rose Kponsenon, Houndonho, Bohicon, September 2, 2015

Growing up in the small lakeside village of Bopa in the 1970s, Séraphine Houngbandan made occasional trips to Abomey's Houndjroto market. During one of these excursions, she first saw a seamstress and, impressed by the woman, her work, and her workshop, begged her father to set her up in an apprenticeship. But he refused and insisted that she continue to make *lio* (balls of akassa, or fermented corn fufu) for sale in the local market and to work alongside her sisters in his fields. Dissatisfied with his response, Houngbandan stole some food from her family and fled on foot to Abomey to find the seamstress, but the woman would not take her on without parental permission, so Houngbandan lied and said she was an orphan. Without any money for contract fees, Houngbandan spent most of her time performing domestic tasks in return for scraps of food instead of learning the craft. Discouraged and hungry, a teenage Houngbandan threatened to throw herself in a well until another resident of Abomey, who was also from Bopa, financed her return to the village. There Houngbandan married, but the relationship between her and husband fell apart after she failed to conceive.[49]

With one marriage behind her and now in her early twenties, Houngbandan returned to Abomey to apprentice under a different master seamstress, but she still could not afford a contract and turned to panhandling for her monthly apprenticeship fees. This period of her life had a profound impact on Houngbandan, who recalled how Abomeans mocked her for her advanced age (for an apprentice), poverty, and "villageois" ways. Eventually someone in town told Houngbandan's patronne (master) that she was homeless, and the woman took her in for a few years while she finished her apprenticeship. But again Houngbandan's progression to master was blocked by libération fees. She eventually met a man who offered to pay them, but this plan also collapsed when the man lost his job and, according to Houngbandan, "became crazy" (*devenir fou*). Houngbandan then met another man and together they moved to Abeokuta, Nigeria, where she worked odd jobs, including as a mason's assistant, hauling bags of concrete on her head. Through this aventure, she saved enough money to buy a sewing machine and open a workshop in Abeokuta, where she found clients among the town's many Béninois migrants. Houngbandan ended up leaving this man after he stole from her, and then she was forced to leave Nigeria when the government expelled migrants in 1983. Back in Abomey, she opened a workshop near the Houndjroto market where she had first seen the woman who had inspired her drive to become a seamstress.

Over the next few decades, her shop gradually became a success, and by 2015 she had liberated over sixty apprentices and had an adopted daughter attending university. Houngbandan ended her narrative of her life by telling how, despite her father's lack of aid and support for her, she had paid for his funeral. She noted "that among all of my father's children, I am the only one with an occupation now, the only one with some value."[50] Tailoring had provided a route for Houngbandan to go from a self-declared exploited village girl to a well-respected maman and a patronne of an important Abomean tailoring shop. Houngbandan, along with many other women, used the craft to tailor new roles for themselves within the community and to create new personas as prominent, independent women.

Houngbandan's path to becoming a grande dame in Abomey was atypical in the number of challenges she faced, but her story was also similar to other oral histories collected from seamstresses and their descriptions of what the craft meant to them personally. Even her framing of her life story as an epic journey of overcoming obstacles, particularly exploitative men, was part of a larger narrative pattern used by seamstresses of a similar age. Unlike the middle-class women who learned sewing in mission and state programs, the women who entered the craft after the 1970s often lacked formal education and were usually the daughters of farmers. They moved from small villages to larger towns to study couture dame under women who either had formal mission or state training or had been trained by someone who did. For these women, opening a workshop was key to their strategy of re-creating themselves in the city. Tailor's workshop was a place where a woman could achieve a level of autonomy, opportunity, and respectability not available to them in other more mobile occupations or even marriage.

Girls and women faced a limited number of choices in choosing a craft or profession, but workshop-based sewing appealed to women across the socio-economic spectrum. Olga Dokponou left school to apprentice in haute couture during the 1983 *année blanche* (a school strike that was so long it forced a "cleared year" where country-wide no students progressed to the next class). Already a teenager and completely idle due to the strike, she saw other young women of her own age making money as seamstresses and decided that the craft was a more stable route to material success than formal education, especially when most of the well-paying positions in the civil service were occupied by men.[51] Other women, like Houngbandan, had little formal education and had left the countryside for the city. Women with no formal education or connections had limited options for supporting themselves, and most chose between tailoring, hairdressing, farming (if one had land), market trading, making and selling prepared foods, working in bars, or finding a man to support them. When asked why she pursued an apprenticeship in tailoring, one woman responded, "You cannot stay stripped to the waist out in the world, so I prefer sewing so I can dress myself and my family."[52] Becoming a seamstress was often a pragmatic choice for women. In oral histories, almost all men, but only a small minority of women, described their interest in clothes and fashion as driving their career choice. Instead, women emphasized the redemptive qualities of the craft and the space of the workshop over their desire to make beautiful things.

One of the most appealing aspects of clothes-making was its new location of production—the workshop—and the possibilities that the space offered to women looking to recraft themselves as autonomous and upstanding community members. Christian missions and domestic education programs stressed that women's work took place in the home and that women's respectability was linked both to their modestly clothed bodily presentation and to their location in the home. In the increasingly anonymous spaces of Bénin's growing cities, women like Houngbandan could ground themselves in a tailor's workshop, a particularly identifiable space, unlike most other working women such as market women and vendors of prepared foods, who sold their goods or plied their trade in the street. Women who sewed couture dame in workshops were literally in walled-off female spaces where they taught the craft to girls and served women clients. The seamstress's workshop became a uniquely female sphere in Bénin, even more so than homes, which rarely contained women's domestic labor since much of the work of cooking and cleaning was done outdoors and which had men, family or otherwise, moving freely in and out of them. As women created the workshop as a feminine and respectable space, they also helped remake the city, creating a feminine alternative to the market and the otherwise male spaces of both the precolonial and colonial cities.

Béninois often contrasted sewing with hairdressing to explain the relationship between mobility, space, and respectability. Hairdressing and tailoring were the two crafts available to women who lacked formal education or other resources. The choice of tailoring might be due to practicality and self-sufficiency. For example, Marié-Rose Kponsenon chose one craft over the other with the justification "if I buy a pagne, I can sew my own blouse, one that I have in my head, that I can make it, but a hairdresser cannot do her own hair."[53] But other women decided to become tailors because of perceptions of mobile hairdressers as lacking in respectability when compared to immobile seamstresses. In a 1971 photograph (fig. 5.7), an Abomean hairdresser braids a child's hair in a courtyard surrounded by children and men selling appliqué tapestries, mostly to tourists.[54] Hairdressers often traveled to people's homes or the spaces in front of them to work, putting them in the enclosed spaces of nonrelative men or, as in the picture, opening them up to their gaze. Seamstress Jeanne Hanou contrasted the mobility of hairdressers with the stability of seamstresses. She explained, "Girls who do hair move about a lot, they crawl along everywhere. But sewing! When a girl comes to her workshop, it's to work, when she leaves it is to go home."[55] The mobility of hairdressers affected perceptions of the women who worked in the craft, leading some people to associate them with sex work. Abomean seamstress Hélène Ahonon taught herself hairdressing before doing an apprenticeship in tailoring. She claimed

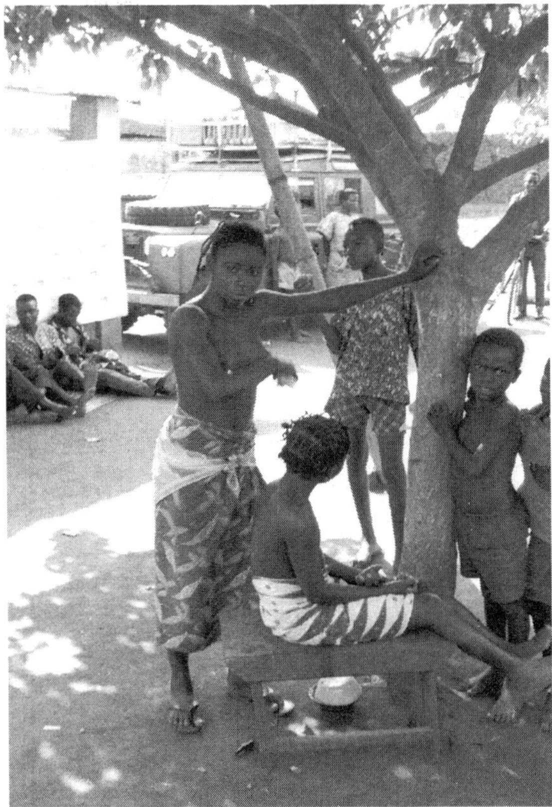

Figure 5.7. Hairdresser in the street, Abomey, Bénin, 1971. Photograph by Eliot Elisofon. EEPA EENG 01332, Eliot Elisofon Photographic Archives, National Museum of African Art, Smithsonian Institution.

to have been a very successful hairdresser but changed her profession because "here, people consider the majority of women hairdressers as prostitutes. . . . I stopped doing hair because people considered me as a prostitute."[56] By opening a tailor's workshop, Ahonon believed, she had changed the community's perception of her and achieved a new level of respectability.

While many seamstresses like Houngbandan were unmarried or divorced, others negotiated with fiancés and husbands to learn couture dame, which both spouses recognized as particularly suited to aspirations of middle-class respectability. In towns and cities, older forms of marriage organized around bridewealth exchange and uniting families gave way to multiple types of relationships, from cohabitation where, after having children, men and women assumed the titles of "husband" and "wife" to elaborate Christian ceremonies among elites.[57] Craft and marriage might overlap when contract and libération fees became part of betrothal negotiations. Husbands and wives usually kept separate accounts, but these same fees might also become part of financial negotiations within a marriage. For example, Jeanette Agadame (fig. 5.4) attended Foyer Sainte Monique to become a seamstress after a conversation with her future fiancé. Agadame's mother sold dried fish in the market in Agbainzoun, and Agadame had imagined that she too would enter into market trade once she left her family home. But then she met and started making plans for the future with a young man in his final year of middle school (*collège*). They decided that if he was going to continue on to Porto-Novo for high school (*lycée*) and eventually become a hunnukún (intellectual), she needed a profession beyond market commerce. Becoming a seamstress seemed like a good fit.[58] Echoing the assertions of missionaries and the realities of women in the craft, Agadame and her fiancé interpreted tailoring as a job particularly suited to a middle-class woman, and while her fiancé prepared himself to enter into a career in the civil service, she trained at a mission institution to become a seamstress. In this way, women used the craft to both buttress and subvert gender roles as domestic women—taking on the role of a middle-class housewife who sewed but also using that skill to establish themselves as entrepreneurial women.

The emplacement of tailoring within specific, legible spaces made it appealing to men and women interested in curtailing the movement and visibility of women in the city. Beyond his middle-class aspirations, Agadame's husband specifically did not want her to engage in commerce because market women traveled. She remembered, "He did not want me to go out like that, he wanted me to stay [in the workshop] where he can see me."[59] Za-Kpota tailor Victoire Glinman abandoned her plan to open a shop and decided to work out of her home after a conversation with her husband. She recalled, "It was a question of jealousy between my husband and me. When I received my diploma, he did not want me to open a workshop on the side of the road." She continued, "If I was on the side of the road, many [men] would see me and it would lure them in."[60] Although Glinman's husband took an extreme position, other women and their husbands agreed that seamstresses' workshops were female spaces, providing fewer opportunities for women to consort with other men or even providing women relief from being exploited or attacked by men. Bohicon tailor Jeanne Hanou was a rarity among seamstresses in the town. She had finished technical school with a certificate in stenography and typing before she married one of Bohicon's most prominent businessmen. Once married, however, her husband no longer wanted her to work as a secretary, and he set her up in an apprenticeship with a local seamstress. Although much older than the other apprentices, she quickly finished and opened up her own shop, complete with fancy glass windows and imported mannequins.[61] When Hanou had worked in the closed spaces of an office with a man and under his authority, perhaps her husband worried about exploitation or consensual adultery—or the perception of it. Yet in her own shop, Hanou was the master.

While the spaces of the seamstress's workshop afforded a measure of bodily autonomy for the master, it also reinforced her ability to exercise authority over her apprentices. Seamstresses began to take on large cohorts of dependent apprentices, increasing their prestige within the artisanat (artisan sector) and the larger community. Apprentices usually called their master maman, even if she was childless, and she achieved a level of respect not usually afforded to childless women. The notion of a woman with children or dependents as more respectable drew not just on notions of Christian motherhood but also on long-standing Fon ideas about the value of motherhood.[62] Seamstresses sometimes required their apprentices to wear *uniforme* (uniforms), materializing their attachment to the workshop and its master and creating equivalency among them. Uniforms were usually made from inexpensive fabrics tailored into shirts and tops or jumper dresses. The visual tableau of similarly dressed bodies reinforced perceptions of the power and prestige of the seamstress, which was made more striking as the numbers of apprentices grew. For example, Agadame liberated more than sixty apprentices before she retired, a Bohicon seamstress claimed to have trained about seventy apprentices, and another Bohicon seamstress, Amélie Gnancadja, liberated over one hundred apprentices during her career.[63] Such large numbers were unique to couture dame shops and vastly exceeded the numbers that men trained in both haute couture shops and taillerie simple stalls, which was usually five or fewer apprentices over the course of a career. For a woman with many apprentices, her networks and prestige grew larger when these new masters took on their own apprentices. When a seamstress became older and no longer worked, former apprentices might stop by and give small cash gifts to their former master to show respect and continue their relationship.[64] These multiple generations of women approached the master seamstress not only as an authority in tailoring but as someone who could provide them advice and help in other aspects of life.

The couture dame workshop became a place that in many ways cloistered seamstresses while also permitting women to assert a measure of power over their own lives and those of their apprentices. Although local authorities and husbands might be better able to surveil women's work, sexuality, and profits in a clearly defined space like a workshop, for women like Houngbandan, Agadame, and Hanou, the possibility of workshop-based production provided a path to social mobility and personal autonomy unafforded by other crafts and professions open to women. It gave them the power to negotiate relationships with fathers, husbands, and other men and permitted them to become a maman to dependent girls. Women used the workshop to carve out new political and economic roles as women entrepreneurs. These spaces also helped remake cities and became one of the only women-centered spaces, a place where women could get together to talk politics or about their neighbors or, perhaps most importantly, to discuss styles and what it meant to wear them. As the patronne of her shop, a seamstress also led the conversations within its walls.

Working in Pagne: Workshop Production and Women's Fashion

A visitor to Bénin at the turn of the twenty-first century would have been struck by the sheer amount of colorful print fabrics worn by men, women, and children. Men wore these fabrics tailored into bounba, as did children, but women's styles varied from women's bounba with unadorned voluminous shirts over wrappers to tight form-fitting ensembles embellished with pipping, flounces, slits, sheer inserts, and other flourishes. This colorful palette of everyday life has recent origins in places like Abomey and Bohicon, where most people did not have the means to purchase the Dutch waxes that had long dominated as coastal prestige fabrics. The newly accessible sartorial regime was rooted in technological developments elsewhere in the world, especially new fabric printing techniques in China, but also to the expansion of the local tailoring industry where women in couture dame workshops began to dominate clothes-making. Seamstresses' expertise over matters of fashion, and also accessible forms of respectability, helped facilitate the spread of fitted prints

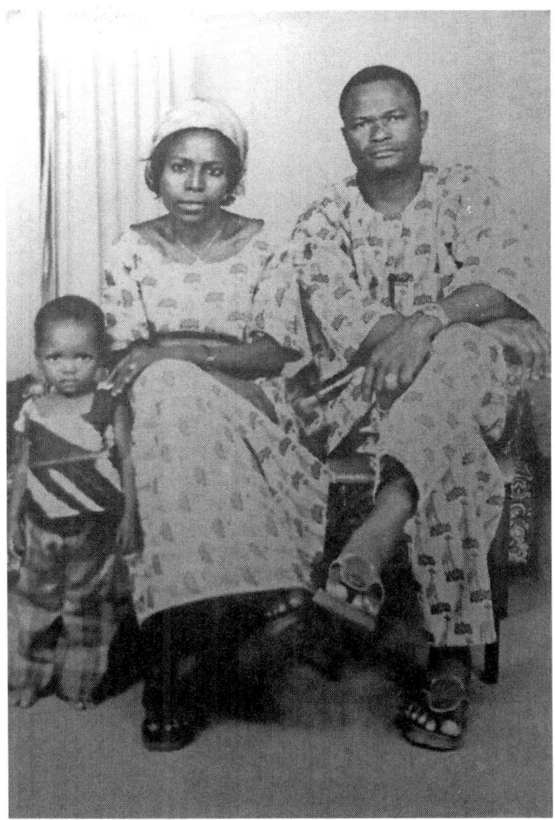

Figure 5.8. Family in matching fabric, undated.
Courtesy of Fidel Ouèjo.

as everyday dress for Béninois women in the final decades of the twentieth century.

The least labor-intensive outfit that seamstresses made and the standard wear for both young and old women was bounba sewn from pagne. In figure 5.8, a Bohicon couple wears men and women's bounbas in a uniform of *même tissu* (same fabric). Similar to men's bounba, women's bounba was fashioned as a two-piece outfit made of the same fabric on top and bottom. Women wore a wrapper on the bottom, carefully tucked or tied at the waist, combined with a tunic that was usually made with a neck wide enough to be pulled over the head. The wide neckline meant it might fall to the upper arm, revealing the tops of the shoulders, although occasionally seamstresses might add a snap to attach the shirt to a bra strap and prevent slippage. Other than occasional changes to sleeve length, women's bounba underwent fewer modifications than the men's version where buttons, zippers, embroidery, and fittedness changed along with the cut of the pants. The two bounbas in the photograph also show how seamstresses used fabric to complement their designs. In the man's bounba, the maker cut and sewed the outfit so that all the giraffes in the pattern faced the same direction while the seamstress who made the women's bounba sewed the sleeves with the giraffe on its side in order to match the way that the pattern would be worn as pagne over the legs. A women's bounba required two pagnes, or four meters—two for the shirt and two worn on the bottom as a wrapper. Since fabric was often sold as a *demi-pièce*, or six meters in length, this left a two-meter pagne that women often used as a head wrapper, a loose piece of cloth to attach children to their back, or a folded length of cloth casually draped over the shoulder to highlight married status. Occasionally, seamstresses sewed the third pagne into clothing that children might wear on days that their mothers wore their bounba, creating an opportunity for expressing relationships through *même tissu*.

While bounba was the standard dress for women and girls of all ages, seamstresses also encouraged clients to order fitted ensembles of a more tailored blouse worn with a matching skirt or wrapper, a style called a *modèle* (French for "design"). The addition of a third pagne, worn in versatile ways as with a bounba, made an outfit *complet* (complete). Blouses might be sleeveless or have tight-fitting or voluminous sleeves of varying lengths. Seamstresses often looked to catalogs from Europe for inspiration. For example, the global trend of puffed sleeves in the late 1980s was equally popular in Béninois modèles, and as one seamstress fondly remembered, "There was a time when we used one meter of cloth to make the sleeves, only the sleeves! During that time, if you did not sew sleeves like that, you did not sew."[65] Women named blouses by the *comin* (collar or neckline), which was usually the part of the outfit that gave seamstresses the most opportunity for creativity in designing and sewing. An especially popular although not trendy shirt was called *hohononcomin*, in which fabric draped from the neckline, making it wearable by women in all stages of pregnancy.[66] Seamstresses used techniques such as honeycomb smocking (*nid d'abeille*) on comin with elastic thread, which allowed women to wear form-fitting styles without buttons or zippers.[67] The popularity of specific styles of blouses changed frequently and earlier styles were later revived, regaining popularity after many years.

Seamstresses often designed modèles as conservative dress meant for older women, but there were also more revealing and form-fitting versions meant for younger women. *Modèles jeunes filles* (young women's designs) consisted of a blouse that was usually much tighter than those created for older women, worn with a matching skirt.[68] As people moved to cities, "youth" categories became more prevalent as more young men and women delayed marriage.[69] Young people in cities also began to wrap their pagnes differently. Instead of gathering the fabric in front, they would pull the fabric taut in the front and tuck it in the back, showing off more of their bodies.[70] Others adopted skirts instead of wrapping pagne. As explored in previous chapters, ordinary women—those who worked as market traders, farmers, and artisans—rarely, if ever, wore skirts, preferring wrappers throughout most of the twentieth century. Middle-class women often wore dresses, and young urbanites and professionals embraced miniskirts beginning in the 1960s. But with an ever-increasing number of seamstresses, skirt wearing became more widespread. Skirts were often tightly fitted, with embellishments along the back seam or around the bottom. As *zemidjans* (taxi-motos) became a more available form of inexpensive transportation, women chose styles that facilitated getting on and off the back of a motorcycle. For example, mermaid skirts were fitted through the hips and thighs with a separate panel below the knees forming a *jupe ovale* (oval skirt). This design allowed wearers to hike up their skirts and grab fabric from the back through their legs, pulling it forward, in order to straddle the backs of motorcycles without revealing any skin above their knees. For young women, designs like this were revealing enough to be fashionable but also allowed a measure of modesty, without the dangers of the "side-saddle" approach to taxi-motos that women in more form-fitting skirts employed.

Similar to the market for menswear, seamstresses and their clients used images and samples to decide upon styles for skirts and blouses. Individuals continued to order French catalogs when they could afford to, but the growth of local photography between independence and the 1990s significantly changed the relationship between the two crafts, facilitating new ways of managing and negotiating women's styles. When seamstresses were particularly happy with a modèle, they called a photographer to take a picture of it, and these photographs were kept in workshop albums to be brought out for clients placing orders.[71] Tailors, seamstresses, and photographers also worked together to produce images of modèles for sale locally, and both clients and clothes-makers purchased these images to inspire designs.[72] Seamstresses used these photographs to advise clients on which designs worked for their body type and to dissuade clients from ordering out-of-style garments.[73] Samples also became more readily available with the influx of acouta beginning in the 1980s, providing clothes-makers with a new source of fabric for backings, linings, and finishes of all sorts.[74] Some tailors and seamstresses made new outfits from salvaged secondhand textiles, while others repaired them into wearable outfits.[75] Acouta vendors were often former seamstresses, which created another overlap between the markets for secondhand and tailor-made. One woman explained that she switched to selling secondhand because she preferred the on-the-spot exchanges of market trading to the drawn-out process of working with clients on made-to-order clothing. She declared, "It annoyed me that you had to work hard and often clients come to tell you that they need it, you have to stay the night to do everything to finish and afterwards they come to take it and they do not pay you."[76] Selling secondhand goods shifted how these women interacted with potential clients and reduced the need to invest in long-term relationship building, while also increasing access to sample garments for the whole community.

The growth of the secondhand market—just one facet of the post-revolution "neoliberal economy" in Bénin—might be perceived as leading to the decline of local clothes-making, yet seamstresses and their clients were adamant that it did not. While occasionally a client might find a particularly nice secondhand garment, acouta was mostly worn around the house or for work, and wearers saved their finer outfits tailored from waxes and prints for occasions like church or ceremonies. Indeed, wardrobes grew significantly larger in the 1980s and 1990s, even as Bénin and many Béninois became poorer amid structural adjustment, austerity measures, and the 1994 devaluation of the CFA. Fabric remained one good that was rarely in scare supply.[77] Foreign companies made imitation wax pagne starting in the 1980s and in the 2000s, and Chinese companies perfected methods to made fabric look like a wax but without using the expensive stamped production process of companies like Vlisco. These new and abundant types of pagne were of differing quality—some approached the price and quality of Vlisco while others were cheaply made with colors that quickly faded—and new notions of prestige emerged around these varying qualities.[78] As a result, clients worked with their seamstresses to order different types of outfits based on the cost of the fabric. Seamstresses might make an expensive wax into a timeless bounba or a simple modèle while clients had less expensive fabrics sewn into risky, fleeting styles or housedresses.

Seamstresses also benefited from new investments in urban infrastructure, and not just from the expansion of road networks or the electrification of workshops and their associated increases in production. During the 1990s, electrical power became more regular, with fewer blackouts, leading to new funerary practices and expectations around the clothing worn to funerals.[79] Consistent electrical supply led local entrepreneurs to open a slew of new morgues, allowing Béninois to store the corpses of their deceased relatives for weeks or months.[80] While funerals had long been important within Fon cultural life, the construction of morgues helped them achieve new levels of complexity, since a longer period between a death and a funeral date allowed more elaborate planning. Part of the planning process included selecting three fabrics for different parts of the ceremony and ordering the fabric from Cotonou or abroad. Invited guests were sold the fabric directly or told where to purchase it so that attendees at the funeral wore a uniforme of même tissu for each part of the multiday ceremony. This, of course, created an abundance of work for tailors and seamstresses, and the wardrobes of many Béninois became filled with outfits ordered for funerals and later integrated into the wearer's everyday looks.

Increased demand for clothing contributed to greater gendered differentiation among clothes-makers, and men's haute couture shops were able to charge higher prices. Clients might frequent multiple tailors and seamstresses, bringing high-quality fabrics or funerary fabrics that they particularly liked to more expensive tailors in haute couture shops. These shops were usually operated by men and sewed more complicated or trendy styles for both male and female clients. By the last decade of the twentieth century, haute couture workshops were occasionally mixed gender, and girls might apprentice under male tailors, a practice that came via coastal workshops.[81] However, most seamstresses had not studied haute couture but mission-derived couture dame with its emphasis on conservative styles like bounba or simple modèle. While women did learn some needlework techniques unique to missions, such as knitting or hand embroidery, there was a popular perception that couture dame shops were unable to make the trendiest styles. Some women exclusively visited couture dame shops, but others used them for their more low-end ensembles or for funerary cloth that they did not want to invest in.

Seamstresses themselves often recognized the limitations of the craft knowledge of couture dame, and many hoped to eventually retrain in haute couture. Like men who traveled for cours de perfectionnement (improvement courses), women could also pay other tailors to follow short courses in their workshops. After two years learning hand sewing of women and children's clothing at a Catholic institution, Victoire Glinman apprenticed herself to a woman in Bohicon in order to learn additional techniques and styles.[82] But, like apprenticeships, these short courses cost money, and women were usually responsible for feeding and clothing their children, leaving them relatively less spare cash to invest in craft knowledge. As a Davougon-trained seamstress stated, "I prefer haute couture, but I did not have the money. After couture dame, if you have the money, you can go into haute couture to learn how to make men's shirts and also pants ... but if you do not have money you are incapable of making it."[83] Indeed, women often felt constrained by their inability to sew certain styles and their lack of options for gaining new competencies.

Popular perceptions of couture dame practitioners as less qualified reduced their profitability, but seamstresses also faced challenges inherited within their craft knowledge that made them less competitive with haute couture shops. Many women identified the hand crank sewing machine as one of the limitations of mission-based couture dame. A treadle machine was easier to operate and resulted in faster stitching versus a hand crank machine, but due to their training and concerns about reproductive health most women continued to use hand-operated machines well into the 1990s. Even after adopting treadle machines, women might return to hand crank machines during pregnancy or when trying to become pregnant. The emphasis on having many apprentices within couture dame also affected productivity in various ways. Apprentices brought with them significant funds in the form of contract and libération fees, which enriched masters. They also did most of the ironing and, depending on their skill level, sewing, leaving advanced skills of design and cutting to masters. But it took time to train girls, and while the appeal of couture dame and the respectability of the workshop led many girls to enter apprenticeships, oftentimes master seamstresses identified girls as lacking aptitude or taste. Seamstresses also remarked that with dozens of teenagers under their supervision as a maman, they spent much of their time solving personal disputes among the girls or managing unplanned pregnancies. Perhaps the most significant effect of couture dame apprenticeship practices was to rapidly increase the number of women operating workshops, which eventually oversaturated the market, leading to many women being unable to find clients and maintain shops. While a few workshops, like Houngbandan's, continued to be successful, the lower profits of couture dame shops prevented most women from investing in expensive embroidery machines or other ways of improving their shops, which were increasingly necessary in a highly competitive tailoring economy.

Seamstresses continue to struggle to access capital for growing their businesses, although they gained some options for acquiring new techniques and styles after Bénin's 1990 National Conference and the transition to democracy. After severe economic decline, financial collapse, and IMF-imposed austerity measures in the 1980s, Béninois staged a general strike against Kérékou's Marxist-Leninist regime, leading to the National Conference in 1990 and free elections the following year.[84] Cloth merchants were an important group in calling for the National Conference, and artisans were one of the civil society groups present, but for ordinary tailors and seamstresses perhaps the largest impact of democratization was the spread of new "sustainable development" programs that taught skills like clothes-making. Now a democratic state, Bénin became a prime site for conscientious donors from the United States and Europe, and nonprofits focused on skill-building proliferated. For example, in the mid '90s, the German Hanns Seidel Foundation ran a center in Abomey where tailors and seamstresses could take ten-day and two-week courses in cutting and sewing, children's clothing, lingerie, and other subjects. Certificates from the program became part of seamstresses' material culture of expertise, alongside their artisanal diplomas and photographs.[85]

Internationally funded nonprofits also continued the colonial-era work of teaching tailoring to indigent boys and girls, creating an ever-increasing pool of semiskilled needleworkers. While Béninois ran some of these nongovernmental organizations with international funding, and others were directly administered by foreigners, all operated under the guise of sustainable development, which, in this case, manifested in the idea that teaching young people to sew would make them self-sufficient and foster entrepreneurship.[86] Similar to colonial and mission programs, nonprofit organizations rarely offered financial incentives to program participants or taught courses in business management. Seamstresses and tailors were often enthusiastic participants in these programs and occasionally picked up techniques that they integrated into their craft knowledge. However, the appeal of these programs was usually that they provided an opportunity for socializing or acquiring a certificate or a smaller tool such as new shears or samples of fabric rather than significant or innovative new techniques.[87] These programs usually spoke more to the interests of donors and their focus on sustainability than to the needs of tailors and seamstresses who already had highly developed systems for knowledge transfer and learning new styles but lacked capital for machinery and work-shop improvement.

By the end of the twentieth century, women outpaced men as both makers and wearers of tailor-made clothes in the cities and towns of southern Bénin, a shift from the dominance of men's labor and men's fashion in the era of independence. This feminization of craft and fashion was embedded in larger national, regional, and global shifts within clothes-making but was also very locally driven by the specific urban politics of Bénin and the choices of girls and young women who flocked to the profession in the hopes of carving out new social roles as respectable women in their communities. Seamstresses traced their craft knowledge to mission education and relied on gendered technologies and practices that often curtailed their productivity and stylistic innovation. Yet poor rural women used the craft for personal uplift, taking on dependent apprentices and establishing themselves as independent business owners within the increasingly anonymous urban spaces of interior Bénin. Their notions of stability and practices of place-making differed significantly from the "adventuring" men of the previous generation, contributing to larger conceptual shifts around embodied labor and the prestige and respectability of the craft.

In couture dame workshops, women made styles that drew on global fashions using catalogues and acouta, but they also commissioned photographs, using the technology to create local systems of sharing designs. But the craft knowledge of couture dame and its roots in mission education presented challenges to seamstresses who hoped to amass the wealth and social capital of previous generations of tailors. Faced with competition from haute couture shops, seamstresses often lamented the limitations of their craft knowledge, technologies, and apprenticeship practices. Immobilized in the workshop and constrained by increasingly rigid systems of apprenticeship, they had few opportunities to learn new methods and styles and often felt compelled to take on apprentices to both heighten their prestige and fill their coffers with contract and libération fees. Ultimately, the feminization of the craft aligns with patterns identified globally—as women enter professions, wages and prestige fall. Yet despite these trends, becoming a seamstress remains a popular choice among Béninoise girls who desire independence and respectability in a country that offers them few political and economic opportunities.

Conclusion

Tailoring in the Twenty-First Century

In June 2015, the Béninois government, financially and logistically supported by the Danes and the International Labor Organization, piloted national artisans' exams in Za-Kpota, a commune about a dozen miles outside of Bohicon. The exam was called the Traditional Exam at the End of Apprenticeship (Examen traditionnel de fin d'apprentissage [EFAT]) and was designed to subsume artisan education under the umbrella of the state and end the system of artisanal diplomas and libération. At a local school in Za-Kpota, apprentice tailors, hairdressers, carpenters, and welders spent an entire day completing the test, which consisted of a practical and a theoretical component. For the practical, apprentice tailors (who supplied their own tools and fabric) were given a scenario in which a client ordered "a simple women's outfit, simple round neck, short sleeves, square back, with two darts in the front, two darts in the back, and a back zipper."[1] EFAT also included a list of measurements for the imaginary client. The apprentices used the measurements and the written description to sew an outfit that they submitted to a panel of local master tailors who judged the apprentice's work to determine whether they passed or failed. The theoretical portion of the exam was administered either in writing or orally and included questions on the primary materials necessary for making specific outfits as well as other questions on management issues, including how to greet clients, keep workspaces clean, and avoid workplace accidents. The young men and women who passed the exam were awarded diplomas a few weeks later in a ceremony presided over by Za-Kpota's mayor.

Standardizing artisan assessments and bringing them under the domain of state control has become a development priority in twenty-first-century Bénin.[2]

Since the Za-Kpota pilot program, artisans and the state have refined the exam process and brought it to the entire country. Apprentices continue to be trained by masters in private workshops, but the state administers the exams and awards those who pass a Trade Qualification Certificate (le certificate de qualification aux métiers [CQM]), a document that supersedes and replaces the handmade artisanal diplomas featured in chapter 4. Some artisans have been vocal supporters of the EFAT and CQM because they believe the new system will mitigate some of the virulent disagreements between artisans over how to assess apprentices and their competencies. They also appreciate the state's recognition of their skill and see formalization and a state-issued document as an official acknowledgment of their expertise. Other interested parties—the international community and parents, especially—hope that the CQM might reduce the power of master artisans and drive down costs associated with apprenticeship and libération, which have grown substantially since the 1970s, even as Bénin's economy has remained relatively stagnant during the same decades.

By 2017, the CQM had reached all of Bénin, including Abomey and Bohicon, and libération had become an extralegal event. But did it disappear? During a research trip in 2021, I spoke with many tailors and seamstresses, some of whom I have known for over a decade and others who were new contacts. Almost all of them were outwardly pleased with the CQM and standardization. A few had given up libération entirely and had shifted to attending the CQM diploma event and then perhaps a small reception hosted by the apprentice's parents. But many artisans also acknowledged that libération had actually become "clandestine," and new artisans were undergoing it each Saturday morning. The libération ceremony had moved from the streets and open spaces where artisans could show off their skills to the interiors of courtyards where masters, apprentices, and their families avoided the condemnation of local authorities. For the community of artisans, diplomas had only been one aspect of libération. The paper document helped confer master status, but blessings, sacrifices to Gu, the palmatoire, and shared food and drink were part of a complex rite that could not be captured through a sterile graduation ceremony run by local bureaucrats. Indeed, artisans have already begun to push back against the CQM, leading the government to make adjustments in response to the "weaknesses" of the exam and its organization.[3] Ultimately, it remains unclear how libération and the community of artisans will endure an onslaught of standardization and formalization.

As this book has shown, tailors and other makers have long adapted to and adjusted their craft to the constantly evolving political, economic, and social landscapes of the nineteenth and twentieth centuries. Indeed, "the spirit of creativity"—a phrase often invoked by tailors—helped explain not only how makers designed and made things for their clients but also how they endured the volatility of conquest, colonization, postcolonial politics, and urbanization. In one of the rare written records of a libération blessing, a master seamstress in 1971 extolled her apprentices with "the spirit of invention; the spirit of beauty," so that the young women might open successful shops and prosper.[4] Whispered in ears or loudly proclaimed to onlooking crowds, the invocation of the *espirit* or *àyì* (spirit, heart, intelligence) necessary to make fine objects hinted at the almost mystical abilities of craftspeople to transform materials—hunks of metal or wood or lengths of fabric—into something practical but also beautiful. The vast majority of tailors maintained that their creativity was in part innate, but many also emphasized that craft knowledge needed to be refined or honed over the course of training and then through a lifetime of work.

Like other types of "spirits" in Bénin—the vodun that are seemingly everywhere—craft knowledge was living and always evolving, and it required a reciprocal relationship through offerings. New materials, technologies, and stylistic flourishes sustained Béninois sartorial culture as tailors gathered them through travel, apprenticeship, trainings, and consuming media. Tailors did not think of themselves as imitating designs of more affluent urban fashion designers or of copying the images found in catalogues; rather, they fed their creativity through encounters and brought together these different elements to create fashion styles that made sense for themselves and their clients. During their processes of designing, cutting, and sewing, and in their interactions with clients, tailors conveyed when and how specific garments should be worn. Their work, knowledge, and expertise over the material world shaped the meanings and uses of clothing in twentieth-century Bénin and the identity-making work of creating clothing.

The craft practices of tailors and their ability to nurture the creative spirit drew upon deep histories of making in the region. In the precolonial kingdom, the palace encouraged, and at times forced, the migration of artisans to Dahomey, bringing individuals, their knowledge, and their technologies into the kingdom's material culture. After the French colonized and attempted to mold a sartorial economy in search of colonial profit, clothes-makers and consumers adopted fabrics, machinery, and techniques largely on their own terms, ignoring the prerogatives of the colonial state. Likewise, tailors were important technological agents who incorporated new technologies and materials in their production methods while developing new artisanal ways to ascertain and express their expertise. Their craft knowledge was never a top-down process, and makers honed clothing styles through regional craft practices of technical and formal domestication, improvisation, and collaboration with other artisans. Knowledge sharing between tailors was sometimes highly organized, especially in the second half of the twentieth century, as artisans systematized new types of apprenticeship and forms of certification. But these exchanges could also be informal. Proximity to one another led to collaboration on new techniques and styles that crossed lines of gender, specialty, or class. Tailors stopped in the ateliers of masters or people they apprenticed with, asking advice on tricky items. Men and women came back from aventure ready to teach others what they had learned. There was, of course, competition among craftspeople when individuals argued or even fought over clients, but there was also comradery and a collective desire to make things even more beautiful.

Understanding this long history of clothes-making provides new insight into the origins of not just production methods, work patterns, and occupational identities but also the enduring popularity of certain styles in Bénin. In the nineteenth century Dahomey kingdom, agricultural labor, dirt-covered bodies, dull dress, and minimal textiles were the purview of the nonelite in the countryside (glètà), who, over the course of the nineteenth century, were increasingly captives from elsewhere. In contrast, the dress of the tòvi, or Dahomean "citizens," was a bricolage of different imported and local elements and employed an extensive use of draped and wrapped fabrics to signify wealth, power, and prestige. Yorùbá-style sandals or Spanish-style hats in eighteenth- and nineteenth-century Dahomey allowed the king to embody his reach and power. While these styles never disappeared, elaborate "Fon dress" took on new valences of power in the sartorial economy of the colonial period. For the descendants of royal families and heads of clan (Dáa), yards of draped fabric, tchanka, and ceremonial clubs (recade) recalled power lost over the course of colonization, but for ordinary people this Fon "ethnic dress" became irrelevant, harkening to an elite style of a highly unequal past.

The relationship between identity and clothing is well established, but introducing the maker into the story reveals how craftspeople's complex identities—in terms of class, ethnicity, craft, and gender—affected the social meanings and uses of clothing. Modèles made by women in missions materialized respectable Christian ideals, and their fit reflected modes of production and techniques emphasized in mission programs as essential to ideal domestic womanhood. Outfits like men's bounba or polyester détè made by adventuring men in independence-era Bénin hinted at global inclusion, even amid a changing world order where it became increasingly clear that Béninois were being left out. These craftspeople used their machines to project Béninois conceptions of "being modern" and profited from their associations with three-piece suits, imported technologies, and bookkeeping. Popular fashions worn in the streets, bars, and churches of the towns and villages of interior Bénin reflected the life experiences of ordinary people living in the world and wearers' personal aspirations for a better life for themselves and their families. In this way, the twentieth-century appeal of the three-piece suit for men or Dutch waxes for women was not embedded in a desire to be European or white but rather to embody new status and possibilities in one's own community. This book has emphasized these fashions as made things and how meaning derives not just from their form but from the processes, knowledge, and materials of their making.

To be sure, tailors have continued to demonstrate their resilience and dynamism in the recent past, discovering new ways to navigate the challenges of neoliberalism and globalization. Growing textile industries abroad, especially in China, contributed to the collapse of African industrial textile and clothing production, whether for export or local consumption, yet African consumers gained access to more fabric and finished clothing as Chinese imports grew.[5] Béninois factories may have closed or reduced production, but Béninois artisanal clothes-makers had more work than ever. Notable changes in the fashion system in West Africa have also created more demand for tailored dress. In the first decade of the twentieth century, Ghanaian and Nigerian publishing companies printed fashion magazines and posters of modèles, which grace the walls of ateliers and provide inspiration for tailors and clients alike. Vlisco, and later other high-end wax brands, launched advertising campaigns to revive interest in their fabric and to recover losses after improvements in Chinese manufacturing. Vlisco billboards depicted their fabric sewn into high fashions, and the company choose Cotonou as the site of its first flagship store in 2007. The images in the advertisements, which were used internationally, depicted styles that had been designed outside of Bénin, but Vlisco also began to promote their textiles in partnership with Cotonou designers by arranging fashion shows and other advertising campaigns. In addition to more images of West African fashion made by international companies, in the past decade some small shops began to promote their styles on social media, reaching a greater audience than ever before. With the spread of phones and inexpensive data, tailors and clients could easily send each other images of outfits and promote individual workshops. These modes of stylistic sharing have mostly replaced earlier systems that included circulating European catalogues or locally made photographs. Béninois consumers have more opportunity to purchase clothing and cloth of varying qualities and to directly access images of new styles from Cotonou, Lagos, Abidjan, or Paris. Demand for the work of a tailor continues to grow and shows no sign of stopping.

This recent history of tailoring reveals how a craft can persist and even grow in a globalized neoliberal economy. But the individual fortunes of tailors are usually much less than for previous generations, and tailors face new onslaughts against their control over craft knowledge and matters of style. Clients' access to a seemingly endless availability of fashion photographs in African fashion magazines and on their phones has diminished the role of the tailor as a mediator of style. For many young tailors, the ability to turn a profit and prosper has also suffered amid an ever-increasing number of craftspeople. While a very few might become well-off, many tailors are just getting by, and women especially often rely on small retail activities like selling candy or hair accessories to supplement their incomes. Despite these recent developments, tailoring remains a common choice for girls and boys looking for a career. In June 2021, the EFAT and CQM quantified new artisans into rolls of test takers, revealing the extent and continued popularity of tailoring. Posted on an exterior wall of the Bohicon Maison des Artisans, the CQM results showed that over a third of the apprentices who took and passed the exam were tailors and seamstresses, although the feminization of the craft continues, and the number of girls and women vastly exceeded the number of boys and men. Indeed, new workshops seem to spring up daily along highways and backroads of southern Bénin.

Addressing how tailors have seen their own positionality through their words and works reveals some of the reasons behind the lasting appeal of tailoring as a career choice and tailored clothing as everyday dress. Clothing was especially important in the construction of identity in Bénin, but other materials—things like sewing machines, urban workshops, artisanal diplomas, textiles, catalogues, and so on—also mattered, affecting not only how Béninois made clothes but also how individual garments took on greater political, social, and cultural meaning. This book has revealed some of the reasons behind the enduring popularity of tailored clothing in Bénin and how tailors and seamstresses took a leading role in the making of selves, cities, and nations in the twentieth century.

GLOSSARY

Fon spellings are those that are officially sanctioned by the Republic of Bénin's programs in literacy in the Fon language. Other terms are French-origin words with meanings that may or may not map onto their usage in France.

acouta: "used," a term for secondhand clothing

adjalabou: boubou consisting of a floor-length shirt with matching pants, "Hausa style"

agbada: style of men's clothing consisting of trousers, a long-sleeved shift, and a wide, floor-length gown worn over the other two pieces, from Yorùbáland

agojie: women warriors in the Dahomey kingdom; Europeans referred to them as "Amazons"

ahi: open-air market, usually every four days

ahosi: wife of the king in the Kingdom of Dahomey

àlɔnúzɔwàtɔ: artisan

anago: alternative name for bounba as well as Yorùbá in general

anato: commoner

année blanche: a school strike (by either teachers or students) that is so long it forces a "cleared year" where country-wide no students progress to the next grade

apprentis: apprentice

artisanat (l'artisanat): artisanship, or the economic sector and social identity of artisans

asen: ceremonial staff

atan: saliva

aventure: "adventure," a pleasurable form of migration

avɔ: pagne, or wrapper in Fon

bas d'éléph: short for "elephant bottoms," bell-bottoms

bazin: brocade, popular fabric for adjalabou

bla: twisting or knotting

bo: power

bociɔ: power object

botoyi: coarsely woven cotton cloth, widespread in the 1940s

bounba: tunic and trousers (men) or tunic and pagne (women) made from matching fabric, often from waxes or prints

boutique: neighborhood store

chef de canton: African appointed by French colonial administration to collect taxes, find laborers, and enforce customary law over a given territory

chokoto: short pants

collectifs des artisans: artisans' associations organized at the local, regional, and national levels

comin: collar or neckline

costume: suit

cours de perfectionnement: "refresher course," or a course in an apprentice's shop or through a nonprofit in which master tailors learn new techniques and/or management skills

couture dame: women's tailor shop, staffed by women and making women and children's clothing

Dáa: title for a head of clan

Dáda: king of Dahomey

demi-pièce: six meters of cloth

détè: Béninois leisure suit with short sleeves, patch pockets, and matching pants

dévɔ: raffia cloth

drill: sturdy fabric such as khaki, often cotton

évolué: in the colonial period, an African who had "evolved" or assimilated into French culture and values

Fá: Yorùbá-derived divination practice common on Abomey Plateau

ganhi: covered market, specifically that of Bohicon

glètà: countryside or bush

gòdó (go): loincloth

grand: big man

grand pagne: three meters of fabric

Gu (Ogun): vodun of metallurgy, artisans, and craft

haute couture: tailoring shop that caters to both male and female clients, usually with higher prices

Houndjroto: Abomey's main market

hunnukún: literally, "one with his eyes open," an educated person or intellectual

Hwetanu: "Annual Customs," ceremony in kingdom

jupe ovale: oval skirt

kanvɔ: cotton cloth

klui klui: fried peanut paste

libération: rite of passage ceremony at end of apprenticeship

lio: balls of akassa, or fermented corn fufu

Maison des artisans (maison): French colonial training center for African artisans

maman: mother, or older woman

même tissu: same fabric, creating a "uniform" among wearers

métis or *métisse:* mixed-race person

mission civilisatrice: civilizing mission

modèle: women's ensemble of matching shirt and skirt

modèles jeune fille: women's ensemble of matching shirt and skirt intended for young women, often tighter or more revealing

nid d'abeille: honeycomb smocking

Nunupweto: "omnipotent" cloth (according to Skertchly) in the Kingdom of Dahomey

nùtomò: sewing machine

nùtɔnú: needle

nutɔtɔ: gender-neutral term for a tailor, literally a proprietor of sewing

Orò: secret societies of men

pagne: wrapper, term used throughout French-speaking West and West Central Africa

palmatoire: ceremonial paddling at libération

pâte: dense maize-based fufu, often poured into molds

patron: master artisan

pièce: twelve meters of cloth, basic unit of imported wax and prints

préfet: person and office of head of (Zou) region, in Abomey

recade: ceremonial club

sodabi: distilled palm wine

tailleurie simple: small-scale tailor's shop focused on repairs, often in open-air market

tchanka: short pants with a panel in between the two legs, widely considered Fon "traditional" men's dress

tenue pique: machine-stitched dress

tò: town

tòvi: "children of the town" or citizens

trois pièces: another name for an agbada

trois poches: "three pocket," another name for a détè

uniforme: "uniform" of wearing the same fabric, often sewn into different styles

villageois: "countryfolk," person from a village or in the style of the village

vodun: Fon religion, "god"

vodunon: priests or priestess to a vodun, literally "wife of vodun"

vodunsi: adherents to a vodun

yokpo yokpo xwé: royal artisans' workshop established by King Agaja of Dahomey

yovo: white person, foreigner

zemidjan: taxi-moto

Zongo: neighborhood in southern Bénin (and Togo and Ghana) where Muslim migrants settled

NOTES

Introduction

1. In 1970, the women would have lived in the Republic of Dahomey
(1960–75). In the precolonial era, parts of Bénin were the Dahomey kingdom
(c. 1600–1894); then came the French colony of Dahomey (1894–1960), the Republic of Dahomey (1960–75), the People's Republic of Bénin (1975–90), and now
the Republic of Bénin (1990–present). In this book, I refer only to people in the
precolonial era as *Dahomeans*. I call people living in this region in the twentieth
century *Béninois* since the modern-day borders of Bénin are the same as those of
the French colony of Dahomey.

2. On clothing as "social skin," see Terence S. Turner, "The Social Skin,"
HAU: Journal of Ethnographic Theory 2, no. 2 (2012): 486–504. For some examples
in Africa, see the essays in Hildi Hendrickson, ed., *Clothing and Difference:
Embodied Identities in Colonial and Post-Colonial Africa* (Duke University Press,
1996).

3. On Atlantic consumption, see Robert S. DuPlessis, *The Material Atlantic:
Clothing, Commerce, and Colonization in the Atlantic World* (Cambridge University Press, 2016).

4. Joanne B. Eicher and Barbara Sumberg argue that "Western dress" is a
misnomer for suits, dresses, trousers, and other tailored, fitted clothing. Instead, "world fashion" or "cosmopolitan dress" better explains them as a global
phenomenon of the twentieth century. Joanne B. Eicher and Barbara Sumberg,
"World Fashion, Ethnic, and National Dress," in *Dress and Ethnicity: Change
across Space and Time*, ed. Joanne B. Eicher (Berg, 1995), 295–306. Béninois often
refer to these styles as *la mode française* (French style), reflecting their particular
history of colonization rather than geographically locating the fashion in France.

5. Examples include Jean Allman, ed., *Fashioning Africa: Power and the Politics of Dress* (Indiana University Press, 2014); Marie Grace Brown, *Khartoum at Night: Fashion and Body Politics in Imperial Sudan* (Stanford University Press, 2017); Karen Tranberg Hansen and Soyini Madison, eds., *African Dress: Fashion, Agency, and Performance* (Bloomsbury, 2013); Andrew Ivaska, *Cultured States: Youth, Gender, and Modern Style in 1960s Dar es Salaam* (Duke University Press, 2011); and Jacqueline-Bethel Tchouta Mougoué, *Gender, Separatist Politics, and Embodied Nationalism in Cameroon* (University of Michigan Press, 2019).

6. The biography of objects as method was articulated by Igor Kopytoff, "The Cultural Biography of Things: Commoditization as Process," in *The Social Life of Things: Commodities in Cultural Perspective*, ed. A. Appadurai (Cambridge University Press, 1986), 64–93. Tim Ingold points out that studies of material culture "take as their starting point a world of objects that has, as it were, already crystallized out from the fluxes of materials and their transformations. At this point materials appear to vanish, swallowed up by the very objects to which they have given birth." Tim Ingold, "Materials against Materiality," *Archaeological Dialogues* 14, no. 1 (2007): 9.

7. Tim Ingold, "The Textility of Making," *Cambridge Journal of Economics* 34 (2010): 92.

8. The phrase "artisanal paths" is also used in Boaventura de Sousa Santos, *The End of the Cognitive Empire: The Coming of Age of Epistemologies of the South* (Duke University Press, 2018). While I am not claiming to have achieved the sort of decolonial epistemological work suggested by de Sousa Santos, I have done my best to develop a method of *knowing with* rather than *knowing about*.

9. A rare full-length history of tailors is R. J. Pokrant, "The Survival of Indigenous Tailoring among the Hausa of Kano City," (PhD diss., University of Cambridge, 1982). There have been a few shorter studies of tailors and seamstresses by anthropologists and art historians; see Suzanne Gott, "'Life' Dressing in Kumasi: African-Print Style in 'Popular Fashion,'" in *African-Print Fashion Now! A Story of Taste, Globalization, and Style*, ed. S. Gott, K. S. Loughran, B. D. Quick, and L. W. Rabine (Fowler Museum at UCLA, 2019); Joanna Grabski, "The Visual City: Tailors, Creativity, and Urban Life in Dakar, Senegal," in *Contemporary African Fashion*, ed. Suzanne Gott and Kristyne Loughran (Indiana University Press, 2010); Karen Tranberg Hansen, "Fabricating Dreams: Sewing Machines, Tailors, and Urban Entrepreneurship in Zambia," in *The Objects of Life in Central Africa*, ed. R. Ross, M. Hingelaar, and I. Peša (Brill, 2013); and parts of Okechukwu Nwafor, *Aso Ebi: Dress, Fashion, Visual Culture, and Urban Cosmopolitanisms in West Africa* (University of Michigan Press, 2021).

10. Johanna Amos and Lisa Binkley note that women are the subject of most of the literature on global needlework across time and space. See Johanna Amos and Lisa Binkley, "Introduction: Stitching the Self," in *Stitching the Self: Identity and the Needle Arts*, ed. Johanna Amos and Lisa Binkley (Bloomsbury, 2020), 4.

11. Early examples include Maurice Delafosse, *Haut-Sénégal-Niger* (Émile Larose, 1912); Auguste Dupuis-Yakouba, "Notes sur la population de Tombouctou (castes et associations)," *Revue d'ethnographie et de sociologie* (1910): 233–36; and Auguste Dupuis-Yakouba, *Industries et principales professions des habitants de la région de Tombouctou* (Émile Larose, 1921).

12. Tal Tamari, "The Development of Caste Systems in West Africa," *Journal of African History* (1991): 221–50; Patrick R. McNaughton, *The Mande Blacksmiths: Knowledge, Power, and Art in West Africa* (Indiana University Press, 1993).

13. Judith Byfield, *The Bluest Hands: A Social and Economic History of Women Dyers in Abeokuta (Nigeria), 1890–1940* (Heinemann, 2002); Victoria L. Rovine, *Bogolan: Shaping Culture through Cloth in Contemporary Mali* (Indiana University Press, 2008); Barbara E. Frank, *Mande Potters and Leatherworkers: Art and Heritage in West Africa* (Smithsonian Institute, 1998); and Barbara E. Frank, *Griot Potters of the Folona: The History of an African Ceramic Tradition* (Indiana University Press, 2021).

14. Edna Bay, *Wives of the Leopard: Gender, Politics, and Culture in the Kingdom of Dahomey* (University Press of Virginia, 1998), 20; and Suzanne Preston Blier, *African Vodun: Art, Psychology, and Power* (University of Chicago Press, 1995).

15. Alexis Adandé and Goudjinou Metinhoué, "Potières et Poterie de Sè (Mono)" (Ministere de l'Enseignement Superièure et de la Recherche Scientifique, République Populaire du Bénin, 1981), 37.

16. William Sewell, *Work and Revolution in France: The Language of Labor from the Old Regime to 1848* (Cambridge University Press, 1980); Steven M. Zdatny, *The Politics of Survival: Artisans in Twentieth-Century France* (Oxford, 1990).

17. Michael Adas, *Machines as the Measures of Men: Science, Technology, and Ideologies of Western Dominance* (Cornell University Press, 1989). See also Paulin Hountondji, "Knowledge Appropriation in a Post-Colonial Context," in *Indigenous Knowledge and the Integration of Knowledge Systems*, ed. Catherine A. Odora Hoppers (New Africa, 2002), 35.

18. Hamid Irbouh, *Art in the Service of Colonialism: French Art Education in Morocco, 1912–1956* (Bloomsbury, 2013); Victoria Rovine, "A Wider Loom? French Colonial Preoccupations with West African Weaving," *African Arts* 52, no. 4 (2019): 66–83.

19. For earlier efforts in Senegal, see Hilary Jones, *The Métis of Senegal: Urban Life and Politics in French West Africa* (Indiana University Press, 2013).

20. Byfield, *The Bluest Hands*.

21. Frederick Cooper, *Decolonization and African Society: The Labor Question in French and British Africa* (Cambridge University Press, 1996), 466.

22. Bill Freund, *The African Worker* (Cambridge University Press, 1988).

23. For example, Claire C. Robertson, *Sharing the Same Bowl: A Socioeconomic History of Women and Class in Accra, Ghana* (University of Michigan Press, 1985); and Luise White, *The Comforts of Home: Prostitution in Colonial Nairobi* (University of Chicago Press, 1990).

24. Anthropologist Douglas J. Falen suggests that NGO-led development in southern Bénin shares many of the same ambiguities as *àzě* (witchcraft). He writes, "Development projects represent the disappearance of money, perceived betrayal, inequality, and shameless exploitation—the very same qualities associated with àzě." Douglas J. Falen, *African Science: Witchcraft, Vodun, and Healing in Southern Bénin* (University of Wisconsin Press, 2018), 58.

25. Comlan Cyr Davodoun has published extensively about the artisanat in Bénin; see, for example, Davodoun, *Développement du mouvement associatif en milieu artisan au Bénin* (Les Editions du Flamboyant, 2006); or Davodoun, *Mieux connaitre l'artisanat au Bénin* (Le Bureau d'appui aux artisans, 2008).

26. Cooper, *Decolonization and African Society*; Alexander Keese, "A Social History of Parastatal Employees in Southern Benin, 1989–1990: Contesting Decline and Unemployment During 'Africa's Second Democratization,'" *ILWCH* 98 (Fall 2020): 77–98; Babacar Fall, *Le travail au Sénégal au XXe siècle* (Karthala, 2011).

27. Monni Adams, "Fon appliqué cloths," *African Arts* 13, no. 2 (1980): 28–41, 87–88; Edna Bay, *Asen, Ancestors, and Vodun: Tracing Change in African Art* (University of Illinois Press, 2008); and Venice and Alastair Lamb, "The Classification and Distribution of Horizontal Treadle Looms in Sub-Saharan Africa," *Textile History* (1980): 22–62.

28. Joshua Grace, *African Motors: Technology, Gender, and the History of Development* (Duke University Press, 2021); Clapperton Chakanetsa Mavhunga, *Transient Workspaces: Technologies of Everyday Innovation in Zimbabwe* (MIT Press, 2014); Abena Dove Osseo-Asare, *Atomic Junction: Nuclear Power in Africa After Independence* (Cambridge University Press, 2019); Laura Ann Twagira, *Embodied Engineering: Gendered Labor, Food Security, and Taste in Twentieth Century Mali* (Ohio University Press, 2021).

29. Laura Ann Twagira argues that to Africanize technology is to underscore Africans as technological agents, as producers of and not simply recipients of technology through diffusion. To Africanize technology is to also be attentive to what agency means in specific historical contexts. Laura Ann Twagira, "Introduction: Africanizing the History of Technology," *Technology and Culture* 61, no. 2 (2020): S1–S19.

30. Giacomo Macola, *The Gun in Central Africa: A History of Technology and Politics* (Ohio University Press, 2016).

31. Two exceptions that explore the cultural and social histories of sewing machines in non-Western contexts include David Arnold, *Everyday Technology: Machines and the Making of India's Modernity* (University of Chicago Press, 2013); and Andrew Gordon, *Fabricating Consumers: The Sewing Machine in Modern Japan* (University of California Press, 2011).

32. Phyllis G. Tortora, *Dress, Fashion, and Technology: From Prehistory to the Present* (Bloomsbury, 2015), 132–34.

33. Catherine E. McKinley, *The African Lookbook: A Visual History of 100 Years of African Women* (Bloomsbury, 2021), xx.

34. Arnold contrasts "small technologies" with big ones such as infrastructure or airplanes to explore the everyday lived experiences of technology in India; see Arnold, *Everyday Technology*.

35. For more on African women's strategic use of photographs, see McKinley, *African Lookbook*.

36. On the typewriter, see Thomas D. Mullaney, *The Chinese Typewriter: A History* (MIT Press, 2017), 27–29.

37. Arnold, *Everyday Technology*, 94.

38. Elizabeth Ann Fretwell, "'Domesticating the Unfamiliar': Afropolitan Dress in the West African Kingdom of Dahomey," *Radical History Review* 144 (October 2022): 19–44.

39. Falen, *African Science*, 65, 68–69.

40. Elizabeth Ann Fretwell, "The Tools of Tailoring as Technologies-in-Use in Twentieth Century Benin, West Africa," *History and Technology* 37, no. 2 (2021): 147–71.

41. Paulin J. Hountondji, ed., *Endogenous Knowledge: Research Trails*, trans. Ayi Kwesi Armah (CODESRIA, 1997).

42. Clapperton Chakanetsa Mavhunga, *The Mobile Workshop: The Tsetse Fly and African Knowledge Production* (MIT Press, 2018), 20.

43. Rudolph Ware reminds us, "Human 'bodies of knowledge' are made, not born . . . brought into the world through concrete practices of corporal discipline, corporeal knowledge transmission, and the deeds of embodied agents." Rudolph Ware, *The Walking Qur'an: Islamic Education, Embodied Knowledge, and History in West Africa* (University of North Carolina Press, 2014), 8. On "knowledge-made-in-common," see Mavhunga, *Transient Workspaces*.

44. Anthropologist Trevor Marchand analyzes mud masons' personalized "knowing-in-practice"—the unique combinations of their skills, forms of knowledge, identities, and personalities—that translate into construction methods. For example, masons take measurements in lengths of an individual's body parts, and the master mason's own concept of space and personal aesthetics play a much greater factor in the final form than standardized blueprints. Marchand's project also reveals how masons have maintained and developed their techniques through social institutions that promote secrecy. Trevor Marchand, *The Masons of Djenné* (Indiana University Press, 2009).

45. Jean Lave, *Apprenticeship in Critical Ethnographic Practice* (University of Chicago Press, 2011), 65–79.

46. Similar to how South African women might use skin lighteners to be seen, assembling a material culture of expertise might be considered a "technology of visibility." See Lynn M. Thomas, *Beneath the Surface: A Transnational History of Skin Lighteners* (Duke University Press, 2020).

47. Grace, *African Motors*, 86.

48. Twagira, *Embodied Engineering*, 146–54.

49. Abena Dove Osseo-Asare, "Writing Medical Authority: The Rise of Literate Healers in Ghana, 1930–70," *Journal of African History* 57, no. 1 (2016): 75.

50. This use of "tradition" is not a reference to "custom" but more along the lines of usage by political historians such as Jan Vansina, *Paths in the Rainforest: Toward a History of Political Tradition in Equatorial Africa* (University of Wisconsin Press, 1990), and recent work on African epistemologies such as Oludamini Ogunnaike, *Deep Knowledge: Ways of Knowing in Sufism and Ifa, Two West African Intellectual Traditions* (Pennsylvania State University Press, 2020), 24.

51. In this way, the history of tailors provides an interesting counter to James C. Scott's arguments on state efforts to render modern populations legible. In this case, it was the tailors themselves who did the work. Scott, *Seeing Like a State: How Certain Schemes to Improve the Human Condition Have Failed* (Yale University Press, 1998).

52. Jean Allman, "Fashioning Africa: Power and the Politics of Dress," in *Fashioning Africa: Power and the Politics of Dress*, ed. Allman, 1–12 (Indiana University Press, 2004), 1.

53. For example, articles in Allman, *Fashioning Africa*, and Ivaska, *Cultured States*; Mougoué, *Gender, Separatist Politics*; and Brown, *Khartoum at Night*.

54. This point was also made by Jonathan Friedman on the impacts of precolonial Kongo aesthetics of elegance on *la sape* in Congo; see Jonathan Friedman, "The Political Economy of Elegance: An African Cult of Beauty," in *Consumption and Identity*, ed. Jonathan Friedman (Harwood Academic, 1994), 170–71. However, much of the literature on African fashion emphasizes its global dimensions.

55. Bay, *Asen, Ancestors*, 4–5.

56. Dana Rush, *Vodun in Coastal Bénin: Unfinished, Open-Ended, Global* (Vanderbilt University Press, 2013), 5.

57. Timothy R. Landry, *Vodún: Secrecy and the Search for Divine Power* (University of Pennsylvania Press, 2019), 111–14.

58. Blier, *African Vodun*, 239–70.

59. The exceptions, of course, are the clothed bodies of Vodun priests and priestesses and those actively undergoing Vodun rituals.

60. C. A. Bayly, *The Birth of the Modern World, 1780–1914* (Blackwell, 2004), 14.

61. Eicher and Sumberg, "World Fashion."

62. Shantrelle P. Lewis, *Dandy Lion: The Black Dandy and Street Style* (Aperture, 2017), 8–9. See also Monica L. Miller, *Slaves to Fashion: Black Dandyism*

and the Styling of Black Diasporic Identity (Duke University Press, 2009); and Didier Gondola, "Dream and Drama: The Search for Elegance among Congolese Youth," *African Studies Review* 42, no. 1 (1999): 23–48.

63. Nwafor, *Aso Ebi.*

64. Christopher L. Richards, *Cosmopolitanism and Women's Fashion in Ghana: History, Artistry and Nationalist Inspirations* (Routledge, 2022), 7.

65. Helen Jennings, *New African Fashion* (Prestel, 2011); Leslie W. Rabine, "Translating African Textiles into U.S. Fashion Designs," in *Contemporary African Fashion*, ed. Suzanne Gott and Kristyne Loughran (Indiana University Press, 2010).

66. For example, in nineteenth-century South Africa, Christian missionaries sought to promote certain styles and fabrics as a way to make rural inhabitants good capitalist consumers or to engender heteronormative domesticities. Jean and John Comaroff, "Fashioning the Colonial Subject: The Empire's Old Clothes," in *Of Revelation and Revolution*, vol. 2, *The Dialectics of Modernity on a South African Frontier* (University of Chicago Press, 1997); Juliette Leeb-du Toit, *isiShweshwe: A History of the Indigenisation of Blueprint in South Africa* (University of KwaZulu-Natal Press, 2017); and T. J. Tallie, *Queering Colonial Natal: Indigeneity and the Violence of Belonging in South Africa* (University of Minnesota, 2019), 119–36. In post-independence Ghana, elite African women in the south led campaigns to clothe "naked" Northerners as part of the nation-building process. Jean Allman, "'Let Your Fashion Be in Line with Our Ghanaian Costume': Nation, Gender, and the Politics of Cloth-ing in Nkrumah's Ghana," in Allman, *Fashioning Africa.*

67. AbdouMaliq Simone, *For the City Yet to Come: Changing African Life in Four Cities* (Duke University Press, 2004), 2.

68. Ivan Gaskell and Sarah Anne Carter, introduction to *The Oxford Handbook of History and Material Culture*, ed. Gaskell and Carter (Oxford University Press, 2020), 6.

69. Marchand, *The Masons of Djenné*; Lave, *Apprenticeship in Critical Ethnographic Practice*; Grace, *African Motors.*

70. The role of headshots in postcolonial bureaucracy is explored in Drew Thompson, "'*Não há Nada*' ('There Is Nothing'): Absent Headshots and Identity Documents in Independent Mozambique," *Technology and Culture* 61 (2020): S104–S134.

71. This interplay between fashion design and photography is addressed in Kerstin Pinther, "Textiles and Photography in West Africa," *Critical Interventions* (2007): 106–18; Nwafor, *Aso ebi*; and Hudita Nura Mustafa, "Portraits of Modernity: Fashioning Selves in Dakarois Popular Photography," *Politique africaine* 100 (2006): 241.

72. Christian M. Geary, *In and Out of Focus: Images from Central Africa, 1885–1960* (Philip Wilson, 2002); Paul Landau, "Empires of the Visual:

Photography and Colonial Administration in Africa," in *Images and Empires: Visuality in Colonial and Postcolonial Africa*, ed. Landau and Deborah D. Kaspin (University of California Press, 2002), 141–71.

1. Wrapped and Draped

1. Frederick E. Forbes, *Dahomey and the Dahomans, Being the Journals of Two Missions to the King of Dahomey, and Residence at His Capital in the Years 1849 and 1850* (1851), 2:108.

2. Richard F. Burton, *A Mission to Gelele, King of Dahome. With Notices of the So Called "Amazons," the Grand Customs, the Yearly Customs, the Human Sacrifices, the Present State of the Slave Trade, and the Negro's Place in Nature. In Two Volumes* (1864), 1:318.

3. Forbes, *Dahomey and the Dahomans*, 2:108.

4. Burton, *A Mission to Gelele*, 1:318.

5. Fashion in Britain had been thoroughly feminized by this time. Men had adopted the three-piece suit as a symbol of modest masculinity, in contrast to earlier, more ornate forms of elite masculine dress now reimaged as symbolic of the aristocratic corruption and excess of ancien régime Europe. David Kuchta, *The Three-Piece Suit and Modern Masculinity: England, 1550–1850* (University of California Press, 2002). On the long history of European ideas around Africans' supposed "irrational" relationships with things, see William Pietz, "The Problem of the Fetish II: The Origin of the Fetish," *RES: Anthropology and Aesthetics* 13 (1987): 23–45.

6. The literature on precolonial Dahomey and the Slave Coast has focused on topics such as the gendered bureaucratic institutions of the state, the political economy of the transatlantic slave trade, and the role of space in concretizing Dahomean power and authority. See I. A. Akinjogbin, *Dahomey and Its Neighbours: 1708–1818* (Cambridge University Press, 1967); Edna Bay, *Wives of the Leopard: Gender, Politics, and Culture in the Kingdom of Dahomey* (University Press of Virginia, 1998); Robin Law, *The Slave Coast of West Africa, 1550–1750* (Oxford University Press, 1991); Patrick Manning, *Slavery, Colonialism, and Economic Growth in Dahomey, 1640–1960* (Cambridge University Press, 1982); J. Cameron Monroe, *The Precolonial State in West Africa: Building Power in Dahomey* (Cambridge University Press, 2014). Others have explored the development of the Fon religion of Vodun and the important place of religion and ritual in state politics and everyday life. Suzanne Preston Blier, *African Vodun: Art, Psychology, and Power* (University of Chicago Press, 1995); Suzanne Preston Blier, *Royal Arts of Africa: The Majesty of Form* (Harry N. Abrams, 1998); Edna Bay, "Belief, Legitimacy, and the Kpojito: An Institutional History of the 'Queen Mother' in Precolonial Dahomey," *Journal of African History* 36 (1995): 1–27; Robin Law, "'My Head

Belongs to the King': On the Political and Ritual Significance of Decapitation in Pre-Colonial Dahomey," *Journal of African History* 30 (1989): 399–415.

7. European ancien régimes used sumptuary laws as "instruments of political, social and economic regulation"; see Philippe Perrot, *Fashioning the Bourgeoisie: A History of Clothing in the Nineteenth Century*, trans. Richard Bienvenu (Princeton University Press, 1994), 15. For a more global approach, see Giorgio Riello and Ulinka Rublack, eds., *The Right to Dress: Sumptuary Laws in a Global Perspective, c. 1200–1800* (Cambridge University Press, 2019).

8. This chapter uses *palace* to refer to both the physical structure and the inhabitants as did Bay, *Wives of the Leopard*, 8. But it also expands this usage to include "policies, individuals, and administrative practices," which Monroe cumbersomely called the "royal palace sphere"; Monroe, *Precolonial State*, 73.

9. Fon trace their origins even farther to the west among the Aja of Tado (Togo). Interview with Nestor Dako-Wegbe, Houawe Zoungonsa (Bohicon), Bénin, December 10, 2014. Robin Law has underscored this origin story as a probable myth created to legitimize the Dahomean Alladahonu ("people of Allada") dynasty within the history of the older (and initially more powerful) Kingdom of Allada. It is more likely that Dahomey emerged from lineage alliances formed in response to pressures from the increasingly important Atlantic trade, although historical evidence is scant for this period. Robin Law, "History and Legitimacy: Aspects of the Use of the Past in Precolonial Dahomey," *History in Africa* 15 (1988): 431–56.

10. John Gillow calls the region from present-day Mauritania to the Cameroon grasslands "the heartland of African textile production"; John Gillow, *African Textiles: Color and Creativity across a Continent* (Thames & Hudson, 2003). Scholars usually categorize West African textiles by processes of weaving or dyeing as opposed to final forms while others associate textile traditions with precolonial political or social formations—Asante *kente*, Bamana *bogolanfini*, and Kano black shiny cloth, for example. Dahomean or Fon textiles are not prominent within this literature, although there are some studies of appliqué; Gillow, *African Textiles*; Colleen E. Kriger, *Cloth in West African History* (AltaMira, 2006); François Thierry Toé, *Textiles et Vêtements du Golfe de Guinée: Enjeux de Conservation et de Médiation* (Riveneuve, 2016); Monni Adams, "Fon Appliqued Cloths," *African Arts* 13, no. 2 (1980): 28–41; Joseph Adandé, "Textiles in Southern Benin," in *Museums & History in West Africa*, ed. Emmanuel Arinze and Claude Daniel Ardouin (James Currey, 2000).

11. Blier, *African Vodun*, 31.

12. Kriger, *Cloth in West African*, 24.

13. Interview with Alphonse Ahouado, Musée d'Abomey, Abomey, September 15, 2015.

14. Colleen E. Kriger, "Mapping the History of Cotton Textile Production in Precolonial West Africa," *African Economic History* 33 (2005): 95.

15. Manning, *Slavery, Colonialism, and Economic Growth*, 68–69; Robert Norris, *Memoirs of the Reign of Bossa Ahádee, King of Dahomy, an Inland Country of Guiney. To Which Are Added, the Author's Journey to Abomey, the Capital; and a Short Account of the African Slave Trade* (Frank Cass, 1968 [1789]), 146.

16. Melville Herskovits conducted fieldwork in the 1930s and observed "old people of both sexes" spinning cotton and described spinning as a "widespread industry," although oral tradition and other European accounts often maintain that spinning was women's work. Melville J. Herskovits, *Dahomey: An Ancient West African Kingdom in Two Volumes* (J. J. Augustin, 1938; Northwestern University Press, 1967), 1:45. If men spun cotton in the 1930s, as claimed by Herskovits, this may have been due to economic depression, cloth shortages, and the turn to *botoyi* (chap. 2).

17. J. A. Skertchly, *Dahomey as It Is; Being a Narrative of Eight Months' Residence in That Country, with a Full Account of the Notorious Annual Customs, and the Social and Religious Institutions of the Ffons; Also an Appendix on Ashantee and a Glossary of Dahoman Words and Titles* (London, 1874), 494.

18. Similar tools for spinning are occasionally used into the twenty-first century. Interview with Juliette Kanlihano, Ahouaja, Abomey, December 11, 2014.

19. Kriger, *Cloth in West African*, 10–11.

20. Marion Johnson, "Technology, Competition, and African Crafts," in *The Imperial Impact: Studies in the Economic History of Africa and India*, ed. Clive Dewey and A. G. Hopkins (Athlone, 1978), 260.

21. Jennifer Morgan, *Laboring Women: Reproduction and Gender in New World Slavery* (University of Pennsylvania Press, 2004).

22. This method of spinning is still practiced today, and locally spun thread is highly valued in the production of wicks for kerosene lamps, often used in night markets.

23. Interview with Juliette Kanlihano, Ahouaja, Abomey, December 11, 2014.

24. Lucie Smolderen, "Textile Production in Dendi: An Ethnographic and Historical Study of a Chain of Production," in *Two Thousand Years in Dendi, Northern Benin*, ed. Anne Haour (Brill, 2018), 76.

25. Interview with Alphonse Ahouado, Musée d'Abomey, Abomey, September 15, 2015; interview with Ernest Fiogbe, Ahouaja, Abomey, September 4, 2015.

26. Suzanne Preston Blier, "Melville J. Herskovits and the Arts of Ancient Dahomey," *RES: Anthropology and Aesthetics* 16 (1988): 133.

27. The debate over whether Dahomey engaged in warfare solely to create tradeable captives was at the heart of the early historiography on the precolonial kingdom.

28. Interview with Ernest Fiogbe, Abomey, September 4, 2015.

29. Bay, *Wives of the Leopard*, 20.

30. Historian Colleen E. Kriger also attributes vertical looms to the forest belt of the Bights of Bénin and Biafra and horizontal looms to the interior; see Kriger, *Cloth in West African*, 21, 70. Interview with Alphonse Ahouado, Musée d'Abomey, Abomey, September 15, 2015.

31. Burton, *A Mission to Gelele*, 2:260; Skertchly, *Dahomey as It Is*, 495; Archibald Dalzel, introduction to *The History of Dahomey: An Inland Kingdom of Africa; Comp. from Authentic Memoirs; with an Introduction and Notes* (London, 1793), xxiv–xxv.

32. This point is also made in Venice and Alastair Lamb, "The Classification and Distribution of Horizontal Treadle Looms in Sub-Saharan Africa," *Textile History* 11, no. 1 (1980): 22–62. However, they attribute the Dahomean loom to Yorùbá origins (Lamb, "Classification and Distribution," 33) while Dahomeans claim the loom came from Asante; see above. The Lambs' argument relies on the idea that the frame is more closely related to the Yorùbá, although frames on Dahomean looms vary in complexity.

33. In Dendi-speaking areas to the north, women spun cotton and men wove. Robin Law and Paul Lovejoy, *The Biography of Mahommah Gardo Baquaqua* (Marcus Wiener, 2007), 111.

34. Herskovits, *Dahomey: An Ancient West African Kingdom*, 1:45–46. Interview with Alphonse Ahouado, Musée d'Abomey, Abomey, September 15, 2015.

35. Kriger, *Cloth in West African*, 20.

36. Skertchly, *Dahomey as It Is*, 323–24; interview with Alphonse Ahouado, Musée d'Abomey, Abomey, September 15, 2015.

37. Dalzel, *History of Dahomey*, xxiv–xxv.

38. Dalzel, *History of Dahomey*, xvii.

39. Hélène d'Almedia Topor, *Histoire économique du Dahomey (Bénin)* (L'Harmattan, 1995), 1:83–84. An example of cloth woven from dyed yarn is the nineteenth-century Royal War Tunic held in the Musée de l'Homme in Paris, France. Blier, *Royal Arts*, 109.

40. Yet Burton felt that the wild product could never be cultivated on a large enough scale since "no amount of demand would produce a regular supply here"; Burton, *A Mission to Gelele*, 2:245.

41. Dalzel, *History of Dahomey,* xxiv–xxv.

42. According to Johnson, red and green dyes were not well known in the region, and weavers acquired these colors by taking apart imported cloth and, later, buying imported dyed yarn. Johnson, "Technology," 261.

43. Interview with Ernest Fiogbe, Ahouaja, Abomey, September 4, 2015.

44. Interview with Barthélemy Adjahouinou, Tindji-Zecko (Za-Kpota), May 27, 2015.

45. Interview with Alladassi Tavi, Tanta (Agbaignzoun), August 25, 2015.

46. Bulfinch Lambe, "Letter from the Great King Trudo Audati's Palace of Abomey, in the Kingdom of Dahomey," November 27, 1724, in *Dahomey and the Dahomans, Being the Journals of Two Missions to the King of Dahomey and Residence at his Capital in the Years 1849 and 1850*, ed. Frederick E. Forbes (London, 1851), 1:184–85.

47. Lambe, "From the Great King Trudo."

48. This supports Bay's conclusion "that individuals could rise in status through merit" in Dahomey. Bay, *Wives of the Leopard*, 14.

49. Patrick R. McNaughton, *The Mande Blacksmiths: Knowledge, Power, and Art in West Africa* (Indiana University Press, 1993), 58–59.

50. In the twentieth century, only postmenopausal women could make and fire pottery for use in vodun shrines. Neil L. Norman, "Powerful Pots, Humbling Holes, and Regional Ritual Processes: Towards an Archaeology of Huedan Vodun, ca. 1650–1727," *African Archaeological Review* 26 (2009): 187–218.

51. Skertchly, *Dahomey as It Is*, 188.

52. Interview with Alphonse Ahouado, Musée d'Abomey, Abomey, September 15, 2015.

53. On the limitations of market approaches for understanding African economies, see Jane I. Guyer, *Marginal Gains: Monetary Transactions in Atlantic Africa* (University of Chicago Press, 2004).

54. Monroe, *Precolonial State*, 41.

55. Monroe, *Precolonial State*, 39.

56. Law, *Slave Coast*, 118–27; Toby Green, *A Fistful of Shells: West Africa from the Rise of the Slave Trade to the Age of Revolution* (University of Chicago Press, 2019), 174.

57. Kriger, "Mapping," 102–3.

58. Norris, *Memoirs of the Reign*, 87.

59. Burton, *A Mission to Gelele*, 38.

60. Skertchly, *Dahomey as It Is*, 323–24.

61. Philip James Shea, "The Development of an Export Oriented Dyed Cloth Industry in Kano Emirate in the Nineteenth Century," (PhD diss., University of Wisconsin–Madison, 1975).

62. Stanley B. Alpern, "What Africans Got for Their Slaves: A Master List of European Trade Goods," *History in Africa* 22 (1995): 6–10.

63. Alpern, "What Africans Got," 10.

64. Gezo transferred the market of Houndjrogondi of Tio to Abomey. Jean-Roger Ahoyo, "Les marchés d'Abomey et de Bohicon," *Les Cahiers d'Outre-Mer* (1975): 165–66.

65. Peter Morton-Williams, "A Yoruba Woman Remembers Servitude in a Palace of Dahomey, in the Reigns of Kings Glele and Behanzin," *Africa: Journal of the International African Institute* 63 (1993): 105.

66. Skertchly, *Dahomey as It Is*, 58.

67. Skertchly, *Dahomey as It Is*, 58.

68. Skertchly, *Dahomey as It Is*, 314.

69. Marion Johnson, "Cloth as Money: The Cloth Strip Currencies of Africa," *Textile History* 11 (1980): 193–202.

70. Green, *Fistful of Shells*, 95–96.

71. Bay, *Wives of the Leopard*, 122–23.

72. Forbes, *Dahomey and the Dahomans*, 1:122.

73. Skertchly, *Dahomey as It Is*, 498, 501.

74. Bay, *Wives of the Leopard*, 158; and Blier, *African Vodun*, 268.

75. "Song against a woman who has done evil, 1931," Dahomean Texts of Songs (copied and commented on, after replaying, by MJH), West Africa Field Trip, 1931, Box 11, Melville J. and Frances S. Herskovits Papers, Sc MG 261, Schomburg Center for Research in Black Culture, Manuscripts, Archives, and Rare Books Division, New York Public Library.

76. Herskovits, *Dahomey*, 265, quoted in Blier, *African Vodun*, 264.

77. Auguste Le Herissé, *L'ancien royaume du Dahomey: Mœrs, religion, histoire* (Emile Larosè, 1911).

78. Elsewhere, Skertchly describes a *joji* as "gallows" adorned with fetishes (32). Skertchly, *Dahomey as It Is*, 73.

79. Zora Neale Hurston, *Barracoon: The Story of the Last "Black Cargo"* (HarperCollins, 2018), 48.

80. Hurston, *Barracoon*, 48.

81. Blier, *African Vodun*, 268–69.

82. Catherine Coquery-Vidrovitch, "La fête des coutumes au Dahomey: Historique Et Essai D'interprétation," *Annales. Histoire, Sciences Sociales* 19 (1964): 696–716.

83. It is important to distinguish "Annual Customs" from "Grand Customs" (*Ahosutanu*), or the weeks-long ceremony that took place two years after the death of a king. Coquery-Vidrovitch argues that only in Grand Customs did human sacrifices exceed five hundred people while about one-tenth the number might be sacrificed on an annual basis. Coquery-Vidrovitch, "La fête des coutumes," 703.

84. Robin Law, "The Slave-Trader as Historian: Robert Norris and the History of Dahomey," *History in Africa* 19 (1989): 220.

85. Norris, *Memoirs of the Reign*, 87.

86. Norris, *Memoirs of the Reign*, 87.

87. Norris, *Memoirs of the Reign*, 87.

88. Dalzel, *History of Dahomey*, xxiii–xxiv.

89. Norris, *Memoirs of the Reign*, 125. Karl Polanyi famously characterized these acts as "redistribution" to theorize his "archaic economy." Polanyi,

Dahomey and the Slave Trade: An Analysis of an Archaic Economy (University of Washington Press, 1966).

90. Norris, *Memoirs of the Reign*, 125.

91. Norris, *Memoirs of the Reign*, 112.

92. Forbes, *Dahomey and the Dahomans*, 2:40; Skertchly, *Dahomey as It Is*, 205.

93. Norris, *Memoirs of the Reign*, 110.

94. Monroe, *Precolonial State*, 55 and 156.

95. Forbes, *Dahomey and the Dahomans*, 2:75.

96. Skertchly, *Dahomey as It Is*, 215.

97. Skertchly, *Dahomey as It Is*, 216–17.

98. Skertchly, *Dahomey as It Is*, 217–18.

99. The royal treasurers or storekeepers were eunuchs housed in the palace called *utunon*. Bay, *Wives of the Leopard*, 270.

100. Law argues that "urbanity was defined not (or not only) by size and concentration of population, but by political autonomy and the role of the town as the seat of administration." Robin Law, *Ouidah: The Social History of a West African Slaving "Port"* (Ohio University Press, 2004), 81. I would add that material culture also defined "urbanity."

101. William Snelgrave, *A New Account of Some Parts of Guinea and the Slave-Trade* (London, 1732), 79–80. Europeans were barred from the capital and seeing the person of the king before this time.

102. Forbes, *Dahomey and the Dahomans*, 1:36, 45.

103. Forbes, *Dahomey and the Dahomans*, 1:77.

104. Interview with Dáa Atchassou, Ahouaja, Abomey, December 10, 2014.

105. On the relationship of *ahisinon* to the state, see Bay, *Wives of the Leopard*, 105.

106. Dalzel, *History of Dahomey*, xvi.

107. Norris, *Memoirs of the Reign*, ix.

108. Interview with Alphonse Ahouado, Musée d'Abomey, Abomey, September 15, 2015.

109. Dalzel, *History of Dahomey*, xvi; Norris, *Memoirs of the Reign*, ix.

110. The king permitted foreigners to wear shoes while in the kingdom. Dalzel, *History of Dahomey*, xvi. This practice is still observed today: When in the presence of the current ceremonial king of Dahomey, all are required to remove their shoes.

111. Interview with Dáa Atchassou, Ahouaja, Abomey, December 10, 2014.

112. Forbes, *Dahomey and the Dahomans*, 2:25–26; Dalzel, *History of Dahomey*, xvii.

113. Lambe, "Letter," 190–91.

114. Skertchly, *Dahomey as It Is*, 487–88.

115. European descriptions of African women's breasts and their role in constructing a racialized other is explored in Morgan, *Laboring Women*, 31–35. For a description see Forbes, *Dahomey and the Dahomans*, 1:28.

116. She was interviewed by anthropologists in the 1950s; Morton-Williams, "A Yoruba Woman," 108.

117. Forbes, *Dahomey and the Dahomans*, 2:64.

118. Aileen Ribeiro, *Fashion and Fiction: Dress in Art and Literature in Stuart England* (Yale University Press, 2006).

119. Skertchly, *Dahomey as It Is*, 204.

120. Forbes, *Dahomey and the Dahomans*, 2:238.

121. Forbes, *Dahomey and the Dahomans*, 2:242. Skertchly identified a number of regiments by their uniforms and insignia. The "Life-guards, or Agbaraya troop" wore "blue tunics, with grey petticoats showing beneath and reaching to the knee. . . . The Gbeto, the elephant hunters . . . were dressed in brown waistcoats, with pink underskirts, with a profuse girdle of leather thongs, which hung down below the skirts. . . . The Tower Gun company. . . [wore] insignia [of] scarlet tassels to their agbaja." Skertchly, *Dahomey as It Is*, 166. In her analysis of the Royal War Tunic, Blier notes that the number of rings indicated the rank of the wearer; see Blier, *Royal Arts of Africa*, 109.

122. Skertchly, *Dahomey as It Is*, 218.

123. Skertchly, *Dahomey as It Is*, 221.

124. Burton, *A Mission to Gelele*, 2:153–54.

125. Burton, *A Mission to Gelele*, 2:50.

126. Skertchly, *Dahomey as It Is*, 263.

127. Forbes, *Dahomey and the Dahomans*, 1:27.

128. Forbes, *Dahomey and the Dahomans*, 1:23.

129. Alphonse Jean René Vicomte de Fleuriot, "Croisières à la côte d'Afrique (1868)," *Le tour du monde* (1876): 243.

130. Bay, *Wives of the Leopard*, 11.

131. Burton, *A Mission to Gelele*, 1:199.

132. Norris, *Memoirs of the Reign*, 102–3.

133. Forbes, *Dahomey and the Dahomans*, 2:214.

134. *Yovo* is sometimes translated as "foreigner," and while this is correct, it is largely associated with white foreigners. For example, the kingdom's position of Yovogan managed coastal trade. Today, light-skinned people are often referred to as yovo while dark-skinned foreigners (from Europe or the United States but not other parts of Africa) might be called yovo as well.

135. Forbes, *Dahomey and the Dahomans*, 2:214.

136. Forbes, *Dahomey and the Dahomans*, 1:219.

137. "No 1396/E Objet: Organisation de l'Enseignement manuel," Rapport au Dahomey, Enseignement Technique et Artisanal – Renseignements, Archives Nationales du Bénin (ANB), 1G/3/6; Dov Ronen, "The Colonial Elite in Dahomey," *African Studies Review* 17 (1974): 56–57. For a story of returnee styling in nearby Lagos, see Okechukwu Nwafor, *Aso Ebi: Dress, Fashion, Visual Culture,*

and *Urban Cosmopolitanism in West Africa* (University of Michigan Press, 2021), 29–31.

138. John M'Leod, *A Voyage to Africa with Some Account of the Manners and Customs of the Dahomian People* (London, 1820), 106.

139. Green writes, "Those who knew how to write and read in European languages were called *yovo*, and were often either of mixed African-European descent, or occasionally of Fon background themselves." Green, *Fistful of Shells*, 308.

140. Burton, *A Mission to Gelele*, 2:52–53.

141. "Au Dahomey (Les fétiches de Kana.–Le dieu de la guerre)," *Supplément illustré du La Petit Journal* 158 (1893): 386.

142. Monroe, *Precolonial State*, 114.

143. Clothing and beards distinguished free people from slaves elsewhere in Africa. See Green, *Fistful of Shells*, 293; and Laura Fair, "Dressing Up: Clothing, Class and Gender in Post-Abolition Zanzibar," *Journal of African History* 39 (1998): 63–94.

144. The illustrated account by d'Albéca contains multiple images of gòdó, while most European publications focused on elite dress. A. L. d'Albéca, *Le France au Dahomey* (Paris, 1895), 123.

145. Dalzel, *History of Dahomey*, 251.

146. Skertchly, *Dahomey as It Is*, 487–88.

147. Adeline Masquelier, introduction to *Dirt, Undress, and Difference: Critical Perspectives on the Body's Surface*, ed. Masquelier, 1–33 (Indiana University Press, 2005).

148. Misty Bastian, "The Naked and the Nude: Historically Multiple Meanings of Oto (Undress) in Southeastern Nigeria," in *Dirt, Undress, and Difference*, 34–60.

149. Dalzel, *History of Dahomey*, xvii.

150. Monroe, *Precolonial State*, 125–45.

151. Manning, *Slavery, Colonialism, and Economic Growth*, 54.

2. Fitting Changes

1. Aho and his brother Rene were the primary informants in Herskovits's research during the 1930s. Justin also served the head of the Abomey palace museum, shaping the narrative of Dahomey's history; "Autour du Mussée historique d'Abomey," *Le Messager du Bénin*, December 1938.

2. Seizures of land by Aho and other Dahomean chefs de canton for their own personal profit led to fifty-one suits against Aho and others by 1937. Aho escaped unscathed from the scandals, although other canton chiefs were forced to resign. Patrick Manning, *Slavery, Colonialism, and Economic Growth in Dahomey, 1640–1960* (Cambridge University Press, 2004), 274.

3. J. Aho was repeatedly accused of sacrificing a young female servant. Rapport politique, année 1937 Archives Nationales du Sénégal (ANS), 2G/37/14.

4. Even many years later, when Aho was no longer chef de canton and was living as an expat in Paris, he continued to make claims on the throne. Manning and others cite how Aho convinced I. A. Akinjogbin that he ought to be recognized as the legitimate king of Dahomey in Paris sometime in 1962. Akinjogbin, *Dahomey and Its Neighbors, 1708–1818* (Cambridge University Press, 1967), 6.

5. Interview with Pascal Adouhouncla, Adandokpodji, Abomey, May 7, 2015.

6. J. F. Reste, *Le Dahomey: Réalisations et Perspectives d'avenir* (Publications du Comité de l'Afrique Française, 1934), 64.

7. A. Annet, Rapport politique, 1939, Porto-Novo, March 23, 1940, ANS, 2G/39/5.

8. Invitation vin d'honneur, October 13, 1935, Abomey, 1935, Archives Nationales du Bénin (ANB), 1G/20/9.

9. Interview with Pascal Adouhouncla, Adandokpodji, Abomey, May 7, 2015.

10. Léonce Grandin, *A l'assaut du pays des noirs. Le Dahomey, par le commandant Grandin* (Paris, 1895), 2:196–97.

11. Sven Beckert, *Empire of Cotton: A Global History* (Vintage, 2015).

12. Historian Marion Johnson first made the argument that, in the late nineteenth century, colonial states and businesses turned to "cotton imperialism"; Marion Johnson, "Cotton Imperialism in West Africa," *African Affairs* 73 (1974): 178–87.

13. "Rapport: Prix du cotton Allen sélectionne FOB Abidjan," Paris, November 3, 1941, Mise en application de la convention du 26 décembre, 1941, Archives Nationales d'Outre-Mer (hereafter ANOM), 1 AFF-ECO/282.

14. Auguste Le Herissé, *L'ancien royaume du Dahomey: Mœrs, religion, histoire* (Emile Larosè, 1911), 43.

15. Rapport Mensuel, Cercle d'Abomey, Février 1912, ANB, 1E2/2-3.

16. Manning, *Slavery, Colonialism, and Economic Growth*, 176–77.

17. Manning, *Slavery, Colonialism, and Economic Growth*, 108.

18. "Song of Ridicule," D59, Dahomean Texts of Songs (copied and commented on, after replaying, by MJH), West Africa Field Trip, 1931, Box 11, Melville J. and Frances S. Herskovits papers, Sc MG 261, Schomburg Center for Research in Black Culture (SCBC), Manuscripts, Archives, and Rare Books Division, New York Public Library.

19. German buyers purchased Dahomean cotton in 1909. Rapport Mensuel, August 1909, ANB, 1E2/4/3/8.

20. Lettre du Governeur Reste au Governeur Général d'AOF, Porto-Novo, Februrary 5, 1930, Correspondance relatifs à l'exposition coloniale (1931), ANB, 1Q/002/00014.

21. Bulletins commerciales des cercles, Abomey, 1er trimestre 1928, ANB, 1Q/003/00023.

22. Richard L. Roberts, *Two Worlds of Cotton: Colonialism and the Regional Economy in the French Soudan, 1800–1946* (Stanford University Press, 1996).

23. Dahomey Field Notes, Accounts 1931–Book Xi, West Africa Field Trip, 1931, Box 10, S. Herskovits papers, Sc MG 261, SCBC.

24. Interview with Juliette A. Kanlihano, Ahouaja, Abomey, December 11, 2014.

25. Interview with Michel Agounkpléto, Adagamé, Lissèzoun, Bohicon, September 2, 2015.

26. Manning, *Slavery, Colonialism, and Economic Growth*, 126.

27. Manning, *Slavery, Colonialism, and Economic Growth*, 125–26.

28. Le Herissé, *L'ancien royaume du Dahomey*, 43.

29. Interview with Amadou Adamou, Zongo, Abomey, May 9, 2015.

30. Nina Sylvanus, *Patterns in Circulation: Cloth, Gender, and Materiality in West Africa* (University of Chicago Press, 2016).

31. Lettre de Witt & Büsch et al. à Monsieur le Lieutenent Gouverneur du Dahomey et Dépendences, Porto-Novo, October 28, 1904, ANB, 1Q/017/00187.

32. Télégramme Lettre Officiel de Lieutenant-Gouverneur à Cercles, March 20, 1936, Cercle de Porto-Novo, Emigration saisonnière des travailleurs vers le Nigeria, ANB, S/6/1/2.

33. Interview with Amadou Adamou, Zongo, Abomey, May 9, 2015.

34. Lettre de la Banque de l'AOF à Président de Chambre de Commerce de Cotonou, June 24, 1933, ANB, 1Q/1/00009. See also Jane Guyer, *Marginal Gains: Monetary Transactions in Atlantic Africa* (University of Chicago Press, 2004).

35. État des jugements, par le tribunal du 1er degré de Cotonou pendant le mois de Janvier 1932, ANB, 1M62/1.

36. État des jugements, par le tribunal du 1er degré de Djougou pendant le mois de Janvier 1932, ANB, 1M62/1.

37. État des jugements, par le tribunal du 1er degré de Allada pendant le mois de Janvier 1932, ANB, 1M62/1. État des jugements, par le tribunal du 1er degré de Zagnanado pendant le mois de Janvier 1932, ANB, 1M62/1.

38. Hilary Jones, *The Métis of Senegal: Urban Life and Politics in French West Africa* (Indiana University Press, 2013), 99–102.

39. Lettre de la Directrice de l'École ménagère à Monsieur l'Administrateur du cercle de Ouidah, Ouidah, May 28, 1912, ANB, 1G/20/1.

40. Mougent, Directrice, Internat des métis, Règlement interieur, Porto-Novo, January 11, 1922, ANB, 1G/12/8.

41. Agoué is a coastal town near Grand Popo while Calavi is about ten kilometers inland from Cotonou—today it is essentially a suburb of Cotonou.

L'inspecteur des écoles, No. 1450 E., Object: envoi de documents en Vue Conseil gouvernement, Porto-Novo, November 3, 1931, ANB, 1G/6/8.

42. No 372E - Décision plaçant en qualité d'enternes les métisses dans les établissements d'enseignement privé, March 15, 1936, Porto-Novo, clipping from *Journal officiel du Dahomey*, ANS, K/154/26.

43. L'inspecteur des écoles, Rapport No. 145 E, Porto-Novo, November 13, 1931, ANB, 1G/6/8. The first public school devoted to girls' domestic education in the AOF opened in 1955 in Côte d'Ivoire; see ANS, 2G/57/80.

44. Untitled document, Abomey, 1935, ANB, 1G/20/9.

45. A. Annet, "Enquête sur la formation de la femme indigène comme ménagère et comme mère de famille. Enseignement ménagèr, 1939," July 24, 1939, ANS, O/307(31).

46. Lettre de le directeur de l'école d'apprentissage à Monsieur le Lieutenant gouverneur du Dahomey, January 8, 1914, ANB, 1G/6/13.

47. Arrêt no 965, September 1924, ANB, 1G/12/8.

48. École professionnelle de Cotonou, Rapport d'ensemble sur le service de l'enseignement pendant l'année, 1929–1930, ANB, 1G/17/8.

49. L'inspecteur des écoles, Rapport No. 145 E, Porto-Novo, November 13, 1931, ANB, 1G/6/8. The programs in shoemaking and tailoring would be closed the following academic year when the school was moved to Cotonou. ANB, 1G/10/8.

50. Arrêt no 1132, Licenciement Sections Tailleurs et Cordonniers École professionnelle, July 18, 1932, ANB, 1G/10/8.

51. Instructions du Lieutenant-Govuverneur du 1er Septembre 1934, ANB, 1G/14/9.

52. Lettre du Brévié au Gouverneur Général du Dahomey, No 192/E, Objet: Maison des métiers au Dahomey, ANB, 2G/3/9.

53. The extensive list includes "blacksmiths, jewelers, carvers and engravers, sculptors and modelers, dyers, potters, basket makers, shoemakers, etc." Desanti, "Arrêt portant création d'une 'Maison des Artisans dahoméens' à Abomey," May 10, 1936, Porto-Novo, ANS, O/45/31.

54. Lettre du governeur du Dahomey aux commandants de cercle, "No 3813, Artisanat dahoméen," July 19, 1938, ANB, 2G/3/6.

55. Rapport de tournée au Dahomey (Tournée du 10 Décembre au 28 Février 1939), Lettre de l'Inspecteur de l'enseignement téchnique et artisanal à le Gouverneur général de l'A.O.F., Dakar, July 18, 1939, ANB, 2G/3/6.

56. Victoria Rovine, "A Wider Loom? French Colonial Preoccupations with West African Weaving," *African Arts* 52, no. 4 (2019): 66–83.

57. Robert Bruce Davies, *Peacefully Working to Conquer the World: Singer Sewing Machines in Foreign Markets, 1854–1920* (Arno Press, 1976), described in Judith

G. Coffin, "Credit, Consumption, and Images of Women's Desires: Selling the Sewing Machine in Late Nineteenth-Century France," *French Historical Studies* 18 (1994): 750.

58. Hélène d'Almedia Topor, *Histoire économique du Dahomey (Bénin)* (Éditions L'Harmattan, 1995), 1:160.

59. A. Charton, "L'artisanat indigène en AOF," Congres de la Société Indigène, 1931, ANS, O/349/31.

60. Nancy Rose Hunt, *A Colonial Lexicon: Of Birth Ritual, Medicalization, and Mobility in the Congo* (Duke University Press, 1999); Lynn M. Thomas, *Politics of the Womb: Women, Reproduction, and the State in Kenya* (University of California Press, 2003).

61. Arrêt No. 1812 I.T., Conakry August 4, 1937, ANS, K/154/26.

62. Office du travail, Procès-verbal de la réunion du 15 fevrier 1935, ANS, K/154/26.

63. This discourse on treadle machines causing miscarriage is found elsewhere in the early twentieth century. See, for an example in the United States, Mary Lillian Read, *The Mothercraft Manual* (Little, Brown, 1919), 70.

64. Ends with "Abitó is a god, Gbajiwó here is the Fa which I have received." D234, Dahomean Texts of Songs (copied and commented on, after replaying, by MJH), West Africa Field Trip, 1931, Box 11, Melville J. and Frances S. Herskovits papers, Sc MG 261, SCBC.

65. "No 1396/E Objet: Organisation de l'Enseignement manuel," Rapport au Dahomey. Enseignement Technique et Artisanal - Renseignements, ANB, 1G/3/6. Also quoted in Dov Ronen, "The Colonial Elite in Dahomey," *African Studies Review* 17 (1974): 56–57.

66. Pierre Verger, Images 7289, 7304, 7333, and 7334/Dahomey/Ouidah/De Souza, Fundação Pierre Verger, Salvador, Brazil, https://pierreverger.org.

67. Rapport commercial et administrative, Cercle d'Abomey, April 1899, ANB, 1E2/2-1/2.

68. Rapport Mensuel, Cercle d'Abomey, avril 1912, ANB, 1E2/2-3/4; Rapport Mensuel, Cercle d'Abomey, November, 1912, ANB, 1E2/2-3/2/11. Clothing prisoners was an ongoing challenge for the local colonial government; see also Rapport 4e trimester, Cercle d'Abomey, 1936, ANB 1E2/4/10/4.

69. Rapport Mensuel, Cercle d'Abomey, July 1912, ANB, 1E2/2-3/2/7.

70. Elisée Soumonni, "Some Reflections on the Brazilian Legacy in Dahomey," *Slavery and Abolition* (2001): 61–71.

71. In an interview, Gabin Akouêdenoudjè, a former clerk in the AOF, described how one attained education. He went to a private Catholic school for his primary school certificate, and as he described it, "I only have a CEPE but I have worked like university graduate." Later, he took a correspondence course

in accounting from the private Parisian technical school Pigiet. Interview with Akouêdenoudjè, Adandokpodji, Abomey, September 4, 2015.

72. Joanne B. Eicher and Barbara Sumberg, "World Fashion, Ethnic, and National Dress," in *Dress and Ethnicity: Change across Space and Time*, ed. Joanne B. Eicher (Berg, 1995).

73. Interview with Nestor Dako-Wegbe, Houawe Zoungonsa (Bohicon), December 10, 2014.

74. David Kuchta, *The Three-Piece Suit and Modern Masculinity: England, 1550–1850* (University of California Press, 2002); Philippe Perrot, *Fashioning the Bourgeoisie: A History of Clothing in the Nineteenth Century*, trans. Richard Bienvenu (Princeton University Press, 1996).

75. Photograph, *Phare du Dahomey*, No 144, May 13, 1937, ANOM.

76. Rouven Kunstmann notes how in neighboring Nigeria, "aristocrats with less power" also appeared within the pages of newspapers wearing suits, as opposed to the agbada and other fancy dress of traditional authorities. Kunstmann, "The Politics of Portrait Photographs in Southern Nigerian Newspapers, 1945–1954," *Social Dynamics* 40 (2015): 524–25.

77. A. Annet, Rapport politique, 1939, Porto-Novo, March 23, 1940, ANS, 2G/39/5.

78. Children and young women wrapped themselves in a single pagne by starting with the pagne placed behind the body, wrapping the two sides over the front of the body, and tying the ends behind the neck. Interview with Gabin Akouêdenoudjè, Adandokpodji, Abomey, September 4, 2015.

79. Interview with Cyprien Fa, Détohou (Abomey), May 3, 2015; interview with Amadou Adamou, Zongo, Abomey, May 9, 2015.

80. On the dynamics of "tradition" in colonial Africa, see Thomas Spear, "Neo-Traditionalism and the Limits of Invention in British Colonial Africa," *Journal of African History* 44 (2003): 3–27.

81. Interview with Cyprien Fa, Détohou (Abomey), May 3, 2015.

82. Interview with Dáa Atchassou, Ahouaja, Abomey, December 10, 2014.

83. For the effects of the war more generally, see Judith A. Byfield et al., *Africa and World War II* (Cambridge University Press, 2015).

84. Manning, *Slavery, Colonialism, and Economic Growth*, 236.

85. Rapport Politique, 1943, May 17, 1944, 2, ANS, 2G/43/21.

86. Lettre de la Direction des Affaires Économiques et du Plan Accords Commerciaux et Douanes to Président of la Chambre de Commerce de Tarare, 9243/AE/4, October 9, 1950, Tissus: cotonnades I, 1948–1950, ANOM, 1 AFF-ECO 649.

87. Rapport Politique, 1944, 1–2, ANS, 2G/44/25.

88. Rapport Annuel sur le Travail et Main d'œuvre, 1943, Porto-Novo, March 23, 1943, ANS, 2G/43/27.

89. Singer Manufacturing Company, *Singer in World War II, 1939–1945* (Singer Manufacturing Company, 1946), 33.

90. "Programme d'importation supplémentaire dans le but d'enrayer le hausse dus prix," Departement des affairs économique et du plan, October 12, 1950, ANOM, 1 AFF-ECO/649/1.

91. Lettre de le secrétaire à la production à Monsieur le Gouverneur général de l'AOF, February 20, 1943, ANOM, 1 AFF-ECO 221.

92. Interview with Alphonse Ahouado, Musée d'Abomey, Abomey, September 15, 2015.

93. Lettre de le Gouverneur générale de l'AOF à Monsieur le ministre des colonies, Dakar, June 27, 1945, ANOM, 1 AFF-ECO 221.

94. Arrêt no 1062, SE/P, Réglementant la culture du coton en Afrique Française, Dakar, March 18, 1942, ANOM, 1 AFF-ECO 282.

95. Interview with Dáa Martin Ayikpé, Avogbannan (Bohicon), May 25, 2015.

96. Leora Auslander, *Cultural Revolutions: Everyday Life and Politics in Britain, North America, and France* (University of California Press, 2009); Lisa Trivedi, *Clothing Gandhi's Nation: Homespun and Modern India* (University of Indiana Press, 2007).

97. Lettre du Gouverneur général de l'AOF à Monsieur le ministre des colonies, no. 3442 SSM/5, Dakar, November 3, 1939, ANOM, 1 AFF-ECO/222.

3. Tailoring Men

1. E. Cayode, "Eloquence du vêtement," *L'aube nouvelle*, April 24, 1966.

2. Frederick Cooper, "Possibility and Constraint: African Independence in Historical Perspective," *Journal of African History* 49, no. 2 (2008): 167–96; Adom Getachew, *Worldmaking after Empire: The Rise and Fall of Self-Determination* (Princeton University Press, 2019).

3. Karin Barber, *A History of African Popular Culture* (Cambridge University Press, 2017). For some case studies, see Andrew Ivaska, *Cultured States: Youth, Gender, and Modern Style in 1960s Dar es Salaam* (Duke University Press, 2011); Elizabeth Harney, *In Senghor's Shadow: Art, Politics, and the Avant-Garde in Senegal, 1960–1995* (Duke University Press, 2004); Paul R. Davis, "An Institution for Post-Independence Art: US-RDA Cultural Policy and *Encadrement Malien* at the Institut National des Arts," *Critical Interventions* (2014): 96–118; and Mike McGovern, *Unmasking the State: Making Guinea Modern* (University of Chicago Press, 2012).

4. Abena Dove Osseo-Asare, "Kwame Nkrumah's Suits: Sartorial Politics in Ghana at Independence," *Fashion Theory* 25, no. 5 (2021): 597–632; Rouven Kunstmann, "Fashioning Nationalism and the Shaping of the Public Sphere in 1950s Nigeria," *Journal of West African History* (2021): 27–54; and Leslie Rabine,

"Photography, Poetry, and the Dressed Bodies of Léopold Sédar Senghor," in *African Dress: Fashion, Agency, Performance*, ed. Karen Tranberg Hansen and D. Soyini Madison (Bloomsbury Academic, 2013).

5. Lisa Lindsay, "Working with Gender: The Emergence of the 'Male Breadwinner' in Colonial Southwestern Nigeria," in *Africa after Gender?*, ed. Catherine M. Cole, Takyiwaa Manuh, and Stephan F. Miescher (Indiana University Press, 2007), 241–52.

6. As chapter 5 will explore, there was a feminization of both fashion and tailoring by the 1970s.

7. James Ferguson, *Expectations of Modernity: Myths and Meaning of Urban Life on the Zambian Copperbelt* (University of California Press, 1999). Ferguson has argued that "modernization" in Africa served as a metonym for the pathway toward a "global status and political economic condition" and that, in Africa, "modern" signified particularly wealthy people and places. James Ferguson, *Global Shadows: Africa in the Neoliberal World Order* (Duke University Press, 2006), 82.

8. In the decades preceding the late 1940s, the colonial state sought to limit cross-border traffic and restrict imports. Worldwide depression in the 1930s and then global war made it difficult for West Africans to access the goods of tailoring, like machinery and textiles, until several years after the end of the Second World War. By the 1970s, mobilities of populations and ideas were once again stifled by national politics, including a 1972 coup d'état that led to Mathieu Kérékou's 1974 declaration of Marxism-Leninism, and by politics in other African states that forcibly repatriated Béninois, including tailors, as part of their own nation-building schemes.

9. Clapperton Chakanetsa Mavhunga, *The Mobile Workshop: The Tsetse Fly and African Knowledge Production* (MIT Press, 2018).

10. In southern Ghana, Tobias Wendl pointed out not only that "photographers and tailors share the same aesthetic values and preferences" but also that many of the early photographers were originally tailors (84–85). Tobias Wendl, "Entangled Traditions: Photography and the History of Media in Southern Ghana," *RES: Anthropology and Aesthetics* 39 (2001): 78–101.

11. Interview with Lékolihoui Djibidisse, Zakpo Adame-Ahite, Bohicon, December 9, 2014.

12. Monica L. Miller, *Slaves to Fashion: Black Dandyism and the Styling of Black Diasporic Identity* (Duke University Press, 2009).

13. Shantrelle P. Lewis, *Dandy Lion: The Black Dandy and Street Style* (Aperture, 2017), 8. See also Didier Gondola, "Dream and Drama: The Search for Elegance among Congolese Youth," *African Studies Review* 42, no. 1 (1999), 23–48.

14. Franz Fanon, *The Wretched of the Earth* (Grove, 1961 [2004]), 158, 161.

15. In this sense, the Black dandies of the 1950s and '60s are very different from the *bluffeurs* of early 2000s Côte d'Ivoire, whose acts of dressing up were self-consciously imitative and illusionary. Sasha Newell, *The Modernity Bluff: Crime, Consumption, and Citizenship in Côte d'Ivoire* (University of Chicago Press, 2012).

16. The importance of tailored, fitted clothing to veteran self-fashioning is most evident within the film *Camp de Thiaroye*, about the uprising in a demobilization camp outside Dakar. *Camp de Thiaroye,* directed by Ousmane Sembène and Thierno Faty Sow (Filmi Domireew, 1988), DVD. On riflemen's uniforms, see Keith Rathbone, "Dressing the Colonial Body: Senegalese Rifleman in Uniform," in *African Dress*, ed. Karen Tranberg Hansen and D. Soyini Madison (Bloomsbury, 2013), 111–23.

17. Interview with Lêgbânon Bénoit Djezandé, Tindji-Adjoko (Za-Kpota), May 27, 2015.

18. Interview with Lazare Agbotounso, Tindji-Assalin (Za-Kpota), August 1, 2015.

19. Gregory Mann argues that demobilized veterans in the French Soudan used parts of their uniforms to upset power dynamics between generations or elder-younger siblings. *Native Sons: West African Veterans and France in the Twentieth Century* (Duke University Press, 2006), 93–95. Mann also contrasts veterans of the Second World War with those of World War I who tended to align themselves with the traditional authority of the chefs de canton. Mann, *Native Sons*, 110.

20. Rapport Politique, 1947, April 15, 1948, 4, ANS, 2G/47/25.

21. The Portuguese family names of the signatories on the petition attest that the prewar traders of the early colonial commercial class came, for the most part, from Aguda communities and that businessmen from places like Abomey and Bohicon had begun to threaten their market dominance. Lettre de la Groupement des Traitants de Porto-Novo à le Gouverneur de Dahomey, Porto-Novo, October 4, 1944, ANB, 1Q/1/0002.

22. Interview with Elisabeth Sodokpa, Dota-Sogbadji, Abomey, June 16, 2015.

23. Interview with Lêgbânon Bénoit Djezandé, Tindji-Adjoko (Za-Kpota), May 27, 2015.

24. For example, a new police station opened in Bohicon in 1949. Rapport Politique, 1949, ANS, 2G/49/36.

25. Bill Freund, *The African City: A History* (Cambridge University Press, 2007), 76–93.

26. Interview with Paul Zoungbowenon, Marché Ganhi de Bohicon, April 24, 2015.

27. Interview with Maurice Béhanzin, Hountondji, Abomey, July 14, 2015.

28. Interview with Gabin Akouêdenoudjè, Adandokpodji, Abomey, September 4, 2015.

29. Timothy Burke, *Lifebuoy Men, Lux Women: Commodification, Consumption, and Cleanliness in Modern Zimbabwe* (Duke University Press, 1996).

30. Interview with Anago Yobode, Dota, Abomey, April 28, 2015; interview with Célestin Kokossou, Kpatalokoli, Bohicon, June 4, 2021.

31. Jennifer Hart, *Ghana on the Go: African Mobility in the Age of Motor Transportation* (Indiana University Press, 2016), 98–99.

32. Interview with Pierrot Akpako, Agbaignzoun Centre, August 25, 2015.

33. Interview with Alain Baba, Zakpo, Adame-Ahito, Bohicon, November 28, 2014, June 5, 2021. In my many years of living in the areas southeast of Abomey, discussion and fear of àzètɔ (witches) thieving body parts was quite common. I personally witnessed a 2007 market riot in Klouekanmé over a stolen corpse. Yet the literature is relatively silent on this. Falen notes rumors of bodysnatching and the arrest of a prominent Abomean for using body parts in ceremonies around 2012 (Douglas J. Falen, *African Science: Witchcraft, Vodun, and Healing in Southern Benin* [University of Wisconsin, 2020], 184–86). I was there at the time and remember the incident well. The man was never charged.

34. Interview with Marc Agbandjaï, Dota, Abomey, April 28, 2015.

35. Interview with Clotaire Blenon, Kpocon, Bohicon, May 4, 2015.

36. Interview with Clotaire Blenon, Kpocon, Bohicon, May 4, 2015.

37. Interview with Clotaire Blenon, Kpocon, Bohicon, May 4, 2015.

38. Jennifer Bajorek, *Unfixed: Photography and Decolonial Imagination in West Africa* (Duke University Press, 2020); Kerstin Pinther, "Textiles and Photography in West Africa," *Critical Interventions* 1, no. 1 (2007): 106–18.

39. The technological and bureaucratic role of these documents and headshots will be explored in the following chapter.

40. Godou Kpodo's version lacks the chalkboards usually placed among the diamonds of letters. Roger Gerards and Suze May Sho, *Vlisco Fabrics* (ArtEZ, 2014).

41. Anne Grosfilley, *African Wax Print Textiles* (Prestel, 2018), 51–55.

42. Interview with Sébastien Djokpe, Marché Ganhi de Bohicon, June 6, 2021.

43. Elizabeth Ann Fretwell, "The Tools of Tailoring as Technologies-in-Use in Twentieth Century Benin, West Africa," *History and Technology* 37, no. 2 (2021): 147–71.

44. "AOF - Programme général des importation pour l'année 1948 en provenance de l'étranger et l'union français," ANOM, 1 AFF-ECO/333.

45. In 1950, French administrators estimated that 95 percent of Singer machines in its overseas territories were these "household" models. "Programme d'importation supplémentaire dans le but d'enrayer le hausse dus prix," Departement des affairs économique et du plan, 12 October 1950, ANOM, 1 AFF-ECO/649/1.

46. Judith G. Coffin, "Credit, Consumption, and Images of Women's Desires: Selling the Sewing Machine in Late Nineteenth-Century France," *French Historical Studies* 18 (1994): 761.

47. In colonial India, local Singer representatives ignored company-wide directives on how to market their products to homemakers and instead focused their efforts on selling household machines to Indian artisan tailors. David Arnold, *Everyday Technology: Machines and the Making of India's Modernity* (University of Chicago Press, 2013), 70–72.

48. "Programme d'importation supplémentaire dans le but d'enrayer le hausse dus prix," Departement des affairs économique et du plan, 12 October 1950, ANOM, 1 AFF-ECO/649/1.

49. "Etude sur l'évolution comparée des prix français et étrangers en 1952," Departement des affairs économique et du plan, 12 October 1950, ANOM, 1 AFF-ECO/652.

50. Interview with Trankilin Alladanon, Bohicon Centre, August 17, 2011.

51. On automobility and "modern" men, see Hart, *Ghana on the Go*, 98–99. On tractors, Laura Ann Twagira, "'Robot Farmers' and Cosmopolitan Workers: Technological Masculinity and Agricultural Development in the French Soudan (Mali), 1945–68," *Gender & History* 26 (2014): 470–71.

52. Paulin J. Hountondji, introduction to *Endogenous Knowledge: Research Trails*, ed. Hountondji, trans. Ayi Kwesi Armah (CODESRIA, 1997), 4.

53. Anthropologist Douglas Falen has noted recent instances of Fon calling technologies from the West *yovò àzě* (white witchcraft) due to their association with white people. He also traces the problematic local associations between yovò àzě and goodness, as opposed to the malevolent forces behind African àzě, although he convincingly dismisses this as a form of internalized racism, focusing rather on how discourses on yovò àzě offer a "critique of the West's failed development policies" (69). Falen, *African Science*, 65–70.

54. Patrick R. McNaughton, *The Mande Blacksmiths: Knowledge, Power, and Art in West Africa* (Indiana University Press, 1993).

55. See chapter 4.

56. Interview with Célestine Dangbé, Azali, Abomey, June 17, 2015.

57. Rapport Politique, 1949, ANS, 2G/49/36.

58. Rapport sur l'activité des services présenté par M. Le Gouverneur Bonfils à l'Assemblée Territoriale, session budgétaire 1954, 45, ANS, 2G/54/107. Non-French companies made most of the fabric that entered through the port of Cotonou by 1950, a significant change from earlier decades. Lettre de la Direction des Affaires Economiques et du Plan Accords Commerciaux et Douanes to President of la Chambre de Commerce de Tarare, 9243/AE/4, 4, October 9, 1950, ANOM, 1 AFF-ECO 649.

59. For example, in 1952, an Ecru with a value of 80 francs was subject to a 15 percent tariff if French or 30 percent if foreign upon entering the AOF, while

the same fabric in the Gold Coast or Nigeria had a 10 percent tariff whether it was British or not. Lettre de Ministre de la france d'outre-mer à Monsieur le président du Syndicat general de l'Industrie cotonnière Française, July 24, 1952, ANOM, 1 AFF-ECO/651.

60. While manufacturers blamed colonial administrators for permitting a flourishing black market, administrators contended that manufacturers failed to make the types of cloth that West Africans wanted to purchase and French firms in particular failed to research their preferences. Rapport Politique, 1950, Porto-Novo, July 9, 1951, ANS, 2G/50/31. Lettre de Gouverneur des colonies à Monsieur le ministre de la france d'outre mer, December 17, 1948, ANOM, 1 AFF-ECO/649.

61. "Le livre de bord de l'exposition organisée par le Syndicat general de l'Industrie cotonnière française en afrique noire," "Textiles" Editions Dotec, Paris, ANOM, 1 AFF-ECO/651.

62. Odile Georg, *Tropical Dream Palaces: Cinema in Colonial West Africa* (Oxford University Press, 2020), 79.

63. "Le livre de bord de l'exposition organisée par le Syndicat general de l'Industrie cotonnière française en afrique noire," "Textiles" Editions Dotec, Paris, ANOM, 1 AFF-ECO/651.

64. J. Binet, "Consommation des articles textiles au Cameroun," ANOM, 1 AFF-ECO/652.

65. Nina Sylvanus attributes the licking and smelling of cloth in Togo to more recent times as a way to detect counterfeits, although there is no evidence that this is a new practice. Nina Sylvanus, *Patterns in Circulation: Cloth, Gender, and Materiality in West Africa* (University of Chicago Press, 2016), 145.

66. In French Cameroon, an administrator noted how cotton drill was less popular in the final decade of colonialism. J. Binet, "Consommation des articles textiles au Cameroun," ANOM, 1 AFF-ECO/652.

67. Phyllis M. Martin, "Contesting Clothes in Colonial Brazzaville," *Journal of African History* 35 (1994): 419.

68. Ursula Klein, *Experiments, Models, Paper Tools: Cultures of Organic Chemistry in the Nineteenth Century* (Stanford University Press, 2002).

69. Interview with Jules Wimêllo, Tindji-Kpozou (Za-Kpota), May 6, 2015.

70. Interview with Donatien Dansi, Adame-Adato, Gnidgazou (Bohicon), December 9, 2014; interview with Nestor Dako-Wegbe, Houawe Zoungonsa (Bohicon), December 10, 2014.

71. Interview with Emiliene Agbo, Adandokpdji Daxo, Abomey, June 8, 2015.

72. Interview with Jules Wimêllo, Tindji-Kpozou (Za-Kpota), May 6, 2015.

73. Interview with Lékolihoui Djibidisse, Zakpo Adame-Ahite, Bohicon, December 9, 2014. Djokpe, one of Djibidisse's brother's apprentices, also recalled

his methods for learning new styles. Interview with Sébastien Djokpe, Marché Ganhi de Bohicon, June 6, 2021.

74. Anthropologist Jean Lave notes similar processes among Liberian tailors in the 1970s. Jean Lave, *Apprenticeship in Critical Ethnographic Practice* (University of Chicago Press, 2011), 70.

75. Karen Tranberg Hansen, *Salaula: The World of Secondhand Clothing and Zambia* (University of Chicago Press, 2000).

76. S. Videhouenou, "Faut-il condamner le commerce de vêtements d'occasion au Dahomey," *L'aube nouvelle*, August 4, 1968.

77. Valentin Alagbe, "Friperie, fripons, et frivolités 'imperialistes,'" *L'aube nouvelle*, September 15, 1968.

78. Agassounon explained that ideas around acouta changed as "today, they have preached the good news of Jesus Christ and he has changed the world and today we see clearly and, like that, everybody wears acouta." Interview with Célestine Agassounon, Soglogon, Bohicon, June 14, 2015.

79. Interview with Sébastien Djokpe, Marché Ganhi de Bohicon, June 6, 2021.

80. Interview with René Allaga, Bohicon market, April 27, 2015.

81. André Chappatte, *In Search of Tunga: Prosperity, Almighty God, and Lives in Motion in a Malian Provincial Town* (University of Michigan Press, 2022), 7.

82. Lorelle Semley, *Mother Is Gold, Father Is Glass: Gender and Colonialism in a Yoruba Town* (Indiana University Press, 2011), 119–20.

83. Interview with Donatien Dansi, Adame-Adate, Gnidgazou (Bohicon), December 9, 2014; interview with Antoine Zohou, Adame-Adate (Bohicon), April 20, 2015.

84. Interview with Antoine Zohou, Adame-Adate (Bohicon), April 20, 2015.

85. Interview with Lazare Agbotounso, Tindji-Assalin (Za-Kpota), August 1, 2015; interview with Donatien Dansi, Adame-Adate, Gnidgazou (Bohicon), December 9, 2014; and interview with Jules Wimêllo, Tindji-Kpozou (Za-Kpota), May 6, 2015.

86. The French army trained Indochinese and Malagasy soldiers as tailors, cooks, and nurses and in other jobs starting in the First World War and extended similar programs to the *tirailleurs sénégalais* during the Second. Richard Standish Fogarty, *Race and War in France: Colonial Subjects in the French Army, 1914–1918* (Johns Hopkins University Press, 2008), 65–66. One woman recalled how her father became a tailor after he was injured and unable to serve in other ways. Interview with Jeanne Hanou, Ahouamé, Bohicon, July 17, 2015.

87. Interview with Lêgbânon Bénoit Djezandé, Tindji-Adjoko (Za-Kpota), May 27, 2015.

88. Interview with Dáa Ganmanssô-Ahéko, Lissazoumé (Agbaignzoun), July 22, 2015.

89. Interview with Célestin Kokossou, Kpatalokoli, Bohicon, June 4, 2021.

90. Interview with Pierrot Akpako, Agbaignzoun Centre, August 25, 2015. Another tailor spent time in Cotonou specifically to learn how to make suits; interview with Lêgbânon Bénoit Djezandé, Tindji-Adjoko (Za-Kpota), May 27, 2015.

91. Interview with Antoine Zohou, Adame-Adate (Bohicon), June 5, 2021.

92. Interview with Sébastien Djokpe, Marché Ganhi de Bohicon, June 6, 2021.

93. Interview with Alain Baba, Zakpo, Adame-Ahito, Bohicon, June 5, 2021.

94. Interview with Celestin Godou Kpodo, Adandokpodji, Abomey, June 1, 2015.

95. Interview with Alain Baba, Zakpo, Adame-Ahito, Bohicon, June 5, 2021.

96. Interview with Célestin Kokossou, Kpatalokoli, Bohicon, June 4, 2021.

97. Celestin Goudou Kpodo worked at the jute sack factory and saved enough money to buy two cars, one of which he drove to Côte d'Ivoire to work there. Interview with Celestin Godou Kpodo, Adandokpodji, Abomey, June 1, 2015.

98. Nestor Djèha, head of the Bohicon taxi station and head of the drivers' union, was originally a tailor. Interview with Donatien Dansi, Adame-Adate, Gnidgazou (Bohicon), December 9, 2014. Interview with Lékolihoui Djibidisse, Zakpo Adame-Ahite, Bohicon, December 9, 2014.

99. Interview with Jules Wimêllo, Tindji-Kpozou (Za-Kpota), May 6, 2015.

100. Interview with Celestin Godou Kpodo, Adandokpodji, Abomey, June 1, 2015.

101. Interview with Jeanne Hanou, Ahouamé, Bohicon, July 17, 2015. A significant number of Dahomeans worked in the other colonies of the AOF, and these civil servants were forced to return to Dahomey at independence. These men, now "foreigners" in countries where many had worked for years and established families, often had to abandon investments and families. Interview with Gabin Akouêdenoudjè, Adandokpodji, Abomey, September 4, 2015.

102. Thélesphore Ahossi was repatriated from Gabon; interview with Ahossi, Lissazoumé (Agbaignzoun), July 21, 2015. The Nigerian expulsions of the early 1980s affected several of my male and female informants. For example, interview with Maurice Béhanzin, Hountondji, Abomey, July 14, 2015; and interview with Lêgbânon Bénoit Djezandé, Tindji-Adjoko (Za-Kpota), May 27, 2015.

103. "La mode: le voile se leve sur les collections printemps - été 1962 de la haute couture," *L'aube nouvelle*, no. 69, March 10, 1962, ANB.

104. Unlike in General Soglo's 1963 coup, in 1965 he did not transfer power to a civilian regime. Instead he declared himself president and ruled for about two years until he was also deposed through a military coup d'état.

105. Michael A. Langkjær, "From Cool to Un-cool to Re-cool: Nehru and Mao Tunics in the Sixties and Post-sixties West," in *Global Textile Encounters*, ed. M. Nosch, Z. Feng, and L. Varadarajan (Oxbow, 2014), 227–36.

106. Philip H. Dougherty, "From the Jungle to Main Street, Emergence of the Safari Suit," *New York Times*, June 26, 1975.

107. The Kareeba suit become the "uniform" of the Jamaican People's National Party in 1972. Ralph Blumenthal, "Kareeba: Jamaica's 'Uniform,'" *New York Times*, March 24, 1976.

108. The détè was not just a Béninois style, and it remains popular there, with the Togolese, and, according to one informant, among the Igbo of Nigeria. Interview with Lêgbânon Bénoit Djezandé, Tindji-Adjoko (Za-Kpota), May 27, 2015; interview with Clotaire Blenon, Kpocon, Bohicon, May 4, 2015.

109. Interview with Célestin Kokossou, Kpatalokoli, Bohicon, June 4, 2021.

110. Interview with Alain Baba, Zakpo, Adame-Ahito, Bohicon, June 5, 2021.

111. Interview with Clotaire Blenon, Kpocon, Bohicon, May 4, 2015.

112. Interview with René Allaga, Marché Ganhi de Bohicon, April 27, 2015.

113. Interview with Sébastien Djokpe, Marché Ganhi de Bohicon, June 6, 2021.

114. E. Cayode, "Eloquence du vêtement," *L'aube nouvelle*, April 24, 1966.

115. His disagreements with the Fon royal families manifested in a split among Fon voters on the national platform. The squabbles between Fon royal and non-royal families are also present in the archival record. For example, see Lettre de Germain Dègan to Ahomadégbé-Tomêtin, October 19, 1950, ANB, 1G/19.

116. Interview with Alain Baba, Zakpo, Adame-Ahito, Bohicon, November 28, 2014.

117. Interview with Celestin Godou Kpodo, Adandokpodji, Abomey, June 1, 2015.

118. Interview with Alain Baba, Zakpo, Adame-Ahito, Bohicon, June 5, 2021.

119. Interview with Clotaire Blenon, Kpocon, Bohicon, May 4, 2015. In 2015, only "old men" wore bounbas that could be pulled over the head.

120. Interview with Lékolihoui Djibidisse, Zakpo Adame-Ahite, Bohicon, December 9, 2014.

121. Interview with Clotaire Blenon, Kpocon, Bohicon, May 4, 2015.

122. Interview with Pierrot Akpako, Agbaignzoun Centre, Auguest 25, 2015.

4. The Material Culture of Expertise

1. "Sous le signe du centimètre," *Daho Express*, no. 621, August 28, 1971.

2. Today, artisans almost always use the French word *libérer* (liberate) to describe the processes of a master condoning a new status on an apprentice. The Fon *flí* (liberate) is rarely used.

3. "Sous le signe du centimètre," *Daho Express*, no. 621, August 28, 1971.

4. This chapter also pushes back against popular characterizations of libéra-tion as a problematic, exploitative, and traditional ceremony that impedes devel-opment in Bénin, a position that recently led the state to render these important

ceremonies illegal. Admittedly this is a very niche point, but it is of particular importance to the tailors at the center of this study. Libération and diplomas were made illegal through a series of laws starting in 2004. See Schweizerische Eidgenossenschaft and Bureau d'Appui aux Artisans, *Le certificate de qualification aux métiers (CQM): Textes fondamentaux, document-cadre d'operationnalisation du dispositive, guide pratique d'organization*, Républic du Bénin, Ministère de l'enseignement secondaire, de la formation technique et professionelle, de la reconversion et de l'insertion des jeunes (MESFTPRIJ), 2013. For a sympathetic review of these laws see Nouatin Guy Sourou et al., "Reforms of Technical Vocational Education and Training System in Benin: An Exploration of a Social Anthropological Field," *LELAM Working Papers* 15 (2020), 1–27.

5. A. Charton, "L'artisanat indigène en AOF," 1, Congres de la Société Indigène, 1931, Archives nationales du Sénégal (ANS), Dakar, O/349/31.

6. Michael Adas, *Machines as the Measures of Men: Science, Technology, and Ideologies of Western Dominance* (Cornell University Press, 1989).

7. Charton, "L'artisanat indigène en AOF."

8. Douglas W. Leonard, *Anthropology, Colonial Policy and the Decline of French Empire in Africa* (Bloomsbury Academy, 2020).

9. Charton, "L'artisanat indigène en AOF."

10. The ethnologist and colonial official Maurice Delafosse identified among the Bambara the *Somono* (fishermen and boatmen), *Noumou* (blacksmiths and potters), *Lorho* (copper jewelers), *Koulè* (wood craftsmen), *Dièli* (griots), *Faunè* or *Founéè* (religious griots and magicians), and *Donso* or *Lonzo* (hunters). Delafosse argued that one found similar castes among all Mandé speakers and "under other names, among most of the peoples of the Soudan." Maurice Delafosse, *Haut-Sénégal-Niger* (Émile Larose, 1912), 139.

11. Melville Herskovits, *Dahomey: An Ancient West African Kingdom* (J. J. Augustin, 1938), 1:49.

12. Herskovits, *Dahomey*, 1:48.

13. Herskovits, *Dahomey*, 1:49–50.

14. Herskovits, *Dahomey*, 1:49–50.

15. On the "colonial humanists," see Gary Wilder, *The French Imperial Nation-State: Negritude and Colonial Humanism between the Two World Wars* (University of Chicago Press, 2005), 55.

16. According to Fadiga, the artisanal traditions of certain groups such as the Maures of Timbuktu and Djenné remained uncorrupted.

17. Bouyagui Fadiga, "Education de l'artisanat indigène," September 25, 1932, ANS, O/349/31.

18. Charton, "L'artisanat indigène en AOF."

19. "Arrêt no 145 Arrête regulating the conditions of admission to the Professional School of Dahomey," January 29, 1930, Archives nationales du Bénin (ANB), Porto-Novo, 1G/12/8.

20. "Arrêt: Réglementant l'organisation et le fonctionnement de la Maison des Artisan Soudanais de Bamako," September 25, 1934, Koulouba, ANS, O/45/31.

21. For example, applicants to the 1956 incoming class of carpenters, masons, and auto mechanics at the Center of Industrial Apprenticeship in Cotonou had to be "sons of artisans or apprentices presented by an employer"—a significant change from earlier technical programs that did not tie admittance to the profession of an applicant's parents. Lettre de H. Diot à la commandant de cercle de Porto-Novo, No. 3923/IAD/3E, August 11, 1956, ANB, 1G/5/3; "Arrêt no 965 Arrête reorganizing the Superior Primary and Professional School of Dahomey," September 1924, ANB, 1G/12/8.

22. Gouverneur général de l'Afrique Occidentale Française to monsieur le ministre des colonies, August 6, 1934, ANS, O/309/31.

23. R. Delavignette, *Soudan, Paris, Bourgogne* (Bernard Grasset, 1935), 57.

24. As critics pointed out, in focusing not on innovation but on revival, these programs failed to address the inability of artisans to compete with cheaper industrial alternatives. "Artisanat indigène en Afrique occidentale française," clipping from *Bulletin d'information et de reseignements*, no. 138, April 5, 1937, Archives nationales d'outre-mer (ANOM), Aix-en-provence, France, GUERNUT/50.

25. While Monroe rejects *artisan* as merely a colonial category, he fails to acknowledge its resonance within the project of the *maison des artisans* itself. He recounts the case of a Dahomean "artist," Jean Dado, who was sent on scholarship to the Bamako center, only to quickly fail at learning "authentic" production methods since he favored to make objects geared towards the lucrative tourist markets. By eliding the difference in status between Soudanais and Dahomean artisans, Monroe may have missed a significant contributing factor that led Dado to quickly abandon the Bamako center. John Warne Monroe, "Surface Tensions: Empire, Parisian Modernism and 'Authenticity' in African Sculpture, 1917–1939," *American Historical Review* 117, no. 2 (2012): 445–75.

26. A. Charton, "L'artisanat indigène—1935."

27. Delavignette, *Soudan, Paris, Bourgogne*, 57.

28. "Arrêt no 145 Arrête regulating the conditions of admission to the Professional School of Dahomey," January 29, 1930, ANB, 1G/12/8.

29. "Recruitement d'artisans métropolitains," Soudan, education artisanale, ANS, O/537/31.

30. Compte Rendu d'activités, septembre-decembre, 1953, AOF, Inspection générale du travail, mission d'études psychotechniques, ANS, 2G/53/113.

31. L'inspecteur d'académie du Dahomey, Porto-Novo, October 9, 1956, ANB, 1G/19/22.

32. Oke Assogba, Minister of National Education, Center of Apprenticeship of INA, Porto-Novo, October 24, 1960, ANB, 1G/26/3.

33. Elizabeth Ezra, *The Colonial Unconscious: Race and Culture in Interwar France* (Cornell University Press, 2000); Catherine Hodeir, *L'Exposition coloniale de 1931* (A. Versaille, 2011).

34. Catherine Hodeir, "Decentering the Gaze at French Colonial Exhibitions," in *Images and Empires: Visuality in Colonial and Postcolonial Africa*, ed. Paul S. Landau and Deborah D. Kaspin (University of California Press, 2002).

35. Eighteen men and three women from Abomey attended. Correspondances relative à l'exposition coloniale (1931), recruitement d'indigènes, objets à exposer, artisans et figurants, 1930–31, ANB, 1Q/2/00013.

36. Inventaire des objets des diverses colonies, l'Afrique occidentale Française, ANOM, AGEFOM//628/1077; Marche de gré à gré, Exposition international paris, 1937, commissairat de l'AOF, artisans et gendarmes indigènes: nourriture rapatiement, ANOM, AGEFOM//590/510.

37. Lettre de le Directeur de l'agence economique du gouvernement General de l'AOF à Monsieur le gouverneur General de l'AOF, Sujet: embarquement artisans expositions 1937, ANOM, AGEFOM//590/510.

38. Lettre de (illegible signature), Exposition Internationale à Paris 1937 à Monsieur le Commissaire, October 2, 1935, L'artisanat à l'exposition, Les artisans indigènes à l'exposition, ANOM, AGEFOM//614/931.

39. Objets d'art et d'artisanat indigènes destinés à être vendus aux visit euros de l'exposition 1937, Dahomey, ANOM, AGEFOM//594/566.

40. The makers of winning objects received the title "un des Meilleurs ouvriers en France—MOF" (One of the best craftsmen in France) and membership in the Society of Best Craftsmen. Nathalie Montargot, "Les Meilleurs Ouvriers de France: Des professionnels en perpétuelle quête d'excellence," *Humanisme et Entreprise* 311 (2013): 61–72. According to the society's website, today, improperly adopting the title of "meilleurs ouvriers de France" is punishable by imprisonment and a 15,000 euro fine. http://meilleursouvriersdefrance.pro.

41. Circulaire a/s de la participation des colonies à la 3e exposition National du Travail à Paris, 1932, ANB, 1Q/029/0043.

42. Reunion de MM. Les directeurs des agencies Economiques des colonies, pays de protectorate et territoires sous mandat français, Expo nationale du travail, 1936, ANOM, AGEFOM//508/155.

43. For the Fourth Exposition in 1936, organizers sought to make the program more inclusive to colonial artisans by introducing the new category of "regional small industries" (*petites industries régionales*). African artisans could, however, still compete in the "French" categories if they felt that their objects were on par with those of their French counterparts. File: 4e, distribution des récompenses palmarès, ANOM, AGEFOM//629/1081.

44. File: Expo nationale du travail, 1936, ANOM, AGEFOM//508/155. By the fifth competition in 1939, there was an entirely separate category of "outre-mer,"

and African artisans were now given the title "Best Craftsmen in Overseas France," although colonial subjects might still submit works in categories for objects in European style. Groupe France Outre-mer, File: 1939 exposition, ANOM, AGEFOM//629/1082.

45. Attachment to Letter from Governor J. Chambon to Commandants de cercle, April 29, 1948, ANB, 1Q/7/00067.

46. Lettre de Governor J. Chambon aux Commandants de cercle, April 29, 1948, ANB, 1Q/7/00067.

47. Lettre de le directeur du contrôle financier à Monsieur le Ministre de la france d'outre-mer, April 25, 1950, File: exposition Nationale du travail, 1949; préparation de l'Exposition, ANOM, AGEFOM//561/241.

48. G. Vermot-Gauchy, Inspection territoriale du Travail du Dahomey-Niger, Rapport Annuel, 1952, 113, ANS, 2G/52/40. F. Neveu, Note to Commandants de Cercles et Chefs de Subdivisions, a/s: Exposition territoriale du Travail, Porto-Novo, No. 22/SG, January 9, 1953, ANB, 2G/3/2.

49. Concours du meilleure ouvrier du Dahomey: fiche de candidature, 1953, ANB, 2G/3/1.

50. F. Neveu, Note to Commandants de Cercles.

51. H. Daunic, Circulaire à Messieurs les participants de la Foire de Bohicon, Cotonou, December 27, 1956, ANB, 1Q/011/00137.

52. "Bientôt la Foire de Bohicon," 2, *France Dahomey*, January 12, 1957.

53. "Que comportera la Foire de Bohicon?," *France Dahomey*, January 5, 1957.

54. On international participation, see "Le Dahomey a la Foire de Milan," *Daho Express*, June 23, 1962; "Le Dahomey a la Foire du Proche-Orient a Tel-Aviv," *Daho Express*, July 7, 1962; "Artisanat le Dahomey a la foire Internationale de Munich," *Daho Express*, August 1, 1973; "Le Bénin à la 14e Foire d'Importation <<Partenaires du Progrès>>," *Ehuzu*, September 10, 1976. On domestic events, see "Exposition des oeuvres du centre cooperatif artisanal a Porto-Novo," *Daho Express*, January 23, 1970; "Foire de Cotonou," *Daho Express*, July 3, 1970; "Exposition d'artisanat de l'Agenece de Cooperation Technique et Culturelle," *Daho Express*, December 18, 1970; "Le premier festival culturel nationale s'ouvre démain," *Ehuzu*, August 26, 1976.

55. Interview with Barthélemy Adjahouinou, Tindji-Zecko (Za-Kpota), May 27, 2015; interview with Alladassi Tavi, Tanta (Agbaignzoun), August 25, 2015; and interview with Ernest Fiogbe, Ahouaja, Abomey, September 4, 2015.

56. Telegramme-lettre-official, No. 7199, Objet: A/S Reglementation du travail des femmes et des enfants, Porto-Novo, December 24, 1936, ANB, S/2/1.7.

57. Carde, Apprentissage, enseignement technique, 1925–1945, ANS, K/49/2.

58. Arrêt No. 191, 1938, Arrêt reglementant le travail des femmes et des enfants dans la colonie du Dahomey, ANB, S/14/3/1.

59. Arrêt No. 191, 1938.

60. Frederick Cooper, *Decolonization and African Society: The Labor Question in French and British Africa* (Cambridge University Press, 1996), 466.

61. Lettre de directeur d'education technique à chef de cercle de Bopa, Ref 719 AM/SM, Porto-Novo, July 28, 1959, ANB, 1G/6/10. See, for example, File: Exposition nationale du travail, Togo, ANOM, AGEFOM//561/244 and File: exposition Nationale du travail, 1949; liquidation de l'Exposition, ANOM, AGEFOM//561/247.

62. Lettre de J. B. Kiesgen, Commandant le cercle de Djougou à Gouverneur de Dahomey, March 31, 1952, ANB, 1G/4/1.

63. R. Cazal, Rapport Annuel, 1946, Dahomey, 3, Inspection du Travail, ANS, 2G/46/47.

64. Pierre Pelisson, Inspection du Travail d'AOF Rapport, 1948, ANS, S/7/4.

65. Pierre Pelisson, Inspection du Travail d'AOF Annual Report, 1948.

66. G. H. Connillière, Dahomey-Niger, Inspection du Travail, Rapport Annuel, 1947, ANS, 2G/47/48.

67. Contrat d'apprentissage: Fadaïro-Angèle, January 29, 1955, Fiche: ordre des convocations, certificats de scolarite, certificats d'apprentisange, ANB, 1G/18/1.

68. Contrat d'apprentissage: Fadaïro-Jossi, January 29, 1955, Fiche: ordre des convocations, certificats de scolarite, certificats d'apprentisange, ANB, 1G/18/1.

69. Contrat d'apprentissage: Montcho-d'Oliveira, January 27, 1955, Fiche: ordre des convocations, certificats de scolarite, certificats d'apprentisange, ANB, 1G/18/1.

70. Contrat d'apprentissage: Montcho-d'Oliveira.

71. Contrat d'apprentissage: Montcho-d'Oliveira.

72. Interview with Alain Baba, Zakpo, Adame-Ahito, Bohicon, November 28, 2014.

73. File: Recensement des hommes de métiers, ANB, 1Q/032/00365.

74. Bureau International de Travail, Programme élargi d'assistance technique, "Rapport au Gouvernement de la Republique du Dahomey sur la situation et l'aide à l'artisnat et aux petites industries," OIT/TAP/Dahomey/R.7 (B.I.T., 1965): 32.

75. Bureau International de Travail, 1965, 32.

76. Bureau International de Travail, 1965, 7.

77. Inspecteur d'Ècoles, No. 1450 E. Objet: envoi de documents en Vue Conseil gouvernement et cons sup ens., Porto-Novo, November 3, 1931, ANB, 1G/6/8; "Arrête année 1932, no 847. Aommaire: diplôme fin apprentissage 'section maconnerie' de l'ècole professionnelle," ANB, 1G/10/8.

78. Copie de certificat d'apprentissage de Adoula, Dossier intégration cadre Chefs d'atelier - enseignement pratique, 1949–1951, ANB, 1G/4/2.

79. Inspecteur d'Ècoles, No. 1450 E.

80. Copie de certificat d'apprentissage de Gbaguidi, Dossier intégration cadre Chefs d'atelier—enseignement pratique, 1949–1951, ANB, 1G/4/2.

81. Copie de diplôme de Gbanouidi, Dossier intégration cadre Chefs d'atelier—enseignement pratique, 1949–1951, ANB 1G4/2.

82. Diplôme de l'Exposition de l'artisanat de Porto-Novo, 1936, ANB, 1Q/021/00219.

83. Agence exposition Paris 1937 AOF, ANOM, AGEFOM//613/922.

84. Interview with Pierrot Akpako (Dakossi), Agbaignzoun Centre, August 25, 2015.

85. Interview with Jules Wimêllo, Tindji-Kpozou (Za-Kpota), May 6, 2015; I found multiple examples of this over the course of my research. Interview with Thérèse Hountondji, Hountondji, Abomey, July 16, 2015.

86. Interview with Alladassi Tavi, Tanta (Agbaignzoun), August 25, 2015.

87. C. Elegbede, "Un profession surchargée: LA COUTURE," *L'aube nouvelle*, April 21, 1968.

88. It is also unclear if *libération* is originally Béninois; artisans in Togo, Nigeria, Ghana, Cameroon, and perhaps elsewhere hold ceremonies as well.

89. Interview with Georges Henri Ayadji, Dokpodji, Abomey, August 21, 2015.

90. Interview with Alain Baba, Zakpo, Adame-Ahito, Bohicon, June 5, 2021.

91. Interview with Abdou Ibrahim Bah, Zongo, Abomey, May 9, 2015.

92. Sandra T. Barnes, "Introduction: The Many Faces of Ogun," in *Africa's Ogun: Old World and New*, ed. Barnes (Indiana University Press, 1989).

93. The object remains at the center of an intense public debate on art restitution to former colonies. The Gu was captured by the French in 1896, and Béninois have demanded its return. Complicating this narrative, however, are the origins of the object since it and its maker (Ekplékendo) were captured by Dahomey in 1860.

94. "Sous le signe du centimètre," *Daho Express*, no. 621, August 28, 1971.

95. Suzanne Preston Blier, *African Vodun: Art, Psychology, and Power* (University of Chicago Press, 1995), 78.

96. Douglas Falen, *African Science: Witchcraft, Vodun, and Healing in Southern Benin* (University of Wisconsin Press, 2018). In areas around Abomey, there are widespread fears of àzètɔ and poisoning. In my experience, most people will not consume food or beverages unless they are opened and served in front of them.

97. "Sous le signe du centimètre," *Daho Express*, no. 621, August 28, 1971.

98. Interview with Célestin Kokossou, Kpatalokoli, Bohicon, June 4, 2021.

99. Florence Bernault, "The Shadow of Rule: Colonial Power and Modern Punishment in Africa," in *Cultures of Confinement: A History of the Prison in Africa, Asia, and Latin America*, ed. Frank Dikötter and Ian Brown (Cornell University Press, 2007), 78.

100. Interview with Léocadie Zehounkpé, Zakpo-Anouame, Bohicon, June 18, 2015.

101. Jennifer Bajorek, *Unfixed: Photography and the Decolonial Imagination in West Africa* (Duke University Press, 2020), 98–103; Kerstin Pinther, "Textiles and Photography in West Africa," *Critical Interventions* (2007): 106–18.

102. Lettre de LeGall à Monsieur le Gouverneur Général (Inspection Général de l'Enseignment), Bamako, March 1937, ANS, 2G/37/72.

103. R. Berthoumieu, Inspection du Travail, Dahomey, Rapport Annuel, 1949, ANS, 2G/49/44.

104. P. Berthoumieu, Inspection Territoriale du Travail, Rapport Annuel, 1954, ANS, 2G/54/32.

105. P. Berthoumieu, Inspection Territoriale du Travail et Des Lois Sociales Rapport Annuel, 1955, ANS, 2G/55/27.

106. Bureau International de Travail, 1965, 11.

107. Bureau International de Travail, 1965, 3.

108. Bureau International de Travail, 1965, 5.

109. Interview with Alain Baba, Zakpo, Adame-Ahito, Bohicon, June 5, 2021.

110. Interview with Christine Agbamandé, Atchia (Zogbodomey), June 23, 2015.

111. Interview with Anago Yobode, Dota, Abomey, April 28, 2015.

112. Bureau International de Travail, 1965; see also Process verbal de reunion, Porto-Novo, March 2, 1972, ANB, 1G/13/11.

113. "Nouveau visage des activites culturelles en RPB," *Ehuzu*, December 11, 1975.

114. "Pour une organisation rationnelle du secteur artisanal," *Ehuzu*, December 17, 1975.

115. Interview with Alain Baba, Zakpo, Adame-Ahito, Bohicon, November 28, 2014.

116. Interview with Alain Baba, Zakpo, Adame-Ahito, Bohicon, June 5, 2021.

117. Afize D. Adamon, *Le renouveau démocratique au Bénin: la Conférence nationale des forces vives et la période de transition* (Harmattan, 1995).

118. Interview with Georges Henri Ayadji and Ernest Fiogbe, Dokpodji, Abomey, August 21, 2015.

119. *Fédération nationale des artisans du Bénin (FENAB)*, September 9–11, 1993; interview with Georges Henri Ayadji and Ernest Fiogbe, Dokpodji, Abomey, August 21, 2015.

120. As former head of the Bohicon tailors' association, Baba allowed me to access the archive of these documents. Interview with Alain Baba, Zakpo, Adame-Ahito, Bohicon, June 5, 2021.

121. Interview with Alain Baba, Zakpo, Adame-Ahito, Bohicon, November 28, 2014.

122. Attestations, CFPA, 1997 and undated; interview with Jeanne Hanou, Ahouamé, Bohicon, July 17, 2015.

123. Interview with Barthélemy Adjahouinou, Tindji-Zecko (Za-Kpota), May 27, 2015.

5. Feminizing the Craft

1. Interview with Marie Félicité Babagbéto, Zakpo-Anouame, Bohicon, June 19, 2015. On the "respectability" of seamstressing in contemporary Accra, see Ann Cassiman, "Stitching Womanhood in the *Zongo*: Seamstress Apprenticeship in Accra," *African Studies Review* 65, no. 3 (2022): 642–68.

2. For example, Claire C. Robertson, *Sharing the Same Bowl: A Socioeconomic History of Women and Class in Accra, Ghana* (University of Michigan, 1985); and Luise White, *The Comforts of Home: Prostitution in Colonial Nairobi* (University of Chicago Press, 1990).

3. During research, I was struck by the stark divergence between how men and most women framed their narratives. I suspect that much of this is due to the recent expansion of evangelical Christianity, especially Pentecostalism, among women and its focus on being "born again." See, for example, Girish Daswani, *Looking Back, Moving Forward: Transformation and Ethical Practice in the Ghanaian Church of Pentecost* (University of Toronto Press, 2015). Women even occasionally wanted to tell their life history in front of their apprentices or asked me to return with a transcript for their apprentices to study, thus passing on the lessons of their lives to a younger generation.

4. See the introduction to chapter 3. E. Cayode, "Eloquence du vêtement," *L'aube nouvelle*, April 24, 1966.

5. Andrew Ivaska, *Cultured States: Youth, Gender, and Modern Style in 1960s Dar es Salaam* (Duke University Press, 2011); Elizabeth Ann Fretwell, "'My Most Beautiful Ornament Is My House': National Womanhood and Urban Modernity in Late Colonial and Postcolonial Senegal, 1956–1968," *Journal of Urban History* 42, no. 5 (2016): 881–99; "La mini jupe . . . en difficulté au Niger," *L'aube nouvelle*, May 19, 1968.

6. Madagascar, Mali, Guinea, Tunisia, and Niger all ran campaigns against minis; see "La mini jupe . . . en difficulté au Niger," *L'aube nouvelle*, May 19, 1968; Pierre François, "Visage authèntique de la femme dahoméenne," *Daho Express*, September 5, 1969; for discussion of minis being outlawed in Malawi, see "Votre page madame," *Daho Express*, September 6, 1969; "Niger: Bandes anti-mini," *Daho Express*, March 19, 1970.

7. For some examples see "Un peu de couture: Un jumper pour mettre en valeur votre robe ou votre pantalon," *Daho Express*, July 11, 1970; and "Patron couture: Robe de jeune fille," *Daho Express*, August 8, 1970.

8. "Je serai femme policier," *Daho Express*, September 26, 1970.

9. Valentin Alagbe, "D'accord pour la mini-jupe, non à l'excentricité," *L'aube nouvelle*, July 6, 1968.

10. Balogun describes Nigerian "beauty diplomacy" through beauty pageants; fashion shows are a similar case. Oluwakemi M. Balogun, *Beauty Diplomacy: Embodying an Emerging Nation* (Stanford University Press, 2020).

11. "Un grand gala: Le syntradouane nous sort de l'ordinarie," *Daho Express*, November 3, 1969; and "Instantanes de la mode," *Daho Express*, November 15, 1969.

12. "Presentation de Mode dans le cadre de la soirée de gala du Lion's Club," *Daho Express*, April 11, 1970.

13. "La gala de la FFD: Un beau success pour la femme Dahoméenne," *Daho Express*, February 21, 1972; "Des idées originales pour être élégante," *Daho Express*, February 26, 1972.

14. Tina Mai Chen, "Dressing for the Party: Clothing, Citizenship, and Gender-Formation in Mao's China," *Fashion Theory* 5, no. 2 (2001): 143–71.

15. Interview with Alladass Sodonou, Zakpo Ahowamey, Bohicon, May 13, 2015.

16. With few natural resources and some of the weakest soils in West Africa, Bénin has consistently been ranked one of the poorest countries in the world.

17. Romain Assongba, "Dassa-Zoume: Remise de diplômes de couture au centre féminin d'enseignement ménager," *Daho Express*, July 2, 1974.

18. Interview with Jeanette Agadame, Agbaignzoun Centre, August 25, 2015.

19. Interview with Marie Félicité Babagbéto, Zakpo-Anouame, Bohicon, June 8, 2021; interview with Antoine Zohou, Adame-Adate (Bohicon), June 5, 2021.

20. Interview with Jeanette Agadame, Agbaignzoun Centre, August 25, 2015.

21. Interview with Lilia Abadahoue, Bohicon centre, August 5, 2011.

22. In 1974, the population of the Zou region was 542,554 inhabitants, with 32,000 in Abomey proper. B. Kayossi, "Pleins feux sur la province du Zou," *Daho Express*, November 27, 1974.

23. The World Bank estimates that in 1960 only 9 percent of Bénin's population lived in cities, but by 2000 about 38 percent of Béninois were urban dwellers. In comparison, in Ghana the numbers were 23 percent in 1960 and 44 percent in 2000, while in all of Sub-Saharan Africa (excluding high-income countries) the numbers were 15 percent in 1960 and 31 percent in 2000. The World Bank, "DataBank: World Development Indicators," accessed August 25, 2023, http://databank.worldbank.org/data/reports.aspx?source=2&series=SP.URB.TOTL.IN.ZS&country=.

24. Obayomi Sacramento, "L'amenagement du Territoire au Dahomey," *Daho Express*, October 13, 1973; Obayomi Sacramento, "Amenagement regional et amenagement national," *Daho Express*, January 9, 1974.

25. PUB, 1988, *Abomey analyses urbaines, Plan d'Urbanisme du Bénin*, Cotonou, quoted in Albert Tingbé-Azalou, "Cultural Dimensions of Urban-Rural Relations in Benin: The Case of Abomey and Its Hinterland," in *Rural-Urban Dynamics in Francophone Africa*, ed. J. Baker (Nordic Africa Institute, 1997), 83.

26. In 1972, the population of the area was 120,000 people, living across 85 villages. "Coup mortel au regionalisme," *Daho Express*, November 13, 1972; "Décret No 74-27 du 13-2-74: Limites et dénominations des circonscriptions administratives de la province du Zou," *Daho Express*, February 25, 1974. By the early 1960s, the national government made Bohicon a *sous-prèfecture*, although it was quickly reincorporated back into Abomey. "Le président Ahomadegbe inaugre la Sous-Prèfecture de Bohicon," *L'aube nouvelle*, March 6, 1965; "Ouverture du commissariat de police de Bohicon," *Daho Express*, September 7, 1973.

27. Archives de Musée Historique d'Abomey, Abomey, Bénin.

28. "Naissance de la République Populaire du Bénin et du parti de la Révolution Populaire du Bénin," *Ehuzu*, November 30, 1975.

29. Mèhou d'Assomption, "Abomey, c'est bientôt," *Daho Express*, November 27, 1974.

30. "Abomey s'apprête pour le 26 Octobre," *Daho Express*, September 3, 1974.

31. While there is no definitive list of these sites, others include Étoile Rouge in Cotonou, Place de la Revolution in Ouando (Porto-Novo), and the public square in Sé. It does not seem like there was much of an attempt to destroy colonial sites and completely rebuild. For example, the main square of Porto-Novo—Place Bayol—is still named after the French colonial governor of Porto-Novo who fought Glèlè's armies.

32. Interview with Gabin Akouêdenoudjè, Adandokpodji, Abomey, September 4, 2015.

33. B. Kayossi, "Pleins feux sur la province du Zou," *Daho Express*, November 27, 1974.

34. Interview with Celestin Godou Kpodo, Adandokpodji, Abomey, June 1, 2015.

35. "Inaguration de l'adduction d'eau d'Abomey-Bohicon," *Daho Express*, October 25, 1972; "L'eau manque à Abomey," *Daho Express*, July 23, 1973.

36. Interview with Célestine Dangbé, Azali, Abomey, June 17, 2015.

37. Interview with Thérèse Hountondji, Hountondji, Abomey, July 16, 2015.

38. For example, Olga Dokponou constructed a workshop on land owned by her mother. Interview with Olga Dokponou, Dota, Abomey, July 15, 2015.

39. Tailor Laurence Dossou-Kpézé opened a workshop on her aunt's land, and after her aunt's death, her cousins chased her out of her workshop and rented it to another tailor who she claimed took all of her clients. Interview with Laurence Dossou-Kpézé, Agblomey, Abomey, June 17, 2015.

40. Interview with Lékolihoui Djibidisse, Zakpo Adame-Ahite, Bohicon, December 9, 2014.

41. Interview with Célestine Dangbé, Azali, Abomey, June 17, 2015.

42. Interview with Olga Dokponou, Dota, Abomey, July 15, 2015.

43. Interview with Marié-Rose Kponsenon, Houndonho, Bohicon, September 1, 2015.

44. Interview with Marc Agbandjaï, Dota, Abomey, April 28, 2015.

45. Interview with Euphrasie Goudou, Agbaignzoun Centre, August 25, 2015.

46. Interview with Edmonde Semassou, Hêtchiditô, Abomey, July 15, 2015.

47. Interview with Antoinette Nonvignon, Bohicon, December 1, 2014.

48. Interview with Anago Yobode, Dota, Abomey, April 28, 2015.

49. Divorce is quite common in Bénin and according to Falen, divorcées make up the majority of second and third wives. Douglas Falen, *Power and Paradox: Authority, Insecurity, and Creativity in Fon Gender Relations* (Africa World Press, 2011), 51, 150–51.

50. Interview with Séraphine Houngbandan, Dota, Abomey, June 16, 2015.

51. Interview with Olga Dokponou, Dota, Abomey, July 15, 2015.

52. Interview with Lilia Abadahoue, Bohicon centre, August 5, 2011.

53. Interview with Marié-Rose Kponsenon, Houndonho, Bohicon, September 2, 2015.

54. Eliot Elisofon, "Hairdresser in Street, Abomey, Bénin," EEPA EENG 01328, Eliot Elisofon Field photographs, 1942–72, Eliot Elisofon Photographic Archives, National Museum of African Art, Smithsonian Institute, Washington, DC.

55. Interview with Jeanne Hanou, Ahouamé, Bohicon, July 17, 2015.

56. Interview with Hélène Ahonon, Dota, Abomey, July 14, 2015.

57. Falen, *Power and Paradox,* 44–46.

58. Interview with Jeanette Agadame, Agbaignzoun Centre, August 25, 2015.

59. Interview with Jeanette Agadame, Agbaignzoun Centre, August 25, 2015.

60. Interview with Victoire Glinman, Tinji Kpozoun Kpakpassa (Za-Kpota), August 17, 2015.

61. Interview with Jeanne Hanou, Ahouamé, Bohicon, July 17, 2015.

62. Falen, *Power and Paradox,* 150–52. See also for nearby Yorùbá, Lorelle Semley, *Mother Is Gold, Father Is Glass: Gender and Colonialism in a Yoruba Town* (Indiana University Press, 2011).

63. Interview with Jeanette Agadame, Agbaignzoun Centre, August 25, 2015; interview with Pascaline Wankpo, Zakpo-Ahito, Bohicon, July 17, 2015; interview with Amélie Gnancadja, Zakpo-Ahito, July 17, 2015.

64. Interview with Marie Félicité Babagbéto, Zakpo-Anouame, Bohicon, June 8, 2021.

65. Interview with Jeanette Agadame, Agbaignzoun Centre, August 25, 2015.

66. Interview with Christine Agbamandé, Atchia (Zogbodomey), June 23, 2015.

67. Interview with Antoinette Nonvignon, Bohicon, December 14, 2014.

68. Interview with Emilienne Agbo, Adandokpodji Daxo, Abomey, June 8, 2015.

69. Seamstresses usually defined "young" as someone childless, unmarried, and in their mid-twenties or younger.

70. Valentin Alagbe, "D'accord pour la mini-jupe, non à l'excentricité," *L'aube nouvelle*, July 6, 1968. During my fieldwork in 2015, there was a pagne wrapping competition in Bohicon where young women were judged on their wrapping skills.

71. Interview with Emilienne Agbo, Adandokpodji Daxo, Abomey, June 8, 2015.

72. Interview with Josephine Agounkpléto, Adagamé, Lissezoun, Bohicon, September 1, 2015. I never encountered this system in Bénin during my various trips from 2006 to 2021. However, at a bus station in Abidjan, Côte d'Ivoire, in 2015, an ambulant vendor selling Polaroid photographs of modèles approached me. In these images, the faces of the models wearing the outfits were scratched out.

73. Interview with Marie Félicité Babagbéto, Zakpo-Anouame, Bohicon, June 8, 2021.

74. Interview with Odette Béhanzin, Marché Sêhi, Bohicon, September 2, 2015.

75. Interview with Solange Kpedé, Agblomey, Abomey, June 16, 2015.

76. Interview with Célestine Agassounon, Soglogon, Bohicon, June 14, 2015.

77. Cloth merchants held an inordinate amount of power in Marxist-Leninist Bénin, and attempts to integrate them into the national economy failed. See John R. Heilbrunn, "Social Origins of National Conferences in Benin and Togo," *Journal of Modern African Studies* 31, no. 2 (1993): 284, 290.

78. Togolese women worked with Chinese manufacturers to perfect the techniques of making imitation wax. Nina Sylvanus, *Patterns in Circulation: Cloth, Gender, and Materiality in West Africa* (University of Chicago Press, 2016).

79. This was due, in part, to regional economic integration within the Economic Community of West African States (ECOWAS), which ensured that Bénin, a country that imports almost all its electricity from neighbors, had access to a regular supply. Indeed, power supply in Bénin was (and is) often more regular than in neighboring Nigeria, a power-exporting country.

80. Interview with Paul Zoungbowenon, Marché Ganhi de Bohicon, April 24, 2015.

81. Interview with Célestine Agassounon, Soglogon, Bohicon, June 14, 2015; interview with Olga Dokponou, Dota, Abomey, July 15, 2015.

82. Interview with Victoire Glinman, Tinji Kpozoun Kpakpassa (Za-Kpota), August 17, 2015.

83. Interview with Lilia Abadahoue, Bohicon centre, August 5, 2011.

84. Heilbrunn, "Social Origins of National Conferences."

85. Attestation de formation, Fondation Hanns Seidel, Centre de Formation Professionnelle d'Abomey (CFPA), interview with Jeanne Hanou, Ahouamé, Bohicon, July 17, 2015.

86. In 2011, I attended a meeting of the Bohicon tailors' association where a French couple proposed their idea for opening an orphanage that would teach indigent youth tailoring and a few other crafts. They did not plan on housing or feeding the children and expected master tailors to volunteer their time to teach the children.

87. Seamstresses' reactions to these programs call to mind the reactions of Ghanaian women to similar instructional programs during the colonial era. See Jean Allman, "Making Mothers: Missionaries, Medical Officers, and Women's Work in Colonial Asante, 1924–1945," *History Workshop Journal* 38 (1994): 23–47.

Conclusion

1. Examen traditionnel de fin d'apprentissage [EFAT], 2015. Courtesy of Fidel Ouèjo.

2. The process for establishing the CQM began in 2005 with Presidential Decree 2005-117. Schweizerische Eidgenossenschaft and Bureau d'Appui aux Artisans, *Le certificat de qualification aux métiers (CQM): Textes fondamentaux, document-cadre d'operationnalisation du dispositive, guide pratique d'organization*, Républic du Bénin, Ministère de l'enseignement secondaire, de la formation technique et professionelle, de la reconversion et de l'insertion des jeunes (MESFTPRIJ), 2013.

3. Isidore Gozo, "Certificat de qualification aux métiers: Les documents de rénovation lancés," *La nation*, April 19, 2024, https://lanation.bj/actualites /certificat-de-qualification-aux-metiers-les-documents-de-renovation-lances.

4. "Sous le signe du centimètre," *Daho Express*, no. 621, August 28, 1971.

5. Ali Zafar, "The Growing Relationship Between China and Sub-Saharan Africa: Macroeconomic, Trade, Investment, and Aid Links," *World Bank Research Observer* 22 (2007): 103–30.

BIBLIOGRAPHY

Archives and Libraries

Bénin

Archives municiples de Bohicon, Bohicon (AMB)
Archives nationales du Bénin, Porto-Novo (ANB)
 Sous-serié 1E, Politique générale, rapports politiques
 Sous-serié 1G, Enseignment
 Sous-serié 1M, Justice
 Sous-serié 1Q, Affaires économiques
 Sous-serié 2G, Science et arts
 Sous-serié 2Q, Industrie, artisanat
 Serié S, Travail et main d'œuvre
Musée Historique d'Abomey, Abomey

Brazil

Fundação Pierre Verger, Salvador

France

Archives de la Planète, Musée Albert-Kahn, Boulogne-Billancourt
Archives nationales d'outre-mer, Aix-en-provence (ANOM)
 Affaires économiques (1AFF-ECO)
 Agence économique de la France d'Outre-Mer–Colonies (AGEFOM)
 La Commission Guernut

Senegal

Archives nationales du Sénégal, Dakar (ANS)
 Serié O, Enseignment de l'A.O.F., 1895–1958.

Sous-serié 2G, Rapports périodiques des gouvernements, administrateurs et chefs de services
Serié K, Travail et main d'œuvre

United States

Brooklyn Museum, New York, NY
National Museum of African Art, Smithsonian Institute, Washington, DC
  Eliot Elisofon Photographic Archives
Regenstein Map Collection, University of Chicago, Chicago, IL
Schomburg Center for Research in Black Culture, Manuscripts, Archives, and Rare Books Division, the New York Public Library, Melville J. and Frances S. Herskovits Papers, Sc MG 261

Newspapers and Periodicals

Daho Express
Ehuzu
France Dahomey
La nation
L'aube nouvelle
Le Dahoméen
Le Messager du Bénin
Le Phare du Dahomey
New York Times
Supplément illustré du La Petit Journal

Oral Histories Collected by Author (Digital Recordings and Transcripts)

Lilia Abadahoue, Bohicon Centre, August 5, 2011
Amadou Adamou, Zongo, Abomey, May 9, 2015
Micheline Adanhou, Lêlê Adatô, May 30, 2015
Antoinette Adingni, Adingnigon (Agbagnainzoun), May 30, 2015
Justine Adjacle, Tindji Adahouémey (Za-Kpota), August 17, 2015
Barthélemy Adjahouinou, Tindji-Zecko (Za-Kpota), May 27, 2015
Dêdo Pierre Adjehounou, Gbecon Houegbo, Abomey, May 3, 2015
Pascal Adouhouncla, Adandokpodji, Abomey, May 7, 2015
Jeanette Agadame, Agbaignzoun Centre, August 25, 2015
Célestine Agassounon, Soglogon, Bohicon, June 14, 2015
Barthélemy Agbamande, Atchia (Zogbodomey), June 24, 2015
Christine Agbamandé, Atchia (Zogbodomey), June 23, 2015
Marc Agbandjaï, Dota, Abomey, April 28, 2015

Emiliene Agbo, Adandokpodji Daxo, Abomey, June 8, 2015

Lazare Agbotounso, Tindji-Assalin (Za-Kpota), August 1, 2015

Abraham Agbowakounou, Hounhoué (Za-Kpota), July 28, 2015

Josephine Agounkpléto, Adagamé, Lissezoun, Bohicon, September 1, 2015

Michel Agounkpléto, Adagamé, Lissèzoun, Bohicon, September 2, 2015

Rigobert Ahissou-Avosse, Dota, Abomey, May 9, 2014

Hélène Ahonon, Dota, Abomey, July 14, 2015

Thélesphore Ahossi, Lissazoumé (Agbaignzoun), July 21, 2015

Alphonse Ahouado, Musée d'Abomey, Abomey, September 15, 2015

Gabin Akouêdenoudjè, Adandokpodji, Abomey, September 4, 2015

Pierrot Akpako, Agbaignzoun Centre, August 25, 2015

Trankilin Alladanon, Bohicon Centre, August 17, 2011

René Allaga, Marché Ganhi de Bohicon, April 27, 2015

Joséph Allanon, Gbinmé (Za-Kpota), July 29, 2015

Dáa Atchassou, Ahouaja, Abomey, December 10, 2014

Georges Henri Ayadji, Dokpodji, Abomey, August 21, 2015

Dáa Martin Ayikpé, Avogbannan (Bohicon), May 25, 2015

Alain Baba, Zakpo, Adame-Ahito, Bohicon, November 28, 2014; June 5, 2021

Marie Félicité Babagbéto, Zakpo-Anouame, Bohicon, June 19, 2015; June 8,
    2021

Dorcas Bagbonon, Marché Houndjroto, Abomey, June 8, 2015

Abdou Ibrahim Bah, Zongo, Abomey, May 9, 2015

Maurice Béhanzin, Hountondji, Abomey, July 14, 2015

Odette Béhanzin, Marché Sêhi, Bohicon, September 2, 2015

Clotaire Blenon, Kpocon, Bohicon, May 4, 2015

Nestor Dako-Wegbe, Houawe Zoungonsa (Bohicon), December 10, 2014

Célestine Dangbé, Azali, Abomey, June 17, 2015

Donatien Dansi, Adame-Adato, Gnidgazou (Bohicon), December 9, 2014

François Dessou, Adjahito, Abomey, July 16, 2015

Antoine Djedatin, Wingnansa (Bohicon), May 22, 2015

Lêgbânon Bénoit Djezandé Tindji-Adjoko (Za-Kpota), May 27, 2015

Lékolihoui Djibidisse, Zakpo-Adame-Ahite, Bohicon, December 9, 2014

Sébastien Djokpe, Marché Ganhi de Bohicon, April 22, 2015; June 6, 2021

Olga Dokponou, Dota, Abomey, July 15, 2015

Laurence Dossou-Kpézé, Agblomey, Abomey, June 17, 2015

Cyprien Fa, Détohou (Abomey), May 3, 2015

Ernest Fiogbe, Ahouaja, Abomey, August 21, 2015; September 4, 2015

Dah Ganmanssô-Ahéko, Lissazoumé (Agbaignzoun), July 22, 2015

Elie Gbeho, Hlanhossougon (Zogbodomey), June 23, 2015

Victoire Glinman, Tindji Kpozoun Kpakpassa (Za-Kpota), August 17, 2015

Amélie Gnancadja, Zakpo-Ahito, Bohicon, July 17, 2015
Celestin Godou Kpodo, Adandokpodji, Abomey, June 1, 2015
Euphrasie Goudou, Agbaignzoun Centre, August 25, 2015
Fidèl Guedjo, Bohicon, November 25–26, 2014; May 2, 2015
Raphaël Guedo, Tindji-Adawémé (Za-Kpota), July 29, 2015
Jeanne Hanou, Ahouamé, Bohicon, July 17, 2015; August 27, 2015
Séraphine Houngbandan, Dota, Abomey, June 16, 2015
Thérèse Hountondji, Hountondji, Abomey, July 16, 2015
Juliette Kanlihano, Ahouaja, Abomey, December 11, 2014
Didier Kloué, Tindji-Kpozoun (Za-Kpota), May 20, 2015
Célestin Kokossou, Kpatalokoli, Bohicon, June 4, 2021
Solange Kpedé, Agblomey, Abomey, June 16, 2015
Marié-Rose Kponsenon, Houndonho, Bohicon, September 1, 2015
Appolinaire Lanteffo, Kpozoun-Zadanou (Za-Kpota), May 6, 2015
Lambert Lokossi, Houndonho, Bohicon, August 26, 2015
Bachrou Nondinonchao, Abomey, June 6, 2021
Antoinette Nonvignon, Bohicon, December 1, 2014
Ichaou Odounharo, Bohicon, November 26, 2014
Edmonde Semassou, Hêtchiditô, Abomey, July 15, 2015
Elisabeth Sodokpa, Dota-Sogbadji, Abomey, June 16, 2015
Alladass Sodonou, Zakpo Ahowamey, Bohicon, May 13, 2015
Alladassi Tavi, Tanta (Agbaignzoun), August 25, 2015
Dah Todaho Houndadjo, Agbadjagon, Bohicon, May 13, 2015
Rufin Togbonon, Abomey, June 7, 2021
Pascaline Wankpo, Zakpo-Ahito, Bohicon, July 17, 2015
Jules Wimêllo, Tindji-Kpozou (Za-Kpota), May 6, 2015
Jean-Mari Wletche, Allahé (Za-Kpota), April 13, 2015
Anago Yobode, Dota, Abomey, April 28, 2015
Léocadie Zehounkpé, Zakpo-Anouame, Bohicon, June 18, 2015
Antoine Zohou, Adame-Adate (Bohicon), April 20, 2015; June 5, 2021
Paul Zoungbowenon, Marché Ganhi de Bohicon, April 24, 2015; June 5, 2021

Published Primary Sources

"Au Dahomey (Les fétiches de Kana.–Le dieu de la guerre)." *Supplément illustré du La Petit Journal* 158 (1893): 386.
Burton, Richard F. *A Mission to Gelele, King of Dahome. With Notices of the So Called "Amazons," the Grand Customs, the Yearly Customs, the Human Sacrifices, the Present State of the Slave Trade, and the Negro's Place in Nature. In Two Volumes.* London, 1864.

D'Albéca, A. L. *Le France au Dahomey.* Paris, 1895.

Dalzel, Archibald. *The History of Dahomey: An Inland Kingdom of Africa; Comp. from Authentic Memoirs; with an Introduction and Notes.* London, 1793.

Delafosse, Maurice. *Haut-Sénégal-Niger.* Émile Larose, 1912.

Delavignette, R. *Soudan, Paris, Bourgogne.* Bernard Grasset, 1935.

Dupuis-Yakouba, Auguste. "Notes sur la population de Tombouctou (castes et associations)." *Revue d'ethnographie et de sociologie* (1910): 233–36.

Dupuis-Yakouba, Auguste. *Industries et principales professions des habitants de la région de Tombouctou.* Émile Larose, 1921.

Forbes, Frederick E. *Dahomey and the Dahomans, Being the Journals of Two Missions to the King of Dahomey, and Residence at His Capital in the Years 1849 and 1850.* 2 vols. London, 1851.

Grandin, Léonce. *A l'assaut du pays des noirs. Le Dahomey, par le commandant Grandin.* Vol. 2. Paris, 1895.

Hardy, Georges. *Une conqête morale: l'enseignement en AOF.* l'Harmattan, 2005.

Lambe, Bulfinch. "Letter from the Great King Trudo Audati's Palace of Abomey, in the Kingdom of Dahomey," November 27, 1724. In *Dahomey and the Dahomans, Being the Journals of Two Missions to the King of Dahomey, and Residence at His Capital in the Years 1849 and 1850,* vol. 1, by Frederick E. Forbes. London, 1851.

Le Herissé, Auguste. *L'ancien royaume du Dahomey: Mœrs, religion, histoire.* Emile Larosè, 1911.

M'Leod, John. *A Voyage to Africa with Some Account of the Manners and Customs of the Dahomian People.* London, 1820.

Morton-Williams, Peter. "A Yoruba Woman Remembers Servitude in a Palace of Dahomey, in the Reigns of Kings Gelele and Behanzin." *Africa: Journal of the International African Institute* 63 (1993): 102–17.

Norris, Robert. *Memoirs of the Reign of Bossa Ahádee, King of Dahomy, An Inland Country of Guiney. To Which Are Added, The Author's Journey to Abomey, the Capital; and a Short Account of the African Slave Trade.* Frank Cass and Company, 1968 [1789].

Read, Mary Lillian. *The Mothercraft Manual.* Little, Brown, 1919.

Reste, J. F. *Le Dahomey: Réalisations et Perspectives d'avenir.* Publications du Comité de l'Afrique Française, 1934.

Skertchly, J. A. *Dahomey as It Is; Being a Narrative of Eight Months' Residence in That Country, with a Full Account of the Notorious Annual Customs, and the Social and Religious Institutions of the Ffons; Also an Appendix on Ashantee and a Glossary of Dahoman Words and Titles.* London, 1874.

Snelgrave, William. *A New Account of Some Parts of Guinea and the Slave-Trade.* London, 1732.

Vicomte de Fleuriot, Alphonse Jean René. "Croisières à la côte d'Afrique (1868)."
    Le tour du monde (1876): 241–304.

Reports and Working Papers

Bureau International de Travail. Programme élargi d'assistance technique,
    "Rapport au Gouvernement de la Republique du Dahomey sur la situation et
    l'aide à l'artisnat et aux petites industries," OIT/TAP/Dahomey/R.7. B.I.T,
    1965.
Davodoun, Comlan Cyr. *Développement du mouvement associatif en milieu artisan au
    Bénin.* Les Editions du Flamboyant, 2006.
Davodoun, Comlan Cyr. *Mieux connaitre l'artisanat au Bénin.* Le Bureau d'appui aux
    artisans, 2008.
Fédération nationale des artisans du Bénin (FENAB). September 9–11, 1993.
Nouatin, Guy Sourou, Esaïe Gandonou, Rubain Bankole, and Ursula Renold.
    "Reforms of Technical Vocational Education and Training System in Benin:
    An Exploration of a Social Anthropological Field." *LELAM Working Papers* 15
    (2020).
Schweizerische Eidgenossenschaft and Bureau d'Appui aux Artisans. *Le certifi-
    cat de qualification aux métiers (CQM): Textes fondamentaux, document-cadre
    d'operationnalisation du dispositive, guide pratique d'organization.* Réublic du
    Bénin, Ministère de l'enseignement secondaire, de la formation technique et pro-
    fessionelle, de la reconversion et de l'insertion des jeunes (MESFTPRIJ), 2013.
"Villes et mairies du Département de Zou." *Newsletter Annuaire de Mairies.* Ac-
    cessed March 2011. http://www.annuaire-mairie.fr/departement-zou.html.
World Bank. "DataBank: World Development Indicators." Accessed August 25,
    2023. http://databank.worldbank.org/data/reports.aspx?source=2&series=
    SP.URB.TOTL.IN.ZS&country=.

Secondary Sources

Adamon, Afize D. *Le renouveau démocratique au Bénin: La Conférence nationale des
    forces vives et la période de transition.* Harmattan, 1995.
Adams, Monni. "Fon Appliqued Cloths." *African Arts* 13, no. 2 (1980): 28–41, 87–88.
Adandé, Alexis, and Goudjinou Metinhoué. "Potières et Poterie de Sè (Mono)."
    Ministere de l'Enseignement Superièure et de la Recherche Scientifique, Répub-
    lique Populaire du Bénin, 1981.
Adandé, Joseph. "Textiles in Southern Benin." In *Museums & History in West Africa,*
    edited by Emmanuel Arinze and Claude Daniel Ardouin. James Currey, 2000.

Adas, Michael. *Machines as the Measures of Men: Science, Technology, and Ideologies of Western Dominance.* Cornell University Press, 1989.

Ahoyo, Jean-Roger. "Les marchés d'Abomey et de Bohicon." *Les Cahiers d'Outre-Mer* 28m no. 110 (1975): 162–84.

Akinjogbin, I. A. *Dahomey and Its Neighbors, 1708–1818.* Cambridge University Press, 1967.

Allman, Jean, ed. *Fashioning Africa: Power and the Politics of Dress.* Indiana University Press, 2014.

Allman, Jean. "'Let Your Fashion Be in Line with Our Ghanaian Costume': Nation, Gender, and the Politics of Cloth-ing in Nkrumah's Ghana." In *Fashioning Africa,* edited by Jean Allman. Indiana University Press, 2004.

Allman, Jean. "Making Mothers: Missionaries, Medical Officers, and Women's Work in Colonial Asante, 1924–1945." *History Workshop Journal* 38 (1994): 23–47.

Alpern, Stanley B. "What Africans Got for Their Slaves: A Master List of European Trade Goods." *History in Africa* 22 (1995): 5–43.

Amos, Johanna, and Lisa Binkley. "Introduction: Stitching the Self." In *Stitching the Self: Identity and the Needle Arts,* edited by Johanna Amos and Lisa Binkley. Bloomsbury, 2020.

Arnold, David. *Everyday Technology: Machines and the Making of India's Modernity.* University of Chicago Press, 2013.

Auslander, Leora. *Cultural Revolutions: Everyday Life and Politics in Britain, North America, and France.* University of California Press, 2009.

Bajorek, Jennifer. *Unfixed: Photography and the Decolonial Imagination in West Africa.* Duke University Press, 2020.

Balogun, Oluwakemi M. *Beauty Diplomacy: Embodying an Emerging Nation.* Stanford University Press, 2020.

Barber, Karin. *A History of African Popular Culture.* Cambridge University Press, 2017.

Barnes, Sandra T. "Introduction: The Many Faces of Ogun." In *Africa's Ogun: Old World and New,* edited by Sandra T. Barnes. Indiana University Press, 1989.

Bastian, Misty. "The Naked and the Nude: Historically Multiple Meanings of Oto (Undress) in Southeastern Nigeria." In *Dirt, Undress, and Difference: Critical Perspectives on the Body's Surface,* edited by Adeline Masquelier. Indiana University Press, 2005.

Bay, Edna. *Asen, Ancestors, and Vodun: Tracing Change in African Art.* University of Illinois Press, 2008.

Bay, Edna. "Belief, Legitimacy, and the Kpojito: An Institutional History of the 'Queen Mother' in Precolonial Dahomey." *Journal of African History* 36 (1995): 1–27.

Bay, Edna. *Wives of the Leopard: Gender, Politics, and Culture in the Kingdom of Dahomey.* University Press of Virginia, 1998.

Bayly, C. A. *The Birth of the Modern World, 1780–1914.* Blackwell, 2004.

Beckert, Sven. *Empire of Cotton: A Global History.* Vintage, 2015.

Bernault, Florence. "The Shadow of Rule: Colonial Power and Modern Punishment in Africa." In *Cultures of Confinement: A History of the Prison in Africa, Asia, and Latin America,* edited by Frank Dikötter and Ian Brown. Cornell University Press, 2007.

Blier, Suzanne Preston. *African Vodun: Art, Psychology, and Power.* University of Chicago Press, 1995.

Blier, Suzanne Preston. "Melville J. Herskovits and the Arts of Ancient Dahomey." *RES: Anthropology and Aesthetics* 16 (1988): 125–42.

Blier, Suzanne Preston. *Royal Arts of Africa: The Majesty of Form.* Harry N. Abrams, 1998.

Brown, Marie Grace. *Khartoum at Night: Fashion and Body Politics in Imperial Sudan.* Stanford University Press, 2017.

Burke, Timothy. *Lifebuoy Men, Lux Women: Commodification, Consumption, and Cleanliness in Modern Zimbabwe.* Duke University Press, 1996.

Byfield, Judith. *The Bluest Hands: A Social and Economic History of Women Dyers in Abeokuta (Nigeria), 1890–1940.* Heinemann, 2002.

Byfield, Judith, Carolyn A. Brown, Timothy Parsons, and Ahman Alawad Sikainga. *Africa and World War II.* Cambridge University Press, 2015.

Cassiman, Ann. "Stitching Womanhood in the *Zongo*: Seamstress Apprenticeship in Accra." *African Studies Review* 65, no. 3 (September 2022): 642–68.

Chappatte, Andre. *In Search of Tunga: Prosperity, Almighty God, and Lives in Motion in a Malian Provincial Town.* University of Michigan Press, 2022.

Chen, Tina Mai. "Dressing for the Party: Clothing, Citizenship, and Gender-Formation in Mao's China." *Fashion Theory* 5, no. 2 (2001): 143–71.

Coffin, Judith G. "Credit, Consumption, and Images of Women's Desires: Selling the Sewing Machine in Late Nineteenth-Century France." *French Historical Studies* 18 (1994): 749–83.

Comaroff, Jean, and John Comaroff. "Fashioning the Colonial Subject: The Empire's Old Clothes." In *The Dialectics of Modernity on a South African Frontier,* vol. 2 of *Of Revelation and Revolution.* University of Chicago Press, 1997.

Cooper, Frederick. *Decolonization and African Society: The Labor Question in French and British Africa.* Cambridge University Press, 1996.

Cooper, Frederick. "Possibility and Constraint: African Independence in Historical Perspective." *Journal of African History* 49, no. 2 (2008): 167–96.

Coquery-Vidrovitch, Catherine. "La fête des coutumes au Dahomey: Historique Et Essai D'interprétation." *Annales. Histoire, Sciences Sociales* 19 (1964): 696–716.

D'Almedia Topor, Hélène. *Histoire économique du Dahomey (Bénin)*. 2 vols. Éditions L'Harmattan, 1995.

Daswani, Girish. *Looking Back, Moving Forward: Transformation and Ethical Practice in the Ghanaian Church of Pentecost*. University of Toronto Press, 2015.

Davies, Robert Bruce. *Peacefully Working to Conquer the World: Singer Sewing Machines in Foreign Markets, 1854–1920*. Arno, 1976.

Davis, Paul R. "An Institution for Post-Independence Art: US-RDA Cultural Policy and *Encadrement Malien* at the Institut National des Arts." *Critical Interventions* (2014): 96–118.

de Sousa Santos, Boaventura. *The End of the Cognitive Empire: The Coming of Age of Epistemologies of the South*. Duke University Press, 2018.

DuPlessis, Robert S. *The Material Atlantic: Clothing, Commerce, and Colonization in the Atlantic World*. Cambridge University Press, 2016.

Eicher, Joanne B., and Barbara Sumberg. "World Fashion, Ethnic, and National Dress." In *Dress and Ethnicity: Change across Space and Time*, edited by Joanne B. Eicher. Berg, 1995.

Ezra, Elizabeth. *The Colonial Unconscious: Race and Culture in Interwar France*. Cornell University Press, 2000.

Fair, Laura. "Dressing Up: Clothing, Class and Gender in Post-Abolition Zanzibar." *Journal of African History* 39 (1998): 63–94.

Falen, Douglas J. *African Science: Witchcraft, Vodun, and Healing in Southern Benin*. University of Wisconsin Press, 2018.

Falen, Douglas J. *Power and Paradox: Authority, Insecurity, and Creativity in Fon Gender Relations*. Africa World Press, 2011.

Fall, Babacar. *Le travail au Sénégal au XXe siècle*. Karthala, 2011.

Fanon, Franz. *The Wretched of the Earth*. Grove, 1961 [2004].

Ferguson, James. *Expectations of Modernity: Myths and Meaning of Urban Life on the Zambian Copperbelt*. University of California Press, 1999.

Ferguson, James. *Global Shadows: Africa in the Neoliberal World Order*. Duke University Press, 2006.

Filippello, Marcus. *The Nature of the Path: Reading a West African Road*. University of Minnesota Press, 2017.

Fogarty, Richard Standish. *Race and War in France: Colonial Subjects in the French Army, 1914–1918*. Johns Hopkins University Press, 2008.

Frank, Barbara E. *Griot Potters of the Folona: The History of an African Ceramic Tra-dition*. Indiana University Press, 2021.

Frank, Barbara E. *Mande Potters and Leatherworkers: Art and Heritage in West Af-rica*. Smithsonian Institute, 1998.

Fretwell, Elizabeth Ann. "'Domesticating the Unfamiliar': Afropolitan Dress in the West African Kingdom of Dahomey." *Radical History Review* 144 (October 2022): 19–44.

Fretwell, Elizabeth Ann. "'My Most Beautiful Ornament Is My House': National Womanhood and Urban Modernity in Late Colonial and Postcolonial Senegal, 1956–1968." *Journal of Urban History* 42, no. 5 (2016): 881–99.

Fretwell, Elizabeth Ann. "The Tools of Tailoring as Technologies-in-Use in Twentieth Century Benin, West Africa." *History and Technology* 37, no. 2 (2021): 147–71.

Freund, Bill. *The African City: A History*. Cambridge University Press, 2007.

Freund, Bill. *The African Worker*. Cambridge University Press, 1988.

Friedman, Jonathan. "The Political Economy of Elegance: An African Cult of Beauty." In *Consumption and Identity*, edited by Jonathan Friedman. Harwood Academic, 1994.

Gaskell, Ivan, and Sarah Anne Carter. Introduction to *The Oxford Handbook of His-tory and Material Culture*, edited by Ivan Gaskell and Sarah Anne Carter. Oxford University Press, 2020.

Geary, Christian M. *In and Out of Focus: Images from Central Africa, 1885–1960*. Philip Wilson, 2002.

Georg, Odile. *Tropical Dream Palaces: Cinema in Colonial West Africa*. Oxford University Press, 2020.

Gerards, Roger, and Suze May Sho. *Vlisco Fabrics*. ArtEZ, 2014.

Getachew, Adom. *Worldmaking after Empire: The Rise and Fall of Self-Determination*. Princeton University Press, 2019.

Gillow, John. *African Textiles: Color and Creativity across a Continent*. Thames & Hudson, 2003.

Ginio, Ruth. *The French Army and Its African Soldiers: The Years of Decolonization*. University of Nebraska Press, 2017.

Gondola, Didier. "Dream and Drama: The Search for Elegance among Congolese Youth." *African Studies Review* 42, no. 1 (1999): 23–48.

Gondola, Didier. *Tropical Cowboys: Westerns, Violence, and Masculinity in Kinshasa*. Indiana University Press, 2016.

Gordon, Andrew. *Fabricating Consumers: The Sewing Machine in Modern Japan*. Uni-versity of California Press, 2011.

Gott, Suzanne. "'Life' Dressing in Kumasi: African-Print Style in 'Popular Fash-ion.'" In *African-Print Fashion Now! A Story of Taste, Globalization, and Style*, edited by S. Gott, K. S. Loughran, B. D. Quick, and L. W. Rabine. Fowler Museum at UCLA, 2019.

Gott, Suzanne, and Kristyne Loughran, eds. *Contemporary African Fashion*. Indiana University Press, 2010.

Grabski, Joanna. "The Visual City: Tailors, Creativity, and Urban Life in Dakar, Senegal." In *Contemporary African Fashion*, edited by Suzanne Gott and Kristyne Loughran. Indiana University Press, 2010.

Grace, Joshua. *African Motors: Technology, Gender, and the History of Development*. Duke University Press, 2021.

Green, Toby. *A Fistful of Shells: West Africa from the Rise of the Slave Trade to the Age of Revolution*. University of Chicago Press, 2019.

Grosfilley, Anne. *African Wax Print Textiles*. Prestel, 2018.

Guyer, Jane. *Marginal Gains: Monetary Transactions in Atlantic Africa*. University of Chicago Press, 2004.

Hansen, Karen Tranberg. "Fabricating Dreams: Sewing Machines, Tailors, and Urban Entrepreneurship in Zambia." In *The Objects of Life in Central Africa*, edited by Robert Ross, Marja Hinfelaar, and Iva Peša. Brill, 2013.

Hansen, Karen Tranberg. *Salaula: The World of Secondhand Clothing and Zambia*. University of Chicago Press, 2000.

Hansen, Karen Tranberg, and D. Soyini Madison, eds. *African Dress: Fashion, Agency, and Performance*. Bloomsbury, 2013.

Harney, Elizabeth. *In Senghor's Shadow: Art, Politics, and the Avant-Garde in Senegal, 1960–1995*. Duke University Press, 2004.

Hart, Jennifer. *Ghana on the Go: African Mobility in the Age of Motor Transportation*. Indiana University Press, 2016.

Heilbrunn, John R. "Social Origins of National Conferences in Benin and Togo." *Journal of Modern African Studies* 31, no. 2 (1993): 277–99.

Hendrickson, Hildi, ed. *Clothing and Difference: Embodied Identities in Colonial and Post-Colonial Africa*. Duke University Press, 1996.

Herskovits, Melville J. *Dahomey: An Ancient West African Kingdom in Two Volumes*. J. J. Augustin, 1938; Northwestern University Press, 1967.

Hodeir, Catherine. "Decentering the Gaze at French Colonial Exhibitions." In *Images and Empires: Visuality in Colonial and Postcolonial Africa*, edited by Paul S. Landau and Deborah D. Kaspin. University of California Press, 2002.

Hodeir, Catherine. *L'Exposition coloniale de 1931*. A. Versaille, 2011.

Hountondji, Paulin J., ed. *Endogenous Knowledge: Research Trails*. Translated by Ayi Kwesi Armah. CODESRIA, 1997.

Hountondji, Paulin J. "Knowledge Appropriation in a Post-Colonial Context." In *Indigenous Knowledge and the Integration of Knowledge Systems*, edited by Catherine A. Odora Hoppers. New Africa, 2002.

Hunt, Nancy Rose. *A Colonial Lexicon: Of Birth Ritual, Medicalization, and Mobility in the Congo.* Duke University Press, 1999.

Hurston, Zora Neale. *Barracoon: The Story of the Last "Black Cargo."* HarperCollins, 2018.

Ingold, Tim. "Materials against Materiality." *Archaeological Dialogues* 14, no. 1 (2007): 1–16.

Ingold, Tim. "The Textility of Making." *Cambridge Journal of Economics* 34 (2010): 91–102.

Irbouh, Hamid. *Art in the Service of Colonialism: French Art Education in Morocco, 1912–1956.* Bloomsbury, 2013.

Ivaska, Andrew. *Cultured States: Youth, Gender, and Modern Style in 1960s Dar es Salaam.* Duke University Press, 2011.

Jennings, Helen. *New African Fashion.* Prestel, 2011.

Johnson, Marion. "Cloth as Money: The Cloth Strip Currencies of Africa." *Textile History* 11 (1980): 193–202.

Johnson, Marion. "Cotton Imperialism in West Africa." *African Affairs* 73 (1974): 178–87.

Johnson, Marion. "Technology, Competition, and African Crafts." In *The Imperial Impact: Studies in the Economic History of Africa and India,* edited by Clive Dewey and A. G. Hopkins. Athlone, 1978.

Jones, Hilary. *The Métis of Senegal: Urban Life and Politics in French West Africa.* Indiana University Press, 2013.

Keese, Alexander. "A Social History of Parastatal Employees in Southern Benin, 1989–1990: Contesting Decline and Unemployment During 'Africa's Second Democratization.'" *ILWCH* 98 (Fall 2020): 77–98.

Klein, Ursula. *Experiments, Models, Paper Tools: Cultures of Organic Chemistry in the Nineteenth Century.* Stanford University Press, 2002.

Klein, Ursula. "Paper Tools in Experimental Cultures." *Studies in History and the Philosophy of Science* 32, no. 2 (2001): 265–301.

Kopytoff, Igor. "The Cultural Biography of Things: Commoditization as Process." In *The Social Life of Things: Commodities in Cultural Perspective,* edited by A. Appadurai. Cambridge University Press, 1986.

Kriger, Colleen E. *Cloth in West African History.* AltaMira, 2006.

Kriger, Colleen E. "Mapping the History of Cotton Textile Production in Precolonial West Africa." *African Economic History* 33 (2005): 87–116.

Kuchta, David. *The Three-Piece Suit and Modern Masculinity: England, 1550–1850.* University of California Press, 2002.

Kunstmann, Rouven. "Fashioning Nationalism and the Shaping of the Public Sphere in 1950s Nigeria." *Journal of West African History* (2021): 27–54.

Kunstmann, Rouven. "The Politics of Portrait Photographs in Southern Nigerian Newspapers, 1945–1954." *Social Dynamics* 40 (2015): 514–37.

Lamb, Venice, and Alastair Lamb. "The Classification and Distribution of Horizontal Treadle Looms in Sub-Saharan Africa." *Textile History* 11, no. 1 (1980): 22–62.

Landau, Paul. "Empires of the Visual: Photography and Colonial Administration in Africa." In *Images and Empires: Visuality in Colonial and Postcolonial Africa*, edited by Paul Landau and Deborah D. Kaspin. University of California Press, 2002.

Landry, Timothy R. *Vodún: Secrecy and the Search for Divine Power*. University of Pennsylvania Press, 2019.

Langkjær, Michael A. "From Cool to Un-cool to Re-cool: Nehru and Mao Tunics in the Sixties and Post-sixties West." In *Global Textile Encounters*, edited by M. Nosch, Z. Feng, and L. Varadarajan. Oxbow, 2014.

Lave, Jean. *Apprenticeship in Critical Ethnographic Practice*. University of Chicago Press, 2011.

Law, Robin. "History and Legitimacy: Aspects of the Use of the Past in Precolonial Dahomey." *History in Africa* 15 (1988): 431–56.

Law, Robin. "'My Head Belongs to the King': On the Political and Ritual Significance of Decapitation in Pre-Colonial Dahomey." *Journal of African History* 30 (1989): 399–415.

Law, Robin. *Ouidah: The Social History of a West African Slaving "Port."* Ohio University Press, 2004.

Law, Robin. *The Slave Coast of West Africa, 1550–1750*. Oxford University Press, 1991.

Law, Robin. "The Slave-Trader as Historian: Robert Norris and the History of Dahomey." *History in Africa* 19 (1989): 219–35.

Law, Robin, and Paul Lovejoy. *The Biography of Mahommah Gardo Baquaqua*. Marcus Wiener, 2007.

Leeb-du Toit, Juliette. *isiShweshwe: A History of the Indigenisation of Blueprint in South Africa*. University of KwaZulu-Natal Press, 2017.

Leonard, Douglas W. *Anthropology, Colonial Policy and the Decline of French Empire in Africa*. Bloomsbury Academy, 2020.

Lewis, Shantrelle P. *Dandy Lion: The Black Dandy and Street Style*. Aperture, 2017.

Lindsay, Lisa. "Working with Gender: The Emergence of the 'Male Breadwinner' in Colonial Southwestern Nigeria." In *Africa after Gender?*, edited by Catherine M. Cole, Takyiwaa Manuh, and Stephan Miescher. Indiana University Press, 2007.

Macola, Giacomo. *The Gun in Central Africa: A History of Technology and Politics*. Ohio University Press, 2016.

Mann, Gregory. *Native Sons: West African Veterans and France in the Twentieth Century*. Duke University Press, 2006.

Manning, Patrick. *Slavery, Colonialism, and Economic Growth in Dahomey, 1640–1960*. Cambridge University Press, 2004.

Marchand, Trevor. *The Masons of Djenné*. Indiana University Press, 2009.

Martin, Phyllis M. "Contesting Clothes in Colonial Brazzaville." *Journal of African History* 35 (1994): 401–26.

Masquelier, Adeline, ed. *Dirt, Undress, and Difference: Critical Perspectives on the Body's Surface*. Indiana University Press, 2005.

Mavhunga, Clapperton Chakanetsa. *The Mobile Workshop: The Tsetse Fly and African Knowledge Production*. MIT Press, 2018.

Mavhunga, Clapperton Chakanetsa. *Transient Workspaces: Technologies of Everyday Innovation in Zimbabwe*. MIT Press, 2014.

McGovern, Mike. *Unmasking the State: Making Guinea Modern*. University of Chicago Press, 2012.

McKinley, Catherine E. *The African Lookbook: A Visual History of 100 Years of African Women*. Bloomsbury, 2021.

McNaughton, Patrick R. *The Mande Blacksmiths: Knowledge, Power, and Art in West Africa*. Indiana University Press, 1993.

Miller, Monica L. *Slaves to Fashion: Black Dandyism and the Styling of Black Diasporic Identity*. Duke University Press, 2009.

Monroe, J. Cameron. *The Precolonial State in West Africa: Building Power in Dahomey*. Cambridge University Press, 2014.

Monroe, John Warne. "Surface Tensions: Empire, Parisian Modernism and 'Authenticity' in African Sculpture, 1917–1939." *American Historical Review* 117, no. 2 (2012): 445–75.

Montargot, Nathalie. "Les Meilleurs Ouvriers de France: Des professionnels en perpétuelle quête d'excellence." *Humanisme et Entreprise* 311 (2013): 61–72.

Morgan, Jennifer. *Laboring Women: Reproduction and Gender in New World Slavery*. University of Pennsylvania Press, 2004.

Morton-Williams, Peter. "A Yoruba Woman Remembers Servitude in a Palace of Dahomey, in the Reigns of Kings Glele and Behanzin." *Africa: Journal of the International African Institute* 63 (1993): 102–17.

Mougoué, Jacqueline-Bethel Tchouta. *Gender, Separatist Politics, and Embodied Nationalism in Cameroon*. University of Michigan Press, 2019.

Mullaney, Thomas D. *The Chinese Typewriter: A History*. MIT Press, 2017.

Mustafa, Hudita Nura. "Portraits of Modernity: Fashioning Selves in Dakarois Popular Photography." *Politique africaine* 100 (2006): 231–47.

Newell, Sasha. *The Modernity Bluff: Crime, Consumption, and Citizenship in Côte d'Ivoire*. University of Chicago Press, 2012.

Norman, Neil L. "Powerful Pots, Humbling Holes, and Regional Ritual Processes: Towards an Archaeology of Huedan Vodun, ca. 1650–1727." *African Archaeological Review* 26 (2009): 187–218.

Nwafor, Okechukwu. *Aso Ebi: Dress, Fashion, Visual Culture, and Urban Cosmopolitanisms in West Africa.* University of Michigan Press, 2021.

Ogunnaike, Oludamini. *Deep Knowledge: Ways of Knowing in Sufism and Ifa, Two West African Intellectual Traditions.* Pennsylvania State University Press, 2020.

Osseo-Asare, Abena Dove. *Atomic Junction: Nuclear Power in Africa after Independence.* Cambridge University Press, 2019.

Osseo-Asare, Abena Dove. "Kwame Nkrumah's Suits: Sartorial Politics in Ghana at Independence." *Fashion Theory* 25, no. 5 (2021): 597–632.

Osseo-Asare, Abena Dove. "Writing Medical Authority: The Rise of Literate Healers in Ghana, 1930–70." *Journal of African History* 57, no. 1 (2016): 69–91.

Perrot, Philippe. *Fashioning the Bourgeoisie: A History of Clothing in the Nineteenth Century*, trans. Richard Bienvenu. Princeton University Press, 1994.

Phelan, Craig. "Trade Unions and 'Responsible Participation': Dahomey, 1958–1975." *Labor History* 3 (2014): 346–64.

Pietz, William. "The Problem of the Fetish II: The Origin of the Fetish." *RES: Anthropology and Aesthetics* 13 (1987): 23–45.

Pinther, Kerstin. "Textiles and Photography in West Africa." *Critical Interventions* 1, no. 1 (2007): 106–18.

Pokrant, R. J. "The Survival of Indigenous Tailoring Among the Hausa of Kano City." PhD diss., University of Cambridge, 1982.

Polanyi, Karl. *Dahomey and the Slave Trade: An Analysis of an Archaic Economy.* University of Washington Press, 1966.

Rabine, Leslie W. "Photography, Poetry, and the Dressed Bodies of Léopold Sédar Senghor." In *African Dress: Fashion, Agency, Performance*, edited by Karen Tranberg Hansen and D. Soyini Madison. Bloomsbury Academic, 2013.

Rabine, Leslie W. "Translating African Textiles into U.S. Fashion Designs." In *Contemporary African Fashion*, edited by Suzanne Gott and Kristyne Loughran. Indiana University Press, 2010.

Rathbone, Keith. "Dressing the Colonial Body: Senegalese Rifleman in Uniform." In *African Dress: Fashion, Agency, Performance*, edited by Karen Tranberg Hansen and D. Soyini Madison. Bloomsbury, 2013.

Ribeiro, Aileen. *Fashion and Fiction: Dress in Art and Literature in Stuart England.* Yale University Press, 2006.

Richards, Christopher L. *Cosmopolitanism and Women's Fashion in Ghana: History, Artistry and Nationalist Inspirations.* Routledge, 2022.

Riello, Giorgio, and Ulinka Rublack, eds. *The Right to Dress: Sumptuary Laws in a Global Perspective, c. 1200–1800*. Cambridge University Press, 2019.

Roberts, Richard L. *Two Worlds of Cotton: Colonialism and the Regional Economy in the French Soudan, 1800–1946*. Stanford University Press, 1996.

Robertson, Claire C. *Sharing the Same Bowl: A Socioeconomic History of Women and Class in Accra, Ghana*. University of Michigan Press, 1985.

Ronen, Dov. "The Colonial Elite in Dahomey." *African Studies Review* 17 (1974): 55–76.

Rovine, Victoria L. *Bogolan: Shaping Culture through Cloth in Contemporary Mali*. Indiana University Press, 2008.

Rovine, Victoria. "A Wider Loom? French Colonial Preoccupations with West African Weaving." *African Arts* 52, no. 4 (2019): 66–83.

Rush, Dana. *Vodun in Coastal Bénin: Unfinished, Open-Ended, Global*. Vanderbilt University Press, 2013.

Scott, James C. *Seeing Like a State: How Certain Schemes to Improve the Human Condition Have Failed*. Yale University Press, 1998.

Sembène, Ousmane, and Thierno Faty Sow, directors. *Camp de Thiaroye*. Filmi Domireew, 1988. DVD.

Semley, Lorelle. *Mother Is Gold, Father Is Glass: Gender and Colonialism in a Yoruba Town*. Indiana University Press, 2011.

Sewell, William. *Work and Revolution in France: The Language of Labor from the Old Regime to 1848*. Cambridge University Press, 1980.

Shea, Philip James. "The Development of an Export Oriented Dyed Cloth Industry in Kano Emirate in the Nineteenth Century." PhD diss., University of Wisconsin–Madison, 1975.

Simone, AbdouMaliq. *For the City Yet to Come: Changing African Life in Four Cities*. Duke University Press, 2004.

Singer Manufacturing Company. *Singer in World War II, 1939–1945*. Singer Manufacturing Company, 1946.

Smolderen, Lucie. "Textile Production in Dendi: An Ethnographic and Historical Study of a Chain of Production." In *Two Thousand Years in Dendi, Northern Benin*, edited by Anne Haour. Brill, 2018.

Soumonni, Elisée. "Some Reflections on the Brazilian Legacy in Dahomey." *Slavery and Abolition* 20, no. 1 (2001): 61–71.

Spear, Thomas. "Neo-Traditionalism and the Limits of Invention in British Colonial Africa." *Journal of African History* 44 (2003): 3–27.

Sylvanus, Nina. *Patterns in Circulation: Cloth, Gender, and Materiality in West Africa*. University of Chicago Press, 2016.

Tallie, T. J. *Queering Colonial Natal: Indigeneity and the Violence of Belonging in South Africa*. University of Minnesota Press, 2019.

Tamari, Tal. "The Development of Caste Systems in West Africa." *Journal of African History* (1991): 221–50.

Thomas, Lynn M. *Beneath the Surface: A Transnational History of Skin Lighteners*. Duke University Press, 2020.

Thomas, Lynn M. *Politics of the Womb: Women, Reproduction, and the State in Kenya*. University of California Press, 2003.

Thompson, Drew. "'*Não há Nada*' ('There Is Nothing'): Absent Headshots and Identity Documents in Independent Mozambique." *Technology and Culture* 61 (2020): S104–S134.

Tingbé-Azalou, Albert. "Cultural Dimensions of Urban-Rural Relations in Benin: The Case of Abomey and Its Hinterland." In *Rural-Urban Dynamics in Francophone Africa*, edited by J. Baker. Nordic Africa Institute, 1997.

Toé, François Thierry. *Textiles et Vêtements du Golfe de Guinée: Enjeux de Conservation et de Médiation*. Riveneuve éditions, 2016.

Tortora, Phyllis G. *Dress, Fashion, and Technology: From Prehistory to the Present*. Bloomsbury, 2015.

Trivedi, Lisa. *Clothing Gandhi's Nation: Homespun and Modern India*. University of Indiana Press, 2007.

Turner, Terence S. "The Social Skin." *HAU: Journal of Ethnographic Theory* 2, no. 2 (2012): 486–504.

Twagira, Laura Ann. *Embodied Engineering: Gendered Labor, Food Security, and Taste in Twentieth Century Mali*. Ohio University Press, 2021.

Twagira, Laura Ann. "Introduction: Africanizing the History of Technology." *Technology and Culture* 61, no. 2 (2020): S1–S19.

Twagira, Laura Ann. "'Robot Farmers' and Cosmopolitan Workers: Technological Masculinity and Agricultural Development in the French Soudan (Mali), 1945–68." *Gender & History* 26 (2014): 459–77.

Vansina, Jan. *Paths in the Rainforest: Toward a History of Political Tradition in Equatorial Africa*. University of Wisconsin Press, 1990.

Ware, Rudolph. *The Walking Qur'an: Islamic Education, Embodied Knowledge, and History in West Africa*. University of North Carolina Press, 2014.

Wendl, Tobias. "Entangled Traditions: Photography and the History of Media in Southern Ghana." *RES: Anthropology and Aesthetics* 39 (2001): 78–101.

White, Luise. *The Comforts of Home: Prostitution in Colonial Nairobi*. University of Chicago Press, 1990.

Wilder, Gary. *The French Imperial Nation-State: Negritude and Colonial Humanism between the Two World Wars.* University of Chicago Press, 2005.

Zafar, Ali. "The Growing Relationship Between China and Sub-Saharan Africa: Macroeconomic, Trade, Investment, and Aid Links." *World Bank Research Observer* 22 (2007): 103–30.

Zdatny, Steven M. *The Politics of Survival: Artisans in Twentieth-Century France.* Oxford University Press, 1990.

INDEX

Aho, Justin, *60*, 61–62, 73, 82–84,
    95, 120
Ahomadégbé–Tomêtin, Justin, 120
Ahonon, Hélène, 180–81
Ahouado, Alphonse, 33, *34*
Akaba, king of Dahomey, 28
Akan, 33, 74
Akouêdenoudjè, Gabin, 80–81, 224n71
Akpako, Pierrot, 97, 112–14, *113*, 123
Alagbe, Valentin, 163
albums. *See* photography
alcoholic beverages, 39, 136, 146,
    147, *148*, 150. *See also* beer; sodabi
    (distilled palm wine)
Alikpanou, Elisabeth, 3–4, 8, 12, 13,
    16, 21
Allada kingdom: Dahomean conquest
    of, 38; Fon migration from, 27, 213n9;
    textile market, 37
Allaga, Rene, 119
Allman, Jean, 16–17
Amazons. *See* agojie
anti-colonialism, 63, 101, 170
Apithy, Sourou Migan, 114, 120
Aplogan, Madam, 125
appliqué, 34–35, 213n10; makers, 12,
    73–74, 76, 180; products, 43, 61, 69
apprenticeship, 3, 6, 15, 99, 100, 107,
    125, 126, 127, 134–39, 141, 157, 174, 179,
    180, 190, 195, 196; age, 135; change to
    taking on numerous apprentices,
    168, 183–84; choosing a master, 112,
    136, 177–78; colonial regulations,
    71, 135; domestic tasks, 137, 166,
    177; examinations, 193; fees, 136,
    178, 183, 194; formalization, 154;
    gendered aspects of, 160, 190, 192;
    gender relations in, 138; as historical
    method, 20, 21; moving to cities, 112,
    113, 114, 116, 161, 179; relationships
    among apprentices, 138, 175–76;

relationships with former masters,
    3, 141, 183–84; violence in, 135, 137,
    149. *See also* liberation; paddling
    (palmatoire)
artisans, 3, 8–10, 11, 12, 16, 20, 21–22,
    67, 75, 86, 125–27, 136, 137, 138–41,
    143, 145, 147, 151, 152–57, 172, 173, 174,
    176, 183, 187, 191, 194, 196; attempts
    to limit number of, 154; attending
    colonial expositions, 131–32;
    colonial education, 71–75; creation
    of diplomas, 140; export market,
    130; hierarchies within, 128–29; and
    labor laws, 135; master status, 138,
    149; NGO interventions, 11, 191,
    193–94, 198, 247n86; in precolonial
    Dahomey, 9, 25, 26, 31–33, 34, 36,
    45, 47, 50, 58; relationship to art, 7,
    18–19, 130; rural, 131; self-regulating
    craft membership, 32, 126, 141, 154–
    56; sending wares to European fairs
    and competitions, 132–33; setting
    up shop, 134; social organization in
    AOF, 128; spatial organization in
    Dahomey, 128; as traditional, 127–30
artisans, discourses on, 8–11, 74–75,
    127–34, 136, 153, 165; colonial
    assessments of products, 132–34;
    occupational identity, 4, 9, 13,
    126, 153
artisans' associations, 12, 20, 97, 120,
    152–56; comparisons with French
    guilds, 10, 153; funding, 152; as
    gatekeepers, 155; membership
    cards, 12, 21, 99, 104, 127, 155, 156;
    organization of, 156; as political
    actors, 154–55; role in certifying
    documentation, 143. *See also*
    Fédération nationale des artisans du
    Bénin (FENAB)
Asante kingdom, 212n10, 215n32

Elizabeth Ann Fretwell is Assistant Professor of African History at Old Dominion University in Norfolk, VA. She received her PhD from University of Chicago and has previously published in *Radical History Review, History and Technology,* and the *Journal of Urban History.*

For Indiana University Press

Sabrina Black, Editorial Assistant
Anna Francis, Assistant Acquisitions Editor
Anna Garnai, Production Coordinator
Samantha Heffner, Marketing Production Manager
Katie Huggins, Production Manager
Nancy Lightfoot, Project Manager/Editor
Alyssa Nicole Lucas, Marketing and Publicity Manager
Bethany Mowry, Acquisitions Editor
Dan Pyle, Online Publishing Manager
Pamela Rude, Senior Artist and Book Designer